One fish, two fish, crawfish, bluefish

The Smithsonian
Sustainable
Seafood
Cookbook

Carole C. Baldwin
and Julie H. Mounts

Illustrations by Charlotte Knox

SMITHSONIAN BOOKS
Washington and London

EXECUTIVE EDITORS: Caroline Newman and
    Carolyn Clark Gleason
TEXT EDITOR: Julie Carlson
RECIPE EDITOR: Susan Stuck
PRODUCTION EDITOR: Joanne Reams
DESIGNER: Janice Wheeler
TYPESETTER: Brian Barth

Library of Congress Control Number:
2003107182
ISBN: 1-58834-169-0

Manufactured in the United States of America
10 09 08 07 06 05 04 03   5 4 3 2 1

The paper used in this publication meets the
minimum requirements of the American
National Standard for Information Sciences—
Permanence of Paper for Printed Library
Materials ANSI Z39.48-1984.

Some recipes in this book are made with raw

fish or raw eggs. These uncooked foods

should not be consumed by pregnant women,

the very young, the elderly, and those with

compromised immune systems.

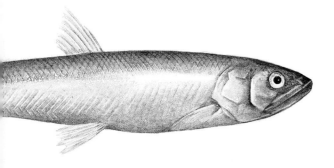

Contents

Acknowledgments

WE EXTEND OUR DEEPEST GRATITUDE TO THE CHEFS who contributed recipes to this compilation. The universal nature of your participation far exceeded our expectations, and your excitement about the project often kept us motivated. From phone and e-mail conversations, it is evident that many of you are concerned about the oceans, and some of you were clearly happy to have a venue to publish recipes for underutilized species. We hope that you will continue to offer such species on your menus and wish you the best of luck in convincing your customers to try them. We hope this book will help. We also hope that it will help educate chefs who do not have time to do the kind of research we did for this book but who want their menus to reflect a high degree of environmental awareness.

We are also indebted to the restaurant owners, office personnel, public relations staff, and the chefs themselves who handled the correspondence associated with this project. At least four or five exchanges of information were required for each chef, and we appreciate the time this took, especially in light of hectic restaurant schedules. In addition to the chefs, we thank Henry Adaniya, Sandra Ardito, Helen Baldus, Carollynn Bartosh, Maggie Boone, Sylvan Brackett, Anna Brenner, Sallie Buben, Dorina Bustamante, Karen Chamberlain, Lanii Chapman, Barbara Dawson, Gay Dochin, Eddie Duangrat, Mimi Rice Duncan, Yukari Hirata Elston, Don Fellner, Jennifer Fite, June Fujise, Norma Galehouse, Gina Gargano, Sally Graves, Susan Hennessey, Stephanie Hersh, Michael Hill, Ebony Hunter, Lori Kahn, Caroline Kasparian, Ellen Kassoff-Gray, Kristine Keefer, Brian Kingsford, Sarah Lagrotteria, Andrea Lazar, Alysa Lebeau, Sandra Le Du, Lori Magaro, Traci Mandell, Monique McCambridge, Ruth Munro, Suzanne Nasuti, Tracy Niporant, Clive O'Donoghue, Françoise Nowak, Ernie Paquette, Lucia Pernot, Audra Poole, Nicole Prevost, Simone Rathle, Aline Reitzer, Robbyn Shim, Peter Shire, Linda Shores, Marcia Smith, Katye Kane Stanzak, Jannis Swerman, Anita Taggersell, Laurie Thomas, Michael Tornatore, Huong Truong, William Truslow, Janet Van Aken, Karen Waltuck, Elizabeth Woodhouse, and Sari Zernich.

The Smithsonian Women's Committee (SWC) provided major funding for our sustainable seafood project, and the quality of the book would not have been the same without these funds. We would particularly like to acknowledge the efforts of Elsa Williams, who represented our proposal through the SWC proposal-review process; we think her enthusiasm about our book helped a lot. Other funding was provided by Tony and Margaret Laliberte, Yvonne Llewellyn, Terry Meiers and Suzie Rodriguez, Sam and Elise Sherer, and William and Eleanor O'Sullivan. Thank you all.

Victor Springer introduced us to the wonderful world of fish art as portrayed by Charlotte Knox. We were captivated by her intriguing designs and vibrant color from the start. We thank Vic for the introduction, Lucy Scherer and Cindy Zarate for helping us arrange the contract with Charlotte, and Anthony Gill and Oliver Crimmen for assisting Charlotte in obtaining fish specimens for illustration. Charlotte, we are so pleased that you agreed to work with us on this project.

Amanda Thornburg and Rachel Romano volunteered many hours to the research phase of this project. We are grateful to them for their willingness to take time out of their college schedules to help. Numerous people helped by providing recommendations of chefs or helping us track them down. Included in this list are Maria Baldwin, Sally Bernstein, Barbara Ainey Brancoli, Sylvan Brackett, David Clark, Lillian Comas-Diaz and Frederick Jacobsen, Jon Dodson, David Foster, Norma Galehouse, Chuck and Arlene Heyward, Wayne Knight, Rick Lang, Janet Magner, Diane Petersen, Camille Richardson, and Roxy Roselle. Others provided information we requested about certain seafood species or information on other sustainable seafood projects, including Dave and Alexandra Baldwin, Bruce Collette, Charles Driggers, Bob Ferri, David Gaudet, Michael Lang, Henry Lovejoy, John McCosker, Patti Parisi, and Charles Robbins. Numerous people provided information or assistance along the way, including Doug Caslow, Jeffrey Clayton, Jerry Finan, Susan Jewett, Dave Johnson, Nicole Krakora, Randall Kremer, Gary Luke, Suzanne Moore, Kris Murphy, Laurence O'Reilly, Tom Orrell, Lisa Palmer, Lynne Parenti, Dave Pawson, Sandra Raredon, Shirleen Smith, Dave Smith, Jiakun Song, Michele Urie, Richard Vari, Stanley and Marilyn Weitzman, and Jeffrey Williams. David Baldwin, Jennifer Dianto, Michael Lang, Darrell Mounts, and Lynne Parenti provided helpful comments on various drafts of portions of this book.

At Smithsonian Books, we are grateful to Vince Burke, who convinced us to work with Smithsonian Books on this project, and Don Fehr, who agreed to publish the book on schedule knowing that doing so would add another burden to his staff. That staff—Caroline Newman, Janice Wheeler, Carolyn Clark Gleason, Joanne Reams, Kiki Forsythe, Nicole Sloan, Matt Litts, and Christian Orcutt—embraced the project enthusiastically, and their good nature about the tight schedule encouraged us to do our part in turning drafts around quickly. Julie Carlson and Susan Stuck provided editorial help with the text and recipe portions of the book, respectively. Lauryn Grant of the Smithsonian Office of General Counsel pleaded our case through Karl ZoBell to Dr. Seuss Enterprises and received permission for us to use as the title of this book an adaptation of the title of the Dr. Seuss children's book *One Fish, Two Fish, Red Fish, Blue Fish*. Our title conveys the thought that there is more than one fish in the sea, and crawfish and bluefish are two relatively underutilized species highlighted here. Thank you, Dr. Seuss.

"We take our oceans for granted. We must view our oceans as a public trust and handle them in a way that ensures that living marine resources are there for our children and for future generations."

—Leon E. Panetta, Chair, Pew Oceans Commission

EARTH'S OCEANS WERE ONCE THOUGHT TO BE inexhaustible sources of food, but they cannot sustain the demands humans have placed on them. Many fish and shellfish species are overfished or otherwise threatened. Conservation initiatives to protect ocean resources are under way throughout the world, but creating, implementing, and enforcing effective global environmental management strategies will require considerable time and cooperation among groups that have different or opposing interests. Until then, consumers can help protect marine resources by making environmentally sound seafood choices.

Choosing seafood wisely requires knowing which species are fished or farmed in a manner that is sustainable—that doesn't risk the future of the species. It is also important to know if seafood was caught in a way that minimizes both the destruction of marine habitat and bycatch (nontarget animals caught and usually killed when fishing for the target species). We initiated this seafood cookbook project because we realized that even as marine biologists who study fish, we were not fully aware of environmental issues surrounding our seafood choices, and we discovered from talking with friends, family, and colleagues that they were equally uninformed. We also recognized that much of what the public hears about seafood is negative publicity focused on species that are overfished or poorly managed (in recent years, for example, orange roughy,

Swordfish

Atlantic swordfish, and Chilean sea bass), with little attention given to promoting well-managed species. Not surprisingly, our research on fisheries management and U.S. seafood consumption revealed that most Americans choose their seafood without much knowledge of current ocean issues.

We believe that most individuals not only care about the ocean environment but also would change their seafood buying and eating habits if they only knew the seriousness of the conservation problems and learned ways to help. We wrote this book to fill these educational gaps—and added a twist: Rather than suggest avoiding consumption of seafood for conservation purposes, we present an array of U.S. seafood species that appear to be fished or farmed in an ecologically sound manner, as well as ways to prepare them provided by top chefs from throughout the country. The premise of the book is that the public, by diversifying its seafood consumption among a broad spectrum of well-managed stocks, can lessen the demand for problematic species. In other words, we encourage individuals to eat more of the well-managed species as well as a broader variety of such species so that none shoulders more of a burden than it can sustain. Should one believe that consumers cannot have such a great effect on marine resources, note that red drum became so popular in the United States as blackened redfish that commercial catches in the Gulf of Mexico increased by more than 10 million pounds in three years in the early 1980s, leading to a collapse of the fishery. Fish populations are dynamic entities, however, and red drum and other overfished species such as Atlantic swordfish are rebounding following the implementation of emergency management plans.

We are a seafood-loving world, and per capita consumption of seafood in the United States continues to rise. Seafood is healthy, low in saturated fat, and often high in the beneficial omega-3 fatty acids. It is thus a desirable part of a diet that, at least in America, has become heavy with saturated fat and trans-fatty acids. We hope that this project will increase public awareness regarding sustainability of the oceans as a food resource, but it is unrealistic to think that people will put the health of the oceans ahead of their own well-being. We believe the public can reap the benefits of a diet rich in seafood and at the same time support marine resource protection. In much the same way that people contribute to resource conservation through recycling programs, individuals can have a positive influence on conservation of marine resources simply by diversifying their seafood selections among well-managed stocks.

Creating this book opened our eyes to a whole new world of seafood choices and illuminated our own habits of relying weekly on the same species, mainly imported farmed Atlantic salmon and shrimp. Neither is a good choice from an environmental perspective (see "Issues Regarding U.S. Seafood"), but seafood markets in the United States rely heavily on their sales. The burden can be spread to a much greater diversity of species. The list of U.S. sustainable seafood species that we compiled and distributed to chefs appears at the back of the book. The derivation of the list is briefly explained in "Issues Regarding U.S. Seafood" and will be described more comprehensively in the Smithsonian's related Web site at www.mnh.si.edu/seafood. The list contains a wonderful diversity of seafood choices, including shellfish and finfish, well-known species as well as many that are underutilized, wild-caught species and those that are farmed, and economical as well as expensive choices. There is no compilation of seafood recipes by professional U.S. chefs that rivals this one, and with a diversity of cuisines and simple as well as more complex dishes, the book should appeal to all cooks. Also included are retail sources for most of the seafood species included in the recipes, a glossary of culinary terms to aid readers who may be unfamiliar with certain technical cooking terms or products, and a list of the chefs. The recipes are divided into sections, each of which provides information about the natural history, commercial importance, and conservation status of the included species, as well as chef-friendly information about their use as seafood. We hope readers will find the information enlightening, the recipes inspiring, the artwork intriguing, and the intent of it all of utmost importance.

WHAT YOU CAN DO

Whether eating out or cooking at home, broaden your seafood selections, using the "Seafood Species" list as a general guide. When preparing recipes from this book, experiment freely, interchanging seafood species based on availability.

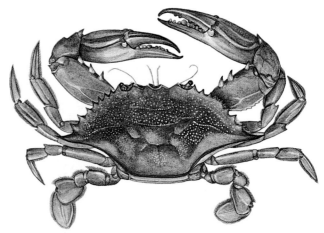

Make sustainable seafood a routine by establishing, for example, a weekly Family Sustainable Seafood Night. Exploring the diversity of well-managed seafood species with family and friends can be an enjoyable adventure, and including children in the fun may help prepare them for a future in which marine conservation issues will be vitally important.

Using information provided in the text portions of this book, familiarize yourself with issues surrounding seafood choices and then question seafood retailers about the identity and history of their products before buying. Ask them, *What is it? Where is it from? How was it caught or was it farmed?* and *Has it been treated with preservatives or antibiotics?* We all would find it much easier to make conscientious seafood choices if seafood products in the United States were better labeled. Letting retailers know that you are educated about and interested in such information may encourage them to include more of it on their packaging or displays.

Stay informed. "Issues Regarding U.S. Seafood" outlines many environmental concerns. Additional information can be found on our Smithsonian seafood Web site and those of numerous conservation organizations. Consumers wishing to stay abreast of policy, media coverage, and fishery council activities related to marine fisheries might consider a free subscription to the Marine Fish Conservation Network's online Fishlink.

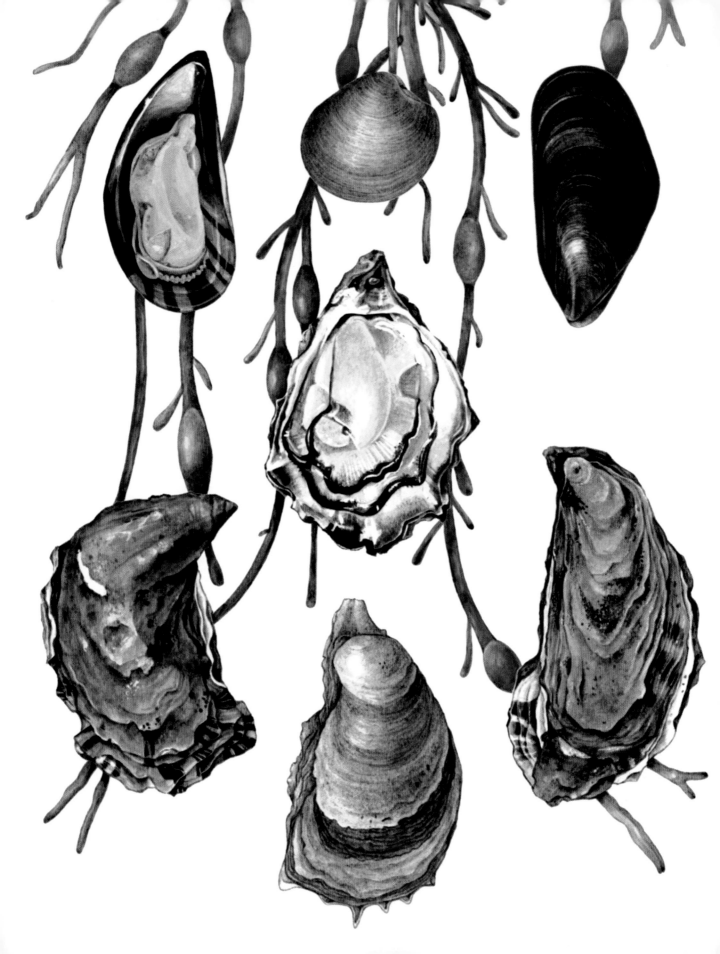

Oysters, Mussels, and Clams

PERHAPS NO GROUP OF SEAFOOD OFFERS A GREATER diversity of flavors and textures than the shellfish known as bivalves. To experience this savory array, the cook must first pry or heat open the bivalve's tightly clasped shells. Within is the briny, slippery oyster, the sweet and softly chewy clam, the rich, succulent mussel.

Unfortunately, wild populations of oysters, mussels, and clams have

Blue mussels *(top left and right)*, hard clam *(top center)*, Eastern oyster *(bottom)*, and Pacific oyster *(left, center, right)*

In the Wild

All bivalves, not just oysters, can produce pearls. They do so by covering foreign particles that make their way inside the shells with layers of "mother of pearl," the smooth, shiny, nacreous material that lines the inside of a bivalve shell. But don't be disappointed if your next oyster, mussel, or clam yields no gem. Most pearls come from tropical Pacific *Pinctada* oysters, not edible U.S. species.

declined in many coastal areas of the United States because of disease, pollution, or heavy fishing pressure. For example, populations of the famed Olympia oyster (the only native west-coast species) are nearly depleted. The good news is that bivalves are now farmed successfully throughout coastal zones of the United States.

From east- and Gulf-coast U.S. farming operations, consumers will find the eastern oyster, hard clam, and blue mussel. On the west coast, farms exist for the European flat oyster, the Pacific oyster, and the small Kumomoto oyster; blue mussels (including Penn Cove mussels) and Mediterranean mussels; as well as various clams such as manila and butter.

Hard clams (*Mercenaria mercenaria*) may be marketed as littlenecks (not the same as the Pacific littleneck, *Protothaca staminea*), topnecks, cherrystones, chowder clams, or quahogs—names that reflect the increasing size categories of clams as they grow. Consumers may also encounter myriad names for oysters in the United States, such as Blue Point, Malpeque, Wellfleet, Chincoteague, Hog Island, Fanny Bay, and Yaquina. Aquagrill in New York City lists more than 130 oyster names on their menu. These names do not reflect the presence of numerous species in U.S. waters—most U.S. varieties are eastern (*Crassostrea virginica*) or Pacific (*Crassostrea gigas*) oysters. Instead, they mostly indicate where the oyster was grown, a characteristic that may subtly affect the flavor. A relatively new "variety" of oyster to appear on the market is the AmeriPure, an eastern oyster that has been subjected to a hot-cold water process to destroy potentially harmful bacteria without opening the shell.

Most of the oysters, mussels, and clams available as seafood to U.S. consumers are farmed, and bivalve farming is considered environmentally sound. If given a choice, select farmed bivalves over harvests of wild populations. Not only have wild populations dwindled, but also commercial harvesting methods for bivalves such as dredging are habitat destructive.

Oysters on the Half Shell with Verjus Mignonette

Makes 1-1/3 cups mignonette, enough for 10 dozen oysters

This mignonette is a takeoff from the traditional French preparation in using red verjus instead of vinegar. Combined with the peppercorns, it goes very well with west-coast oysters and provides an accent to their crisp, clean flavors.

Oysters from California, Oregon, or Washington (as many as you want)

❧ Verjus Mignonette

Shuck the oysters (see page 10) and put about 1 teaspoon of the verjus mignonette on each oyster.

Serve on a bed of ice.

❧ Verjus Mignonette

1-1/4 cups verjus (sour liquid pressed from unripe grapes), preferably red verjus

1/4 cup minced shallots

1-1/2 teaspoons coarsely ground or cracked black pepper

2 teaspoons kosher salt

1 teaspoon Champagne vinegar

In a medium bowl, combine the verjus, shallots, pepper, salt, and vinegar. Whisk to blend.

Jeffery Powell is Chef de Cuisine at PlumpJack Squaw Valley Inn, Olympic Valley, California.

Oysters

Eastern, Kumomoto, Pacific, and European Flat

SCIENTIFIC NAMES: *Crassostrea virginica* (eastern), *C. sikamea* (Kumomoto), *C. gigas* (Pacific), and *Ostrea edulis* (European flat)

OTHER NAMES: Kumomoto oysters are also called Kumamotos.

U.S. DISTRIBUTION: The eastern oyster ranges from the Gulf of Mexico to the Gulf of Saint Lawrence in Canada. Pacific oysters range from California to Alaska. Eastern, Pacific, Kumomoto, and the European flat oyster are now cultivated in coastal areas throughout the United States.

WHAT TO LOOK FOR: When buying live oysters, make sure they're still alive. The shells must be closed tightly or should close when tapped. Use your nose too: If oysters smell sulfurous, avoid them. Shucked oysters (sold in jars) should have a creamy color surrounded by clear liquid. Avoid oysters that look bloated; water has been added for extra weight.

If harvesting your own oysters, it's best to do so only during the "r" months (September through April) because the oysters may be spawning during the spring and summer, rendering them less firm and less appetizing on the plate. Also, avoid eating raw oysters from the warm waters of the Gulf of Mexico and southeastern United States during the summer months because of the risk of serious illness from *Vibrio* bacteria. Culturing oysters now produces nonspawning oysters year-round. Live oysters are usually sold by the piece or by the dozen, graded by size.

COOKING METHODS: Oysters are served raw on the half shell or fried, grilled, baked, or used in chowders or stews.

Kumomoto Oysters and Sashimi Tuna with a Cilantro-Lime Glaze

Serves 2

An Asian glaze is drizzled on oysters topped with fresh tuna in this Japanese-inspired version of oysters on the half shell.

10 Kumomoto oysters in shell
    (scrubbed free of dirt and debris)
1/2 pound sashimi-grade yellowfin tuna
3 tablespoons chopped cilantro,
    plus sprigs for garnish
1 tablespoon chopped mint
1/4 cup freshly squeezed lime juice
1/4 cup honey

3 tablespoons mirin
    (Japanese seasoning wine)
3 tablespoons rice-wine vinegar
1 teaspoon sambal oelek
    (Indonesian chile sauce)
2 teaspoons salt
1 tablespoon pineapple juice
1 tablespoon wasabi powder

To make the cilantro-lime glaze, combine the cilantro, mint, lime juice, honey, mirin, vinegar, sambal oelek, and salt in a small mixing bowl. Place in the refrigerator to chill. In a very small bowl, combine the pineapple juice and wasabi and incorporate evenly.

Shuck the oysters using an oyster knife: Hold an oyster with the rounded side down and insert the knife between the shells to pry the oyster open. Use the knife to scrape free the meat attached to the top shell. Remove the top shell, leaving the oyster on the bottom half shell. Rinse with water to remove any grit left from the shell. Cut the tuna into 10 thin strips. Place a tuna strip on top of each oyster. Spoon 1 teaspoon of the glaze on top of each oyster. (Extra glaze will keep a few days in the refrigerator.) Finish with a small dot of the wasabi. Place crushed ice on a deep plate and top with cilantro leaves (this will keep the oysters cold and prevent sliding). Place all of the oysters on top and serve immediately.

Craig Deihl is Executive Chef of Cypress Grille in Charleston, South Carolina.

Oysters Kathryn

2 dozen plump, salty oysters, preferably freshly shucked, shells reserved

One 7.8-ounce can artichoke hearts (or frozen or cooked fresh artichokes), chopped very finely

1 egg

3/4 cup heavy cream

1/2 cup plain bread crumbs

1/2 cup freshly grated Parmesan

Juice of 1 lemon

1 teaspoon chopped garlic

1/2 teaspoon chopped fresh basil

Salt and freshly ground black pepper

2 lemons, cut in half

Serves 4

Special Equipment: 4 pie pans filled with rock salt

Mix the artichokes, egg, cream, bread crumbs, cheese, lemon juice, garlic, basil, and salt and pepper in a large mixing bowl. Cover and chill for at least 30 minutes.

Preheat the oven to 400°F. Wash oyster shells well and pat dry. Drain the oysters and put 1 on each shell, 2 if small. Set oysters in each pan of rock salt. Place 1 heaping tablespoon of the artichoke topping on each oyster. Bake for 15 to 18 minutes until well browned. The shells will be extremely hot.

Carefully place the hot pans of rock salt onto heatproof dinner plates. Garnish each serving with a lemon half. For a nice touch, wrap each lemon half in a 4-inch square of cheesecloth and tie closed. Juice squeezes through the fabric, but seeds do not.

Tommy DiGiovanni is Executive Chef of Arnaud's Restaurant in New Orleans, Louisiana.

Sesame-Crusted Oysters, Miso-Wasabi Vinaigrette, Enoki Mushrooms, and Scallions

Serves 2
as an appetizer

12 eastern (Maryland or Blue Point)
oysters (shucked oysters
from a jar are fine)
Peanut or canola oil, for frying
2 tablespoons flour
1 egg, beaten
2 cups panko (Japanese bread crumbs)

1/4 cup black sesame seeds
1/4 cup white sesame seeds
2 leaves red-leaf lettuce
1 package enoki mushrooms
2 teaspoons sliced scallions
✣ Miso-Wasabi Vinaigrette

Shuck the oysters and place them in a shallow pan. Pour enough oil into a large deep skillet to fill it 1 inch deep. Heat the oil to 360°F. While the oil is heating, sprinkle the oysters with flour and mix around. Add the egg and mix. In a shallow dish, mix the panko and sesame seeds. Remove the oysters from the first pan and roll them in the bread crumb–sesame mixture. When the oil is hot, fry the oysters until golden brown, about 2 to 3 minutes. Place the oysters on a plate covered with paper towels to drain the excess oil.

To serve, place a lettuce leaf on each of 2 dinner plates. Place hot oysters to one side of each plate. Cut open the package of enoki mushrooms, place them on the other side of the plate, and sprinkle with the sliced scallions. Serve with the Miso-Wasabi Vinaigrette on the side for dipping.

✦ Miso-Wasabi Vinaigrette

1/4 cup rice-wine vinegar

2 tablespoons red miso
(fermented soybean paste)

2 tablespoons wasabi powder,
dissolved in 2 tablespoons
white wine or water (or enough
to make a paste)

2 teaspoons sesame oil

1 teaspoon minced fresh ginger

1 teaspoon minced shallots

1 teaspoon light soy sauce

1/2 teaspoon minced garlic

1/4 cup heavy cream

1/2 cup olive oil

Salt and freshly ground
white pepper

Whisk together the vinegar, miso, wasabi, sesame oil, ginger, shallots, soy sauce, and garlic. Slowly add the heavy cream and olive oil, whisking to emulsify. Season with salt and white pepper to taste.

Sandy Ingber is Executive Chef of Grand Central Oyster Bar in New York City.

Storing Oysters, Mussels, or Clams

When you get home, unwrap the shellfish and put them in a colander. Set the colander in a large bowl, which will catch drips as well as allow air circulation. Lay some damp paper towels over the shellfish and place the assembly in the coldest area of your refrigerator, probably the lower shelf, toward the back.

Do not be tempted to create a seawater home and plunge shellfish into salted water, and be sure not to let the shellfish become submerged in freshwater, either—that includes not on top of or under ice, which will melt and collect at the bottom of the bowl, possibly suffocating some of the shellfish. Eat them within a day or two of purchase. Scrub the shells under cold running water with a stiff brush just before cooking. Discard any oysters, clams, or mussels that do not close.

Caesar Salad with Spicy Fried Oysters

Serves 6
as a first course
or 4 as an
entrée

This salad is fairly easy to do, but it does require last-minute preparation, as the oysters must be fried and served immediately. Parmesan shards are very thin triangular slices carefully shaved from a large wedge of Parmesan cheese. Their size and shape give a sense of drama to the salad's presentation. If this is not practical for you, grated fresh Parmesan works as well taste-wise, but use a fine Parmigiano-Reggiano.

1/2 gallon select shucked oysters
    (about 40 oysters)
1/3 cup salt
2 tablespoons cayenne pepper
4 teaspoons filé powder
    (available in grocery stores)
1 tablespoon onion powder
1 tablespoon garlic powder
1 tablespoon ground white pepper
1 tablespoon paprika

1 tablespoon freshly ground black pepper
2 cups all-purpose flour
6 cups peanut oil
8 cups (about 3/4 pound) romaine lettuce,
    washed, dried, and cut into
    1/2-inch-wide ribbons
1/4 cup Parmesan shards
✦ Caesar Dressing
✦ Croutons

Combine the salt, cayenne pepper, filé powder, onion powder, garlic powder, white pepper, paprika, and black pepper. Stir to mix well. Add 2 tablespoons of this spice mixture to the 2 cups of flour. Stir to mix well. (Stored in a tightly covered container in a cool place, the remaining spice mixture will keep for 2 months. If you fry oysters often, having the spice mixture already made will be handy.)

Pour the peanut oil into a heavy skillet that is large enough for the oil to be 1-1/2 inches deep but not more than halfway up the sides. Heat the oil to 350°F on a frying thermometer. Working with a dozen oysters at a time, sprinkle them with 1/2 teaspoon spice mixture and toss to coat evenly. Then toss the oysters quickly in the spice-flour mixture, coating them well but shaking to remove any excess flour. Do not leave the oysters sitting in the flour or they will get soggy.

Drop the oysters gently into the hot oil. Do not crowd the skillet by adding too many at once. The oysters should not touch each other. If you put in too many, the temperature of the oil will drop and the finished oysters may be greasy. Move them around with a slotted spoon so that they don't stick to the skillet or each other. Fry the oysters for 45 to 60 seconds. When they are done, they should be golden brown. It is important not to overcook them, because they will lose their delectable juices. If you suddenly hear popping and sputtering from the skillet, remove the oysters immediately—that's a sign that they're beginning to overcook. Otherwise, remove the oysters with a slotted spoon when they are golden brown and place them on a paper towel to drain, changing the towel if it begins to get saturated with oil. (Oysters actually need no cooking to be eaten, as on the half shell. When frying, they are ready when they float to the top; however, most people like to cook them a little longer so that they get extra crispy and more golden brown.)

To serve, toss the lettuce and 3/4 cup Caesar Dressing in a large bowl. Divide the lettuce among 6 or 4 plates, depending on whether the salad is a first course or an entrée. Sprinkle the Croutons, oysters, and Parmesan shards over the lettuce.

❧ Caesar Dressing

1/3 cup red-wine vinegar	1 tablespoon Dijon mustard
1 large egg yolk	1/2 cup peanut oil
3 anchovy fillets, crushed	1/2 cup extra-virgin olive oil
2 tablespoons minced garlic	1/4 teaspoon salt
1 tablespoon finely minced onion	1/4 teaspoon freshly ground black pepper
1 tablespoon freshly squeezed lemon juice	

In a bowl, blender, or food processor, combine the vinegar, egg yolk, anchovies, garlic, onion, lemon juice, and mustard. Whisk or process these ingredients together. Slowly whisk in the peanut oil and olive oil or very slowly pour them into the blender or food processor, spoonful by spoonful. Be careful not to add the oil too quickly, which could break the emulsion. Add the salt and pepper. Tightly covered, the dressing will keep in the refrigerator for 1 week. If it separates, whisk to bring it back together.

❧ Croutons

1 baguette	Salt and freshly ground black pepper
1/2 cup extra-virgin olive oil	to taste

Preheat the oven to 350°F. Slice the baguette into 2 dozen 1/2-inch-wide slices, leaving the crust on; toss with the olive oil and salt and pepper. Spread the croutons on a baking sheet and bake for 10 to 15 minutes, or until they are browned and crisp. Toss them once or twice while baking so that they brown evenly. Remove from the oven and reserve.

Louis Osteen is Chef/Owner of Louis's at Pawleys in Pawley's Island, South Carolina. He is the author of *Charleston Cuisine* (Algonquin Books, 1999), from which this recipe was adapted.

Oyster Stew with Sherry and Country Ham

Serves 8

The cream in this recipe is optional and can be replaced by more milk if you prefer. How rich you make the broth depends on you and your taste. The stew without the oysters will keep in the refrigerator for two or three days. It can easily be made ahead for a special dinner party and the oysters added at the last minute.

40 shucked oysters of any variety,
    with their liquor
2 tablespoons butter
1 medium onion, finely chopped
1 medium leek (white and pale
    green parts), cut in half lengthwise,
    then cut into thin half moons
    and washed
5 cups whole milk

1 cup heavy cream
1-1/2 cups diced sweet potatoes
1-1/2 cups diced celery
6 tablespoons dry sherry
1/2 cup diced country ham
1/2 teaspoon ground mace
Salt and freshly ground white pepper
1 tablespoon chopped fresh parsley

Melt the butter in a large saucepan over medium-low heat. Add the onion and cook slowly until it is almost soft; add the leek. Continue cooking slowly until the leek is tender but has not given up all its pale green color.

Stir in the milk and cream. Slowly bring the mixture to a simmer without boiling (boiling causes the soup to curdle). Add the sweet potatoes and simmer until they are just tender but retain their shape. Add the celery and simmer until just tender and still bright green.

Stir in the sherry, country ham, and mace. Simmer for a minute or so. Season with salt and white pepper to taste. Add the oysters and their liquor and simmer gently, only until the edges of the oysters have curled a bit. Ladle the oyster stew into 8 warm bowls, garnish with chopped parsley, and serve.

Susan McCreight Lindeborg is Chef/Partner of Majestic Café in Alexandria, Virginia.

Baked Oysters with Bacon, Wilted Greens, and Bread Crumbs

Serves 6

30 eastern oysters on the half shell,
    freshly shucked (Apalachicola,
    Blue Point, Pemaquid or Malpeque)
Rock salt or coarse kosher salt
2 pounds fresh spinach (crinkly organic
    if possible) or substitute watercress
    or a mixture of green herbs
    and lettuces
1 tablespoon olive oil
3 ounces slab (unsliced) bacon,
    cut into small dice
2 leeks, trimmed, cleaned, quartered,
    and cut into thin slices

1 shallot, quartered and sliced
1 clove garlic, finely chopped
2 lemons, one zested and juiced,
    one cut into wedges
1 day-old baguette, crust trimmed and
    coarsely ground in food processor
1 stick (8 tablespoons) unsalted
    butter, melted
1 scrape of nutmeg
Salt and freshly ground white pepper

Preheat the oven to 500°F. Line a large baking sheet with sides with rock salt or coarse kosher salt. Set the oysters in their half shells on the salt.

Fill a saucepan 3/4 full with water, add a handful of kosher salt, and bring to a boil. Drop the spinach or other greens into the boiling water for 30 seconds. Drain and plunge into a bowl of ice water. Remove and squeeze dry. Finely chop and set aside.

Heat the olive oil in a large sauté pan over medium heat. Add the bacon and sauté until cooked only halfway. Remove the bacon from the pan. Into the same pan, add the leeks, shallot, and garlic; gently soften over low heat. Transfer the leek mixture to a mixing bowl and add the chopped greens, reserved bacon, lemon juice and zest, bread crumbs, melted butter, nutmeg, and salt and pepper. Stir, taste, and adjust seasonings. Spoon the mixture onto the oysters, trying not to compress but just loosely covering them. Put the baking sheet with the oysters on the top shelf of the oven and roast until golden, about 6 to 8 minutes.

Protecting your hand with an oven mitt, quickly transfer the hot oysters to plates. Serve with lemon wedges and a crisp, dry white wine such as a Sancerre.

Frank Stitt is Chef/Owner of Highlands Bar and Grill, Bottega, Chez Fonfon, and Café Bottega in Birmingham, Alabama.

Roasted Oysters with a Mushroom-Truffle Crust

Serves 4

COOK'S STRATEGY: You can cook the Duxelles and form the cylinder of truffle butter up to a day in advance.

20 oysters in their shells
2 sticks (16 tablespoons) butter, softened
2 cups fresh bread crumbs
1/4 cup white truffle oil (you may also add minced fresh truffle)

Salt and freshly ground black pepper
Rock salt, for lining baking sheet
Seaweed or other decorative green, for garnish
❖ Duxelles

Combine, in order, the butter, bread crumbs, truffle oil, salt and pepper, and Duxelles. Roll up mixture in plastic wrap or wax paper in a cylinder shape with the diameter equivalent to that of the oyster shells. Refrigerate until firm.

Preheat the broiler. Line a baking sheet with sides with rock salt. Shuck the oysters (see page 10), leaving them on the bottom shell, and place on the baking sheet. Cut the roll of truffle crust into 1/4-inch-thick slices and lay a slice on top of each oyster. Broil until light golden brown, about 6 to 8 minutes. Transfer the hot oysters to plates garnished with salt and seaweed. Serve immediately.

❖ Duxelles

1 teaspoon butter or olive oil
1 tablespoon minced shallots
1 tablespoon minced garlic
8 ounces mushrooms (shiitake, chanterelle, or porcini, or a mixture) ground in a food processor

2 teaspoons salt
20 grinds black pepper
1/2 cup white wine

Melt the butter in a sauté pan over medium-high heat. Add the shallots and garlic; cook for 1 minute to release aroma. Add the mushrooms and salt and pepper and cook for about 1 minute. Stir in the wine and cook until the pan is nearly dry. Remove from the heat and let cool.

Jeremy Marshall is Executive Chef of Aquagrill in New York City.

Thai Mussels

Serves 4

2 pounds Penn Cove mussels, cleaned and debearded
1 cup coconut milk
2/3 cup sake
2 teaspoons freshly squeezed lime juice

2 teaspoons Thai fish sauce
1 teaspoon Thai red curry paste
1 teaspoon minced garlic
1 teaspoon minced fresh ginger
1 teaspoon chopped fresh basil, plus whole leaves for garnish

In a large bowl, whisk together the coconut milk, sake, lime juice, fish sauce, curry paste, garlic, ginger, and chopped basil. Heat a large heavy saucepan over high heat for about 30 seconds. Add the mussels and coconut broth. Bring to a boil and lower the heat to medium low. Cover and simmer until the mussels fully open, about 5 minutes. Discard any mussels that do not open. Divide the mussels among 4 bowls and pour broth over mussels. Garnish with basil leaves. Serve with plenty of crusty bread.

Charles Ramseyer is Executive Chef of Ray's Boathouse in Seattle, Washington, and author of *Ray's Boathouse: Seafood Secrets of the Pacific Northwest* (Documentary Media, 2003).

Mussels

Blue, Penn Cove, and Mediterranean

SCIENTIFIC NAMES: *Mytilus edulis* (blue), *M. trossulus* (blue—also known as Penn Cove Mussels), *M. galloprovincialis* (Mediterranean)

U.S. DISTRIBUTION: Maine is the largest U.S. producer of blue mussels. Washington State and, to a lesser extent, California produce both blue mussels and Mediterranean mussels.

WHAT TO LOOK FOR: Cultivated mussels have thin, black-to-slightly-brown shells and plumper meats than wild mussels. They also are virtually free of grit. Avoid any mussels with an off odor. If the shells are open and don't close after you squeeze them together or tap them hard on a counter or sink, or if you can slide the shells from side to side, the mussel is dead and should be discarded. The flesh may vary in color naturally from whitish to orange.

About 20 to 25 blue mussels generally make up a pound; some smaller harvests may run up to 40 per pound. Plan on about half a pound of mussels per person for appetizers and a pound or more per person for a main course.

COOKING METHODS: Shortly before cooking, rinse the mussels under cold running water. Yank off the "beards"—little tufts of coarse fibers sticking out the side. Mussels are usually steamed in some aromatic liquid to open them. French cooks steam mussels in a white-wine and herb broth; Italians favor wine or water with garlic and tomatoes. The flavor of mussels also stands up well to the intensity of Thai seasonings.

Mussels with Garlic, Mustard, Rosemary, and Cream

Serves 6
as an appetizer,
4 as an entrée

4 to 5 dozen medium to large, very fresh,
    cultivated mussels
2 teaspoons butter
4 cloves garlic, minced
1 large shallot, minced
3 cups heavy cream
1/2 cup dry white wine
    (Sauvignon or Chenin Blanc)

8 rosemary sprigs, 4 inches long each
1 bay leaf
2 teaspoons grainy mustard,
    such as Pommery
1/2 teaspoon sea salt
1/2 teaspoon cracked black pepper
Crusty bread

Wash and debeard the mussels. (Cultivated mussels are generally very clean.) In a non-reactive saucepan over medium-high heat, melt the butter and add the garlic and shallot; cook until they start to brown. Pour in the cream and white wine and bring to a boil. Cook liquid quickly to reduce by one-fourth: you should have about about 2-1/2 cups liquid. Add the mussels, rosemary, bay leaf, and mustard. Cover and cook for 3 to 4 minutes until all mussels open. Discard any that do not open. Add the salt and pepper, and pick out the bay leaf and rosemary sprigs.

Serve in large warmed bowls with crusty bread to sop up the briny sauce.

Robert Kinkead is Chef/Owner of Kinkead's in Washington, D.C., and Colvin Run Tavern in Vienna, Virginia.

Mussels with Lime and Basil

Serves 6

I prefer to use the farm-raised mussels such as Great Eastern or Prince Edward Island mussels. They are cleaner and more uniform than wild mussels. The combination of lime and basil brings to mind Thai cooking, but it is something I have always liked and used. This dish may also be made with an assortment of shellfish: clams, mussels, oysters, and/or shrimp.

2 pounds mussels, washed and debearded
2 tablespoons finely chopped shallots
1/2 cup white wine
1 cup cream

Juice of 3 limes (approximately
    3 tablespoons)
3 tablespoons unsalted butter
1/4 cup basil leaves, sliced into thin strips

Place the mussels, shallots, and white wine in a large, nonreactive saucepot with a tight-fitting lid. Cover and steam over high heat until mussels are all open. Remove the mussels as they open and keep them warm. Discard any that fail to open. Over high heat, reduce the liquid that remains in the pot by half. Add the cream, lime juice, and butter and boil until slightly thickened. Add the basil and taste. Adjust the seasoning with lime, salt, or cream if necessary. Divide the mussels between 6 soup plates. Ladle the sauce over the mussels and serve.

David Waltuck is Chef/Owner of Chanterelle in New York City and author (with Melicia Phillips) of *Staff Meals from Chanterelle* (Workman Publishing Company, 2000).

Manila Clams and Shrimp with Chile, Lemongrass, and Black-Bean Sauce

Clams

Hard Clam, Pacific Littleneck, Manila, Butter

SCIENTIFIC NAMES: *Mercenaria mercenaria* (hard clam), *Protothaca staminea* (Pacific littleneck), *Tapes philippinarum* (manila), *and Saxidomus giganteus* (butter)

OTHER NAMES: Hard clams are sold under the names littlenecks, topnecks, cherrystones, chowder clams, and quahogs, which reflect increasing size categories of a single species.

U.S. DISTRIBUTION: Hard clams are local to Atlantic coastal areas. Pacific littlenecks, manila clams (a Japanese clam introduced from Asia), and butter clams are Pacific, but all species are now farmed. Hard clams are farmed on the west coast as well as the east coast.

WHAT TO LOOK FOR: For hard clams, tender and sweet littlenecks usually have shells measuring less than 2 inches across. A little larger, topnecks and cherrystones are also quite tender. The largest and toughest clams—chowder clams and quahogs—are often chopped and used in soups, stews, sauces, and chowders.

Fresh clams should smell clean, like the sea. The shells of live hard clams should be tightly closed or should close when tapped; if not, discard them. Live clams are available year-round.

COOKING METHODS: Small, very fresh hard clams can be enjoyed raw on the half shell. Enjoy the briny yet sweet flavor of larger ones by steaming, roasting, grilling, or sautéing the clams or by using them in classic chowders. Manila and butter clams are good steamed or raw. Pacific littlenecks are small clams suitable for steaming.

Serves 4

12 manila clams, washed
12 U.S.-trawled or -farmed shrimp, 16–20 count, peeled and deveined
Oil for sautéing
1 small onion, diced
2 teaspoons minced garlic
2 teaspoons minced fresh ginger
1/4 pound fresh lemongrass, sliced
4 teaspoons Chinese fermented black beans, rinsed and drained
1/2 cup sherry
1 to 2 tablespoons Thai chile sauce
1/2 pound snow peas
1 vine-ripened tomato, diced
1 pound penne pasta, cooked
1 stick (8 tablespoons) unsalted butter
1/2 cup chicken broth
Salt and freshly ground black pepper

Heat oil in a sauté pan over medium heat, add the clams and shrimp, and sear. Add the onion, garlic, ginger, lemongrass, and fermented black beans. Add the sherry and stir to deglaze. Add the chile sauce, snow peas, tomatoe, pasta, butter, and chicken broth. Cover the pan and simmer until the clams are open and butter is melted. Season with salt and pepper. If you like, add more Thai chile sauce for desired heat.

Divide the pasta among 4 pasta bowls and ladle the clams, shrimp, vegetables, and sauce on top. Serve immediately.

Alan Wong is Chef/Owner of Alan Wong's and The Pineapple Room in Honolulu, Hawaii.

Clam Roast with Spicy Sausages

Bonnet-pepper sausages are so spicy that we use them as an ingredient rather than eat them by themselves. They give this clam roast a serious kick while adding their unique flavor to the broth. Choose small, tightly closed clams to roast. Some clams open faster than others; if most clams have opened, remove the stubborn ones to a cutting board. Hold each clam hinge-side down between your thumb and forefinger. Wedge the blade of a paring knife between the shells and apply a little pressure. If the clam does not readily open, you should discard it.

Serves 4

48 small hard clams (littlenecks)

4 bonnet-pepper sausages or
    1 pound hot Italian sausage

4 large onions

2 heads Belgian endive, coarsely
    chopped (1-1/2 to 2 cups)

1 jalapeño pepper, seeded and chopped

1 to 2 bonnet peppers, seeded
    and chopped, optional

2 tablespoons minced garlic

1/2 teaspoon dried hot red pepper flakes

1-1/2 cups chopped canned tomatoes
    in heavy purée

3/4 cup dry white wine

1 stick (8 tablespoons) unsalted butter,
    cut into small pieces

3 scallions, cut into fine julienne

1 lemon, quartered

Preheat the oven to 500°F. Bring a pot of water to a boil. Drop the sausages in and parboil for 8 minutes to rid them of excess fat. Drain and set sausages aside on a cutting board. Allow the sausages to cool for about 10 minutes, then cut them on a diagonal into 1/2-inch-thick slices.

Peel the onions, cut them in half vertically through the root, and cut a V in the bottom of each half to remove the root. Slice each half into thin slivers.

Lay out the clams in a single layer in a flameproof baking dish or roasting pan. In a bowl, combine the onions, endive, jalapeño peppers, bonnet peppers (if using), garlic, and red pepper flakes. Sprinkle over the clams. Pour the chopped tomatoes and wine over the clams too. On the stovetop over high heat, bring the mixture in the pan to a boil. Dot the clams with the butter and place the pan in the oven. Roast the clams for 8 minutes. Turn the clams and roast for about 5 to 10 minutes longer until the clams open.

To serve, place 12 clams in each of 4 large heated bowls and pour the broth over them. Evenly distribute the vegetables and sausages. Garnish with the scallions and lemon wedges.

Johanne Killeen and George Germon are Chef/Owners of Al Forno Restaurant in Providence, Rhode Island. This recipe is adapted from their cookbook *Cucina Simpatica*, copyright © 1991 Johanne Killeen and George Germon and reprinted by permission of HarperCollins Publishers Inc.

Wood-Roasted Clams with Saffron, Tomatoes, and Garlic

Serves 4
as an appetizer
or lunch entrée

Cooking over a wood fire frees you from the complexities of the kitchen, with all of its gadgets and devices, and inspires simplicity, allowing you to focus on the natural flavors of the food. When you are experimenting with open-hearth cooking, whether indoors or outside, remember that temperature and timing are crucial. Plan to burn the wood for one to two hours beforehand to ensure a hot bed of coals. Alder, cherry, apple, and fir are common woods used in the Pacific Northwest. When the fire is ready, set a metal grate strong enough to support a large pot or skillet in place 8 to 12 inches above the coals. The grate also acts as an excellent grill for large-cut pieces of vegetables such as peppers, onions, corn, or squash.

One of my favorite recipes for clams includes saffron, garlic, and tomatoes. Although this recipe is prepared in the wood-burning brick oven at the restaurant, a conventional outdoor grill works well, with wood chips added to the coals. The juice from the clams mixes with the oil and vinegar, creating a rich-flavored broth that is an excellent dipping sauce for a crusty piece of bread. Mussels also work well in this recipe. Use the same amount, but reduce the cooking time to three to four minutes. Enjoy this dish with a glass of Pinot Gris.

4 pounds Pacific littleneck clams in their
    shells, scrubbed, or 2-1/2
    pounds mussels
1 cup cherry tomatoes, halved, or 1/2 cup
    sun-dried tomatoes, coarsely chopped
2 shallots, thinly sliced crosswise
1 tablespoon minced garlic

Juice of 1 lemon
1/2 cup chopped fresh Italian flat-leaf parsley
Four 1/2-inch-thick slices hard-crusted
    country bread, toasted and rubbed
    with garlic, for serving
❧ Saffron Vinaigrette

Using mesquite or other wood chips, prepare a very hot grill. (The temperature should be at 600° to 700° F, very hot for a quick cooking time.) For added smoky flavor, cover the grill. Put the clams in a 12-inch ovenproof skillet. Add the tomatoes, shallots, and garlic. Pour the Saffron Vinaigrette over the clams and vegetables. Cover the skillet, place on the grill, and cover the grill. Cook the clams for 5 to 6 minutes. Uncover the grill and skillet and continue to cook the clams until they open, transferring them as they do to a covered container to keep warm. Discard any clams that do not open during the cooking process. Add the lemon juice to the vinaigrette in the skillet and cook for 30 seconds. Stir in the parsley.

Divide the clams among 4 bowls and pour the hot vinaigrette over them. Serve with the toasted bread.

❧ Saffron Vinaigrette

1/2 cup Chardonnay vinegar or
　　other white-wine vinegar
6 to 7 saffron threads
1/3 cup extra-virgin olive oil

1/3 cup vegetable oil
1 teaspoon salt
Heaping 1/2 teaspoon freshly
　　ground black pepper

In a nonreactive saucepan, combine the vinegar and saffron threads; bring to a simmer over medium heat. Remove from heat and let cool. Whisk in the oils and salt and pepper; set aside.

Cory Schreiber is Chef/Owner of Wildwood in Portland, Oregon. This recipe is adapted from his cookbook *Wildwood: Cooking from the Source in the Pacific Northwest* (Ten Speed Press, 2000).

THE SWEET, BUTTERY, SLIGHTLY FIRM SEAFOOD
that U.S. consumers know as a scallop is the large, circular muscle that holds
together the two beautiful fan-shaped shells of this unique swimming bivalve.
In many other countries, the scallop roe is savored as well, and it is becoming
increasingly popular everywhere to eat the entire scallop, much as we do with
oysters, mussels, and clams.

Two types of scallops are typically available to U.S. consumers: the Atlantic
sea scallop and the much smaller American bay scallop. Catches of sea scallops
off the northeastern U.S. coast remain high (approximately 47 million pounds
in 2001), but most of these scallops are dredged, a fishing method that is habitat destructive. Alternative sources are farmed sea scallops from New England
and Newfoundland, where production is limited, and "diver scallops," which
are handpicked in places that large boats with dredges cannot access.

Bay scallops in U.S. waters have largely been depleted. Only 6,000 pounds
were landed in 2001, down from more than 2 million pounds in 1982—such a

Various scallops;
adductor muscle
of bay scallops
(loose)

In the Wild

Scallops swim by quickly opening and clapping closed their shells, a movement that expels water forcefully enough to propel the scallop on a short flight through the water. Unlike their nonswimming bivalve relatives—oysters, mussels, and clams—the exercising scallops thus "body build" the large adductor muscle so popular in seafood recipes.

dramatic change that now a large percentage of the American bay scallops sold in the United States comes from China, which successfully farm raises more than 100,000 tons each year. In North America, bay scallops are farmed both in New England (as Taylor bay scallops) and in Nova Scotia using environmentally friendly systems of nets, ropes, and buoys, but as with farmed sea scallops, production is limited. Nantucket bay scallops are still available in some retail markets during the winter months, but they are dredged, landings are extremely small, and prices are high.

Unlike other bivalves, scallops do not survive well out of water, and the scallop muscle that we eat is usually sold already shucked from the shell. To prolong the shelf life of shucked scallops, sodium tripolyphosphate is added. This preservative alters the flavor of the scallop and causes it to absorb water, increasing the apparent weight and freshness of the scallop. Sea scallops labeled as "dry scallops," "day-boat scallops," "top of the catch," or "last of the catch" are typically not treated with chemicals, but those scallops are, unfortunately, dredged.

The most environmentally sound and chemical-free scallop choices, then, are farmed or diver sea scallops and farmed bay scallops such as Taylor bay scallops. An additional benefit of Taylor bay scallops is that they are shipped alive in the shell immediately after they are harvested—a true prize for chefs.

Sea-Scallop Ceviche with Tomatoes and Arugula

Serves 4

Ceviche was on my first menu at Nora's and is still a mainstay. It is low in fat and very refreshing. It originated in Latin America, where it is made with firm, white-fleshed fish. I also like to make it with shrimp and squid. If you want to make the ceviche more substantial, add thin slices of red onion and avocado. A citrusy Sauvignon Blanc makes a nice accompaniment.

1 pound diver sea scallops
3 limes, juiced
Grated zest of 1 lime
1 serrano or jalapeño chile, seeds removed, thinly sliced
2 tablespoons minced cilantro
1/2 teaspoon ground cumin
2 scallions, trimmed and chopped

Sea salt and freshly ground black pepper
1 teaspoon olive oil, optional
Arugula or other greens, for garnish
1/4 pound cherry tomatoes, for garnish

Rinse the scallops in cold water and remove tough side muscle if present. If the scallops are very large, slice them horizontally into 1/2-inch-thick rounds; otherwise leave them whole. Put them in a glass (not metal) bowl, and pour in the lime juice to cover. Marinate the scallops in the refrigerator for 3 to 4 hours, preferably overnight. They should be opaque and "cooked" through.

Drain off and discard most of the juices accumulated around the scallops, leaving about 2 tablespoons. Add lime zest, sliced chile, cilantro, cumin, and scallions, stirring to combine. Season to taste with salt and pepper. Add a small amount of olive oil to balance the flavor if it is too acidic. Spoon some of the ceviche onto each of 4 small plates. Garnish with arugula and some cherry tomatoes.

Nora Pouillon is Chef/Owner of Restaurant Nora and Asia Nora in Washington, D.C., and author of *Cooking with Nora* (Random House, 1996). In April 1999, Restaurant Nora became America's first certified organic restaurant.

Scallops

Atlantic Sea Scallop, American Bay Scallop

SCIENTIFIC NAMES: *Placopecten magellanicus* (sea scallop), *Argopecten irradians* (bay scallop)

U.S. DISTRIBUTION: Sea scallops are found in deep coastal waters from Maine to North Carolina. Bay scallops are found in shallow waters from Nova Scotia to Cape Hatteras.

WHAT TO LOOK FOR: Fresh scallops have a sweet and briny aroma; reject those with a hint of iodine or sour smell. Look for scallops that are firm and slightly translucent and ivory to pinkish white in color. There are 20 to 30 sea scallops to a pound, though some sea scallops can be larger. It takes 60 to 100 bay scallops to make one pound.

Avoid processed, "soaked" scallops, which have been treated with a chemical to improve shelf life. Soaked scallops will feel "soapy" and not have the sweet, rich taste of "dry" (untreated) scallops.

COOKING METHODS: Sweet, firm, and moist, scallops adapt to any number of cooking methods. Raw, they make a superb ceviche. Grill, sear, or sauté scallops just until the outer surface of the muscle turns solidly opaque—by then the insides will be cooked but still moist. Sautéed small scallops take only 2 or 3 minutes to cook; larger sea scallops will take no more than 4 to 5 minutes. Do not crowd the skillet or the scallops will give off their liquid and steam rather than sauté.

Bay-Scallop Ceviche with Blackened Tomatillo–Truffle Sauce

Serves 12 as an hors d'oeuvre or 4 as an appetizer

COOK'S STRATEGY: The ceviche is best made one day before serving. You can prepare the sauce at the same time.

1 pound Taylor bay scallops
   (or diver sea scallops)
1 cup freshly squeezed lime juice
1/4 cup freshly squeezed orange juice
3 tablespoons finely diced red onion

2 tablespoons finely diced serrano chiles
1 tablespoon kosher salt
2 tablespoons crushed plantain chips
   plus additional whole chips
❧ Blackened Tomatillo–Truffle Sauce

In a bowl, combine the lime juice, orange juice, onion, chiles, and salt. Add the scallops and toss to combine. Cover and refrigerate for 24 hours. Drain and discard all liquid.

In a medium bowl, combine the Bay-Scallop Ceviche with most of the Blackened Tomatillo–Truffle Sauce. Cover and refrigerate for 20 minutes to marinate.

When ready to serve, drain the scallops of excess liquid and toss with the remaining sauce. Adjust the seasoning, adding salt and pepper if necessary. Divide the ceviche on soup spoons laid on a platter. Sprinkle with crushed plantain chips just before serving. Accompany with bowls of plantain chips.

Note: plantain chips can be purchased at most supermarkets and Latin American markets. If you prefer to make them yourself, buy very green plantains and slice them thinly, using a mandoline. Fry them in oil heated to 350°F until crisp.

✦ Blackened Tomatillo–Truffle Sauce

3 tablespoons extra-virgin olive oil

1/2 pound fresh tomatillos,
    husks removed and rinsed

1/2 pound ripe plum tomatoes

1 red onion, peeled and quartered

1 jalapeño chile

4 cachucha chiles (small, hot
    Dominican chiles) or other
    small, mild chiles

1 bunch fresh cilantro leaves

1/2 cup freshly squeezed lime juice

3 tablespoons truffle oil

Kosher salt and freshly ground
    black pepper

Heat 1 tablespoon of the olive oil in a large sauté pan over medium-high heat. Add the tomatillos, tomatoes, onion, jalapeño, and cachuchas. Cook, tossing frequently, until the tomatillo skins are blackened. Remove from the pan and cool to room temperature. For the best texture, grind the mixture in a meat grinder with a medium blade. Otherwise, pulse mixture briefly in a food processor until the vegetables are chopped but still chunky. Transfer to a bowl and combine with the lime juice, truffle oil, remaining 2 tablespoons olive oil, and salt and pepper. Taste for seasoning, cover, and refrigerate for up to 1 day.

Guillermo Pernot is Chef/Partner of ¡Pasión! in Philadelphia. Used with permission from *¡Ceviche!*, copyright © 2001 by Guillermo Pernot and Aliza Green, photographs © by Steve Legato, published by Running Press Book Publishers, Philadelphia and London.

Seared Sea Scallops with Green Garlic and Morels

**Serves 6
as an appetizer**

12 large diver sea scallops
2 cups chicken broth
2 tablespoons unsalted butter
4 ounces green garlic (young garlic that
    resembles a scallion; scallion greens or
    garlic chives may be substituted),
    washed and cut into 1-inch pieces
Salt and freshly ground black pepper
1 shallot, minced

1 cup fresh morels, cleaned (sliced in half,
    checked over, and rinsed)
1/2 cup dry vermouth
1 cup heavy cream
1 tablespoon chopped fines herbes
    (parsley, chives, tarragon, and chervil)
2 tablespoons grapeseed oil
Fava leaves, optional
Sea salt for garnish

Simmer 1 cup of the chicken broth with 1 tablespoon of the butter. Add the green garlic and cook until it is tender. Season with salt and pepper; set aside to cool.

In a sauté pan, melt the remaining 1 tablespoon butter over medium-low heat. Add the shallot and cook until translucent. Add the morels, the vermouth, and the rest of the chicken broth and reduce until almost dry. Add the cream and reduce by half. Finish with the fines herbes and salt and pepper to taste. Set aside and keep warm.

Heat a heavy-bottomed sauté pan over medium-high heat. Season the scallops with salt and pepper. Add the oil and sear the scallops on the flat side until golden brown. Turn the scallops over and sear the other side until golden brown.

Place 2 fava leaves, if using, at the bottom of each plate. Spoon a few tablespoons of the morel sauce around the leaves. Top with a spoonful of the cooked green garlic and then 2 seared scallops. Garnish with a light sprinkling of sea salt and serve immediately.

Barbara Lynch is Chef/Owner of No. 9 Park in Boston, Massachusetts.

Maine Diver Scallops in Chardonnay Sauce

16 Maine diver scallops
Salt and freshly ground black pepper
3 tablespoons clarified butter

1 pound snow peas
1 tablespoon olive oil
�֍ Chardonnay Sauce

Serves 8

Slice each scallop horizontally into 2 pieces. Salt and pepper each side. Heat the clarified butter in a large frying pan. When hot, add the scallops, searing them on one side only. Remove once the bottoms are golden.

Julienne the snow peas lengthwise. Put the olive oil in a pot over high heat. Do not let the oil burn. When the oil is hot, put the julienned peas in the pot and stir well. Sauté about 1 minute; the peas need to stay crispy. Season to taste with salt and pepper.

To serve, place 2 tablespoons of the Chardonnay Sauce in each of 8 warmed soup plates. Add 4 pieces of scallops to each. Divide the julienne of snow peas among them as decoration and garnish.

�֍ Chardonnay Sauce
1 tablespoon olive oil
3 to 4 shallots, julienned
1 lobster head, optional
1 cup Chardonnay
1/2 cup mussel juice (left over from
    cooking mussels), shellfish stock,
    or clam juice

1/2 pound white mushrooms, halved
1 cup crème fraîche
Salt and freshly ground black pepper

Heat 1/2 tablespoon of the oil in a saucepan over low heat. Cook the shallots until soft, but do not allow them to brown. Add the lobster head, if using, and smash it. Add the Chardonnay and mussel juice. Simmer to reduce by half over low heat. In another pan, heat the remaining 1/2 tablespoon olive oil and add the mushrooms. Cover and cook for 5 minutes at high heat. Add the contents of the first pot and the crème fraîche to the mushrooms. Lower the heat to low and cook for about 20 more minutes. When the sauce has thickened, strain through a fine-mesh sieve. Season to taste with salt and pepper.

Michel Richard is Executive Chef/Owner of Citronelle in Washington, D.C. He is the author of *Home Cooking with a French Accent* (William Morrow and Co., 1993)

Sea Scallops with Papas Chorreadas and Romaine

Serves 4

"Chorreadas" is a Spanish word that describes the way you pour a sauce and it flows over the dish. Here I make a creamy sauce that has a tiny jolt of heat from the crushed red pepper flakes in the Jack cheese and some sweetness from the tomatoes. In my interpretation, the sauce is served both under and over the potatoes. In addition, the untraditional accompaniment of romaine leaves adds a soft green hue. This recipe also works well with any white, flaky fish, shrimp, or lobster.

COOK'S STRATEGY: Begin by boiling the potatoes. While they are cooking make the Chorreadas Sauce. Sear the scallops just before serving.

1-1/2 pounds diver sea scallops
2 tablespoons olive oil
Kosher salt
Black pepper freshly cracked from a mill
4 large Idaho potatoes, scrubbed and
    quartered lengthwise into wedges

Extra-virgin olive oil
Chopped fresh herbs, optional
✦ Chorreadas Sauce

Boil the potatoes in salted water until tender, about 30 minutes. Drain.

Heat 1 or 2 large nonstick skillets (so the scallops are not crowded) and add 2 tablespoons of the oil. Lightly season the scallops with the salt and pepper just before cooking. When the oil is quite hot, sear the scallops over medium-high heat until golden on the bottom. Turn them over and cook about 20 seconds more. Remove them to a warm wire rack set over a plate.

Pour the Chorreadas Sauce with the lettuce onto 4 warm plates. Place the potato wedges on the sauce and drizzle the potatoes lightly with extra-virgin olive oil. Season the potatoes with salt and pepper. Spoon the remaining warmed sauce over the potatoes. Garnish with some chopped fresh herbs if desired. Place the scallops on top of the sauce and serve.

❋ Chorreadas Sauce

3 tablespoons butter

1 red onion, finely chopped

3 vine-ripened tomatoes, peeled,
    seeded, and diced

Kosher salt and freshly ground
    black pepper

2/3 cup heavy cream

6 ounces pepper Jack cheese
    (Monterey Jack with jalapeños),
    grated (about 1-1/2 cups)

2 handfuls of thinly sliced romaine lettuce

In a large sauté pan over medium-high heat, melt the butter. When it foams a little, add the onion and cook until lightly caramelized, about 8 minutes. Add the tomatoes, season with salt and pepper, and cook for 7 minutes; the sauce will develop a stewlike consistency. Stir in the cream, bring to a simmer, and then stir in the cheese. Cook for another 3 minutes to allow the components to meld. Divide the sauce in half and put half in a small pot and keep warm. Place the other half in a warm bowl, add the romaine leaves, and gently stir until the leaves are warmed.

Norman Van Aken is Executive Chef/Owner of Norman's in Coral Gables, Florida. He is the author of four cookbooks, the most recent titled *New World Kitchen: Latin American and Caribbean Cuisine* (Ecco, 2003).

Grilled Sea Scallops with Black-Eyed Peas, Cabbage, Tomatoes, and Slab Bacon

Serves 4

This recipe gives a hint of a hearty meal to come, but actually it is quite light. For those inclined naturally to lighten things up, or for those with dietary considerations, you may omit the bacon. Although grilling lends a specific character to the scallops, it is not a necessity. If grilling is impractical, the scallops may be cooked by broiling in the oven. Place the scallops on a lightly oiled baking sheet under a preheated broiler and broil for two minutes on each side. Don't forget a chilled glass of Sauvignon Blanc, one with enough acidity to balance the richness in flavor of the scallops and bacon.

1-1/2 pounds diver or farm-raised
    sea scallops, side muscle removed
1/2 cup dried black-eyed peas, washed,
    picked over, and soaked
    in water for 12 hours
2 teaspoons salt, plus more for seasoning
1/2 pound hickory-smoked slab bacon
3 tablespoons peanut oil

1 pound green cabbage
    (discolored and tough outer
    leaves removed), cored, quartered,
    and sliced 1/4-inch thick
Freshly ground black pepper
2 vine-ripened tomatoes, peeled,
    seeded, and chopped
1 bunch watercress, stems trimmed,
    washed and dried
Lemon wedges for garnish

Drain the soaked black-eyed peas in a colander. Rinse the peas with cold water and drain thoroughly before cooking.

Bring 1 quart of cold water and the 2 teaspoons salt to a boil in a 3-quart saucepan over high heat. Add the black-eyed peas. Adjust the heat and simmer the peas uncovered about 40 minutes, until tender but slightly firm to the bite. Drain the cooked peas in a colander and set aside at room temperature until needed.

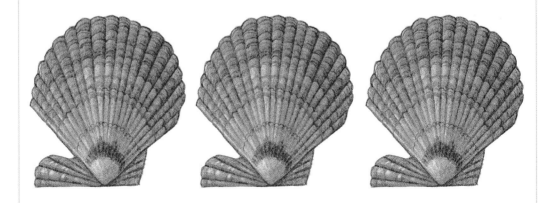

Preheat the oven to 325°F. Trim the rind and excess fat from the bacon. Slice the bacon into strips, then cut into 3/8-inch cubes. Spread on a baking sheet with sides and bake for 30 minutes. Transfer the cooked bacon to paper towels to drain. Keep the drained bacon at room temperature until needed.

In a large, nonstick sauté pan, heat 1 tablespoon of the peanut oil over medium-high heat. When hot, add the cooked bacon and sauté for 30 seconds. Stir in the cabbage, season with salt and pepper, and heat for 2 minutes. Add 2 tablespoons of water and braise the cabbage and bacon for 3 to 5 minutes. Add the cooked black-eyed peas and chopped tomatoes, season with salt and pepper, and continue to heat until the mixture is hot, about 2 to 3 minutes. Keep warm while preparing the scallops.

Combine the scallops with the remaining 2 tablespoons peanut oil. Season with salt and pepper. Thread the scallops onto 4 skewers. Grill the scallop skewers for 4 minutes (for tender and delicious scallops, do not overcook) over a medium gas or charcoal fire. Turn the skewers only once while cooking. Remove from fire.

Portion the cabbage mixture onto each of 4 warmed large soup or pasta plates. Remove the grilled scallops from the skewers and place a portion onto the cabbage on each plate. Garnish with the watercress and lemon wedges. Serve immediately.

Marcel Desaulniers is Chef/Owner of The Trellis Restaurant in Williamsburg, Virginia. He is co-host of the PBS shows *Cook-Off America* and *Grilling Maestros* and is the author of numerous books, including *Death by Chocolate* (Rizzoli, 1992), *The Trellis Cookbook* (Grove Press, 1988) and *Salad Days* (Simon and Schuster, 1998).

Thai-Curry Sea Scallops with Black-Rice Cakes and Green-Papaya Salad

Serves 4

COOK'S STRATEGY: The black rice requires 1-1/2 hours of cooking and then needs to cool. Begin cooking the rice well before cooking the scallops, which take only a few minutes to cook. The Thai-Curry Paste can be prepared a day or two in advance.

20 large diver sea scallops
2 teaspoons peanut oil or canola oil
2/3 cup chicken broth
1/2 cup coconut milk
2 tablespoons cornstarch dissolved
    in 2 tablespoons water

Salt
❧ Thai-Curry Paste
❧ Black-Rice Cakes
❧ Green-Papaya Salad

Heat the oil to smoking in a large nonstick skillet over medium-high heat. Remove the skillet from the heat and quickly add scallops to the pan, one by one. Return pan to the heat and sear scallops on one side, then the other. The process should take about 4 or 5 minutes; the scallops will be medium rare. Transfer the scallops to a warm platter and discard excess grease from the pan. Add 3 tablespoons of the Thai-Curry Paste and sauté briefly. Pour in the chicken broth and cook rapidly to reduce by half. Stir in the coconut milk and continue to simmer, adding the cornstarch and water, drop by drop, until the sauce is thick enough to coat a spoon. Season to taste with salt. Reserve and keep warm until ready to serve.

Set a Black-Rice Cake in the center of each of 4 plates. Arrange 5 scallops around each rice cake. Pour the sauce over the scallops and top with Green-Papaya Salad.

❧ Thai-Curry Paste
1/4 pound peeled fresh galangal
    (available at Asian markets)
1/4 pound peeled fresh ginger
1/4 pound peeled fresh turmeric
    (available at Asian markets)
1/2 pound shallots, sliced

1 head garlic, cloves peeled and chopped
1 bunch fresh cilantro
Juice of 2 limes
5 Thai bird chiles
Peanut oil

Place the galangal, ginger, turmeric, shallots, garlic, cilantro, lime juice, and chiles in a blender or food processor and grind. Add just enough peanut oil to make a paste. Continue to grind until the paste is smooth. This recipe makes about 2 cups of curry paste. Transfer the extra curry paste to a plastic container and freeze for later use.

✦ Black-Rice Cakes

2 cups glutinous Thai black rice

1/4 cup yellow Thai-curry paste (available at Asian markets) or leftover Thai-Curry Paste from recipe above

Put 4-1/2 cups water and the curry paste in a blender and mix for a few seconds. Pour the mixture into a stockpot and bring to a simmer. Add the rice and cook until tender and creamy, about 90 minutes. Spread evenly on a baking sheet to the height of the sides to cool. Use a biscuit cutter to cut out rice cakes.

✦ Green-Papaya Salad

1/2 green papaya, peeled, seeded, and julienned

1 zucchini, julienned

1 yellow squash, julienned

1/2 carrot, julienned

2 Thai bird chiles, thinly sliced

Juice of 1 lime

1 clove garlic, chopped

2 tablespoons Thai fish sauce

Toss all ingredients together in a mixing bowl.

Christine Keff is Chef/Owner of Flying Fish and Fandango in Seattle, Washington.

Octopus and Squid

ALTHOUGH THEY LOOK VERY DIFFERENT FROM their fellow mollusks, because they lack external shells, octopus and squid are closely related to oysters, clams, mussels, and scallops. Squid, with its slightly chewy texture and light flavor, is already a popular seafood species among Americans (think fried calamari), but fewer home cooks are familiar with preparing octopus. Although octopus can be tough if not prepared properly, anyone can cook it in delicious ways at home. The elegant recipes provided here by Roberto Donna of Galileo, Charlie Palmer and Dante Boccuzzi of Aureole, Brad Thompson of Mary Elaine's at the Phoenician, and Nobuo Fukuda of Sea Saw provide some great ideas for introducing octopus into your kitchen.

Octopus *(center)* and northern shortfin squid *(top left and bottom right)*

In the Wild

Octopus and squid differ behaviorially from the bivalves in being excellent swimmers and predators. One reason that octopus and squid are so effective at stalking and attacking prey is that they are smart: Along with the cuttlefish and chambered nautilus, these otherwise primitive creatures have the most complex brain of any invertebrate (animal without a backbone). In fact, researchers have observed octopus learning hunting strategies from each other and believe that they can communicate with other octopuses by rapidly changing their patterns of body color.

Squid is easier to find in retail seafood markets than octopus because the commercial fishery for squid is far better developed. In 2001, only 109,000 pounds of octopus were landed from U.S. waters, whereas in the same year, the 190 million pounds of California market squid caught made this species the most important seafood in the California commercial fishing industry by value. The Atlantic longfin inshore squid (winter squid), as well as the northern shortfin squid (summer squid), also are heavily fished.

Octopus is an ecologically sound seafood choice because the animals are caught in pots, a method that has no negative effect on the environment. When purchasing squid, choose California market squid when possible. The population appears stable off the west coast, and the brightly lit purse seines in which they are caught attract squid but little bycatch and do not destroy bottom habitat. Populations of the other squid species have been overfished, are fished with more destructive methods such as trawling, or may not even be available to consumers because they are sold as bait.

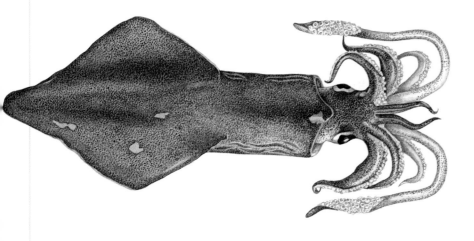

Octopus and Tomato Salad with Wasabi Aïoli

Serves 4

24 thin slices boiled octopus (available at Asian markets)

3 medium heirloom tomatoes, each cut into 8 slices

1 shallot, thinly sliced

2 medium balls fresh mozzarella cheese, preferably buffalo mozzarella each cut into 12 slices

2 tablespoons fruity extra-virgin olive oil

2 teaspoons yuzu (Japanese citron) juice (available at Japanese markets)

Pinch of sea salt and freshly cracked mixed peppercorns

2 cups baby arugula

✤ Wasabi Aïoli (2 tablespoons)

Layer the tomatoes, shallot, cheese, and octopus—in that order—around the perimeter of a serving dish. Drizzle with the olive oil and yuzu juice. Sprinkle with salt and pepper. Mound the arugula in the center. Dot each slice of octopus with a little Wasabi Aïoli.

✤ Wasabi Aïoli

1 clove garlic, pressed with a garlic press

1 egg yolk

1 teaspoon fresh wasabi (or wasabi paste in a tube from an Asian market)

1/2 cup olive oil

Salt

In a bowl, combine the garlic, egg yolk, and wasabi. Slowly whisk in the olive oil until the mixture reaches a mayonnaise-like consistency. Add salt to taste.

Nobuo Fukuda is Chef/Owner of Sea Saw in Scottsdale, Arizona.

Octopus

SCIENTIFIC NAMES: Various species of *Octopus*, usually *Octopus vulgaris*

OTHER NAMES: Octopus may be sold in the United States by its Spanish name, pulpo.

U.S. DISTRIBUTION: Atlantic, Gulf, and Pacific coasts

WHAT TO LOOK FOR: In U.S. markets, it's rare to find whole fresh octopus (but see Retail Sources). If you do, it usually weighs around 2 pounds. The flesh should be shiny, with a bluish or gray tint. You are more likely to find raw or cooked frozen arms. Asian seafood markets are often a good source for octopus.

COOKING METHODS: The predatory octopus has a hard beak that should be removed, along with the eyes, before cooking. European and Asian cooks have secrets for tenderizing octopus (Roberto Donna shares one in his recipe on page 48), but lengthy simmering in liquid is the time-honored approach.

Carpaccio of Saffron-Braised Octopus

Serves 10

COOK'S STRATEGY: This recipe takes two days to prepare. The fish stock, which takes about thirty minutes to make, should be made before proceeding with the rest of the recipe. The terrine and octopus cooking liquid need to chill overnight.

4 pounds fresh octopus arms
2 teaspoons saffron threads, plus more
    for garnish
Salt and freshly ground black pepper
1 stalk celery, julienned
1/2 small red onion, julienned

1 cup baby arugula
3 tablespoons lemon oil
3 tablespoons freshly squeezed lemon juice
➤ Fish Stock (5 quarts)

In a large saucepan, combine the octopus, 5 quarts of Fish Stock, and 2 teaspoons saffron. Season with salt and pepper. Simmer until the octopus is tender, about 4 hours. Drain the octopus, reserving the cooking liquid.

Line a 10-by-3-by-2-1/2-inch terrine mold with plastic wrap, allowing the plastic wrap to drape over the edge by 3 inches. While the octopus is still hot, straighten the arms, cutting if necessary, to fit along the length of the lined mold. Alternate the widths of the arms as necessary and press to fit evenly into the mold. Pour some of the reserved cooking liquid into the mold to cover the octopus. Cover with plastic wrap, place two 1-pound weights on top, and refrigerate overnight. Taste the remaining cooking liquid and add salt if needed. Strain the liquid through a fine-mesh sieve into a bowl. Cover and refrigerate overnight to set the natural gelatin.

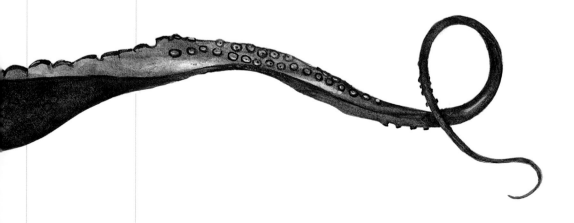

The next day, invert the terrine mold onto a cutting board. Remove the mold, discard the plastic wrap, and cut the octopus into thin slices. Return the slices to the refrigerator to keep cold. Cut the gelée (chilled cooking liquid) into little cubes.

To serve, lay the slices of octopus down on a plate and spoon gelée on the side. In a small bowl, toss the celery, red onion, and arugula with the lemon oil and lemon juice and season with salt and pepper. Place the salad on top of the octopus. Sprinkle with a few strands of saffron.

✦ Fish Stock
2 pounds fish bones, from lean, white-fleshed fish
1 head garlic, cloves peeled

1 onion, chopped
3 sprigs fresh thyme

Combine all ingredients and 5 quarts water in a large pot. Bring to a simmer and cook for 20 minutes. Strain. Makes about 5 quarts.

Chef Charlie Palmer, author and restaurateur, has established restaurants in Las Vegas, Sonoma, and New York, including Aureole, from which he and Executive Chef Dante Boccuzzi submitted this recipe. Palmer is the author of *Great American Food* (Random House, 1996) and *Charlie Palmer's Casual Cooking* (William Morrow and Co., 2001).

Basquaise-Style Seafood Salad

Serves 4

COOK'S STRATEGY: Simmer the octopus and make the Tomato Confit Petals first, as they take a couple of hours to cook.

1/2 pound fresh octopus arms
6 ounces squid
1 pound small hard clams, scrubbed
8 large U.S.-trawled or -farmed shrimp
Court bouillon
Piment d'espelette or other
    small hot chile
Olive oil
Freshly squeezed lemon juice
Salt and freshly ground black pepper
Paprika
1/2 cup white wine

1 tablespoon butter
1 sprig thyme
4 ounces chorizo, cut into 1/4-inch slices
6 fingerling potatoes, boiled, peeled,
    sliced 1/4-inch thick
2 pequillo peppers, cut into
    1/8-inch-wide strips
1 bunch parsley, leaves roughly chopped
4 imported black olives, flesh
    removed in 4 strips
1 teaspoon finely chopped garlic
✦ Tomato Confit Petals

Simmer the octopus in court bouillon for 2 hours until tender. Cool and remove dark skin. Slice the octopus arms into 1/4-inch cross sections and lay on a small tray. Sprinkle with piment d'espelette, olive oil, and lemon juice. Cover with plastic wrap.

Clean the squid and slice the bodies into very thin cross sections. Heat 1 tablespoon olive oil in a large skillet over high heat. Quickly sauté the squid. Season with salt, pepper, paprika, piment d'espelette, and olive oil. Reserve.

Heat the wine, butter, and thyme in a pot. Add the clams and let them steam until they open. Remove the clams. Reduce the cooking liquid by half, strain, and reserve. Remove the clams from their shells and keep covered.

In a skillet over medium-high heat, sauté the chorizo slices. Drain off any oil from the skillet. Keep the chorizo warm.

To serve, arrange the octopus slices around the center of each plate. In a bowl, combine the Tomato Confit Petals, potatoes, pequillo peppers, clams, and squid with the reserved clam juice, lemon juice, olive oil, and parsley. Season with salt and pepper. Spoon the mixture inside the octopus ring. Quickly sauté the shrimp in a little olive oil. When almost cooked, add olive strips, garlic, and additional lemon juice and parsley. Top each plate with 2 shrimp and a slice of chorizo. Spoon pan juices over each serving.

✦ Tomato Confit Petals

2 tomatoes, peeled, seeded, and quartered   1/4 cup olive oil

Preheat the oven to 200°F. Put the tomato quarters in a small baking dish and pour the olive oil over them. Slow roast until wrinkled and intensely flavored, about 2 hours. Tomato confit may be prepared several days in advance.

Bradford Thompson is Chef de Cuisine of Mary Elaine's
at The Phoenician in Scottsdale, Arizona.

Octopus Salami with Potato and Basil Salad on Sardinian Bread with Tomatoes

Serves 8 as an antipasto

COOK'S STRATEGY: Octopus cannot be rushed. Here it simmers for forty-five minutes and then is chilled for six hours, allowing plenty of time to prepare the accompaniments.

3 pounds fresh octopus (frozen may
    be used but fresh is preferred)
4-1/4 cups dry white wine
1 large onion, chopped
1 carrot, sliced
4 stalks celery, sliced
1 bunch Italian flat-leaf parsley

1 bay leaf
1 teaspoon black peppercorns
Juice of 2 lemons
1/4 cup salt
✤ Potato and Basil Salad
✤ Sardinian Bread with Tomatoes

Special Equipment: 2 wine-bottle corks

Rinse the octopus in fresh water a few times before removing the mouth and eyes. Grab the octopus at the head and smash it a few times over your work table in order to break some of the very hard fibers; this will help to make the octopus tender after cooking.

Place the wine corks and all the ingredients for the octopus in a large stockpot, and add the octopus. (The corks help to make the octopus tender.) Bring to a boil and simmer for 45 minutes. Remove the pot from the heat and allow the octopus to cool in the liquid for 10 minutes. Place the octopus in a linen or cheesecloth bag large enough to hold the octopus with room to be tied at the top, and squeeze all the liquid out of it. Tie it very tightly and place it in the refrigerator with a weight on top of it for at least 6 hours.

To serve, thinly slice the Octopus Salami and fan the slices on a platter. Spoon the Potato and Basil Salad on top of the octopus. Place Sardinian Bread with Tomatoes alongside.

✤ Potato and Basil Salad
1 pound Red Bliss potatoes, cubed
1 cup olive oil
Juice of 2 lemons
1 clove garlic
14 basil leaves
4 teaspoons chopped Italian
    flat-leaf parsley

2 slices white bread
1 hard-cooked egg
5 gherkins
1/3 cup sliced imported black
    olives, such as kalamata

Boil the potatoes in a large pot of water until tender, about 10 to 15 minutes. Drain and rinse under cold water. Place all remaining salad ingredients in a blender except the black olives and blend for 1 minute. Mix the potato cubes with the sliced black olives and dress with the dressing.

❧ Sardinian Bread with Tomatoes

1/2 pound grape or cherry tomatoes, each cut in half

1/2 cup olive oil

1/2 teaspoon chopped fresh oregano

Salt and freshly ground black pepper

4 carasau bread (or 4 pieces of pita bread, each sliced horizontally to make two rounds and toasted until crispy)

In a bowl, toss the tomatoes with the olive oil, oregano, and salt and pepper. Just before serving, top the carasau or pita with the tomato mixture.

Roberto Donna is Chef/Owner of Galileo, Laboratoria del Galileo, Barolo, Vivo, and Il Radicchio in Washington, D.C., and Cesco in Bethesda, Maryland. He is the author of *Cooking in Piedmont* (Food Concepts Marketing Corporation, 1997).

Grilled Calamari with Warm White-Bean Salad

Squid

California Market Squid

SCIENTIFIC NAME: *Loligo opalescens*

OTHER NAMES: Opalescent inshore squid

U.S. DISTRIBUTION: California coast

WHAT TO LOOK FOR: Squid (2 to 3 ounces each) can be frozen, thawed, and refrozen and still retain good flavor and texture. Under the purplish-brown thin skin, there should be no discoloration on the main body or mantle. The squid should look shiny and firm. Smell it: Squid should have a faint ocean perfume. Whole and cleaned squid are available.

COOKING METHODS: Be adventurous with squid. Many of us go for fried calamari on a restaurant menu, but it's easy to do at home. Panfried or grilled squid adds flavor and texture to seafood salads and rice and pasta dishes.

Squid have a transparent internal shell called a "pen" that should be removed before cooking, along with the hard, beaklike mouth and eyes. The rest of the body, as well as the arms and tentacles, can then be cooked. For tender, not rubbery, squid, follow the "2-or-20 minute" rule. Cook squid very quickly in a very hot pan for no more than 2 minutes; if it cooks any longer and becomes tough, continue cooking at a much lower heat with the addition of some aromatic broth for about 20 minutes, by which time the squid will be tender again.

Serves 6 as an appetizer

This is one of our most popular menu items, and, although our menu changes daily, this dish is always on (as long as fresh calamari is available). The grilled calamari and white-bean salad are accented with a bit of parsley-garlic oil just before serving.

COOK'S STRATEGY: To ensure that the beans are completely tender, start simmering them at least two hours before serving. It takes a while to skewer the squid, but only minutes to cook them.

1 pound fresh calamari (squid), cleaned and separated, preferably not skinned
1 lemon
Kosher salt and freshly ground black pepper
Extra-virgin olive oil, for brushing

Several leaves frisée lettuce, torn
3 cups arugula
Splash of vinegar
18 to 24 imported olives
➤ White Beans
➤ Parsley-Garlic Oil

Special Equipment: Several 6-inch wooden skewers, soaked in water for 20 minutes

Remove strips of zest from the lemon with a vegetable peeler. Stack the strips and cut into fine julienne with a large knife. Put the lemon julienne in a small pot of cold water, bring to a boil, and drain immediately. Rinse with cold water. Set aside.

Prepare a charcoal or gas grill. Skewer the squid bodies and heads in groups of 3 using 2 wooden skewers, once through the bottom and once through the top of each. Season with salt and pepper and brush with oil. Grill until the squid begin to firm up slightly and take on color. Flip and grill on the other side.

Just before serving, toss the frisée and arugula with salt, pepper, a splash of vinegar, and some extra-virgin olive oil. Warm the beans with some of their cooking liquid, some extra-virgin olive oil, and salt and pepper. Arrange the Grilled Calamari with the White Beans and the greens. Sprinkle with the olives, Parsley-Garlic Oil, and julienned lemon zest.

✤ White Beans

1 cup (4 ounces) "rice beans" (tiny white beans) or great northern beans

1 sprig fresh sage leaves
1 to 2 cloves garlic
Kosher salt

Combine the beans, sage, and garlic in a large pot. Add cold water to cover by about 4 inches and bring to a boil. Reduce the heat to a very low simmer and cook for about 2 hours, or until the beans are completely tender. Season lightly with salt and store in their liquid.

✤ Parsley-Garlic Oil

1/2 clove garlic
Kosher salt
1/2 cup extra-virgin olive oil

1/2 bunch Italian flat-leaf parsley, finely chopped

Combine the garlic and pinch of salt in a mortar and pound to a paste with a pestle. Transfer to a stainless-steel bowl. Whisk in the oil, a little at a time, to form a homogeneous mixture. When all the oil is added, stir in the parsley and season with salt.

Craig Stoll is Chef/Owner of Delfina in San Francisco, California.

Roasted Squid with Bread Crumbs and Oregano

Serves 4

Fresh squid from Monterey Bay are inexpensive but luxurious. We roast them in the pizza oven, which cooks them quickly and gives them an incredible flavor. If you don't have a wood-burning oven, this is still quite delicious cooked in a conventional oven. If tiny squid are available, simply clean them and roast them whole.

1-1/4 pounds fresh squid
Salt and freshly ground black pepper
3 tablespoons extra-virgin olive oil

1/2 cup fresh bread crumbs
1 teaspoon chopped fresh oregano
❧ Aïoli (Garlic Mayonnaise)

Preheat the oven to 400°F. To clean the squid, separate the head from the body and cut free the tentacles, trimming off and discarding the eyes and beaklike teeth. Starting at the tip of the body, with the back of a paring knife, push out and discard the insides and the transparent pen or quill from within. Cut the body into 1/4-inch rings. Season the rings and tentacles with salt, pepper, and 2 tablespoons of olive oil. (If using pre-cleaned squid bodies, rinse and cut into rings.)

Toss the bread crumbs with the remaining tablespoon of olive oil and toast in the preheated oven until golden, stirring them after 5 minutes to help them brown evenly. Toss with the chopped oregano while still warm and reserve.

Turn the oven up to 500°F or have your wood-burning oven ready to go. Lay the seasoned squid on a baking sheet with sides (the squid give off liquid as they cook). Bake for 5 minutes, until the squid are nicely roasted and lightly browned. Remove the baking sheet from the oven and pour off the liquid.

To serve, arrange the squid on a platter and sprinkle with the bread crumbs. Thin the Aïoli a bit with water and drizzle over the top.

❧ Aïoli (Garlic Mayonnaise)
3 cloves garlic, peeled (feel free to use
    more or fewer garlic cloves,
    depending on their size—use your
    taste and preference to judge)
Salt

1 egg yolk, lightly beaten
3/4 cup pure olive oil
1/4 cup extra-virgin olive oil
    (extra-virgin olive oil adds flavor but
    can be overpowering by itself)

Mash the garlic to a smooth paste in a mortar with a pinch of salt. Take out one-third of the paste and set aside. To the rest of the garlic add 1 teaspoon water, 1/4 teaspoon salt, and the egg yolk, stirring well. Combine the two types of olive oil. Slowly whisk in the olive oil, a few drops at a time. As the mixture begins to thicken, begin adding the oil in a slow, steady stream. If the aïoli becomes too thick, thin it with a bit of water and continue. After all the oil has been mixed in, taste for salt and garlic and adjust accordingly. Refrigerate until needed. Aïoli should be used the day it is made, preferably within a few hours; otherwise, the fresh garlic flavor dissipates and becomes unpleasant.

Alice Waters is Owner of Chez Panisse Restaurant in Berkeley, California. She is the author or co-author of eight books, including *Chez Panisse Café Cookbook,* copyright © 1999 by Alice Waters, from which this recipe was adapted and reprinted by permission of HarperCollins Publishers Inc.

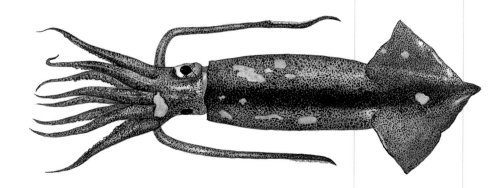

Squid Sauté

Serves 5 as an appetizer, 4 as an entrée

1-1/2 pounds squid, cleaned (those with bodies approximately 4 to 5 inches long are best)
15 cloves garlic, peeled
1/2 cup olive oil
1 teaspoon salt
1 teaspoon freshly ground black pepper
2 large vine-ripened tomatoes, peeled, seeded, and diced
1 large bunch oregano, leaves only, chopped

Cut the squid bodies into thin (1/4-inch) rings, remove beaks from the heads, and leave the tentacles whole. Wash, dry, and place in a mixing bowl. Purée the garlic with 1/4 cup of the olive oil in a blender until smooth. Pour over the squid. Add the salt and pepper, tossing well to combine.

Heat a dry, medium skillet over high heat. Add a generous tablespoon of the remaining olive oil and heat until almost smoking. Pour in one-third of the marinated squid and sauté for 30 seconds. Stir in one-third each of the tomatoes and oregano and cook about 2 minutes longer, just until the tomatoes dissolve and the garlic colors slightly. Transfer to a platter, wipe out the skillet, and repeat 2 times.

Serve with flour tortillas as an appetizer or over rice and beans as an entrée.

Mary Sue Milliken and Susan Feniger are Chef/Owners of the Border Grill restaurants in Santa Monica, Pasadena, and Las Vegas, as well as Ciudad in downtown Los Angeles. They are authors of five cookbooks (four dedicated to the Latin kitchen), hosts of *Too Hot Tamales* and *Tamales World Tour* programs on the Food Network, and radio hosts of *Hot Dish* features heard daily in southern California.

Fried Calamari with Garlic, Hot Red Pepper, and Basil

4 pounds fresh California market squid (calamari), cleaned, bodies cut into 1/2-inch pieces
Canola oil, for frying
2 cups all-purpose flour
1/4 cup cornstarch

1 tablespoon salt
1 garlic clove, finely chopped
1 teaspoon dried hot red pepper flakes
2 tablespoons extra-virgin olive oil
1/4 cup chopped fresh basil leaves

Serves 6 as large appetizer portions

Add canola oil to a deep fryer and preheat to 350°F. Thoroughly combine the flour, cornstarch, and salt. Toss the calamari with the flour mixture and shake off the excess. This may need to be done in 3 batches, depending on the size of your fryer. Fry the calamari for about 2 minutes or just until golden. Shake off the excess oil and place calamari into a bowl.

Sprinkle the hot calamari with the garlic, red pepper flakes, olive oil, basil, and salt. Quickly toss together and serve.

Mark Gordon is Executive Chef of Rose's Café in San Francisco, California.

Crisp-Fried Calamari with Green Mayo and Molho Campanha

Serves 6

Molho Campanha is a Brazilian vinaigrette that includes finely chopped vegetables.

COOK'S STRATEGY: Prepare the vivid Green Mayonnaise and Molho Campanha before starting the calamari, which only take a minute to cook.

2 pounds fresh squid (calamari), cleaned, bodies sliced into rings
Flour
Peanut or soybean oil for frying
Salt and freshly ground black pepper
Chopped fresh parsley, for garnish
✦ Green Mayonnaise
✦ Molho Campanha

In a deep, heavy-bottomed saucepan, heat enough oil to fry the calamari safely. Heat to about 350°F. The oil can be tested with a small piece of bread: At the correct temperature the bread will sizzle immediately and turn brown within a minute or so. When the oil is hot, toss the calamari rings in the flour. Coat entirely, shaking off the excess flour. Fry the calamari in batches if necessary until crisp and golden brown, about 1 to 1-1/2 minutes. Drain well. Season to taste.

To serve, spread a spoonful of Green Mayonnaise in the center of each of 6 serving plates and place equal amounts of the Crisp-Fried Calamari over it. Stir the Molho Campanha very well and ladle about 1/4 cup of it on top of each portion of calamari. Sprinkle with chopped parsley.

◈ Green Mayonnaise

3 scallions, including some of the
    green, finely chopped
2 tablespoons chopped fresh parsley
2 tablespoons chopped fresh cilantro
1 tablespoon snipped chives
1 tablespoon capers, drained,
    rinsed, and chopped

1 sour pickle, chopped
1 tablespoon chopped pickled
    jalapeño chiles
1-1/2 cups mayonnaise
Salt and freshly ground black pepper

In a food processor, combine the scallions, parsley, cilantro, chives, capers, pickle, and jalapeños; process until very fine. Add mayonnaise and season to taste.

◈ Molho Campanha

1/2 red onion, finely chopped
2 medium vine-ripened tomatoes,
    finely chopped
1 bunch parsley, minced

1 green pepper, finely chopped
1/2 cup red-wine vinegar
1 cup extra-virgin olive oil
Salt and freshly ground black pepper

In a bowl, combine the red onion, tomatoes, parsley, green pepper, vinegar, and olive oil. Season to taste and set aside.

Christine Keff is Chef/Owner of Flying Fish and Fandango in Seattle, Washington.

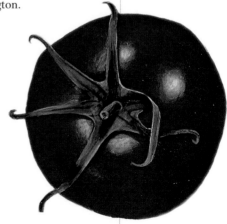

SIMPLY PREPARED, CRABMEAT IS ARGUABLY THE BEST the ocean has to offer: sweet, delicate, and succulent. This delicacy, however, is housed within a veritable fortress of crab shell that must first be picked or cracked away. Once you learn that the crabmeat you're after is the muscle that powers the ten legs of a crab (and thus is hidden within them and around their bases), the tedious picking process will make sense.

Recipes for three species of crabs are included here: the blue crab, stone crab, and Dungeness crab. Blue crabs live along the east and Gulf coasts and have been harvested commercially as far north as Connecticut. Both the hard and soft-shell stages of blue crabs are valued by chefs. Stone crabs are familiar

Stone-crab claws

In the Wild

Unlike most animals, a crustacean such as a crab, lobster, or crawfish doesn't increase in size simply by growing larger; it must lose its outer shell to grow. The old shell cracks, and the soft animal backs out of it. It can take several hours for a blue crab to finish molting and several days for the new shell to harden—during which time the crab is vulnerable to predators. The soft-bodied crab known as a "soft-shell crab" is the molting stage of a blue crab. If you love the taste of crabmeat but don't want to pick it out yourself (or pay a premium price for someone else to do it), give soft-shell crabs a try.

to consumers as "stone-crab claws" because only one claw, not the whole crab, is harvested commercially. The stone-crab industry is built around the amazing fact that crustaceans can drop a whole or partial appendage and then regenerate it. Stone crabs are caught in traps, and one claw is removed; the crab is then released to grow a new claw, which takes about a year.

Dungeness crabs are the only west-coast crab included here, and populations appear to be plentiful. The fishery for them is well managed, and only mature male crabs may be harvested. This is not the case for blue crabs in the Chesapeake Bay, where large harvests of females are thought to have contributed to dramatic declines of crabs in recent years. In other parts of its range, blue-crab populations appear relatively stable. The unusual single-claw-only fishery for stone crab has resulted in remarkably steady landings, most coming from the Gulf coast of Florida.

All three crab species are typically caught in traps or pots, an ecologically sound fishing method because it results in little bycatch and damage to habitat. In winter months, however, in high-salinity lower estuarine or coastal areas off the mid-Atlantic states, dredges with large metal teeth may be used to harvest female blue crabs that have burrowed prior to spawning. This practice not only is habitat destructive but also may prevent females from laying their eggs. Consumers can try to avoid dredged blue crabs by not purchasing live crabs during the winter, but unfortunately most of this catch is processed and the resulting meat is not labeled as originating from dredged crabs.

The snow-crab legs and king-crab legs popular in seafood markets are from overfished populations that are apparently beginning to recover in U.S. waters under Alaskan fishery management plans. Although they could be an ecologically sound choice in the future, for now choose Dungeness crab, blue crab (keeping in mind the concerns noted above), and stone crab instead.

Lump Crabmeat Cakes with Crawfish and Tomato Coulis

Serves 4

The fragrant Opal-Basil Cream Sauce garnishes the crab cakes.

1 pound lump blue-crab meat, picked free
   of shell fragments
1 egg white
2 tablespoons mayonnaise, preferably homemade
1 pinch celery seed
1 pinch cayenne pepper
1 cup white bread crumbs
1/4 to 1/2 cup cracker meal
2 tablespoons grapeseed or vegetable oil
➤ Crawfish and Tomato Coulis
➤ Opal-Basil Cream Sauce

Preheat the oven to 375°F. Combine crab, egg white, mayonnaise, celery seed, and cayenne. Form into 8 cakes and roll lightly in a mixture of bread crumbs and cracker meal. Heat the oil in an ovenproof skillet over medium-high heat. Sear the crab cakes until golden brown on both sides. Transfer the pan to the hot oven for 3 to 4 minutes to finish cooking the crab cakes.

To serve, spoon Tomato Coulis and 6 crawfish tails into each of 4 soup plates. Garnish each with 2 crab cakes. Pour a little Opal-Basil Cream Sauce over the crab cakes.

(Continued)

Crabs

Blue Crab, Stone Crab, Dungeness Crab

SCIENTIFIC NAMES: *Callinectes sapidus* (blue), *Menippe mercenaria* (stone), and *Cancer magister* (Dungeness)

U.S. DISTRIBUTION: Blue crabs are found along the east and Gulf coasts. The fishery for Dungeness crab reaches from the Gulf of Alaska to central California. Stone crabs are a Florida specialty.

WHAT TO LOOK FOR: Whole hard-shell blue crabs (4 ounces to a pound) come live or cooked (fresh or frozen). Male blue crabs, called "Jimmies," are the largest and most expensive. "Jumbo" or "jumbo lump" crabmeat contains the largest unbroken pieces of white meat from the body. "Lump," "backfin," or "special" are names for smaller pieces. "Claw" is darker-colored meat. Crabmeat is often pasteurized to extend shelf life; just-picked unpasteurized meat has a more delicate flavor. Soft-shell blue crabs are sold fresh (sometimes alive) or frozen.

Most Dungeness crabs (1 to 3 pounds) are cooked right after harvest and frozen in a briny solution. If you are buying whole cooked Dungeness crabs, look for those without damaged shells. Dungeness-crab meat is divided into three categories: "fry-legs" is the most expensive, followed by "broken leg meat" and "body meat."

Stone crab claws are always sold cooked.

When buying live crabs of any type, choose moving and feisty individuals—and then handle with caution!

COOKING METHODS: Hard-shell crabs are almost always steamed or boiled. Soft-shell crabs are best panfried or sautéed to crisp the soft outer shell and preserve the marvelous sweet flesh inside. Crabmeat finds its way into crab cakes, gratins, fillings, soups, and sauces.

Crawfish and Tomato Coulis

24 large cooked crawfish tails,
   peeled and deveined
3 tablespoons olive oil
3 shallots, finely chopped
2 cloves garlic, finely chopped

6 large yellow tomatoes, peeled,
   seeded, and diced
1 bay leaf
2 sprigs fresh thyme
Salt and freshly ground white pepper

In a medium saucepan, heat the olive oil over medium heat. Add the shallots and cook for 1 minute without browning. Add the garlic and cook for another 30 seconds. Add the tomatoes, bay leaf, thyme, and salt and white pepper to taste. Cook for 15 minutes over a low to medium heat. Discard the bay leaf and thyme. Puree the tomato sauce in a blender until smooth. Season again, if necessary. Pour the coulis into a saucepan, add the crawfish tails, and reheat gently.

Opal-Basil Cream Sauce

1 cup white wine
1/4 cup dry vermouth, such as Noilly Prat
2 shallots, minced
1 cup heavy cream

Salt and freshly ground black pepper
1/2 tablespoon finely chopped fresh
   opal basil (sweet basil
   may be substituted)

In a small saucepan, heat the white wine, vermouth, and shallots. Simmer until only 2 or 3 tablespoons liquid remain. Add the cream to the wine mixture and reduce by half to a saucelike consistency. Add salt and pepper to taste. Stir in the basil just before serving.

Robert Waggoner is Executive Chef of Charleston Grill in Charleston, South Carolina.

Jumbo Lump Crab Cakes with Baby Arugula and Roasted Sweet Peppers

Serves 6

1 pound jumbo lump blue-crab meat, picked free of shell fragments

1/3 cup mayonnaise, preferably homemade

1/3 cup capers, drained

7-1/2 tablespoons extra-virgin olive oil

1/2 teaspoon dry mustard

1/8 teaspoon cayenne pepper

Salt and freshly ground black pepper

2 slices brioche, crusts removed, sliced into small cubes (1/2 cup)

3 cups baby arugula

3/4 cup roasted red bell peppers, cut into 1/4-inch strips

1/4 cup freshly squeezed lemon juice

In a large mixing bowl, combine the mayonnaise, capers, 1 tablespoon of the olive oil, the mustard, cayenne, and salt and pepper; mix well. Gently stir in the crabmeat and brioche cubes—be careful not to break up lumps of crab. Gently pat the mixture into 6 crab cakes.

Heat a 10-inch nonstick sauté pan over medium heat. Add 1/2 tablespoon of the olive oil and brown the crab cakes on both sides, about 5 minutes. Meanwhile, in a bowl toss the arugula with the peppers, lemon juice, and the remaining 6 tablespoons olive oil. Season to taste.

On 6 plates, put arugula and peppers in the center and top with a crab cake. Serve immediately.

Todd Gray is Chef/Owner of Equinox in Washington, D.C.

Creamed Crab on Brioche with Wild Mushrooms and Thyme

**Serves 4
as an appetizer**

I still get a craving for the creamed crab I used to savor on the days I worked at Dan and Louis Oyster Bar, my family's restaurant in Portland since 1919. This dish is traditionally prepared by heating the crabmeat in a béchamel sauce and spooning it on top of a piece of toast. I use heavy cream instead of béchamel sauce. The cream requires time to reduce, but it has just the right consistency to bind the crabmeat. Wild mushrooms, another great accompaniment to crab, give this dish a rich flavor that will warm your soul on a cold winter's day. Dried mushrooms may be substituted for fresh mushrooms: Use 2 ounces (dried mushrooms are more concentrated), skip the wilting step, and add the dried mushrooms along with the wine. This dish is great paired with Pinot Noir.

8 ounces fresh lump blue-crab meat,
    picked free of shell fragments
4 ounces fresh wild mushrooms, such as
    morels, black trumpet, or chanterelles,
    or 1 portobello mushroom,
    about 4 ounces
1 teaspoon unsalted butter
3 shallots, minced
1/4 cup dry white wine
2 cups heavy cream
1/3 cup grated Asiago or pecorino cheese
1 tablespoon grated lemon zest

1 tablespoon freshly squeezed lemon juice
2 teaspoons minced fresh Italian
    flat-leaf parsley
2 teaspoons minced fresh thyme
2 teaspoons salt
1 teaspoon freshly ground white pepper
Four 1/2-inch-thick slices brioche or
    crusty country bread
2 tablespoons olive oil
10 cups (10 ounces) mixed baby greens
✣ Red-Wine Vinaigrette

Wipe the mushrooms clean. If using wild mushrooms, leave whole; if using portobello, dice. In a large sauté pan or skillet, melt the butter over medium heat. Add the shallots and cook, stirring, for 1 minute. Add the mushrooms and cook until they wilt and reduce in size, 3 to 4 minutes. Stir in the wine and simmer until

reduced by half. Add the cream and cook over medium-high heat until the cream is reduced by half. Stir in the crabmeat, cheese, and lemon zest and juice; cook for 1 minute. Blend in the parsley, thyme, and salt and pepper; remove from heat. The mixture should be thick and creamy. If the mixture is too thin, return to heat and cook until thickened.

Preheat the broiler. Brush both sides of the bread with the olive oil. Broil on each side until lightly browned.

To serve, place a slice of bread on each plate and top with one-quarter of the crab mixture. Toss the mixed greens with 1/4 cup Red-Wine Vinaigrette and place one-quarter on each serving of crab.

✤ Red-Wine Vinaigrette

1/3 cup extra-virgin olive oil

3 tablespoons red-wine vinegar

1 teaspoon Dijon mustard

1/2 teaspoon salt

1/2 teaspoon freshly
    ground black pepper

In a medium bowl, combine all the ingredients and whisk lightly. The vinaigrette can be made up to 5 days ahead and refrigerated. Makes about 1/2 cup vinaigrette.

Cory Schreiber is Chef/Owner of Wildwood in Portland, Oregon. This recipe is adapted from his cookbook *Wildwood: Cooking from the Source in the Pacific Northwest* (Ten Speed Press, 2000).

Sautéed Soft-Shell Crabs on Asparagus

Serves 4

Soft-shell crabs are, for me, one of America's greatest delicacies. I particularly enjoy serving them to European visitors, most of whom appreciate the introduction to this delightful treat not available where they live. Be sure to buy your soft-shell crabs from a reliable fishmonger. These crabs are only good for forty-eight hours to three days after they have shed their hard shell, and the closer you can consume them to the moment of their shedding, the softer and more flavorful they are. The crabs are lightly sautéed here, which makes them tastier and lower in calories than if deep-fried, which is how they are often prepared in restaurants. I serve them with a mixture of asparagus, tarragon, and red onion.

4 large soft-shell crabs
    (about 1 pound)
8 asparagus stalks (about 6 ounces)
    with tight, firm heads
1 large vine-ripened tomato
    (about 12 ounces)
2 tablespoons unsalted butter

3/4 cup chopped red onion
1/2 teaspoon salt
1/2 teaspoon freshly ground black pepper
2 tablespoons peanut oil
1 teaspoon finely chopped garlic
1 teaspoon finely chopped fresh tarragon

Peel the lower third of the asparagus stalks and cut each stalk in half crosswise; each half will be about 3 inches long. Then cut each half lengthwise into 4 to 6 strips. Using a sharp vegetable peeler, peel the tomato, cut in half, and seed it. Alternatively, blanch, peel, and seed the tomato. Cut the tomato flesh into 1/2-inch pieces. You should have about 1-1/2 cups.

Heat 1 tablespoon of the butter until hot in a skillet. Add the onion and sauté it for 1 minute over high heat. Add the asparagus, 1/4 teaspoon of the salt, 1/4 teaspoon of the pepper, and 2 tablespoons water. Bring the mixture to a strong boil and cook it, covered, for 1 minute. Most of the water will have evaporated at this point. Transfer the asparagus to a bowl and set it aside.

Heat 1 tablespoon of the oil in the unwashed skillet. When it is hot, add the tomato pieces, the remaining 1/4 teaspoon salt, the garlic, and the tarragon. Sauté over high heat for about 45 seconds, just long enough to warm and slightly soften the tomato. Transfer the tomato mixture to a bowl and set it aside.

Clean the crabs: Lift up the skirt or apron of each crab and twist it off. Cut off and discard a strip from the front part of the shell that includes the eyes and antennae. Lift up the top shell at both ends to expose the sponge-like lungs on either side, pull them off, and discard them. Pat the crabs dry with paper towels.

Heat the remaining tablespoon each of butter and oil in the skillet. When they are hot, add the crabs in 1 layer and cook them over high heat for about 2 minutes on each side.

To serve, divide the asparagus among 4 plates and arrange 1 crab in the middle of each plate, on top of the asparagus. Spoon the tomatoes on top and around the crab on each plate. Pour any juices that may have accumulated in the skillet on top of the crabs.

Jacques Pépin is a well-known chef, food columnist, cookbook author, and cooking teacher. This recipe was adapted from his book *Jacques Pépin's Table* (Bay Books, formerly KQED Books and Tapes, 1995). Two recent books include *Jacques Pépin Celebrates* (Alfred A. Knopf, 2001) and the autobiography *The Apprentice: My Life in the Kitchen* (Houghton Mifflin, 2003). Jacques appeared on public television with Julia Child in their series *Julia and Jacques Cooking at Home*, and he now hosts that network's *Jacques Pépin Celebrates* with his daughter, Claudine.

Panfried Soft-Shell Crabs with a Ragoût of Spring Vegetables

Serves 4

I think of this recipe as one that captures the changing of the seasons. It takes a little time because each of the green vegetables needs to be blanched separately, but the final dish is well worth the effort.

4 soft-shell crabs, cleaned
   (see page 66, instructions
   by Jacques Pépin)
1 cup buttermilk
1/2 tablespoon Tabasco sauce
1/2 cup yellow cornmeal
1/2 cup all-purpose flour
1/2 teaspoon baking soda
1/2 teaspoon salt
1/2 teaspoon freshly ground black pepper

1/4 cup peanut oil, plus extra as needed
2 sticks plus 2 tablespoons
   (18 tablespoons total)
   unsalted butter, plus extra as needed
1 tablespoon red-wine vinegar
3 tablespoons freshly squeezed lemon juice
1 tablespoon chopped fresh Italian flat-leaf
   parsley or chervil
❧ Ragoût of Spring Vegetables

Place the cleaned crabs in a nonreactive dish. Mix the buttermilk and Tabasco and pour over the crabs. Cover the pan with plastic wrap and refrigerate for 1 hour, turning the crabs occasionally. Combine the cornmeal, flour, baking soda, 1/4 teaspoon of the salt, and 1/4 teaspoon of the pepper and mix well. Drain the crabs and carefully dredge them in this breading mixture, shaking off the excess. Place the crabs on a wire rack over a baking sheet.

Heat the peanut oil and 2 tablespoons of the butter in a heavy skillet over medium-high heat. When hot, carefully place 2 or 3 of the crabs in the skillet, white-side down. Panfry the crabs for 1-1/2 to 2 minutes on each side or until they are a nice golden brown. Panfrying is an alternative to deep-frying that uses less fat and is a good bit simpler. Panfrying also produces a lighter, more intensely flavored soft-shell crab than the traditional deep-frying method.

Transfer the crabs to a platter lined with paper towels. (You may keep the crabs warm in a 200°F oven while you finish frying the others, but be sure to move quickly so they don't dry out.) You may have to add more oil and butter to the pan as you continue to fry the remaining crabs.

When the last crab has been fried, carefully pour all the fat out of the skillet, retaining any small browned bits. Combine the vinegar, lemon juice, and 3 tablespoons water in a small bowl. Add to the skillet and simmer for 30 seconds. Add the remaining 1/4 teaspoon each of salt and pepper and stir to combine. Cut the remaining 2 sticks of butter into 8 pieces and add to the skillet all at once; whisk to incorporate. Add the chopped parsley or chervil, stir, and pour into a sauceboat.

Divide the Ragoût of Spring Vegetables among 4 plates and top each with a soft-shell crab. Serve immediately. Pass the butter sauce separately.

✦ Ragoût of Spring Vegetables

1 cup haricots verts or baby green beans
1 cup asparagus, sliced on the
    diagonal into 1/2-inch-long pieces
1 cup shelled green peas
1 cup snow peas, stem ends removed
1 cup fiddlehead ferns, skins removed
5 tablespoons unsalted butter
3 cups sliced sweet onions, such as
    Wadmalaw, Vidalia, or Maui
    (about 1 pound)

1 cup fresh morels
1 cup chicken broth
1/4 cup heavy cream
1 cup mixed red and yellow
    sweet cherry tomatoes, halved
1 tablespoon chopped fresh chervil
1 tablespoon chopped fresh basil
1 tablespoon chopped fresh thyme
1 teaspoon salt

Bring a saucepan of salted water to a boil. Drop in the haricots verts and briefly boil for 1 minute to set their color. Remove from the saucepan with a slotted spoon and refresh by rinsing with cold water. Set aside to dry. Follow the same procedure to blanch asparagus, green peas, snow peas, and fiddleheads.

Melt 2 tablespoons of the butter in a heavy-bottomed saucepan over medium heat. Add the onions and morels and sauté for 4 minutes, stirring occasionally. Add the blanched vegetables and continue to sauté for a minute or 2. Remove vegetables from the pan; reserve. Add the chicken broth and cream to the pan and stir to combine. Raise the heat to medium high and briskly simmer the mixture for 5 to 7 minutes or until the liquid is reduced by half.

With the mixture still simmering, add the remaining 3 tablespoons of butter, the reserved vegetables, tomatoes, and herbs. Cook, stirring occasionally, for 4 minutes or until the mixture thickens. Immediately remove the pan from the heat. Add the salt and stir to combine well.

Louis Osteen is Chef/Owner of Louis's at Pawleys in Pawley's Island, South Carolina. He is the author of *Charleston Cuisine* (Algonquin Books, 1999), from which this recipe was adapted.

Dungeness-Crab Salad with Meyer Lemon, Endive, and Watercress

Serves 6

Dungeness crab, Meyer lemons, and endive are all in season in the wintertime in the Bay area, so a simple, elegant salad like this one naturally suggests itself.

1 large Dungeness crab
   (about 1-3/4 pounds)
2 large handfuls watercress
   (about 1 bunch)
2 shallots

2 Meyer lemons
Salt and freshly ground black pepper
1-1/2 teaspoons Champagne vinegar
6 tablespoons extra-virgin olive oil
4 Belgian endives

Bring a large pot of salted water to a boil. Add the crab and cook for 13 minutes. Drain and let cool. Lift the carapace and clean the crab of all the "butter" and gills inside. Break the crab in half. Separate the legs from the body and crack them open. Extract all the leg meat carefully; try to keep it intact. Next, split the body and pick out all its meat. Go through all the crabmeat after it is picked to remove any stray shell fragments. Set the crabmeat aside in the refrigerator.

Remove any tough stems from the watercress. Wash and dry it well. Peel and finely dice the shallots. Carefully peel the zest from both the lemons with a sharp vegetable peeler, being sure to take only the yellow peel and none of the bitter white pith. If you do end up with some pith, pare it away. Chop the zest and combine it with the shallots in a small bowl. Season generously with salt and pepper. Squeeze the lemons and add about 5 tablespoons of the juice to the bowl with the shallots and lemon zest. Add the Champagne vinegar, mix well, and let sit for at least 1/2 hour to macerate. Whisk in the olive oil; taste for salt, pepper, and acidity, and adjust as needed.

When you are ready to serve the salad, remove any blemished outer leaves from the endives. Cut them in half lengthwise and remove the cores, then cut lengthwise into strips. Put them in a serving bowl with the watercress, crab, and Meyer lemon vinaigrette and toss well. Arrange on a platter or individual plates and serve immediately.

Alice Waters is Owner of Chez Panisse Restaurant in Berkeley, California. This recipe was adapted from her book *Chez Panisse Fruit,* copyright © 2002 by Alice Waters, illustrations copyright © 2002 by Patricia Curtan, and reprinted by permission of HarperCollins Publishers Inc.

Cracked Dungeness Crab with Garlic, Parsley, and Olive Oil

Serves 2

I like to serve the crab with a side plate of capellini, which I cook for two minutes in the crab-boiling water and then toss in a frying pan with heated olive oil, garlic, maras pepper, and salt. Diners use this capellini to sop up every bit of juice at the bottom of the crab plate. I often add the crab butter from the shell and the tomalley from the center of the crab, if it's sweet, to the capellini.

Maras or Aleppo pepper is relatively mild red chile that gives moderate heat. It can be purchased at spice shops and food stores that carry Middle Eastern products. You can use dried hot red pepper flakes but reduce the amount to a generous pinch.

1 live Dungeness crab
3/4 teaspoon kosher salt plus more
    for cooking water
3 tablespoons extra-virgin olive oil
2 heaping teaspoons minced garlic

3/4 teaspoon maras (Aleppo) pepper
    or 1 pinch dried hot red pepper flakes
1/2 cup Chardonnay wine
3 tablespoons chopped fresh Italian
    flat-leaf parsley

Bring a large pot of water to a boil. Add enough salt to make it taste like the sea. Use tongs to drop in the crab to avoid being pinched by the claws. Bring the water back to a boil and set a timer for 6 minutes per pound of crab. Prepare a bowl of ice water large enough to hold the crab. When the timer rings, remove the crab from the pot and plunge the crab into the ice water. Cool for about 5 minutes or until you can clean the crab without burning your fingers.

Pull the carapace off the crab and remove the white gills. Throw these away. Scrape out the crab butter and orange tomalley from the center of the body, taste it, and save if it's sweet. Break the crab in half. Remove the legs and claws. With a pestle or a wooden mallet, crack the narrow edge of each leg segment—not the flat part of the leg. Crack the claw on its flat sides and don't forget the knuckle. Give each body half a few whacks and cut each half in half. Alternatively, buy a whole, cooked, cracked crab.

In a 10-inch frying pan with a cover, heat the olive oil. Add the garlic, 3/4 teaspoon salt, and the maras pepper (or a smaller pinch of red pepper flakes). When the garlic begins to turn golden, add the cracked crab and toss in the oil. Immediately add the Chardonnay and parsley. Cover the pan and let the crab steam for 2 to 3 minutes depending on the size of the crab. The liquid should reduce a little bit. Taste for seasoning.

To serve, divide the crab between 2 soup plates and pour the pan juices over it.

Patricia Unterman is Owner/Executive Chef of Hayes Street Grill in San Francisco, California, and author of the new third edition of Patricia Uterman's *San Francisco Food Lover's Guide* (Ten Speed Press, 2003).

Dungeness-Crab and Mussel Chowder with Chile 'n' Cheddar Crackers

Serves 8

An Oregon Pinot Gris goes well with this.

COOK'S STRATEGY: The Chile 'n' Cheddar Crackers can be made a few days ahead and stored in an airtight container.

1 pound Dungeness-crab meat
1-1/2 pounds fresh mussels,
    rinsed and debearded
1/2 cup diced bacon or pancetta
    (1/4-inch dice)
3 tablespoons minced garlic
3 tablespoons minced shallots
1 tablespoon fresh thyme leaves
1 teaspoon sambal oelek
    (Indonesian chile sauce)
1 teaspoon grated lemon zest

1/4 cup olive oil
1/4 cup all-purpose flour
1 bottle Pinot Gris
3 cups fingerling potatoes, cut into
    3/8-inch coins and parboiled
2 leeks, trimmed, washed, and cut
    into 1/2-inch dice
Salt and freshly ground black pepper
1/2 cup heavy cream
❧ Chile 'n' Cheddar Crackers

In a large nonreactive saucepan, sauté the bacon, garlic, shallots, thyme, sambal oelek, and lemon zest in the olive oil for 7 minutes over medium heat, stirring frequently. Gradually add the flour, stirring well, and then add the mussels and the Pinot Gris. Cover and bring to a low boil. As the mussels open, remove them from the broth; leave them in the shell, refresh them with a quick dip in cold water and reserve. Add the potatoes and leeks and continue cooking at a low simmer, stirring occasionally, until the leeks and potatoes are tender, 20 to 25 minutes. Season the chowder to taste with salt and pepper, whisk in the heavy cream and fold in the Dungeness-crab meat and mussels.

Serve the chowder in shallow bowls with a stack of Chile 'n' Cheddar Crackers.

✦ Chile 'n' Cheddar Crackers

3 cups all-purpose flour

1 tablespoon mild pimentón
de la Vera or paprika

1 teaspoon ground chipotle chile

1/2 teaspoon kosher salt, plus
more for sprinkling

1/2 teaspoon cream of tartar

1/2 teaspoon baking soda

3 ounces organic sharp cheddar cheese,
coarsely grated (about 3/4 cup)

1 stick (8 tablespoons) unsalted butter,
1/2 stick cut into 1/4-inch
cubes, 1/2 stick melted

1 tablespoon maple syrup

Combine the flour, chile powders, salt, cream of tartar, baking soda, cheese, and cubed butter in a large bowl; mix well. Gradually stir in 2/3 cup water and the maple syrup, mix to bring together into a stiff dough, and knead by hand to form a smooth dough, 4 to 5 minutes. Divide in two, wrap in plastic wrap, and allow the dough to rest for 20 to 30 minutes. Preheat the oven to 400°F.

Roll each piece of dough out on a floured board into a rectangle, 1/8 inch thick. Double the ends back to the center and then fold closed like a book. Roll each of these layered doughs out until 1/8-inch thick and prick all over with a fork. Cut with a pastry cutter into desired shapes and transfer to parchment-lined baking sheets. Sprinkle with kosher salt. Bake until nicely browned, 10 to 15 minutes. Brush the crackers with the melted butter and transfer to a wire rack to cool.

Greg Higgins is Chef/Owner of Higgins Restaurant and Bar in Portland, Oregon. He has contributed to cookbooks such as *Wild about Game* (Broadway Books, 1998) and the *Northwest Beautiful Cookbook* (Collins Publishing, 1993).

Stone-Crab Trio

Each serves 6

A stone-crab soufflé, stone crab au gratin, and Joe's mustard sauce for stone-crab claws are presented here.

STONE-CRAB SOUFFLÉ

3 cups stone-crab meat, picked
    free of shell fragments
4-1/2 tablespoons butter
4-1/2 tablespoons flour
Celery salt

Freshly ground black pepper
1-1/2 cups milk
5 eggs, separated
1 teaspoon chopped fresh parsley
1 teaspoon freshly squeezed lime juice

Preheat the oven to 375°F. Melt the butter in the top of a double boiler. Stir in the flour and celery salt and pepper to taste. Gradually stir in the milk. Remove from the heat and add the crabmeat. Beat the egg yolks well and add to the crab mixture. Return the mixture to the heat and cook slowly for 20 minutes. Beat the egg whites until stiff peaks form. Remove the crab mixture from the heat and fold in the beaten egg whites. Pour the mixture into 6 individual buttered soufflé dishes. Sprinkle with parsley and drizzle the lime juice over the top of each.

Place soufflé dishes in a baking pan with sides. Pour hot water into the pan until it reaches a point one-quarter of the way up the sides of the dishes. Bake for 45 minutes or until the tops of the soufflés are golden brown. Serve at once.

STONE CRAB AU GRATIN

1-1/2 cups stone-crab meat, picked
    free of shell fragments
3 tablespoons butter, plus extra
    for dotting
3 tablespoons flour

1 cup hot milk or cream
1/2 cup grated sharp cheddar cheese
1 teaspoon Worcestershire sauce
1 tablespoon freshly squeezed lemon juice
1/2 cup bread crumbs

Preheat the oven to 350°F. Melt 3 tablespoons butter in the top of a double boiler and stir in the flour. Add the hot milk, stirring constantly. Stir in the cheese, Worcestershire sauce, and lemon juice. Pour the mixture into a small gratin dish. Sprinkle the bread crumbs on top and dot with butter. Bake until the crumbs are a light golden brown, about 20 minutes.

CRACKED STONE-CRAB CLAWS WITH JOE'S MUSTARD SAUCE

1 to 2 dozen cooked stone-crab claws
1 cup mayonnaise
1 tablespoon plus 1/2 teaspoon
   dry mustard

2 teaspoons Worcestershire sauce
1 teaspoon A.1. Steak Sauce
2 tablespoons light cream
1/8 teaspoon salt

Mix the mayonnaise, mustard, Worcestershire sauce, A.1. sauce, cream, and salt; chill. Use as a dipping sauce for the cracked stone-crab claws. Covered, the sauce will keep for 3 to 4 days in the refrigerator.

Andre Bienvenu is Executive Chef of Joe's Stone Crab in Miami Beach, Florida.

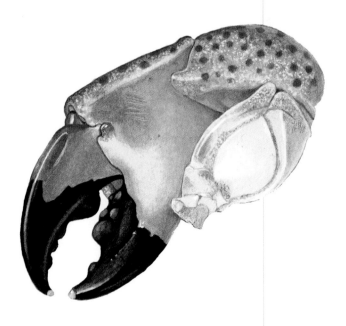

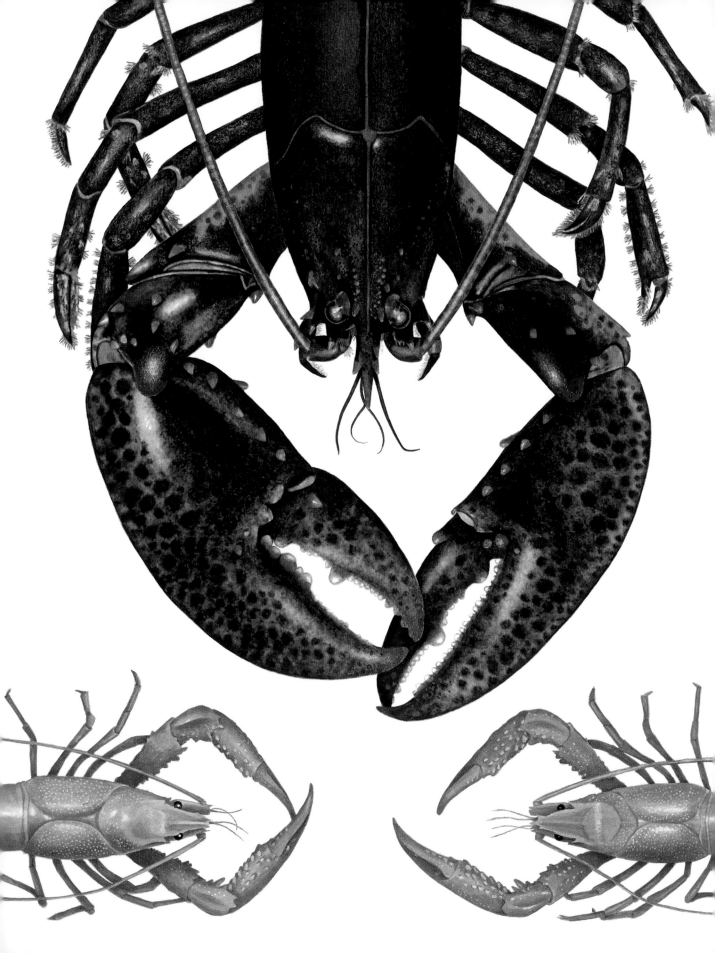

IN 1622 THE PILGRIMS REPORTED THAT CONDITIONS were so bad in New England that they resorted to eating lobster out of desperation. Imagine their surprise if they could have known that lobster would become the delicacy it is considered today. Crawfish, however, has long been revered both by gourmet cooks and regular folks. Crawfish look like miniature American lobsters and are closely related to them, though crawfish usually inhabit fresh water and lobsters are marine. Both have delicious, firm, sweet, and rich flesh in the tail and claws.

American, or Maine, lobsters are caught in traps, and the fishery for them

American lobster *(top)* and crawfish *(bottom)*

In the Wild

Although crawfish also eat plants, they can be vicious predators that use their pincers and tailfans as weapons. Lying in wait for prey, the nocturnal crawfish will remain motionless with its claws open until a hapless fish swims too close and the crawfish launches itself forward to make the kill. Crawfish will even resort to cannibalism: The aggressive red swamp crawfish and white river crawfish, in particular, will attack and eat their vulnerable molting "soft-shell" kin.

off the northeastern United States is well managed though intensive (landings exceeded 71 million pounds in 2001). It may help the lobster population that lobster traps are not as efficient as previously thought: It was recently discovered that only a small percentage of lobsters in a given area is actually captured.

There are nearly 600 species of crawfish worldwide, with about 70 percent of those occurring in North America, many in Kentucky and Louisiana. Crawfish are now farm raised in many places, including Louisiana, California, and China. In Louisiana, more than 10 million pounds were produced in 2001. The red swamp crawfish is the most commonly raised species. Unlike some other farm-raised aquatic species, crawfish are not fed specially formulated diets; rather, they are often grown in rice ponds after the harvest; the rice-plant residue provides nutrition to the crawfish, and the crawfish increase the farm's productivity.

Many American consumers will have tried crawfish only boiled and eaten straight from the shell, but live or steamed whole crawfish and fresh or frozen shelled and deveined crawfish tails are now available. Soft-shelled (molting) crawfish are also available through some retail markets. Crawfish are considered a Swedish national obsession, and traditional crawfish feasts are held there every August. They have also long been popular in French cuisine as *écrevisses*; cooks looking for additional recipes may want to consult French cookbooks.

Prices for U.S.-farmed crawfish can fluctuate based on weather, and readers should be advised that packaged frozen crawfish tails sold in the United States may be from China and thus may have been treated with a potent antibiotic, chloramphenicol, that is prohibited in U.S. farming operations.

U.S. farm-raised crawfish and American lobster are ecologically sound seafood choices and can be substituted for shrimp in many recipes.

Crawfish Etouffée

Serves 4

Serve the étouffée over steamed white rice.

1 pound cooked and peeled
   crawfish tails
1 stick (8 tablespoons) butter
2 cups chopped onions
1 cup chopped celery
1/2 cup chopped green
   bell peppers
2 teaspoons minced garlic

2 bay leaves
1 tablespoon flour
1 cup water
1 teaspoon salt
Pinch of cayenne pepper
2 tablespoons finely chopped
   parsley
3 tablespoons chopped scallions

In a large sauté pan over medium-high heat, melt the butter. Add the onions, celery, and bell peppers and sauté until the vegetables are wilted, about 10 to 12 minutes. Add the crawfish, garlic, and bay leaves and reduce the heat to medium. Cook the crawfish for 10 to 12 minutes, stirring occasionally. Dissolve the flour in the water. Add to the crawfish mixture and stir thoroughly to combine. Season with salt and cayenne pepper. Cook, stirring, until the mixture thickens, about 4 minutes. Stir in the parsley and scallions and continue cooking for 2 minutes.

Emeril Lagasse is Executive Chef/Proprietor of eight restaurants in New Orleans, Las Vegas, Orlando, and Atlanta. He has authored or coauthored seven cookbooks, including *Louisiana Real and Rustic* (William Morrow and Co., 1996), from which he provided this recipe. Emeril hosts the Food Network's *Essence of Emeril* and *Emeril Live.*

Crawfish

SCIENTIFIC NAME:
Procambarus clarkii (red swamp crawfish)

OTHER NAMES: Crayfish, crawdads, mudbugs

U.S. DISTRIBUTION:
Louisiana is the U.S. capital for farming crawfish.

WHAT TO LOOK FOR:
Crawfish are sold live or cooked. Live crawfish should be very active; discard sluggish or inactive ones. One pound contains between 15 and 20 crawfish, yielding about 2-1/2 ounces of crawfish meat.

The shells of cooked crawfish will be brilliant red and should have no cracks. Shelled crawfish meat, available fresh or frozen, is white with red coloring on the surface. It may have a small bit of flavorful orange-tinged "fat" at the head end of the meat.

COOKING METHODS: When you get live crawfish home, place them in a large bowl, cover with a wet towel, and use that day. Crawfish are most often boiled in an aromatic broth, and the succulent meat is eaten right from the shell. Shelled crawfish meat is versatile and can be used like crabmeat or cooked shrimp in sauces, pasta dishes, salads, and stir-fries.

Crawfish Fricassée on Fresh Linguine with Tarragon- and Armagnac-Scented Jus

Serves 4

In the restaurant we serve the dish with a Riesling white-wine sauce with the linguine and caviar. You can also add peas, broad beans, and any other spring vegetables.

COOK'S STRATEGY: The linguine can be rolled and cut a day in advance if desired, or store-bought fresh linguine may be substituted. Peel the crawfish two hours in advance to leave enough time to make the Tarragon- and Armagnac-Scented Jus. Remove the orange zest in advance to let it dry.

2 pounds crawfish, cooked or uncooked, tails peeled, shells reserved to make the Tarragon- and Armagnac-Scented Jus, and claws reserved if desired for garnish
1 tablespoon butter

Tarragon leaves for garnish
2 tablespoons cream
2-1/2 tablespoons cold butter, diced
✤ Tarragon- and Armagnac-Scented Jus, 1 cup
✤ Fresh Linguine

In a sauté pan over moderate heat, sauté the crawfish tails in 1 tablespoon of butter. Bring the Tarragon- and Armagnac-Scented Jus to the simmering point, add the cream, whisk in the diced cold butter, correct seasoning, and keep warm. Add the crawfish claws, if using, to the tails and cook for 10 seconds. Add the tarragon and 1 cup of the Tarragon- and Armagnac-Scented Jus, cover, and cook for 2 to 3 minutes. Correct seasoning. Warm the linguine and correct seasoning. Arrange a mound of linguine in the center of each of 4 plates, surround pasta with crawfish tails and claws, then spoon the sauce around.

✤ Tarragon- and Armagnac-Scented Jus

Crawfish shells, reserved from main recipe, about 1/2 cup of those reserved to finish the Jus.
1-1/2 tablespoons olive oil
1 onion, chopped
1/2 cup diced fennel
1/4 cup diced celery
2 cloves garlic, minced
1 large or 2 medium vine-ripened tomatoes, peeled, seeded, and diced
1/3 cup tomato purée

2/3 cup white wine
2 tablespoons Armagnac
1 orange, zest removed and dried
1 bay leaf
1 sprig fresh thyme
2/3 cup fish stock
1 tablespoon butter, cut into small pieces
1 tarragon sprig
Salt and freshly ground black pepper
1 pinch cayenne

Chop all but about 1/2 cup of the crawfish shells into 1/2-inch pieces. In a heavy pan over moderate heat, sauté chopped crawfish shells in the olive oil until a reddish color and roasted aroma have developed. Remove with a slotted spoon and reserve. In the oil from cooking the crawfish shells, sauté the onion, fennel, celery, and garlic for 5 minutes; no color should develop. Add tomatoes and tomato purée and simmer gently for 25 minutes. Add the sautéed crawfish shells, the white wine, Armagnac, orange zest, bay leaf, thyme, and fish stock. Bring to a boil, simmer 15 minutes, and strain through a fine sieve or a chinois. Pour liquid into a very hot pan and reduce by one-third. Add the reserved 1/2 cup crawfish shells. Whisk in butter and tarragon and season to taste with salt, pepper, and cayenne. When cool, refrigerate if not using immediately. Remove the remaining crawfish shells before serving.

✦ Fresh Linguine

2 cups Italian "oo" pasta flour
   (or substitute 2 cups White Lily flour
   or 1-1/2 cups all-purpose flour
   plus 1/2 cup cake flour)
1 whole egg

2 egg yolks
1 pinch salt
1 pinch saffron
1 tablespoon olive oil

Sift the flour. Blend the egg, egg yolks, and salt together in a mixing bowl. Mix the saffron, oil, and 1 tablespoon water in a small pan and warm through to dissolve. Add the oil mixture to the eggs. Mix in the flour. Transfer to a mixer fitted with a dough hook and mix slowly. When bound together, knead by hand. Refrigerate for 1 hour.

Prepare the linguine using a pasta machine. Roll on No. 2, then put through linguine roller and cut pasta to 12-inch lengths. When ready, cook in a large pot of salted water until al dente.

Jonathan Wright is Executive Chef of The Grill Room Windsor Court Hotel in New Orleans, Louisiana.

Gnocchi with Crawfish Tails and Morels

Serves 6 as an appetizer

COOK'S STRATEGY: Boil the crawfish several hours in advance. Save the cooking water and make the Crawfish Sauce, which may be prepared up to the point of whisking in the butter and brandy. A couple of hours before serving, bake the potatoes, form the gnocchi, and sauté the morels. About fifteen minutes before serving, bring a large pot of water to a boil to cook the gnocchi. Warm the crawfish tails and morels, finish the sauce, chop the herbs for the garnish, and you're ready to serve.

3 pounds live crawfish
1 cup white wine
1 carrot, diced large
2 stalks celery, diced large
1 onion, coarsely chopped
3 cloves garlic
1 bay leaf, 1 sprig fresh thyme, and several peppercorns and coriander seeds tied in a sachet

1/2 cup salt
1 tablespoon finely chopped chervil
1 tablespoon finely chopped parsley
1 tablespoon finely chopped tarragon
➤ Gnocchi
➤ Crawfish Sauce
➤ Morels in Cream

Rinse the crawfish well. Pour 2 gallons water into a large pot and add the wine, carrot, celery, onion, garlic, herb sachet, and salt. Bring to a boil and simmer for 20 minutes. Return to a boil, add the crawfish, turn the heat off, and let sit for 12 minutes. Remove the crawfish from the water and let cool. Twist the heads to separate from the tail and peel the shells from the tail. Remove the bile vein from tails. Reserve the tails, and save the heads and shells to use in the Crawfish Sauce.

About 15 minutes before serving, bring a large pot of salted water to a boil. Cook the Gnocchi until they float, about 2 minutes. Drain and add the Gnocchi to the Morels in Cream and toss well. Add the crawfish tails and toss again. Spoon the mixture into the center of a bowl and sprinkle with the chervil, parsley, and tarragon. Drizzle some of the Crawfish Sauce around.

Gnocchi

4 medium russet potatoes
Coarse salt
1 whole egg
2 egg yolks

2 tablespoons butter, melted
1-1/2 cups all-purpose flour
Salt and freshly ground black pepper

Preheat the oven to 350°F. Rinse the potatoes and poke holes in them. Cover a small baking sheet with sides with coarse salt. Place potatoes on the salt. Bake until the potatoes are tender, about 1 hour.

Working with warm potatoes, scoop out the flesh and press through a ricer onto a smooth work surface. Gently make a well at the center and add the egg, egg yolks, and butter. Working with your fingers, add the flour and salt and pepper in small batches, rolling until a dough is achieved. Cut the dough into 6 pieces and roll each on lightly floured surface into a 1/2-inch-thick log. Cut 1-inch-long pieces from the logs and roll on a gnocchi board or tines of a fork. Reserve on a floured tray until ready to cook.

Crawfish Sauce

Reserved crawfish heads and shells
    from main recipe
2 tablespoons olive oil
1 onion, chopped
2 stalks celery, diced
1 carrot, diced
1 bulb fennel, trimmed and diced
6 cloves garlic
2 tablespoons tomato paste

1-1/2 cups brandy
1 cup white wine
2 gallons cooking liquid from cooking
    the crawfish or chicken broth or water
1 bay leaf, 1 sprig thyme, and several
    peppercorns and coriander
    seeds tied in a sachet
1 to 2 tablespoons cold unsalted butter
Salt and freshly ground black pepper

In a large roasting pan on top of the stove, roast the crawfish heads and shells over high heat with olive oil. Add all the onion, celery, carrot, fennel, and garlic; cook until lightly colored. Turn heat to medium and add the tomato paste. Add the brandy off the fire, stirring to loosen any caramelized bits. Return the pan to the heat, and cook to reduce the liquid. Pour in the wine, and reduce once again. Add the water (or broth or cooking

(Continued)

liquid) and herb sachet. Simmer for 45 minutes. Strain well, pushing all the liquid out of the shells. Transfer the liquid to a large saucepan and cook over low heat until reduced by two-thirds and a sauce consistency has been achieved. To finish, whisk in a little cold butter and brandy (a few drops), then season with salt and pepper. Extra sauce may be frozen and used again for this recipe or in a gumbo or étouffée.

✦ Morels in Cream

2 tablespoons butter

1 tablespoon finely chopped shallots

1 pound fresh morels, rinsed 3
    times and diced

Salt and freshly ground black pepper

1-1/2 cups heavy cream

Heat the butter in a sauté pan over medium heat. Add the shallots and cook until softened, 2 to 3 minutes. Add the mushrooms and season with salt and pepper. Cook until tender, 3 to 5 minutes. Remove the mushrooms from the pan, and let the juice reduce by half. Add the cream and reduce by half again. Return the mushrooms to the pan and reserve.

Bradford Thompson is Chef de Cuisine of Mary Elaine's at The Phoenician in Scottsdale, Arizona.

Crawfish Cognac with Andouille Grits

Serves 4

24 large cooked crawfish tails, peeled
1 tablespoon plus 1 teaspoon
    commercial Creole seasoning
1/2 stick (4 tablespoons) butter
1 tablespoon minced garlic
1/2 leek (white part only), halved
    lengthwise and thinly sliced
1/2 pound assorted wild mushrooms,
    chopped
1 cup Cognac

1/2 cup veal stock (or chicken broth)
1/2 cup stock, made with crawfish or
    other shellfish, or clam juice
2 large, vine-ripened tomatoes, peeled,
    seeded, and diced
1 teaspoon minced fresh thyme
Kosher salt and freshly ground
    black pepper
✦ Andouille Grits

Season the crawfish on both sides with 1 tablespoon of the Creole seasoning. In a large skillet, melt 2 tablespoons of the butter over medium-high heat. Add the garlic and sauté for 30 seconds. Add the leek and sauté for 30 seconds. Add the crawfish and mushrooms and cook for 1-1/2 minutes. Remove the skillet from the heat and add the Cognac, being careful of a possible flare-up. Return the skillet to the heat; add both stocks and tomatoes and cook for 1 minute. Stir in the remaining 1 teaspoon Creole seasoning and the thyme. Gradually add the remaining 2 tablespoons butter and stir until melted. Season with salt and pepper.

Serve the Crawfish Cognac over the Andouille Grits.

✦ Andouille Grits

1 cup stone-ground grits
4 ounces andouille sausage, diced

2 tablespoons butter
Salt and freshly ground black pepper

In a saucepan, bring 5 cups water to a boil and then gradually stir in grits. Simmer, covered to prevent evaporation, for about 1 hour. While the grits are cooking, sauté the sausage for about 5 minutes. Add the sausage and butter to the cooked grits. Season with salt and pepper.

Tory McPhail is Executive Chef at Commander's Palace in New Orleans, Louisiana.

Southern Bouillabaisse

Serves 2

The bouillabaisse is served with grilled sourdough crostini topped with a spicy rouille.

6 littleneck clams

6 mussels

4 ounces striped bass

2 large stone-crab claws

6 cooked crawfish, tail meat removed
   from shell, shells reserved

1/4 pound farm-raised or diver sea scallops

3 small carrots

2 stalks celery

5 Roma tomatoes

3 large cloves garlic

1 bulb fennel, feathery fronds removed
   and stems reserved

2 bay leaves

4 sprigs thyme, leaves removed
   and stems reserved

4 sprigs basil, leaves removed
   and stems reserved

1/2 cup vegetable broth, optional

1 leek

1 orange

1 lemon

2 large shallots

1 tablespoon butter

4 tablespoons extra-virgin olive oil

1 teaspoon Spanish saffron

6 sprigs Italian flat-leaf parsley, leaves
   removed and stems reserved

Salt and freshly ground black
   pepper to taste

✢ Rouille

✢ Crostini

Scrub the clams. Scrub and debeard the mussels. Cut the striped bass into four 1-ounce pieces. Crack the stone-crab claws with back of knife. Set all the seafood aside in the refrigerator.

Combine the crawfish shells, 1 carrot, 1 stalk celery, 2 tomatoes (crushed), 1 clove garlic, trimmings from the two outer leaves of the fennel bulb, 1 of the bay leaves, 1 thyme stem and the basil stems, and, if using, vegetable broth in a large, nonreactive saucepan. Trim and discard the dark green leaves from the leek. Add the lighter green leaves to the saucepan (save the white section for later). Add water to cover the vegetables, bring to a boil, reduce to a simmer, and cook for 40 minutes. Strain. Store in the refrigerator.

Cut an X on the bottom of the 3 remaining tomatoes and drop into a pan of boiling water for a few seconds; remove. Peel, seed, and quarter the tomatoes. With a sharp vegetable peeler, peel 3 strips of orange zest, without any bitter white pith. Do the same for the lemon.

Take the remaining part of the fennel bulb and cut it in half. Remove the core. Turn the bulb on its side and slice into thin strips. Split the leek in half lengthwise, with root attached, and wash thoroughly. Place the flat side on cutting board and slice the leek into 1/2-inch-thick half moons. Peel the 2 carrots and thinly slice. Peel the remaining celery stalk of its strings and slice into thin moon-shaped pieces about 1/4-inch thick. Finely chop the shallots and the remaining 2 cloves garlic.

Arrange the bouillabaisse ingredients next to the stovetop in this order: butter, oil, shallots, garlic, vegetables, seafood, herbs, and salt and pepper. In a large, heavy-bottomed nonreactive saucepan, heat 1/2 tablespoon of the butter and 2 tablespoons of the olive oil over medium-high heat. Add the shallots and garlic and cook for 2 minutes, stirring constantly and not allowing them to brown at all. Add the sliced fennel, carrots, celery, and leeks. Stir in the remaining bay leaf, the remaining thyme stems, the saffron, orange zest, and lemon zest. Cook for 3 or 4 minutes until tender. Add the clams and tomatoes. Cook for about 2 more minutes. Add the reserved broth and turn the heat to high, cover, and cook for 1 more minute. Add the mussels, striped bass, stone-crab claws, crawfish tails, and scallops. Cover and cook for 2 more minutes. Chop fennel fronds, thyme leaves, basil leaves, and parsley. Remove lid and add remaining 1/2 tablespoon butter, 2 tablespoons olive oil, the chopped herbs, and salt and pepper. Carefully stir and remove from heat.

Arrange the seafood and vegetables in 2 bowls. Add broth to fill the bowls three-quarters full. The orange and lemon zest strips may remain or can be removed. Place the just-grilled Crostini on the edge of the bowls, drizzle with Rouille, and serve immediately.

❧ Rouille

1 jalapeño pepper	2 egg yolks
1 red bell pepper	1 lemon, juiced
1 poblano pepper	1/2 cup olive oil
2 large cloves garlic	1/2 cup canola oil
Salt	

Char the 3 peppers under the broiler or over an open flame. Peel, seed, and purée the peppers in a blender. Crush the garlic with salt to a smooth paste in a mortar with a pestle; transfer to a small mixing bowl. Add the egg yolks, pepper purée, and lemon juice. Slowly

(Continued)

American Lobster

SCIENTIFIC NAME: *Homarus americanus*

OTHER NAMES: Maine lobster

U.S. DISTRIBUTION: American lobster thrives in the cold waters of the North Atlantic. Maine is the lobster capital.

WHAT TO LOOK FOR: Lobsters (usually 1-1/4 to 3 pounds, but sometimes larger) are sold alive because their flesh deteriorates quickly after they die. When buying lobsters, pick the most aggressive of the bunch; they are meatier and taste better. The longer a lobster sits in the store's tank, the less it eats and the more lethargic it becomes. The lobster's claws are secured with rubber bands, not only to protect you from a pinch but also to prevent the lobsters from attacking each other. Allow 1 to 1-1/2 pounds of live lobster, yielding 3 to 4 ounces of cooked meat, per person.

COOKING METHODS: It's best to cook lobster the day you buy it. The most common approach is to boil or steam it alive. For recipes that call for sautéing lobster pieces, it's easiest to kill the lobster by making a deep cut in the middle of its head with a chef's knife before proceeding with the recipe. Crushed lobster shells lend tremendous flavor to stocks, soups, and sauces (strain them out before serving).

drizzle the oils in, whisking vigorously until the oil is incorporated. Taste and adjust seasoning. If the rouille is too thin add more olive oil; if too thick, add water or lemon juice. This recipe makes more than needed for 4 crostini. The recipe can be halved, or the extra can be refrigerated and whisked to re-emulsify.

➤ Crostini
4 slices sourdough bread
Olive oil

Drizzle the bread with olive oil and broil or grill to toast.

Chris Hastings is Executive Chef/Owner of the Hot and Hot Fish Club in Birmingham, Alabama.

Lobster Spring Rolls with Cilantro Oil and Thai-Inspired Spicy Sweet Sauce

The recipe for the Thai-Inspired Spicy Sweet Sauce can be halved or the extra sauce can be kept for one or two months in the refrigerator; the sauce also can be used as a stir-fry sauce for vegetables and meat.

Serves 8 as an appetizer

COOK'S STRATEGY: The Cilantro Oil and Spicy Sweet Sauce can be prepared a day or two in advance. Assemble the spring rolls up to twenty-four hours before serving and fry them at the last minute.

1 pound cooked lobster meat, chopped
1 teaspoon toasted sesame oil
2 large carrots, julienned
1 medium daikon (Asian radish), julienned
10 snow peas, julienned
1-inch piece fresh ginger, peeled and finely chopped

1 teaspoon oyster sauce
1 tablespoon soy sauce
8 spring-roll wrappers (wheat flour)
1 egg yolk, beaten
Vegetable oil for frying
✦ Cilantro Oil
✦ Thai-Inspired Spicy Sweet Sauce

In a large sauté pan, heat the sesame oil over medium-high heat. Add the carrots, daikon, and snow peas and stir-fry for 1 minute. Add the ginger, oyster sauce, and soy sauce and stir to combine. Remove the vegetables from the heat.

In a large bowl, combine half of the vegetable mixture with the lobster meat. Divide the mixture into 8 equal portions, squeezing out any extra moisture.

On a dry work surface, lay one spring-roll wrapper. Using your hands, roll one of the portions of vegetable and lobster mixture in a cylinder and place in the center of the top edge of the wrapper. Brush the egg yolk down the left and right edges of the wrapper and fold the edges over to cover the ends of the filling. Roll the filling down the length of the wrapper, tucking in the outside edges to make a tight roll. Seal the seam with more egg yolk. Repeat with the remaining wrappers and filling. The rolls can be fried immediately or kept covered with a towel in the refrigerator for up to 24 hours before frying. Pour 2 inches of vegetable oil into a heavy skillet and heat over medium-high heat until the oil reaches 350°F on a deep-fry thermometer. Carefully lower the rolls into the hot oil and deep fry for 5 minutes, or until golden brown on all sides. Using tongs, remove the spring rolls from the oil and drain on paper towels.

(Continued)

To serve, slice the Lobster Spring Rolls in half, cutting on the diagonal. Arrange them on dinner plates, surrounded with the remaining stir-fried vegetables. Drizzle the Cilantro Oil and warm Thai-Inspired Spicy Sweet Sauce over the rolls. If the sauce has cooled, it can be used as a dipping sauce rather than drizzled over the rolls.

✴ Cilantro Oil

1 cup vegetable oil or blended olive oil
(such as 90% soya oil, 10% olive oil)

1 bunch cilantro

Bring a saucepan of water to a boil and drop the cilantro into the boiling water for a few seconds. Remove and refresh in ice water. Squeeze the blanched cilantro dry. In a blender, blend the oil and cilantro on high speed for 30 seconds; strain through a fine-mesh sieve.

✴ Thai-Inspired Spicy Sweet Sauce

2 cups sugar
1/4 cup soy sauce

1/2 small hot chile, minced, or
1/2 teaspoon dried hot red pepper flakes
1 clove garlic

Mix all ingredients and 2 cups water in a saucepan, bring to a boil, and cook for 1 to 2 minutes, stirring occasionally.

Jonathan Cartwright is Executive Chef of The White Barn Inn Restaurant in Kennebunkport, Maine.

Lobster Capellini

Long, thin, capellini-like "noodles" are created from lobster and scallops, simmered in a kelp dashi (broth), and seasoned with Vinegar-Soy Sauce.

Serves 4

2 live American lobsters, 1-1/4 to 1-1/2 pounds each (only the tail meat will be used; reserve head and claws for another use)

2 sushi-grade diver sea scallops

1 egg white

1 tablespoon potato starch

1 tablespoon grated mountain yam (available at Asian markets)

1 teaspoon sake

Salt and freshly ground white pepper to taste

One 4-to-5-inch piece kombu (dried kelp)

2 tablespoons diced vine-ripened tomato

2 tablespoons diced fresh cucumber

2 tablespoons diced yellow bell pepper

1 ounce farmed white-sturgeon caviar

4 micro basil leaves

❧ Vinegar-Soy Sauce

Using a very sharp knife, make a deep cut in the center of each lobster head. Separate the tail from the head. Using a sharp knife or kitchen shears, make a cut along the underside of the tail and remove the tail meat. Place the lobster tail meat, scallops, egg white, potato starch, mountain yam, sake, and salt and pepper in a food processor. Pulse until the mixture is a smooth purée. Transfer the mixture to a pastry bag fitted with a small-hole tip.

In a large saucepan over medium heat, bring the kombu and 3 quarts water to a simmer. Pipe the purée into this kelp dashi, forming long, thin noodles (just like capellini) and simmer until cooked through, about 1 to 2 minutes.

Make an ice bath and place cooked capellini in it until chilled. Remove with a slotted spoon and drain on paper towels.

To serve, divide the capellini among 4 serving bowls, pour Vinegar-Soy Sauce on top, and garnish with tomato, cucumber, yellow bell pepper, caviar, and basil.

❧ Vinegar-Soy Sauce

2 tablespoons white balsamic vinegar

1 tablespoon rice vinegar

6 tablespoons extra-virgin olive oil

1 teaspoon grated garlic

1 teaspoon shoyu (light soy sauce)

Salt and freshly ground white pepper to taste

Place all ingredients in a mixing bowl and stir until thoroughly combined.

Masaharu Morimoto is Chef/Owner of Morimoto Restaurant in Philadelphia, Pennsylvania. He is the Iron Chef Japanese on the Food Network's *Iron Chef*, and he hosted that network's award-winning special, *Morimoto Raw*.

Lobster with Ginger and Scallions

Serves 2 or more

I am indebted to my good friend, Chef C.K. Sau, for teaching me to cook Lobster with Ginger and Scallions, a dish that was originally and still is most often prepared with fresh live crabs. I have modified C.K.'s technique for cutting and cooking the lobster but have duplicated the sauce as he taught me. As part of a large Chinese dinner, with other featured dishes, this recipe cooks enough lobster for five or six people. But for our American style of eating lobster, it is just right for two people. The recipe can be made twice, but it cannot be doubled.

2 live Maine lobsters, 1-1/4 to
    1-1/2 pounds each
1/4 cup peanut oil (approximately)
1 thumb-size piece of fresh ginger
    (1/2 ounce), peeled and julienned
2 cloves garlic, very thinly sliced
4 or 5 scallions, cut diagonally into
    1-inch pieces, white part cut in
    half lengthwise as well
1/2 cup chicken broth

1/3 cup Chinese cooking wine
2 tablespoons soy sauce
2 teaspoons sugar
1/2 teaspoon freshly ground
    white pepper
2 teaspoons cornstarch mixed with
    1 tablespoon water
2 teaspoons rice vinegar
1 teaspoon dark sesame oil

Using a very sharp knife, make a very deep cut in each lobster in the middle of the head. Use a Chinese cleaver or a large French knife to split the lobster in half lengthwise. Remove and discard the head sac and intestine. Remove the claws and knuckles, cutting the knuckle close to where it meets the carcass. Break the knuckle away from the claw and cut it with your cleaver on one side so that the lobster meat is easy to extract when cooked. Using the backside of your knife, crack the center of the claw on both sides. Remove the green tomalley (and roe, if present) and place in a small bowl; break them into small pieces using a fork. Cover and reserve. Quarter the lobster by cutting down, in one swift motion, where the tail and carcass join. Next, cut each piece in two; keep the cut in the same direction as when you quartered the lobster. Repeat this process with the other lobster. From each lobster you will have 8 pieces from the tail and carcass, plus 2 claws and 2 knuckles. Place the pieces of lobster on a plate, shell-side down, making it easier to slide them into the hot wok or pan.

If you do not have a wok and/or a hot gas fire to work with, this recipe can be produced in a heavy skillet or sauté pan. You will need at least a 12-inch pan (14-inch is even better), which you will put over heat as high as possible. The cooking time will be longer than with a wok, but it is hard to pinpoint exact times (this is true even with a wok) because the intensity of heat varies from one home kitchen to the next.

Be sure to have all ingredients cut, measured, and ready to go before beginning. Preheat the wok or pan over a very high heat until it is smoking hot. Add 3 tablespoons of peanut oil and immediately slide the pieces of lobster into the wok. Stir the pieces only enough to ensure that all pieces cook evenly. Pay special attention to the claws, which take the longest to cook. When they are done, the remaining pieces will also be done. After 2 to 3 minutes, depending on the heat in your wok or pan, the lobster pieces will be red and slightly charred and the lobster will be cooked to about 80% of its doneness. Remove the wok from the heat and, using tongs or a slotted spoon, lift the pieces out of the wok or pan and place on a platter. Keep warm.

Add a tablespoon of peanut oil to the wok or pan, as needed. Place the wok back on a high heat, and add the ginger, garlic, and scallions. Stir fry for barely 1 minute, until the ginger, garlic, and scallions are cooked but not browned. Add the chicken broth, cooking wine, soy sauce, sugar, pepper, and the reserved tomalley and roe. Reduce the heat to medium so the mixture simmers but is not boiling profusely. Add the lobster pieces and cook for 2 minutes, moving the pieces around so they cook evenly. Again, pay special attention to the claws so they cook thoroughly.

Mix the cornstarch and water into a smooth paste and slowly add to the sauce in the wok, stirring constantly to prevent clumps from forming. As soon as the cornstarch is all added, stir in the rice vinegar and sesame oil. Stir the lobster to coat each piece evenly with the sauce, as well as the ginger and scallions.

To serve, transfer the lobster pieces to a warm platter and spoon any extra sauce and pieces of ginger and scallion over the lobster. Accompany with steamed rice and a side vegetable such as broccoli, eggplant, or snow peas.

Jasper White is Chef/Owner of Summer Shack in Boston and Cambridge, Massachusetts, and Mohegan Sun, Connecticut. This recipe is adapted from his book *Lobster at Home* (Scribner, 1998).

Lobster Tempura with Creamy Stone-Ground Grits

Serves 4

A white-wine sauce with yellow tomatoes and tarragon is spooned over the grits as a foundation for the lobster.

COOK'S STRATEGY: The grits require an hour of cooking, so start them first. Then reduce the wine for the White-Wine Sauce. Meanwhile, steam the lobsters and remove the meat. Fry the lobster and then finish the sauce and grits.

4 small fresh live Maine lobsters or
    cooked Maine lobster tails
Salt and freshly ground white pepper
1 cup all-purpose flour
1 cup heavy cream

1 medium green tomato, peeled,
    seeded, and cut into cubes
Oil, for frying
❖ White-Wine Sauce
❖ Creamy Stone-Ground Grits

If using live lobsters, steam or boil for 5 minutes. Remove and separate tail from rest of body. (The claws are not used in this recipe so you may reserve them for another use, but they will need an additional 5 minutes of cooking). Remove the lobster meat from the shells. Salt and pepper each tail and cut in half, lengthwise. Toss them each in the flour, then the cream, then back in the flour once again.

Drop the lobster tails and green tomato into a small deep fryer in which oil has been heated to 375°F. Cook until brown, approximately 1 minute.

To serve, spoon some Creamy Stone-Ground Grits in each of 4 soup plates. Spoon 2 tablespoons of the White-Wine Sauce over the grits. Gently set the Lobster Tempura and fried tomatoes on top of the grits.

❖ White-Wine Sauce

2 cups white wine, preferably
    Chardonnay
1/2 cup dry vermouth, preferably
    Noilly Prat
3 shallots, chopped fine
1 stick (8 tablespoons) cold unsalted
    butter, diced

Salt and freshly ground white
    pepper to taste
1 large yellow tomato, peeled,
    seeded, and diced
2 tablespoons fresh tarragon leaves

In a small saucepan, heat the white wine, vermouth, and shallots over medium heat. Simmer until reduced to 3 tablespoons of liquid. With a small whisk, whisk in the butter cubes a little at a time over low heat. Add salt and pepper to taste. Stir in the tomato and tarragon just before serving.

✦ Creamy Stone-Ground Grits

2-1/4 cups chicken broth
2-1/2 tablespoons unsalted butter
1/2 cup stone-ground grits

1 to 2 cups heavy cream
Salt and freshly ground white pepper
1 teaspoon grated lemon zest

Bring the chicken broth and butter to a boil in a heavy-bottomed saucepan. Stir in the grits and return to a boil. Reduce the heat, allowing the grits to cook for another 15 minutes at a low boil, until the grits are thick and have absorbed most of the liquid. Stir occasionally to keep the grits from sticking. Add 1/2 cup of the heavy cream and reduce the heat, allowing the grits to cook slowly for another 10 minutes. As the liquid is absorbed, add more cream, cooking the grits until thick and creamy, total cooking time of at least 1 hour. The grits should be thick and full-bodied. Season with salt and pepper to taste, and fold in the lemon zest just before serving.

Robert Waggoner is Executive Chef of Charleston Grill in Charleston, South Carolina.

Baked Stuffed Lobster

Serves 2 to 4

The legendary Baked Stuffed Lobster is a true New England classic and has been served for most of the past century in the older Boston hotels. A big, juicy lobster is split and filled with big chunks of fresh briny seafood, broken crackers, and sweet butter, then baked until the stuffing is crisp and golden.

2 live Maine lobsters, weighing 1-1/2 to 2-1/2 pounds each (for a medium-size main course, serve half of a 2-pound lobster for each guest)

4 ounces peeled raw Maine shrimp or raw scallops (one or the other or a combination), cooked crabmeat, or cooked lobster meat, cut roughly into 1/2-inch dice

1 medium onion, finely diced (1/4 to 1/2 inch)

1 stick (8 tablespoons) unsalted butter plus 3 tablespoons melted butter for brushing

2 teaspoons chopped fresh tarragon

2 tablespoons chopped Italian flat-leaf parsley

3 ounces Ritz crackers (3/4 tube), crumbled, or 3 ounces crumbled common crackers, oyster crackers, or dried cornbread

Kosher or sea salt

Freshly ground black pepper

Preheat the oven to 425°F. Combine the onion with the stick of butter in a 9-inch frying pan and place on a medium heat. Cook for 5 minutes until the onion is soft but not browned. Stir in the tarragon and parsley. If you are using raw shrimp or scallops for your stuffing, add them with the herbs and cook for 1 minute. Remove from the heat and let the mixture cool a little. If you are using cooked lobster or crabmeat, remove the pan from the heat as soon as you stir in the herbs. Add the lobster or crabmeat to the buttery onions after they are off the heat. Season with salt and pepper and set aside while you split the lobsters. Keep the crumbled crackers separate, for now, as it is best to mix the stuffing at the last minute to prevent it from becoming soggy.

Using a very sharp knife, make a very deep cut in each lobster in the middle of the head. With a Chinese cleaver or a large French knife, split the lobster in half lengthwise. Remove and discard the head sac and intestine. Remove the green tomalley (and roe, if present), place in a small bowl, and break into small pieces using a fork. Using the back side of your knife, crack the center of the claw on one side only. Repeat this process with the second lobster. Season the lobster lightly with salt and pepper. Place the 2 halves of each lobster side by side (tails pointing out so that the halves form a shape kind of like a butterfly), on a large roasting pan or sheet pan.

The tomalley and roe are optional for the stuffing (I always use them, myself). If you want to include them, mix them into the onion and seafood mixture. Now gently fold the broken crackers into the mixture and divide it evenly between the body cavities (not over the tail) of the 2 lobsters. If you are serving 1 lobster per person, spread the stuffing over the center so the lobster looks whole again. Do not pack the stuffing tightly or it will affect the even baking of the lobster. Brush the melted butter over the exposed tail meat, over the stuffing, and on the claws.

Bake in the preheated oven until the lobster is cooked through and the stuffing is crisp and golden. Use the following recommended times as a guideline. Serve at once.

Baking times in a preheated 425°F oven

1-1/2 pounds	17 minutes
1-3/4 pounds	20 minutes
2 pounds	24 minutes
2-1/2 pounds	30 minutes

Jasper White is Chef/Owner of Summer Shack in Boston and Cambridge, Massachusetts, and Mohegan Sun, Connecticut. This recipe is adapted from his book *Lobster at Home* (Scribner, 1998).

Lobster and Crab Cakes

Serves 4

Lobster adds a rich twist to the classic crab cake. At the Sapphire Grill, we serve these with a wasabi tobiko aïoli.

1/2 cup finely diced cooked lobster meat
1 pound blue-crab meat (lightly picked
    through to remove shell fragments
    but not crumbled)
Grated zest of 1 lemon
2 eggs
2 tablespoons finely diced assorted
    peppers
2 tablespoons minced shallots

1/4 cup grated Romano
1/3 cup half-and-half
1 teaspoon kosher salt
1/2 teaspoon nutmeg
1/4 teaspoon cayenne pepper
1 cup fresh bread crumbs
1/2 bunch scallions, chopped
2 tablespoons butter
2 tablespoons olive or canola oil

In a large mixing bowl, gently combine all ingredients except the butter and oil, making sure not to break up the crabmeat. Chill the mixture for at least 30 minutes before forming cakes.

Divide the crab mixture into 4 portions and form each into a cake. In a large sauté pan over medium heat, heat the butter and oil until bubbly. Saute the crab cakes about 4 minutes, then carefully flip each cake with a spatula and sauté on the other side for another 4 minutes, until the cakes are lightly browned. Remove the cakes from the pan and drain on a plate lined with paper towels before serving.

Christopher Nason is Executive Chef and Proprietor of
Sapphire Grill in Savannah, Georgia.

Winter Squash Bisque with Lobster

2 live lobsters, 1 to 2 pounds each
1 tablespoon extra-virgin olive oil
2 cloves garlic, chopped
1 large onion, diced
6 cups fish stock or chicken broth
2 small or 1 large butternut squash,
    peeled, seeded, and diced
1 tablespoon chopped fresh thyme leaves

1-1/2 cups heavy cream
1 tablespoon soy sauce
2 teaspoons frozen orange-juice concentrate
Salt and freshly ground black pepper
1/2 cup crème fraîche or sour cream,
    for garnish
Fresh thyme sprigs, for garnish

Serves 6

Heat the olive oil in a stockpot over high heat until hot. Add the garlic and onion and sauté for about 2 minutes. Add the stock or broth and bring to a boil. Meanwhile, prepare the lobsters: Using a very sharp knife, make a very deep cut in each lobster in the middle of the head. When the stock is boiling, add the lobsters, cover the pot with a lid, and cook the lobsters just until they are cooked through, about 10 minutes. Remove the lobsters from the stock and let cool.

Add the squash to the stock and cook over medium heat until tender, about 10 minutes. Once the lobsters are cool enough to handle, remove the meat from the claws and tail. Dice the meat and set aside. Place the shells back in the soup, add the thyme and cream, and simmer over medium heat for about 20 minutes. Strain the soup through a fine-mesh sieve into another pan, pushing squash solids through sieve. Gently warm over medium heat. Add the soy sauce and orange-juice concentrate, mix well, and season to taste with salt and pepper.

To serve, divide the reserved lobster meat among 6 bowls. Ladle the hot soup over the lobster meat and garnish with a dollop of crème fraîche and thyme sprigs.

Caprial Pence is Executive Chef/Proprietor of Caprial's Bistro in Portland, Oregon. She has written numerous cookbooks, including *Caprial's Cafe Favorites* (Ten Speed Press, 1994) and *Caprial Cooks for Friends* (Ten Speed Press, 2000), and is the host of the PBS program *Caprial! Cooking for Friends.*

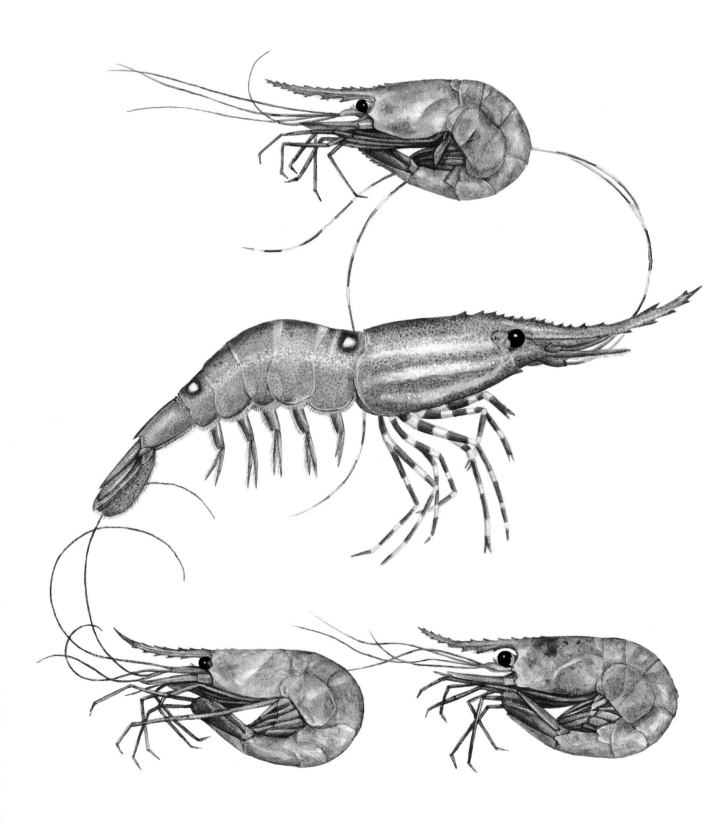

Prawns and Shrimp

LONG BEFORE FORREST GUMP AND HIS FRIEND BUBBA entertained the world with their long list of every shrimp dish they'd ever had ("There's shrimp kabobs, shrimp creole, shrimp gumbo, shrimp cocktail, deep-fried shrimp, stir-fried shrimp . . ."), shrimp was gradually increasing in popularity in the United States. By 2001 shrimp had exceeded canned tuna for the first time as America's top seafood choice, with a record consumption of 3.4 pounds per person. Shrimp as seafood may need no introduction, but few Americans probably know much about the origins of the shrimp they consume.

Most shrimp sold in the United States are farm-raised species from southeast Asia or Ecuador or trawled shrimp from warm-water areas of Central and South America. Environmental problems associated with coastal farming and trawling of shrimp are serious enough (see "Issues Regarding U.S. Seafood") that conservation organizations uniformly suggest that consumers avoid imported farmed and trawled shrimp.

The shrimp and prawns highlighted here are somewhat less contentious. Two featured species are found in cold water: Northern pink shrimp (also called Maine shrimp and deepwater prawns), found in the North Atlantic, North Pacific, and Arctic oceans, and spot prawns (also known as spot shrimp or Alaskan prawns), which live from Alaska to southern California as well as in Asian waters. Northern pink shrimp and spot prawns are taken by trawls with special nets to minimize bycatch, and spot prawns may be captured with ecologi-

Spot prawn *(center)* and northern pink shrimp *(top and bottom)*

In the Wild

What's in a name? The terms "prawn" and "shrimp" have confused many consumers. Some people use "prawn" to differentiate the sometimes freshwater shellfish *Macrobrachium* from its saltwater kin (e.g., *Litopenaeus* or *Farfantepenaeus* species in the United States). Others call all large or jumbo shrimp "prawns." And still others use "prawn" to identify a crustacean that is part of the lobster family. The "prawn" of Great Britain and other countries is essentially the same animal as the shrimp of the United States. The northern pink shrimp highlighted here (*Pandalus borealis*) is also called deepwater prawn, and the spot prawn (*Pandalus platyceros*) is also called spot shrimp. Because of the confusion with multiple common names for a species, many retailers as well as scientists and those managing fisheries and creating policy use scientific names. Although scientific names seem strange to many because they are Latin, they reduce confusion by providing a single name recognized around the world for every species. Scientific names for every seafood species included in the recipes are given in "Seafood Species."

cally sensitive traps. The warm-water species included are U.S.-farmed Pacific shrimp and U.S. wild-caught white, brown, and pink shrimp, harvested from North Carolina to Texas. Given their popularity, there is no great need to highlight warm-water shrimp, and they are included in only a few recipes in this book.

Relative to some foreign farms, U.S. shrimp-farm operations are well regulated, with substances like the toxic chloramphenicol strictly prohibited. U.S.-farmed shrimp are also processed and frozen almost immediately after harvesting, so they are never treated with iodine or other chemicals sometimes used on commercially caught shrimp. Relative to other shrimp-trawling industries, U.S. shrimp trawling is also more ecologically sound because bycatch-reduction devices and turtle-excluder devices are required on trawl nets.

U.S.-farmed or -trawled shrimp can be difficult to find in U.S. seafood markets, or they may be present but not labeled as such (labels such as "tiger shrimp" and "gulf shrimp" do not indicate U.S. shrimp). Confusion may also arise because labels on many imported frozen shrimp packages contain the erroneous information that they constitute an environmentally sound choice because the shrimp were farmed rather than caught in the ocean. Spot prawns are available year-round, but much of the spot-prawn catch is sold to Japan, where it is popular in sushi bars. Northern pink shrimp are available fresh seasonally in northeastern seafood markets and have become available quick frozen and vacuum packed for sale throughout the year. Shrimp farmed in Texas can be ordered in frozen 5-pound blocks, and U.S.-trawled shrimp is available seasonally through many markets. At certain times of the year, Farm-2-Market offers Louisiana white shrimp caught in cast nets, the most ecologically sound method of shrimping but one that provides limited quantities.

Spot Prawns with Garlic, Chiles, and Tomato Confit

Serves 10

I recommend serving the prawns in the shell and encouraging your guests to get their hands involved in eating these delicious prawns. The shell imparts a lot of flavor to the sauce and also helps the prawns stay firm and not become mealy. The warm Yellow-Tomato Sauce provides a base for the prawns. Make the Tomato Confit in advance—one day ahead is great—and make the Yellow-Tomato Sauce a couple of hours before cooking the prawns. A California Chardonnay goes well with this dish.

30 large spot prawns
2 tablespoons extra-virgin
    olive oil
4 shallots, sliced
4 cloves garlic, sliced
2 chiles de arbol, sliced
✤ Tomato Confit
Salt and freshly ground
    black pepper

Juice of 2 lemons,
    for seasoning
10 opal basil leaves,
    cut into thin ribbons
10 green basil leaves,
    cut into thin ribbons
15 parsley leaves,
    thinly sliced
✤ Yellow-Tomato Sauce

Heat a heavy-bottomed sauté pan until almost smoking. Quickly sauté the spot prawns in olive oil, about 2-1/2 minutes. Add the shallots, garlic, chiles, and Tomato Confit and sauté an additional 2-1/2 minutes. Toss often and season with salt and pepper.

To serve, place a spoonful of warm Yellow Tomato Sauce in the base of each of 10 large soup bowls. When the prawns are done pull the pan off the flame and season with the lemon juice and a little more good olive oil. Toss in the herbs and place prawn mixture in the center of the bowls.

(Continued)

Prawns and Shrimp

Northern Pink Shrimp, Spot Prawns, U.S.-Farmed Shrimp, and White, Brown, and Pink (Warm-water) Shrimp

SCIENTIFIC NAMES: *Pandalus borealis* (northern pink), *P. platyceros* (spot prawn), *Litopenaeus vannamei* (U.S.-farmed Pacific shrimp), *L. setiferus* (white), *Farfantepenaeus aztecus* (brown), *and F. duorarum* (pink)

U.S. DISTRIBUTION: Northern pink shrimp live in cold deep waters of the Atlantic and Pacific. Spot prawns occur off the west coast. White, brown, and pink shrimp are caught from North Carolina to Texas; the latter is also the producer of most U.S.-farmed shrimp.

WHAT TO LOOK FOR: Most of the U.S. catch is frozen right after harvest without impairing quality. Once thawed, quality can deteriorate quickly. Shrimp that have been in the store's case for more than 2 days begin to smell fishy or develop an ammonia scent.

Retailers purchase shrimp according to the number of shrimp per pound. Very large shrimp are sometimes labeled "U/15" or "U/20," meaning fewer than 15 or 20 in a pound. This list shows the relationship between numbers per pound and size names:

U/15	Colossal
16/20	Super-jumbo
21/25	Jumbo
26/30	Extra-large
31/35	Large
35/40	Medium
40+	Cocktail or salad

Northern pink shrimp are cocktail (90/500 count!), whereas spot prawns can be super-jumbo to colossal. The U.S. warm-water shrimp range from medium to colossal.

COOKING METHODS: Shrimp is delicious fried, stir-fried, grilled, boiled, steamed, or smoked. If a recipe calls for peeled shrimp, an inexpensive plastic shrimp-peeling tool that facilitates removing the shell and dark vein of a shrimp can be purchased at supermarkets.

❧ Tomato Confit

6 Roma tomatoes, blanched and peeled
3 shallots, sliced
A few sprigs of fresh basil

Extra-virgin olive oil to cover,
    approximately 1-1/2 cups

Scatter the shallots and basil on the bottom of an ovenproof pan into which the tomatoes will fit snugly. Place the tomatoes in the pan and pour on enough oil to almost cover them. Cover with plastic wrap and then aluminum foil and poke 6 holes in the wrap to let off steam. Cook in a 250°F oven for 6 hours until the tomatoes are slightly shriveled like prunes and glossy. The tomato flavor will be very rich and intense.

❧ Yellow-Tomato Sauce

1 red onion, sliced thin
2 dried chiles, such as chiles de arbol
2 cloves garlic, sliced
2 sprigs basil
2 sprigs oregano

6 yellow tomatoes (about 2 pounds)
Salt and freshly ground black pepper
2-1/2 cups chicken broth
2 cups extra-virgin olive oil

In a stainless steel roasting pan, scatter the red onion, chiles, garlic, and fresh herbs. Core the yellow tomatoes and place them on top of the vegetables. Season tomatoes liberally with salt. Pour over the broth and the olive oil. The liquid should almost but not quite cover the tomatoes. Cook in a 400°F oven for 1 to 1-1/2 hours, until the tomatoes are blistered and cooked through. The cooking time will depend greatly on the ripeness and size of the tomatoes. When they are done, remove the pan from the oven and pour the whole mixture into a blender. Process the mixture until it is a smooth purée. Add salt and pepper as needed and set aside.

Suzanne Goin is Chef/Owner of Lucques and A.O.C. in Los Angeles, California.

Paprika Prawns with Tequila-Lime Mojo

COOK'S STRATEGY: Assemble the Paprika Prawns on skewers a day in advance. You can make the Tequila-Lime Mojo at that time as well.

Serves 6

36 spot prawns (16–20 per pound)
1 tablespoon minced garlic
1 lemon, zest grated
2 limes, zest grated

2 tablespoons paprika
1/2 cup oil (25% olive oil/75% canola oil)
Salt and freshly ground black pepper
✦ Tequila-Lime Mojo

Special Equipment: 6 wooden or metal skewers

Clean the prawns and remove the shells, except for the tails. Thread 6 skewers with 6 prawns to a skewer. Combine the garlic, zests, paprika, and oil and pour over skewered prawns. Marinate for 24 hours.

Preheat the grill to medium. Season the prawns with salt and pepper. Grill the skewers about 1 minute per side.

Drizzle some of the Tequila-Lime Mojo over the grilled Paprika Prawns and serve.

✦ Tequila-Lime Mojo
3/4 cup chicken broth
1/4 cup tequila
1 lime, zest removed and chopped
1/3 medium red onion, diced

1/4 cup freshly squeezed lime juice
1/4 cup honey
1 teaspoon chopped cilantro
Salt and freshly ground black pepper

In a small saucepan, combine chicken broth and tequila. Cook rapidly until 1/2 cup remains. Allow the liquid to cool. Place remaining ingredients in a bowl and add chicken-broth reduction. Mix well and season as needed. Makes 1-1/2 cups.

John Toulze is Executive Chef of the girl & the gaucho in Glen Ellen, California, and the girl & the fig in Sonoma and Petaluma, California.

Grilled Northern Pink Shrimp with Fava-Bean Cassoulet and Barbecued Onions

Serves 4

This dish is a throwback to summer barbecues where the flavors meld in the air through thick plumes of smoke. I love the texture of grilled shrimp and, although small, the northern pink shrimp packs more sweetness than any of its jumbo-sized cousins. Granted, these aren't your garden-variety shrimp. Smaller varieties like this are rarely skewered and grilled, but I think the result is worth the patience, a succulent "shrimp toast" of sorts that is packed with flavor. These spectacular shrimp are available fresh from about January through April, but that's just when spring is at least thinking about peeking through the blinds and the warmth of summer is not too far away. To me, the shrimp matches perfectly with the salty sweet pancetta and meaty fava beans, but putting them with any fresh spring vegetable is bound to produce fantastic results as well.

This is a take on one of my favorite preparations of shrimp in Spain—gambas al ajillo—in which shrimp are sautéed with garlic and Spain's secret ingredient, pimentón. Pimentón dulce (sweet paprika) is made from the smoke-roasted and ground piquillo peppers grown in Spain. It has an irreplaceable flavor that gives the dish zest and life beyond the common backyard barbecue. And what would a barbecue be without a sauce? I match the shrimp and beans not with a thick, tomato-and-molasses Southern-style sauce, but rather a Yankee interpretation. The sauce does not, in fact, contain any tomato, yet has all the characteristics of a sweet-and-sour barbecue. It matches wonderfully with the young, tender beans and herbs accompanying delicate shrimp.

COOK'S STRATEGY: Start by marinating the onions for the Barbecued Onions, then marinate the shrimp. Next prepare the Fava-Bean Cassoulet and the Croutons. Grill the onions and then the shrimp.

200 (about 1-1/2 pounds) northern pink
    shrimp (Maine shrimp)
2 teaspoons pimentón dulce
    (Spanish sweet paprika)
Salt and freshly ground black pepper

3 tablespoons extra-virgin olive oil
✢ Croutons
✢ Fava-Bean Cassoulet
✢ Barbecued Onions

Special Equipment: About 30 wooden skewers, soaked in water for 20 minutes

Peel and devein the shrimp, season with pimentón and salt and pepper, and skewer 6 to 7 shrimp on each wooden skewer. Drizzle the shrimp with olive oil and set aside to marinate for 20 minutes. Light a charcoal or gas grill.

Grill the shrimp over the hottest part of the fire, being careful not to burn them. Cook 15 seconds on one side then flip the shrimp for an additional 15 to 20 seconds.

To finish, set a crouton on each of 4 plates and pile one-quarter of the Fava-Bean Cassoulet on top. Spoon some of the sauce from the beans over the top, enough for the Crouton to soak up and become soft again. Lay skewers of Grilled Shrimp across the beans (or remove the skewers if you prefer) and top with the Barbecued Onions. Garnish with a drizzle of the onion barbecue marinade and top with more fresh herbs if you wish. Serve immediately.

✤ Croutons

4 slices bread, cut on a bias 1/2-inch thick
    by 5 inches long from a crusty
    French baguette

1/4 cup extra-virgin olive oil
Salt and freshly ground black pepper

Brush the sliced bread with the oil. Season with salt and pepper and toast under a broiler until browned just around the edges. The resulting crouton should be crunchy and chewy, but not hard.

✤ Fava-Bean Cassoulet

3 pounds fresh fava beans
    (1/2 pound shelled)
1 pound fresh cranberry beans,
    shelled (or fresh black-eyed peas)
3 tablespoons extra-virgin olive oil
1 cup diced pancetta or bacon
4 shallots, finely chopped
4 cloves garlic, thinly sliced
1 teaspoon pimentón dulce
    (Spanish sweet paprika)

A pinch of dried hot red pepper flakes
1/4 cup white wine
1 red bell pepper, roasted over an open
    fire, peeled, seeded, and chopped
15 cherry tomatoes, preferably
    Sweet 100s, halved
16 chives, snipped into 1-inch
    lengths
16 parsley leaves
Salt and freshly ground black pepper

Remove fava beans from their shells and blanch in boiling salted water for 2 minutes. Plunge the beans into an ice bath. Drain beans, slit tough outer skin with a knife,

(Continued)

and remove tender, bright green bean from within; set aside. Blanch the cranberry beans in the same manner, cooking slightly longer until softened, about 4 to 5 minutes. Drain beans and set aside. While the beans are cooking, place a heavy-bottomed pan over medium heat. Sauté the pancetta in the olive oil until it renders most of its fat and becomes fragrant and slightly crispy, about 8 minutes. Add the shallots and garlic and reduce heat to medium low. When the vegetables begin to show color add the pimentón and red pepper flakes. Toast for 15 seconds, then stir in the white wine. Do not drain the fat; it will emulsify with the wine and create a sauce to use later. Remove the pan from the heat and set aside.

When ready to serve, warm the pancetta mixture in a sauté pan over medium heat; add the beans and peppers and cook for 2 minutes. Remove to a mixing bowl and fold in the tomatoes, chives, and parsley leaves. Season with salt and pepper.

✦ Barbecued Onions

3 tablespoons freshly squeezed
    lemon juice
1 tablespoon balsamic vinegar
1 clove garlic, minced
1 tablespoon chopped fresh oregano
3 tablespoons brown sugar
1/2 teaspoon salt
1/4 teaspoon freshly ground black pepper

3-1/2 tablespoons extra-virgin olive oil
1-1/2 tablespoons pistachio oil
    (such as Castelmuro brand
    from France)
2 Vidalia onions (or other sweet onions),
    cut into 1/2-inch slices and
    separated into rings

Put the lemon juice, balsamic vinegar, garlic, oregano, brown sugar, and salt and pepper together in a small bowl and whisk to dissolve the sugar and salt. Whisk in the olive oil and pistachio oil. Add the sliced onions to this sauce and marinate for 30 minutes.

Place the onion rings on the grill. Cook for 2 or 3 minutes until they soften and blacken around the edges. Remove the onions from the grill and re-marinate them in the barbecue marinade.

Ryan Hardy is Executive Chef of The Coach House in Edgartown, Martha's Vineyard, Massachusetts.

Mixed Shellfish Paella

Serves 8

1 pound squid, cleaned, bodies
    cut into rings

1 pound medium or large raw
    U.S. wild-caught or farmed shrimp,
    peeled and deveined

1 pound live mussels, scrubbed and
    debearded, or 1-1/2 pounds
    small live clams

1 frying chicken, about 3-1/2 pounds,
    or 2-1/2 pounds chicken parts

1/4 cup olive oil

1 medium onion, finely chopped

4 cloves garlic, minced

2 teaspoons salt

Freshly ground black pepper to taste

1 large red bell pepper, roasted, peeled,
    seeded, and diced

1/2 cup sliced scallions

1/2 teaspoon saffron threads, or
    more to taste

3 cups short-grain rice
    (preferably Spanish or Italian)

6 cups warm chicken broth

1 cup fresh or frozen peas

Special equipment: A 14-inch flameproof earthenware cazuela or paella pan

Divide the chicken into parts. Then, with a heavy cleaver or large knife, chop each breast half into 3 pieces, each leg into 4 pieces, and each wing in half. Remove the wing tips and reserve, along with the back and neck, for stock (add shrimp shells to the stock, too). The giblets can go in the stock or the paella as you like. Combine the oil, onion, and garlic in the paella pan and place over low heat. When the onion begins to sizzle, increase the heat to medium. Add the chicken pieces a few at a time and cook until lightly browned, sprinkling them with a little of the salt and pepper as they cook. As they brown, move the chicken pieces to the outside of the pan to make room for more in the center.

When all the chicken has lost its raw color, add the squid, peppers, scallions, and remaining salt. Crumble in the saffron. Stir in the rice, cooking for a minute or so to coat it with the oil. Add warm broth to within 1 inch of the rim of the pan (not all the broth may be needed). Arrange the shrimp over the top and the mussels or clams in a ring around the outside, hinged side down. Cover and cook at a lively simmer until the rice is just tender, about 20 minutes; scatter the peas over the top halfway through the cooking time. The paella may seem a little soupy when it first comes off the fire, but the rice will absorb the excess liquid in a few minutes. Serve the paella directly from the pan at the table.

Jay Harlow is a Northern California food writer, culinary instructor, and author or co-author of twelve books including *West Coast Seafood* (Sasquatch Books, 1999) and *The California Seafood Cookbook* (Aris Books, 1983). This recipe was adapted from his paella recipe at www.sallys-place.com.

Red Thai Curry Shrimp with Golden Pineapple and Jasmine Rice

Serves 10

Before opening TenPenh, my partners and I traveled extensively in Southeast Asia to research menu items and to purchase furnishings and decorative items for the new restaurant. While in Bangkok, I took a cooking class at the Mandarin Oriental Hotel where I learned to make traditional Thai curry from scratch, the old-fashioned way. It is the number-one-selling dish at TenPenh.—Jeff Tunks

COOK'S STRATEGY: The Curry Paste and Curry-Coconut Sauce can be made a day or two in advance. About an hour before dinner, peel the shrimp. Start cooking the rice about half an hour in advance; when the rice is nearly done, quickly sauté the shrimp and warm the sauce.

100 fresh shrimp (26–30 shrimp per pound), U.S. trawled or farmed
1 tablespoon olive oil
3/4 cup diced fresh golden pineapple (1/2-inch cubes)

Kaffir lime leaf, julienned
✦ Curry-Coconut Sauce
✦ Jasmine Rice

Peel and devein the shrimp. Heat the olive oil in a saucepan over medium heat. Sauté the shrimp until they are almost pink. Add the Curry-Coconut Sauce and the diced pineapple. Cook for about 5 minutes.

To serve, place a mound of rice in the center of each plate. Pour Curry Shrimp over rice. Garnish with the kaffir lime leaf.

✦ Curry-Coconut Sauce

Four 10-ounce cans coconut milk
2/3 cup palm sugar or brown sugar

3/4 cup fish sauce
✦ Curry Paste

Combine the coconut milk, sugar, fish sauce, and 2 cups Curry Paste over low heat in a medium saucepan. Simmer for 45 minutes. Reserve. Any extra Curry-Coconut Sauce can be stored in the refrigerator for 1 or 2 weeks.

❧ Curry Paste

3/4 cup Thai dried red chiles (prik haeng)
    or Chinese dried chiles
1 cup chopped lemongrass
1/4 cup chopped galangal or young ginger
1-1/2 cups chopped garlic

1-1/2 cups chopped onion
1/2 tablespoon shrimp paste
1/2 cup olive oil
Scant 1 teaspoon coriander seeds, toasted

Purée all ingredients in a blender. Pour the mixture into a large, heavy saucepan and cook over low heat for about 4 hours. Makes about 2 cups; any extra may be stored in the refrigerator for 1 to 2 weeks.

❧ Jasmine Rice

3 cups raw jasmine rice

Place the rice in a sieve and wash thoroughly under cold running water. Transfer the rice to a large saucepan with a tight-fitting lid. Add 3-3/4 cups cold water. Bring the water to a boil and boil uncovered for 15 seconds. Cover tightly and reduce the heat to low. Cook for 15 minutes. Remove from the heat and let stand 10 minutes before lifting the lid.

Jeff Tunks is Executive Chef of TenPenh and DC Coast in Washington, D.C. Cliff Wharton is Chef de Cuisine at TenPenh.

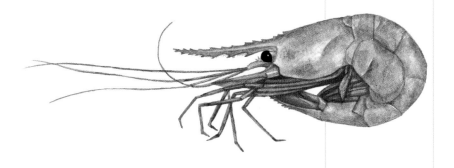

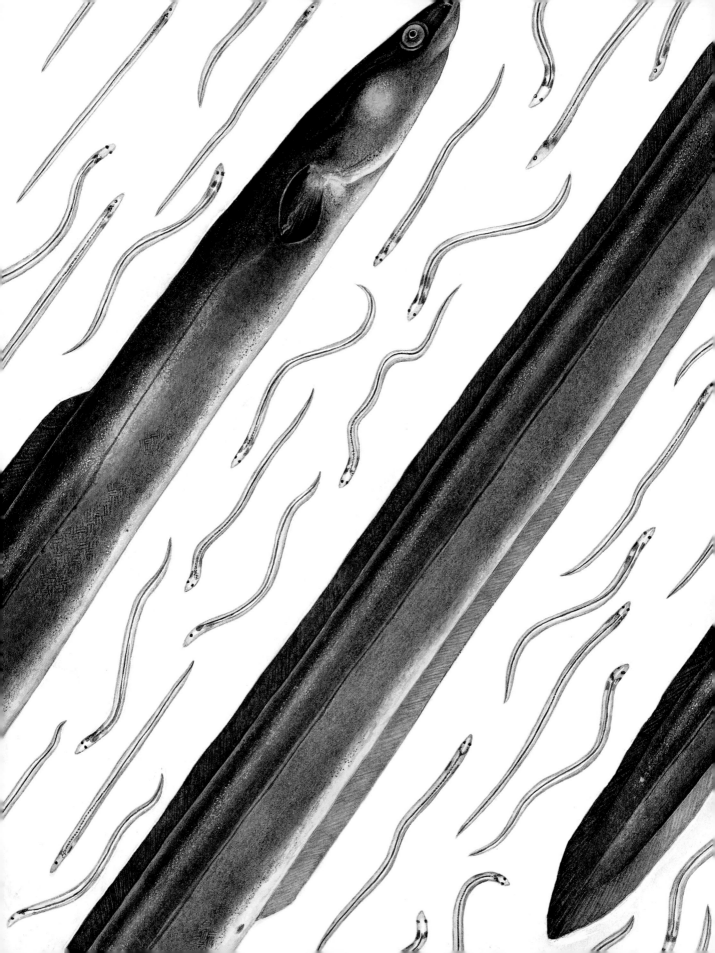

Eel and Farmed White Sturgeon

EEL AND STURGEON, THE MOST PRIMITIVE BONY
fishes on the American seafood scene, are among the most prized outside of
the United States. Recipes provided here are for the American eel and the fillets
and eggs (caviar) of farm-raised white sturgeon. In the wild, the two species
have opposite lifestyles: American eels live and mature in freshwater and then
return to the ocean to spawn; the white sturgeon matures in the ocean and
then returns to freshwater to spawn.

American eel is extremely popular in European and Asian cuisines, but in
the United States it is primarily an ethnic holiday specialty. Much of the eel
caught in the United States is exported to Europe, and there is a huge demand
for glass eels (the transparent young or larval stage) in Japan, where they have
developed an aura of epicurean indulgence like that of caviar or truffle. Rich
in flavor, with high levels of omega-3 fatty acids and a white, firm flesh when
cooked, adult eel is among the most delicious fish species. In Europe, it is
often served in a green sorrel sauce, in a white cream sauce, or fried; Mario

Anguilla eel—
adult and elvers

In the Wild

Oddly, inexplicably, and regardless of how far north the eel has lived most of its life, an American eel will only spawn in the warm waters of the Sargasso Sea, south of Bermuda and east of the Bahamas. Following the southern migration and spawning, the adults die and the newly hatched eels begin the journey northward as transparent larvae or glass eels, then transform into miniature pigmented eels called elvers. At this stage, the eel seeks freshwater, and so great is the instinct to reach it that elvers have been observed slithering snakelike up nearly dry, vertical, creek-bed walls to gain access. Many years later (females mature in approximately ten to twenty years), the cycle begins again.

Batali of Babbo here suggests baking it in a simple tomato sauce, and Armando Maes of Rose Pistola grills it. As noted by Pat Camuso of *Outdoor Magazine,* if you don't eat American eel, "someone in Korea, Japan, or downtown New York City will."

White sturgeon are the largest freshwater fish in North America: they can weigh more than 1,500 pounds and live for more than 100 years. The species is now farmed in California, and loyal consumers of osetra, sevruga, or beluga caviar from the Caspian Sea may find, as one *New York Times* reporter has, that caviar from farm-raised white sturgeon rivals the best Russian osetra. The flesh of the farmed white sturgeon also is excellent—very firm and somewhat fatty. It is often smoked but can be panfried, grilled, baked, braised, or poached; it also holds up well in fish chowders. For a special presentation, you might try Bob Hurley's elegant recipe for pan-roasted sturgeon fillets.

From an environmental perspective, both American eel and farmed white sturgeon are good seafood choices. Although declines in populations of American eel have been reported, annual U.S. landings have remained relatively stable (approximately 1 to 1.5 million pounds) for the past fifty years. Eels are caught in baited pots or various small nets such as seines or fyke nets, none of which is habitat destructive or results in considerable bycatch. In the wild, most of the world's sturgeon species are threatened or endangered in at least some parts of their range, and many are believed to be nearing extinction. Farming of white sturgeon is considered environmentally sound, however, and consumers wishing to try white-sturgeon caviar or fillets should choose products from farmed fish.

Eel Livornese

Serves 4

Eel is perhaps the most traditional of all Christmas Eve dishes, guaranteed to bring you good luck and prosperity throughout the holiday season. I find the rich flavor and silken texture to be similar to the best of smoked sable and sturgeon, without the salinity.

1 piece eel flesh, 1-1/2 pounds
1 cup Gaeta olives
1/4 cup capers, drained
1 generous pinch dried hot red
    pepper flakes

1 cup dry white wine
Salt and freshly ground
    black pepper
❧ Tomato Sauce

Preheat the oven to 450°F. To clean the eel: Make a cut skin-deep behind the head and pectoral fins. Using a fish skinner or pair of pliers, pull the skin off the eel. After skinning, gut the eel and wash off the flesh under running water.

In a 12-inch ovenproof skillet, combine 2 cups of Tomato Sauce, the olives, capers, red pepper flakes, and wine and bring to a boil over medium heat. Rinse the eel, pat dry, and cut it into 4 equal portions. Season the eel with salt and pepper and place in the skillet with the sauce. Transfer the skillet to the oven. Bake for 12 to 15 minutes, until just cooked through.

To serve, place a portion of eel on each of 4 plates and spoon some of the sauce over each.

❧ Tomato Sauce

1/4 cup extra-virgin olive oil
1 Spanish onion, chopped
4 garlic cloves, peeled and thinly sliced
3 tablespoons chopped fresh
    thyme leaves, or 1 tablespoon
    dried

1/2 medium carrot, finely shredded
Two 28-ounce cans peeled
    whole tomatoes, crushed
    by hand and juices reserved
Salt to taste

American Eel

SCIENTIFIC NAME: *Anguilla rostrata*

OTHER NAMES: Anguilla eel, common eel, Atlantic eel, silver eel, freshwater eel. Young (juvenile) eels are called glass eels or elvers.

U.S. DISTRIBUTION: Adults live in freshwater drainages of the eastern United States. Most eels are caught in rivers during the freshwater stage of their lives.

WHAT TO LOOK FOR: Eels should be live in the store or freshly killed. Market size is usually 2 to 8 pounds. Established fish shops, especially those catering to ethnic communities, are likely to carry fresh eel.

COLOR, TASTE, AND TEXTURE: The white to off-white flesh is considered a delicacy by many. The flavor is both rich and delicate, and the texture is moderately firm.

COOKING METHODS: Eel is best when grilled, sautéed, smoked, fried, or simmered in a stew. Unagi is Japanese smoked freshwater eel.

TIP: Buy from someone who knows how to kill and skin eel.

(Continued)

In a 3-quart saucepan, heat the olive oil over medium heat. Add the onion and garlic and cook until soft and light golden brown, about 8 to 10 minutes. Add the thyme and carrot and cook 5 minutes more, until the carrot is quite soft. Add the tomatoes and juice and bring to a boil, stirring often. Lower the heat and simmer for 30 minutes until as thick as hot cereal. Season with salt and serve. This sauce will keep for 1 week in the refrigerator or up to 6 months in the freezer. The recipe makes about 4 cups sauce.

Mario Batali is Chef/Owner of Babbo in New York City. He hosts *Molto Mario* and *Mario Eats Italy* on the Food Network and is the author of *The Babbo Cookbook* (Clarkson N. Potter, 2002), *Simple Italian Food* (Clarkson N. Potter, 1998), and *Mario Batali Holiday Food* (Clarkson N. Potter, 2000).

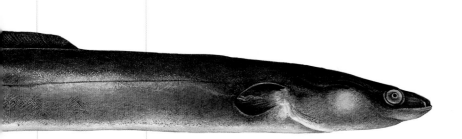

Grilled Eel with Salsa Verde

The grilled eel is served with a simple traditional Italian sauce. Mesquite charcoal or even wood creates a smoky flavor in this dish because of the high natural oil content of the eel.

1 whole eel (1 to 2 pounds),
   preferably cleaned
1/4 cup olive oil

Salt and freshly ground black pepper
✦ Salsa Verde

Cut the eel into 3-ounce fillet portions or have your local fishmonger fillet them ahead of time. Take the prepared portions and roll them in half of the oil. Season with salt and pepper. Preheat a charcoal or gas grill, then place the eel on the grill rack and proceed to cook for approximately 3 minutes (2 minutes on 1 side and 1 minute on the other side).

To serve, lay the cooked eel pieces on deep plates and place a generous spoonful of Salsa Verde on top of each.

✦ Salsa Verde
1 bunch parsley
1 hard-cooked egg
1 teaspoon capers
6 canned anchovy fillets

1 slice day-old bread
3/4 cup extra-virgin olive oil
   (light, fruity-style oil)

Roughly chop the parsley and place in a blender. Then add all other ingredients except for the olive oil. Turn the blender on and add olive oil and blend until oil is completely incorporated and the mixture is relatively smooth but still maintains a chunky consistency. Store the sauce in the refrigerator for up to 3 days.

Armando "Tiny" Maes is Executive Chef of Rose Pistola in San Francisco, California.

Kumomoto Oysters with Farmed White-Sturgeon Caviar and Sake

Farmed White Sturgeon

SCIENTIFIC NAME:
Acipenser transmontanus

U.S. DISTRIBUTION: Native American white sturgeon is farmed in California.

WHAT TO LOOK FOR: Farmed sturgeon are harvested at 15 to 20 pounds. The flesh is pale pink with light orange strips of fat. Steaks and fillets should glisten and smell fresh, not muddy. Farmed-sturgeon caviar comes in a range of colors, including black, gray, cream, olive, and gold, the various colors representing different grades. Individual eggs should be about 2-1/2 to 3 mm in diameter.

COLOR, TASTE, AND TEXTURE: Among the meatiest of fish, the ivory-colored cooked sturgeon has been compared to veal. It holds together well during cooking yet is fork-tender when eaten. The caviar resembles osetra, not too salty and with a light aftertaste.

COOKING METHODS: Grilling, smoking, braising, and sautéing are well suited to fillets or steaks of this unusual fish. Serve the caviar as you would any fine caviar—on blinis or toast points, with scrambled eggs, or as a garnish for raw oysters.

Serves 4

16 Kumomoto oysters
1 ounce U.S.-farmed white-
    sturgeon caviar
1/3 cup dry sake
 Seaweed, cooked briefly in boiling
    water and chilled in cold
    water, for presentation

Lemon wedges
Fresh parsley sprigs

Open the oysters and leave in half shell. Top each with 1 teaspoon of the sake and then top with 1/2 teaspoon of the caviar. Put ice on an oyster platter and top with a small amount of the blanched seaweed. Arrange the oysters on the seaweed. Garnish with lemon wedges and parsley sprigs.

Sandy Ingber is Executive Chef of Grand Central Oyster Bar in New York City.

Eastern Oysters with Sauerkraut and Farmed White-Sturgeon Caviar

I like large, meaty oysters for cooking. Pemaquid oysters from Maine are among my favorites. For years I made this dish using a chiffonade of fresh savoy cabbage, which is also very good, when it occurred to me that the acidity and crunch of sauerkraut would work well with both the oysters and the caviar. This dish is one that sounds odd but tastes perfectly natural.

I suggest pairing the oysters with a dry Riesling because the steely, mineral aromas stand up to the brininess of the oysters, and the petrol flavors and richness counter the acidity of the sauerkraut.

Serves 2

10 large Eastern oysters (such as Pemaquid or Malpeques), shucked, all of the shells and juice reserved
1 to 2 ounces U.S.-farmed white-sturgeon caviar
1/4 cup sauerkraut (not canned), 2 tablespoons of the juice reserved

Lemon juice
1/2 cup heavy cream
2 tablespoons butter
1 tablespoon chopped chives
1 tablespoon chopped dill

Put the oysters and their juice into a small, nonreactive sauté pan. Cook over moderate heat for just a minute or until the edges of the oysters curl very slightly. Lift the oysters out of the pan with a slotted spoon and set aside in a warm place. Warm half of the cleaned oyster shells in the oven while preparing the rest of the dish. Increase the heat and reduce the oyster juice, adding the sauerkraut juice plus a squirt of lemon juice. When reduced by about one-third, add the cream and butter; continue to reduce, adding the sauerkraut, until the sauce is fairly thick. Return the oysters and whatever liquid they have given off to the pan just to reheat. Add chives and dill.

To serve, spoon an oyster and a little sauce into each warmed oyster shell. Top with a tiny bit of caviar.

David Waltuck is Chef/Owner of Chanterelle in New York City and the author (with Melicia Phillips) of *Staff Meals from Chanterelle* (Workman Publishing Company, 2000).

Pan-Roasted Farmed White Sturgeon, Warm Lentil Salad with Pancetta and Wild Mushrooms, Wilted Frisée, and Pinot Noir Glaze

Serves 4

I love cooking fish, and I love red wine. Most of all I love showing people how to pair the two. Sturgeon is a rather dense, full-flavored, meaty fish with a relatively high fat content. Roasting, then using the glaze to finish, is the perfect bridge for the red wine. The wild mushrooms and lentils add an earthiness that scream for a nice Pinot Noir.

The muddy or musty flavor that one often finds in wild sturgeon is eliminated in good farmed sturgeon. At The Fishery in Sacramento, Ken Beer has a "flow through" system from fresh groundwater to the sturgeon ponds. It then goes to catfish ponds and then as irrigation for local agriculture. This system eliminates the need for antibiotics, a rising concern in the fish-farming industry.

COOK'S STRATEGY: Prepare the lentils, mushrooms, and pancetta before cooking the fish. Make the Pinot Noir Glaze and Wilted Frisée, and then while the sturgeon is cooking, finish the Warm Lentil Salad with Pancetta and Wild Mushrooms.

4 farmed white sturgeon fillets, 6 ounces each
3 tablespoons olive oil
Salt and freshly ground black pepper
✤ Warm Lentil Salad with Pancetta and Wild Mushrooms
✤ Wilted Frisée
✤ Pinot Noir Glaze

Preheat oven to 400°F. Place a large, ovenproof sauté pan over medium heat. Season the sturgeon fillets with salt and pepper. Put the olive oil in the pan, add the fish, and brown the fillets on all sides. Place the pan in the oven and cook the fish for approximately 6 minutes or until done in the center. Remove the pan from the oven and keep the fish warm.

Place a portion of the Warm Lentil Salad with Pancetta and Wild Mushrooms in the middle of each plate. Center the Wilted Frisée on top and place a piece of the sturgeon on top of the frisée. Top each serving with a bit of the Pinot Noir Glaze. Serve and enjoy.

✤ Warm Lentil Salad with Pancetta and Wild Mushrooms

1 pound green French lentils
4 tablespoons olive oil
3 cups loosely packed wild mushrooms (chanterelles, morels, oyster, shiitake, or whatever combination is preferred; or seasonal domestic mushrooms may be substituted)
1 teaspoon chopped garlic
2 tablespoons finely chopped shallots
2 tablespoons chopped fresh fines herbes
Salt and freshly ground black pepper
1/4 cup Madeira
2 cups chicken broth
4 ounces pancetta, sliced thinly and diced

Place lentils in a medium saucepan and cover with cold water. Bring to a boil and simmer until tender but not mushy; check after 10 minutes. When cooked, drain lentils and cool on a sheet pan. Gather and reserve.

Place a large sauté pan over high heat and add the olive oil. When the oil is hot, add the mushrooms. Stir mushrooms rather vigorously with a wooden spoon to coat and continue stirring as they give up their liquid. When this liquid has mostly evaporated, add the garlic, shallots, and fines herbes. Stir for 1 minute longer, season to taste with salt and pepper, add the Madeira, and add 1 cup of the chicken broth. Bring to a simmer and reduce by one-half. Reserve.

Place the diced pancetta in a small pan over low heat and cook slowly until much of the fat has rendered but the pancetta is not crisp—drain and reserve.

Combine the lentils, pancetta, and wild mushroom mixture with the remaining cup of chicken broth, bring to a simmer, and let cook slowly to meld the flavors.

✦ Wilted Frisée

6 cups frisée (stems trimmed), washed

1 tablespoon olive oil

1/4 cup sherry vinegar

Salt and freshly ground black pepper

2 tablespoons chicken broth

Toss the frisée with the oil, sherry vinegar, and salt and pepper. Heat in a sauté pan over medium heat until warm; add the chicken broth and cook until the frisée wilts, about 30 seconds.

✦ Pinot Noir Glaze

4 cups Pinot Noir

1 tablespoon chopped shallots

2 cups good veal stock

1 teaspoon cold butter

Bring the wine and shallots to a simmer in a small saucepan and reduce to 1 cup. Add the veal stock and reduce to 1/2 cup of liquid. Stir in the butter until it emulsifies and there is a sheen on the glaze.

Bob Hurley is Chef/Owner of Hurley's Restaurant and Bar in Yountville, California.

HERRING AND SHAD, CLOSE RELATIVES OF SARDINES and anchovies, are silvery, streamlined fishes with large scales and forked tails. The spawning run of American shad, which begins in the southern Atlantic states in February, is a harbinger of spring for many seaside communities, and its roe is a seasonal delicacy. Many Americans know herring only as canned sardines or smoked, salted kippers, but fresh herring has a rich taste and soft texture when pickled or cooked. Likewise, fresh shad is delicious.

The herring and shad species included here are Atlantic herring, Pacific herring, and American shad. Atlantic herring are widely distributed in the North Atlantic, including along the eastern U.S. coast south to South Carolina. Believed to be the world's most numerous fish, schools of millions of migrating Atlantic herring can span as far as 17 miles. Landings in the United States alone exceeded 1.7 billion pounds between 1991 and 2001. Despite these large harvests, fresh herring can be difficult to find in the United States; in New York, locally caught herring is most abundant from November through March.

Pacific herring are similar to Atlantic herring in appearance (silvery with a bluish-green back), size (typically about 1 foot in length), and commercial importance (landings for the ten-year period 1991 to 2001 exceeded 1.2 billion pounds). Ninety percent of Pacific herring landed is caught for the roe, most of which is exported to Japan.

One stock of Atlantic herring, the Thames-Blackwater drift-net fishery, has received the Marine Stewardship Council's certification of sustainability, and although the Atlantic herring stock off Georges Bank collapsed in the 1970s from heavy fishing by foreign fleets, it is now considered recovered. Both

Atlantic herring

In the Wild

American shad can travel amazingly long distances. During their five-year average lifespan, one fish may migrate as far as 12,000 miles. Most shad die after spawning because of the tremendous energy exerted during migration, although some shad survive to repeat the spawning migration as many as two more times. A program to improve the shad population in the Chesapeake Bay is trying to relieve some of the additional strains that people have imposed on spawning shad. In addition to enhancing natural populations with hatchery-raised fish, the shoreline communities are attempting to open 1,400 miles of blocked streams and rivers that prevent shad from migrating to their spawning grounds. Passages constructed through blocked streams include sloped channels, pools, and even an elevator on the Susquehanna River to transport fish over a dam.

Atlantic and Pacific herring are good seafood choices because they are fast growing and abundant, and very little bycatch and habitat damage are involved with the midwater trawls, seines, or gillnets used in herring fisheries.

Unlike herring, American shad return to freshwater streams to breed. The commercial fishery coincides with spawning runs from Saint Johns River, Florida, to the Connecticut River, although there is a moratorium on catching American shad in parts of the Chesapeake Bay, which has a recovering population. In the 1870s American shad were introduced to the Pacific coast, where they support both game and commercial fisheries. Except for the noted problems in Chesapeake Bay, which appear to be improving with record numbers of spawning shad returning to the Susquehanna River in recent years, shad appears to be a good seafood selection.

Herring Trio

Each serves 4

I grew up close to the ocean in Stockholm and have many memories of all the seafood we could catch and eat. One of the strongest memories is of my father and grandfather taking me out to fish in early summer. When a school of herring comes close to shore—you don't have to go out very far—you can simply roll down a string of silver hooks, and then you jerk a bit until you feel the string getting heavier and heavier. You reel it in and you have five, six, or ten shiny silver striped herrings in the boat. A few hours later you are cleaning 20 pounds or so of herrings. You fry them in butter with some fresh dill, lemon, and Swedish caviar (smoked cod roe) and serve them on a cracker. It is a great delicacy and moreover a genuine food experience. When you are old enough, you rinse it down with some Aquavit—"Skal!"

COOK'S STRATEGY: The Pickled Herring needs to be prepared two days in advance whether used alone or as a component of the two other dishes.

PICKLED HERRING

4 fillets fresh herring
1 cup white-wine vinegar
2 cups salt
2 bay leaves

2 black peppercorns
1 carrot, sliced
1 red onion, sliced
1/2 leek

Bring 3 cups of water, the vinegar, salt, bay leaves, peppercorns, carrot, and onion to a boil in a saucepan. Let simmer for 3 minutes and add the leek. Remove the pan from the heat and let the mixture cool. Place the herring fillets in a container with an air tight lid. Pour the pickling mixture over and cover. Refrigerate for 48 hours. The herring may then be sliced and used as is or used in the 2 following recipes.

(Continued)

Herring

Atlantic Herring, Pacific Herring

SCIENTIFIC NAMES: *Clupea harengus* (Atlantic), *C. pallasii* (Pacific)

OTHER NAMES: Atlantic herring are also called common herring or sea herring; Pacific herring may be called California herring. Small fresh herring (3 to 4 inches long) are often sold as sardines. Smoked herring is known as kipper. Rollmops are rolled, pickled herring fillets secured with toothpicks.

U.S. DISTRIBUTION: Atlantic and Pacific coasts

SEASON: Atlantic herring are harvested off the northeastern United States year-round using different types of gear. In New York, fresh herring may be available from November to April.

WHAT TO LOOK FOR: Fresh herring—when you can find them—are sold as whole fish that average about 1 pound. A swath of blue or blue-green skin runs down their backs and their sides and belly shine with silver scales. Pick fish that show no signs of bruising or rough handling. Oil-rich herring has a short shelf life. If the fish smell unpleasantly strong, don't buy them.

COLOR, TASTE, AND TEXTURE: The soft, dark or off-white flesh is sought by those who appreciate a pronounced fish flavor. When marinated or brined, the flesh firms up considerably.

COOKING METHODS: Fresh herring can be fried, grilled, broiled, or baked. It can also be smoked or pickled.

American Shad

SCIENTIFIC NAME: *Alosa sapidissima*

OTHER NAMES: Atlantic shad, poor man's salmon

U.S. DISTRIBUTION: Native to the east coast but introduced to the west coast in the 1800s

SEASON: Spring, when the fish make their way up rivers to spawn

WHAT TO LOOK FOR: To best experience the elegant taste of shad flesh, look for boned shad fillets. A shad fillet will have sections of flesh missing—not an indication of an inept filleter but the unavoidable result of removing the enormous number of bones of the shad. The roe is sold by the set or pair, or "roe shad" may be sold whole.

COLOR, TASTE, AND TEXTURE: The light-colored flesh has a rich, buttery flavor and soft texture. The prized roe is reddish brown with a creamy texture that becomes sandy if overcooked.

COOKING METHODS: Native Americans were the first to dine on planked shad. Cooked on a wooden plank set next to an open fire, the rich shad was subtly flavored by the wood and smoke, and the bones softened during the long cooking process. Grilling over a fire is still a favored method for the succulent boned fillets. Panfrying, baking, or broiling is also recommended. The roe is usually pan-fried in butter or bacon drippings, broiled, poached, or sautéed.

HERB-GARLIC HERRING

2 fillets pickled herring, cut into pieces
1 tablespoon snipped fresh chives
1 tablespoon finely chopped fresh tarragon
1 tablespoon finely chopped fresh dill
1 clove garlic, minced
1/2 tablespoon mayonnaise
1 tablespoon sour cream
Salt and freshly ground black pepper

Combine the chopped herbs and garlic with the mayonnaise and sour cream in a bowl. Add salt and pepper to taste. Fold in the herring.

GRANDFATHER'S HERRING

2 fillets pickled herring
2 tablespoons sweet, Swedish-style mustard
2 tablespoons sour cream
1 teaspoon red-wine vinegar
1/2 teaspoon sugar
Salt and freshly ground black pepper
1 hard-cooked egg, chopped
1 tablespoon chopped leeks
1 tablespoon chopped pickled cucumber
4 chives

Combine the mustard, sour cream, vinegar, and sugar in a bowl. Season to taste with salt and pepper. Slice herring into 1/2-inch pieces and arrange on a plate, keeping shapes of fillets. Spread with the sauce. Arrange egg, leeks, and pickled cucumber on top in separate rows. Garnish with chives and sauce.

Roger Johnsson was Chef de Cuisine of Aquavit in Minneapolis, Minnesota. He now resides in Sweden.

Shad-Roe Omelette with Bacon-Butter Sauce

1/2 set shad roe, medium size,
    about 3 ounces
2 eggs
1/2 teaspoon salt

1/4 teaspoon white pepper
1 tablespoon canola oil
2 slices brioche, toasted
✦ Bacon-Butter Sauce

Serves 1

Preheat the oven to 400°F. Clean the membrane from the shad roe, being careful not to rupture the egg sacs. Separate the egg sacs so that there are 2 individual pieces. Lightly oil roe and season with salt and pepper, and roast in the oven for 5 minutes. Remove from oven and pat excess oil from the roe.

Heat an 8-inch skillet on the stove until very hot. Meanwhile whisk the eggs with salt and pepper until the bubbles on top are each the size of a pinhead. Add the oil to the skillet and swirl to coat evenly. Add the eggs and shake the pan; this helps the egg cook evenly and makes a thinner omelet. When the omelette has set around the edge but is still some-what wet in the middle, place the shad roe on the omelette slightly off center and roll the omelette around the roe. Place the skillet into the oven to finish cooking, about 2 minutes.

Remove skillet from the oven and place omelette on a cutting board. Slice on a bias into medallions. Spoon Bacon-Butter Sauce onto a plate and set the omelette medallions on top. Put 2 slices of toasted brioche on the plate and serve.

✦ Bacon-Butter Sauce

1/2 pound bacon, sliced into 1/4-inch pieces
2 sticks (16 tablespoons) butter, at room
    temperature, cut into 1-inch cubes

2 tablespoons vegetable broth or water

Heat a skillet over medium heat and brown the bacon completely; drain thoroughly. Combine the bacon and all except one cube of butter in a food processor. Blend, then remove from processor and store in refrigerator. Bring the vegetable broth and the remain-ing cube of butter to a boil. Add 3 tablespoons of the bacon butter and shake pan. Once butter begins to melt, whisk gently to emulsify. (The remaining bacon butter can be stored in the refrigerator for up to 1 month.)

Dale Reitzer is Chef/Owner of Acacia in Richmond, Virginia.

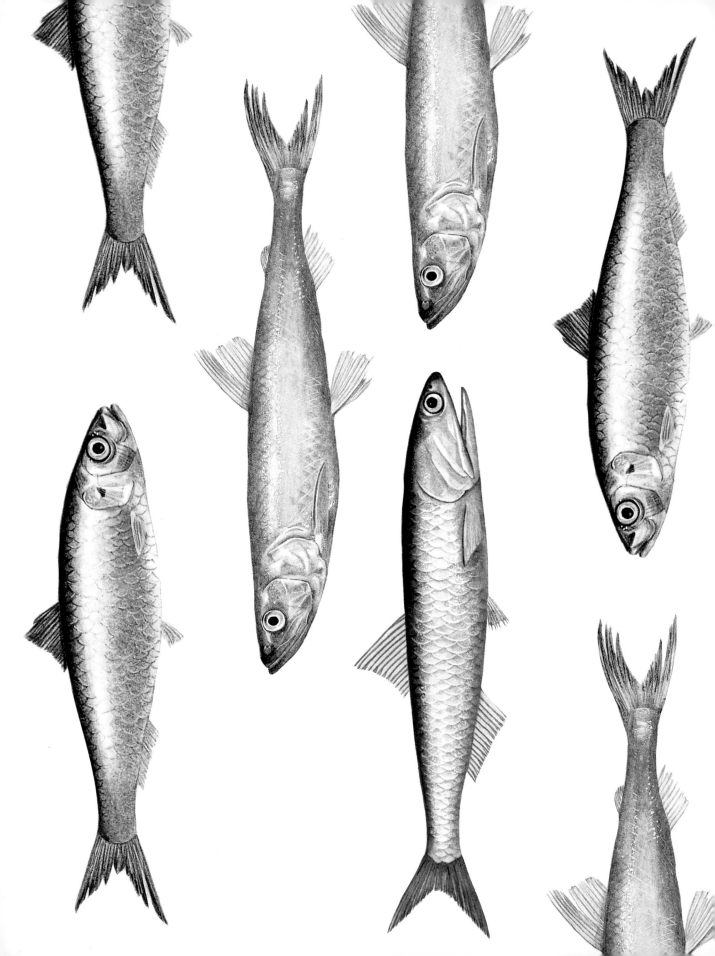

Sardines, Anchovies, and Smelts

SARDINES AND ANCHOVIES, ALONG WITH HERRING, shad, pilchards, and splat, are members of the clupeoid fish group, which throughout history has been the most important group of fishes to humans worldwide as sources of food, oil, fertilizer, and animal feed. During the twentieth century, clupeoids composed, by weight, an astonishing 30 to 40 percent of all commercially caught marine fishes. Although heavily fished commercially for centuries, no clupeoid species is endangered, but the abundance of some species has fluctuated unpredictably or as a result of fishing pressure or environmental disturbances. Smelts, which are not clupeoids but are instead related to salmon and trout, are included here because of a general similarity in size and appearance.

Sardines are most closely related to herring, and the two names are sometimes used interchangeably. Sardines available in U.S. markets are typically the Pacific sardine, Spanish sardine, or the European pilchard (which does not live in U.S. waters and so is not discussed further here). The Pacific sardine formerly supported the largest commercial fishery in the Western Hemisphere, at one time accounting for about 25 percent of all fish landed in the United States. The species later virtually disappeared from the northern part of its range (Point Conception, California, to southeastern Alaska). But after a moratorium on catching them was implemented in California in 1967, the Pacific sardine

European pilchard *(top and bottom left and top right),* smelts *(with green backs),* northern anchovy *(middle, facing up)*

In the Wild

Two alternating twenty-five-year cycles of Pacific climate change have recently been linked to variations in populations of sardines and anchovies. The warm El Viejo, nicknamed the "sardine period," is like a mild El Niño, and the cool La Vieja "anchovy cycle" is similar to a mild La Niña. Both can affect ocean circulation, winds, and patterns of rainfall from Indonesia to the west coast of South America—literally half of the world. During the "anchovy," or cooler phases, stronger ocean currents supply more nutrients to the eastern Pacific, helping to support large populations of anchovies. During the warmer regime, sardines rule throughout Pacific waters.

made a remarkable comeback: More than 900 million pounds were taken off the California, Oregon, and Washington coasts between 1991 and 2001. The Spanish sardine fishery is much smaller, with approximately 12 million pounds taken between 1991 and 2002, mostly from Florida.

Fresh Pacific sardines are sold in many west-coast markets and have recently become available at certain seafood counters in other parts of the country, including the east coast. They are popular with professional chefs, easy for the home chef to cook, and, along with Spanish sardines, environmentally sound seafood choices.

The only anchovy species of commercial importance in the United States is the northern anchovy. Landings for the period 1991 to 2001 exceeded 131 million pounds, most from off California. Most anchovies are processed into fishmeal or used as bait for tuna, but some are salted or salted and canned in oil for human consumption. Fresh anchovies are popular in European cuisine, but they are not common in U.S. seafood markets. "White anchovies," which are marinated in white vinegar and only lightly salted, are available in the United States. The northern anchovy is a good seafood choice because populations appear to be in good condition, and the haul nets used to catch them result in little bycatch or habitat damage.

Fresh smelts available at U.S. grocery stores and seafood counters are usually the Atlantic rainbow smelt, which lives in the north Atlantic and northwest Pacific. Other species that may be found in U.S. markets are the Arctic rainbow smelt, the Eulachon smelt, and the European smelt. Marketed smelts are usually small, about 4 inches long, and they are sometimes deep fried whole (or dressed) so that the entire fish is eaten. The flesh is tender and sweet. Except for a population of the Atlantic rainbow smelt that became landlocked in Lake Michigan and nearly disappeared when a mysterious epidemic struck there, smelts are the subject of few conservation issues.

Sardine Sampler

Serves 4

This sardine sampler features a trio of intriguing plates including a refreshing salad of beets, apples, and house-cured sardines; delicate oil-poached sardines in grape leaves; and a robust dish of grilled sardines skewered on rosemary sprigs. Although the preparation may seem somewhat extensive, your efforts will be rewarded. The result is a stunning appetizer that is truly impressive and delicious. And if you are short on time, choose one to create— each component of the sampler is a tasty appetizer in itself—and multiply the ingredients by four. The Oil-Poached Sardines can even be prepared a day ahead.

SARDINE AND BEET SALAD

8 whole fresh sardines, gutted

1/4 cup kosher salt, plus more
    to taste

1/4 cup sugar

Grated zest and juice of 1 lemon

2 sprigs parsley, finely chopped

1/2 bunch dill, finely chopped

1 medium red beet

1 Granny Smith apple

1/2 small yellow onion

Freshly ground black pepper

2 tablespoons sour cream
    or crème fraîche

1 teaspoon Dijon mustard

    Scale and wash the sardines carefully, so as not to break the skin. Fillet the fish and remove the pin bones. Combine the salt with the sugar, lemon zest, parsley, and half of the dill. Sprinkle half of this mixture on a plate, lay the sardines on top, and cover with the remainder of the mixture. Refrigerate for about 2 hours.

    In the meantime, boil the beet in salted water until soft. Cool and peel. Cut the apple, beet, and onion into 1/4-inch dice. Remove the sardines from the cure. Wash quickly, dry on paper towels, and cut the fillets into 1/4-inch pieces.

    To serve, add the diced sardines and the remaining chopped dill to the apple, beet, and onion. Season with salt, pepper, and lemon juice. Fold in the sour cream and mustard.

(Continued)

Sardines, Anchovies, and Smelts

SCIENTIFIC NAMES: *Sardinops sagax* (Pacific sardine), *Sardinella aurita* (Spanish sardine), *Sardina pilchardus* (European pilchard), *Osmerus mordax mordax* (Atlantic rainbow smelt), *O. m. dentex* (Arctic rainbow smelt), *Thaleichthys pacificus* (Eulachon smelt)

OTHER NAMES: Smelts may also be called whitebait, jacksmelt, grunion, cucumberfish, and candlefish.

U.S. DISTRIBUTION: Pacific sardines range from Alaska to California. Northern anchovies can be found from California to Canada. Atlantic rainbow smelts are found in the north Atlantic.

SEASON: Fresh Pacific sardines are becoming available year-round; fresh anchovies are available all year, but rarely in U.S. markets. Smelts are most available in spring.

WHAT TO LOOK FOR: All of these fish should smell fresh, not as if you're standing downwind from the cannery. Look for firm, unbruised fish with shiny skin and bright eyes.

COLOR, TASTE, AND TEXTURE: When cooked, smelts have white, soft flesh with a mild yet distinctive flavor. Sardines and anchovies have a stronger flavor and soft, off-white flesh when cooked.

COOKING METHODS: Smelts can be fried, broiled, baked, or grilled on skewers. Sardines and anchovies can be broiled, grilled, or panfried.

OIL-POACHED SARDINES

4 whole fresh sardines, gutted
Salt
4 grape leaves, blanched
1 sprig dill
1 lemon, half cut into 1/4-inch slices,
    the other half juiced
1 cup olive oil

1 clove garlic
2 sprigs thyme
5 black peppercorns
1 bay leaf
Salt and freshly ground black
    pepper to taste
Dill sprigs and julienned lemon zest

Scale and wash the sardines carefully so as not to break the skin. Fillet the sardines, leaving the 2 fillets attached by the tail. Close the fillets and season generously with salt. Lay a grape leaf on the work surface and place a sardine at the base of the leaf. Roll once from the bottom up. Fold in sides toward the center and continue to roll upward. Wrap the remaining sardines in the remaining grape leaves. Place them in a stainless-steel or glass dish, lay the dill sprig and lemon slices on top, and sprinkle with lemon juice. Heat the olive oil with the garlic, thyme, peppercorns, and bay leaf until it simmers. Pour the hot oil over the sardines and allow to cool to room temperature. Once cooled, place the sardines in the refrigerator for at least 12 hours before serving.

To serve, transfer the wrapped sardines to plates. Unfold, leaving the leaves on the plates. Garnish with dill sprigs and julienned lemon zest.

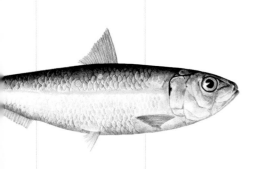

GRILLED SARDINES

8 whole fresh sardines, gutted
1 quart milk, optional
1 clove garlic, crushed
2 tablespoons olive oil

8 fine sprigs of rosemary
Salt and freshly ground black pepper to taste
1 lemon

Scale the sardines carefully so as not to break the skin. Fillet the fish, leaving the fillets attached by the tail. For a milder flavor, soak the sardines in cold milk for 1 hour before continuing with the recipe. Marinate the sardines with the garlic and olive oil for about 1 hour. Preheat a charcoal or gas grill to medium high. Prepare the rosemary skewers by sharpening one end with a knife. This makes it easier to pierce through the skin of the fish. Roll the fillets toward the tail and spike the rosemary skewer through. Grill the sardines quickly for about 1 minute on each side.

Season with salt and pepper and drizzle with lemon juice to serve.

Variation: Bake sardines in a hot oven or pan sear on the stovetop in olive oil.

Jean Alberti is Executive Chef/Partner of Kokkari
Estiatorio in San Francisco, California.

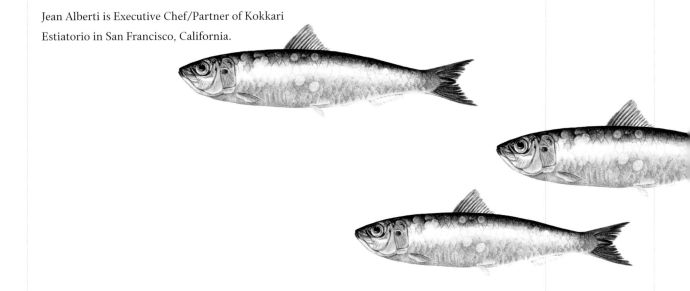

Grilled Sardines with Salsa Verde and Fingerling Potatoes

Serves 4

COOK'S STRATEGY: Begin preparing the Confit Tomatoes first, as they require about three hours in the oven. The confit can be made in advance, stored in the refrigerator, and warmed through when ready to use.

8 to 12 fresh sardines, gutted
  and heads removed
1/4 cup extra-virgin olive oil
1 clove garlic, minced
Salt and freshly ground black pepper

12 fingerling potatoes
1 bunch watercress
❧ Confit Tomatoes
❧ Salsa Verde

Open the sardines (see page 136) and rub with 2 tablespoons of the olive oil and the garlic. Season with salt and pepper; set aside. Blanch the potatoes in boiling salted water until soft. Drain, cool, and slice in half lengthwise. Toss the potatoes with the remaining 2 tablespoons oil and salt and pepper; keep warm and set aside. When ready to grill the sardines, light a charcoal grill or preheat a gas grill. Grill sardines skin-side down over hot coals for 2 to 3 minutes.

Place 3 or 4 fingerling potatoes in the center of each of 4 salad plates. Arrange 2 to 3 sardines on each plate. Top the sardines with 2 halves of Confit Tomatoes. Toss the watercress with 2 tablespoons of the Salsa Verde and garnish each plate with a few sprigs. Drizzle each plate with a tablespoon or 2 of Salsa Verde and serve without delay.

❧ Confit Tomatoes

4 vine-ripened summer tomatoes
Olive oil

Salt and freshly ground black pepper

Preheat the oven to 250°F. With the tip of a sharp knife, cut an X on the bottom of each tomato. Dunk the tomatoes in boiling water for 15 seconds. Cool briefly and slip off the tomato skins. Cut the tomatoes in half and lightly squeeze out excess juice and seeds. Place the tomatoes in a shallow casserole dish, drizzle with olive oil, and season with salt and pepper. Bake the tomatoes for almost 3 hours, until they are slightly dried and shriveled. Set aside.

❧ Salsa Verde

1 cup fresh Italian flat-leaf parsley

6 sprigs fresh thyme, leaves picked

5 sprigs fresh tarragon, leaves picked

6 sprigs fresh oregano, leaves picked

1 clove garlic

1 teaspoon dried hot red pepper flakes

1 tablespoon capers

2 canned anchovy fillets

1 cup olive oil

Juice of 1 lemon

Combine all ingredients in a blender and process to a coarse purée.

Debbie Gold and Michael Smith are Chef/Owners of Forty Sardines in Overland Park, Kansas.

Grilled-Sardine and White-Bean Crostini

Serves 4

Fish with beans is a recurring theme on our menus. This particular combination is rich and satisfying. The creamy, understated bean purée is a great foil for the intense flavor of grilled sardines. The slight acidity in the shallot oil helps balance the dish.

COOK'S STRATEGY: The Shallot Oil and the White-Bean Purée can be made a day in advance.

4 large, whole fresh sardines
Olive oil
Salt and freshly ground black pepper
Chopped Italian flat-leaf parsley
Radishes, halved or quartered,
    sprinkled with salt

Oil-cured olives
❧ Crostini
❧ White-Bean Purée
❧ Shallot Oil

If you can convince your fishmonger to fillet the sardines for you, have him do it! Ask him to butterfly them, leaving the two sides attached along the back.

If you are filleting your own sardines, here's how to do it: Place a cutting board in the sink or span the top of the sink. Lay a sardine on the cutting board under gently running cold water. Using a sharp paring knife, scrape each side of the sardine from tail to head to loosen any scales. Cut off the head and then cut open the belly. Pull out the innards and rinse. Hold the fish belly-up and head pointing away from you. Slit the belly open the rest of the way to the tail, using your thumb. Then, run your thumb from the head to the tail along one side of the backbone, loosening it from the flesh. Do the same along the other side of the backbone. Grasp the backbone at the head and pull free from the body all the way to the tail. Cut the backbone at the tail, leaving the tail still attached. Lay the sardine open and trim off the edges of the belly. Rinse very gently. Lay fillets on a paper towel and blot dry.

On a plate or in a shallow pan, drizzle olive oil and sprinkle with salt and pepper. Lay the sardines flesh-side down in the pan. Brush the skin side with more oil and sprinkle liberally with salt and pepper. Preheat a grill to high and then brush the grates with oil. Lay the sardine fillets on the grill, skin-side down. When you can see that they are cooking, after about 3 minutes, gently slide an oiled spatula under the fillet, loosen from the grill, and turn 90°. Allow fish to finish cooking, another 1 or 2 minutes: the skin should caramelize. Flip the fish over and cook for 30 seconds more. Remove to a fresh plate or shallow pan, skin-side down. Spoon the Shallot Oil, including the solids, over the sardines and allow to sit for up to half an hour.

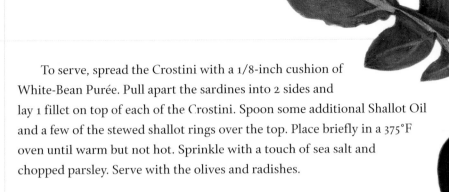

To serve, spread the Crostini with a 1/8-inch cushion of White-Bean Purée. Pull apart the sardines into 2 sides and lay 1 fillet on top of each of the Crostini. Spoon some additional Shallot Oil and a few of the stewed shallot rings over the top. Place briefly in a 375°F oven until warm but not hot. Sprinkle with a touch of sea salt and chopped parsley. Serve with the olives and radishes.

✤ Crostini

1 loaf day-old country-style bread   Coarse sea salt
Extra-virgin olive oil

Cut 8 slices of bread, each slightly thicker than 1/4 inch, on the diagonal so that each slice is long enough to accommodate 1 sardine fillet. Spread the bread out on a baking sheet and brush both sides with olive oil, saturating well. Sprinkle 1 side lightly with coarse sea salt. The bread may be grilled or toasted in a 375°F oven. Grill or toast until crostini are lightly browned and crispy on the outside but still chewy on the inside.

✤ White-Bean Purée

5 garlic cloves, peeled and   1 cup white beans, cooked, with their
   lightly smashed   cooking liquid (use water, not stock)
1/4 cup extra-virgin olive oil   Salt

Combine the garlic and oil in a heavy-bottomed saucepan. Cover and heat over low heat. Cook for about 20 minutes until the garlic begins to dissolve but do not let it brown. Add the white beans and their cooking liquid and season lightly with salt. Continue cooking over a medium-low flame until the liquid is almost all reduced. Purée in a food processor until smooth. Check and adjust salt if necessary. This can be made a day ahead and brought to room temperature before using.

(Continued)

✦ Shallot Oil

1/2 cup extra-virgin olive oil

2 large shallots, peeled and thinly sliced

1 to 2 garlic cloves, peeled and lightly
    smashed with the side of a knife

2 sprigs thyme

1-1/2 tablespoons Champagne vinegar

Salt and freshly ground black pepper

Combine the oil, shallots, garlic, and thyme in a saucepan. Keep the flame very low so as not to color the shallots or garlic. Heat the mixture over a low flame for about 20 minutes. Remove from heat, add the vinegar, and season well with salt and pepper. This can be made a day ahead and kept refrigerated. Allow to warm to room temperature before using.

Craig Stoll is Chef/Owner of Delfina in San Francisco, California.

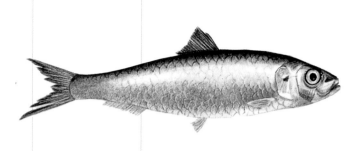

Fresh Sardines with Baby Artichokes, Sauce Niçoise

Sardines certainly bring connotations of strong, oily, canned fish to most people's minds. I am passionate about sardines—since my first travels to Europe as a teenager, I haven't been able to get enough of them. From an environmental standpoint, they are an absolute dream; they reproduce rapidly and are abundant, and thus my inspiration for this recipe.

My first experiences of sardines were in the South of France, and I still believe that they lend themselves to the flavors of the Mediterranean. Whenever I question the composition of a dish, I look to the naturally occurring geography to guide me. The South of France has an abundance of fennel, tomatoes, basil, and garlic and they marry beautifully with the oily little sardine of the Mediterranean. Of course, most of the sardines we use in California come from the Monterey area, which is also home to the prickly artichoke. I have been cooking this dish for many years, and it is always a crowd pleaser. Support our sustainable fisheries and enjoy a delicious dish while doing so!

COOK'S STRATEGY: Begin the Oven-Dried Tomatoes at least three hours before you plan to serve. Blanch the fennel, haricots verts, and fava beans, peel the favas, and then prepare the artichokes and garlic.

12 to 16 fresh sardines, filleted, pin bones removed
30 baby artichokes
Extra-virgin olive oil
1 head garlic, cloves peeled
2 vine-ripened tomatoes, seeded and cut into large dice
1 bulb fennel, trimmed, diced small and blanched
1/4 cup Niçoise olives, pitted and finely chopped
3 tablespoons balsamic vinegar

Salt and freshly ground black pepper
1/2 bunch fresh basil, stemmed, leaves cut into thin ribbons
1/4 pound haricots verts (thin green beans), blanched
4 scallions, thinly sliced
2 pounds fava beans in the pod, shelled, blanched, and peeled
Grated zest of 3 lemons
1/4 bunch Italian flat-leaf parsley, stemmed, leaves finely chopped
✢ Oven-Dried Tomatoes

Peel back and snap off the tough outer leaves of the baby artichokes. Trim the stems and tops. Slice 1/8-inch thick and place in lemon water until ready to sauté. Heat 1 or 2 tablespoons olive oil in a sauté pan over medium-high heat. Drain the artichokes and sauté until cooked through. Keep warm.

(Continued)

Put the garlic cloves in a small saucepan and cover with cold water. Bring to a boil and drain. Repeat this process 3 times. Cool the garlic and thinly slice.

In a large sauté pan, slowly warm the diced tomatoes, garlic slices, fennel, and olives in some olive oil. Season to taste with vinegar and salt and pepper. At the last possible moment, add the basil, haricots verts, scallions, and fava beans. Cook until heated through.

Quickly sauté the sardines in olive oil until the skin begins to crisp on 1 side; turn the sardines over for a quick minute.

Spoon baby artichokes into center of plates. Lay 2 sardines on top of each. Spoon the Sauce Niçoise around and garnish with the Oven-Dried Tomatoes, lemon zest, and parsley.

✦ Oven-Dried Tomatoes

5 Roma tomatoes   Salt and freshly ground black pepper to taste
1/4 cup olive oil

Preheat the oven to 200°F. Bring a saucepan of water to a boil. Cut an X on the bottom of each Roma tomato. Plunge tomatoes into the boiling water for about 8 seconds to loosen skins. Remove the tomatoes with a slotted spoon and plunge into ice water. Peel the tomatoes. Cut the outsides of tomatoes from centers and place on a baking sheet. Drizzle with the olive oil and season with salt and pepper. Bake for 2 to 3 hours or until slightly dried. Set aside.

Traci Des Jardins is Chef/Co-Owner of Jardinière in San Francisco.

Fried Anchovies with Green Olives and Lemon

1 pound fresh anchovies
(approximately 16 to 20 small
anchovies), cleaned
1 cup milk
Salt and freshly ground black pepper
1/2 cup pitted imported green olives

1 cup flour
1 lemon, thinly sliced
(like silver dollars)
4 to 6 cups olive oil for frying

Serves 4 to 6
as an appetizer

Dip the anchovies in the milk for just a minute. Place them into a bowl and season
with salt and pepper. Repeat with the olives, then dump the flour into the bowl, making
sure to coat everything with the flour. Preheat the oil in a pot to 325°F. Shake the anchovies
and the olives to get rid of the excess flour, and then place them into the oil. Fry for about
5 minutes or until the anchovies and olives are nice and crisp. For the lemons, repeat the
process but fry them for about half of the time. Lay the fried anchovies, olives, and lemons
on a napkin to let the excess oil drain. Serve immediately while they are hot.

Armando "Tiny" Maes is Executive Chef of Rose Pistola in San Francisco, California.

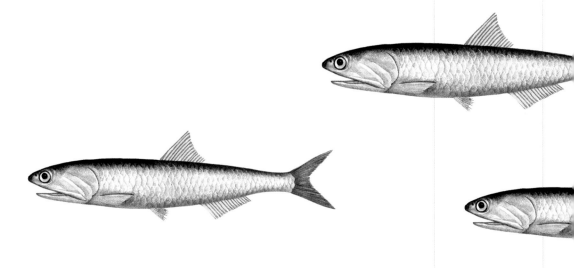

White Anchovies on Grilled-Radicchio Salad with Gorgonzola

Serves 6

24 oil-packed white anchovy
fillets (such as Boquerones)
Snipped chives
Olive oil, optional

Balsamic vinegar, optional
❧ Grilled-Radicchio Salad with Gorgonzola

Divide the Grilled-Radicchio Salad among 6 plates, lay 4 anchovy fillets on top of each, and sprinkle with chives. If you like, drizzle with olive oil and your favorite balsamic vinegar.

❧ Grilled-Radicchio Salad with Gorgonzola

3/4 cup crumbled Gorgonzola
cheese (about 3 ounces)
2 tablespoons grapeseed oil
1 tablespoon freshly squeezed lemon juice

Sea salt and freshly ground black pepper
to taste
❧ Marinated Radicchio

Drain the Marinated Radicchio very well. Preheat a gas grill to medium. Place the drained radicchio over a medium-to-cool grill and cook until tender. Try not to burn the leaves and be careful because it can flare up. Toss the radicchio with the cheese, oil, and lemon juice. Adjust the seasoning with salt and pepper.

❧ Marinated Radicchio

1/2 cup freshly squeezed
lemon juice
1/2 cup plus 1 tablespoon sugar

1/3 cup canola oil
1 small clove garlic, chopped
2 heads radicchio, quartered

Whisk together the lemon juice, sugar, oil, and garlic. Pour over the quartered radicchio and let sit in the refrigerator for 8 hours.

Dale Reitzer is Chef/Owner of Acacia in Richmond, Virginia.

Crispy Smelts with Tomatoes, Olives, and Capers

Serves 4

Contrary to what many people may believe, smelts are very mild fish. The spicy arugula, acidic vinaigrette, and mild smelts make a nice spring appetizer.

1 pound fresh whole or dressed
   smelts, washed
4 cups canola oil
1 cup peeled and diced tomatoes
1/2 cup kalamata olives, pitted
1 tablespoon capers
1 teaspoon chopped garlic
1 tablespoon red-wine vinegar

3 tablespoons extra-virgin olive oil
1 teaspoon sliced fresh basil
Salt and freshly ground white
   pepper to taste
1 cup all-purpose flour
2 cups arugula, washed

Heat the canola oil in a heavy medium-sized pot to 350°F. While the oil is heating, in a stainless-steel bowl, combine tomatoes, olives, capers, garlic, and vinegar. Slowly whisk in the olive oil to finish the vinaigrette. Next add the basil and season with salt and pepper. Set aside.

In another bowl, add the flour and season with salt and pepper. Next add the smelts to the seasoned flour and toss lightly to coat each fish. When the canola oil is at 350°F, add the floured smelts and cook until done, about 3 to 4 minutes. When the smelts are done, remove them from the oil and place on a plate lined with paper towels to drain the oil.

Place the arugula in the bowl containing the vinaigrette, toss, and then divide onto 4 plates. Place the smelts on top and spoon tomatoes, olives, and capers over. Drizzle a little vinaigrette from the bottom of the bowl around the plate.

Rob Klink is Executive Chef of Oceanaire Seafood Room in Washington, D.C.

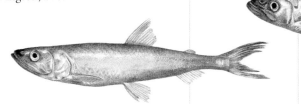

CHANNEL CATFISH AND TILAPIA ARE DELICIOUS, economical fish that you can feel good about eating: They are raised in plentiful quantities in environmentally sound farms in the United States. The channel catfish is highly regarded for its mild, slightly firm white fillets, and tilapia is known for its similarly flavored white or pinkish and more delicate flesh.

The channel catfish is part of a huge order of fishes known as siluriforms, which make up more than 75 percent of all freshwater fish species worldwide. Tilapia comprises various species of perchlike cichlid fishes. Native to Africa, tilapia has been introduced into more than eighty-five countries.

Tilapia was originally raised in the United States in the 1980s as live fish for aquaria. In the 1990s, it became available to U.S. consumers as fresh or frozen fillets from imported farmed fish. Farmed tilapia is inexpensive and mild in flavor, and fillets in markets and restaurants are usually in excellent shape because the fish are transported alive to processing plants and processed quickly. Not surprisingly, there has been a rapid increase in consumption of tilapia by American consumers, with tilapia entering the U.S. top-ten seafood

Tilapia *(top)*, channel catfish *(bottom)*

In the Wild

The "whiskers" on catfish are in fact barbels that extend from the mouth and help detect food such as small fish, crawfish, snails, or clams. Catfish also have retractable and poisonous thorny spines along the front edge of the dorsal and pectoral fins that, when locked into place, make the fish hard for a predator to swallow. Many such spines from ancient channel catfish have been found by archaeologists. One specimen from Lake Huron was found by radiocarbon dating to be 3,000 years old.

list for the first time in 2001. The fish is now farmed in many American states, including New York, Virginia, Florida, Missouri, Texas, and California, although imported tilapia still accounts for a large percentage of U.S. consumption.

Catfish farming is environmentally sound and one of the great U.S. aquaculture success stories. It represents the largest U.S. fish aquaculture industry, with leading states in the business including Mississippi, Arkansas, Alabama, and Louisiana. In 2001, catfish ranked fifth in seafood species consumed in the United States (after shrimp, tuna, salmon, and pollock), and it is the only species in the top five for which U.S. consumption is based almost entirely on a U.S.-farmed product.

In some countries, tilapia farming has been detrimental because when the highly carnivorous fish escape into the wild, they outcompete native species. Tilapia farming in the United States, however, is generally considered environmentally sound, in part because the fish are typically confined to the farms by the environment: Tilapia require very warm, fresh water, which they are provided in the farming ponds. In the United States, this heated pond water is warmer than any fresh- or saltwater bodies of water adjacent to the farms, and fish that escape do not fare well. Escapes are unlikely at the largest U.S. producer of farmed tilapia—an indoor facility in Virginia.

Reduced-Fat Catfish Fry

Serves as many as you would like

Fried fish is frowned upon by many health-conscious people simply because it contains a lot of fat. Yet the fat absorbed by the fish during cooking can be reduced, as shown in this recipe. Even more important, the traditional menu can be altered to reduce the overall fat. The British Fish 'n' Chips, for example, is simply fried fish and French fries. The latter usually soak up more cooking oil than the fish, especially if cooked by the twice-fried method. In the South, the traditional fish-fry menu usually contains hush puppies, which are nothing but fried cornpone, along with the fried fish and the fried French fries. So give some thought to the menu if you want to reduce the fat at a fish fry, or take a tip or two from the serving suggestions following this recipe.

Catfish fillets or small whole fish
    (allow 1/2 pound of fish per person)
Peanut oil for deep frying
Salt and freshly ground black pepper

Tabasco sauce, optional
White stone-ground (fine)
    cornmeal or flour

Heat 3 or 4 inches of oil to 375°F in a cast-iron Dutch oven or other suitable pot. When the oil is almost hot enough, sprinkle the fish lightly on both sides with salt and pepper, along with a little Tabasco sauce, if wanted. Put about 1 cup of cornmeal into a small brown bag or a suitable container. (If you can't obtain fine stone-ground meal made from whole-kernel corn, use ordinary wheat flour.) Place a few fillets into the bag and shake it, coating all sides of the fish. Shake off the excess meal. When the oil is hot, put a few fillets into the pot. Do not overcrowd. Cook for a few minutes. The fillets are done when they float, but let them brown for another half minute or so. Carefully pick up the smallest fillet (larger ones take the longest to cook) with tongs and hold it over the pot to drain some of the oil. Then place the fillet on a large brown bag. Drain the rest, 1 by 1. Do not pile up or overlap the fillets; use more than 1 bag if necessary. (This brown bag will soak up a lot of grease from the fish. Several thicknesses of paper towel can be used,

Catfish

SCIENTIFIC NAME: *Ictalurus punctatus*

OTHER NAMES: In the wild, channel catfish are sometimes called bullheads, spotted cats, white cats, or channel cats.

U.S. DISTRIBUTION: Catfish are farmed in more than half the states, with the bulk of production in the South. Mississippi alone produces about 70 percent of the catfish consumed in this country.

WHAT TO LOOK FOR: Catfish (1-1/2 to 3 pounds) are sold all over the country. The fish should have only a mild aroma. Make sure fillets look moist, and the flesh should be white, not gray or beige. Good-quality frozen fillets are often available.

COLOR, TASTE, AND TEXTURE: Catfish is mild in flavor and a little sweet. The flesh is firm and has a moderate flake. The reputation of catfish having a muddy taste is a thing of the past, and farm-raised fish are of excellent quality.

COOKING METHODS: Endlessly adaptable, catfish is equally at home simply panfried or as the center of elegant recipes. Catfish fillets have no bones.

TIP: Catfish don't have scales and are always skinned before eating.

(Continued)

but brown bags really work better.) When the first batch of fish is done, let the oil heat back to 375°F and cook another batch, and so on.

To recap: If you want to reduce the grease without losing flavor, be sure to follow the above steps closely, for these reasons: (1) a light coating of meal or flour will not soak up much oil, whereas some of the batters are grease traps; (2) cooking the fish at a high temperature (and peanut oil can be heated quite hot before it starts smoking) tends to seal the surface of the fish, keeping the pieces from soaking up oil; (3) proper dripping over the pot and draining on the brown bags will minimize the oil that you actually eat with the fish. This last step is more important than most people realize. Merely taking the fish up in a wire basket and piling them onto a serving platter can result in noticeably greasy fish, especially those on the bottom of the pile.

Another way to reduce the fat from a fish fry is to rethink the menu. I got onto this some time ago in North Florida, where fried fish may be served for breakfast, along with grits and sliced tomatoes. Since I don't care much for grits, even when they are called polenta, I hit upon the idea of using instead whole-kernel hominy topped with tomato-based salsa. Hominy is available in canned form in most supermarkets; dried hominy can be obtained from Southwest markets, but it requires soaking and long cooking to make it tender. Each partaker puts a couple of fillets or small whole fish on half his plate, then spoons on some hominy and tops it with his choice of salsa (hot, medium, or mild). The plate is completed with sliced rounds of raw jícama, all garnished with a wedge or 2 of fresh lime. Lemon can be used, but the green lime makes a better color scheme with yellow hominy.

A. D. Livingston is the cooking columnist for *Gray's Sporting Journal* and has written more than a dozen cookbooks. This recipe has been adapted from his *Outdoor Life's Complete Fish and Game Cookbook* (Stackpole Books, 1989).

Glengarry Glen Fish

Serves 4

Playwright David Mamet, Pulitzer Prize–winning author of Glengarry Glen Ross, *became a regular at Five Spice Café, but when he first came in, he asked for a dish with no sugar and no oil. I made this dish up in a minute and a half, later adding the orange juice after he okayed it.*

COOK'S STRATEGY: The fish and vegetables can be steamed at the same time.

4 catfish fillets, 8 ounces each
2-1/2 tablespoons yellow Indian
    curry powder
2-1/2 tablespoons ground cumin
2-1/2 tablespoons minced garlic
2 tablespoons minced fresh ginger

3 tablespoons Thai fish sauce
    (Squid brand preferred)
3 tablespoons orange juice
2 tablespoons dry sherry
2 cups steamed rice
❧ Steamed Vegetables

Special Equipment: 2 bamboo steamer baskets

Combine the curry, cumin, garlic, ginger, fish sauce, orange juice, and sherry in a small bowl. Rub the seasoning on both sides of the fish. Place fish on a lightly oiled plate or on parchment paper and insert into a Chinese steamer basket with strongly boiling water underneath. Steam until cooked, about 5 to 6 minutes.

To serve, make a circle of rice around the edge of a plate, put the Steamed Vegetables inside the rice circle, and place the fish on top.

❧ Steamed Vegetables
1 cup broccoli florets
1 cup sliced onions
12 to 16 baby corn spears
1 cup sliced red bell peppers
4 teaspoons Chinese fermented
    black beans, chopped

4 teaspoons minced garlic
2 tablespoons Thai fish sauce or soy sauce
Freshly ground black pepper to taste

Toss the ingredients well and place in a second steamer basket on top of the fish. Steam for 5 to 6 minutes to desired doneness.

Jerry Weinberg is Chef/Owner of Five Spice Café in Burlington, Vermont.

Cajun Grilled Catfish with Fresh Tomato and Cilantro Salsa

Serves 2

COOK'S STRATEGY: The Cajun Seasoning keeps well and can be stored for future use in this and other Cajun-inspired recipes. Make the salsa at least two hours in advance to develop maximum flavor. The catfish preparation itself is very quick.

2 catfish fillets, 10 ounces each
Soybean oil

➤ Cajun Seasoning
➤ Fresh Tomato and Cilantro Salsa

Preheat a gas grill to medium-high heat. Spread 2 or 3 tablespoons Cajun Seasoning in a shallow dish. Pour some soybean oil into a separate shallow dish. Dip both sides of a catfish fillet in the Cajun Seasoning and shake off any excess. Then dip the fillet into soybean oil and shake off any excess oil. Place the catfish fillet directly onto the gas grill and cook, turning halfway through cooking with a spatula, until both sides are dark brown and the fish is just cooked (white) in the center. Fillets will take 5 to 10 minutes, depending on the thickness. The fish will turn dark brown very quickly. Once it does, carefully transfer it to a cooler part of the grill to complete cooking.

Using a spatula, carefully transfer fish to a warm plate, skin-side down. Top with a generous mound of Fresh Tomato and Cilantro Salsa and serve.

❧ Cajun Seasoning

1 cup sweet Hungarian paprika

2 tablespoons onion powder

2 tablespoons garlic powder

1/2 teaspoon salt

1/2 teaspoon freshly ground
    black pepper

1-1/2 teaspoons cayenne pepper

1-1/2 teaspoons freshly ground
    white pepper

1/2 teaspoon dried oregano leaves

1/2 teaspoon dried thyme leaves

In a mixing bowl, whisk all ingredients until thoroughly incorporated. Store in a glass jar. This recipe makes plenty of seasoning for future use.

❧ Fresh Tomato and Cilantro Salsa

2 vine-ripened tomatoes, seeded
    and cut into 1/4-inch dice

2 tablespoons finely diced red onion

3 tablespoons finely chopped cilantro

1 jalapeño pepper, minced

2 tablespoons freshly squeezed lime juice

1 tablespoon extra-virgin olive oil

1/4 teaspoon salt

1/8 teaspoon freshly ground black pepper

At least 2 hours before serving, combine all ingredients in a large mixing bowl.

Sandy Ingber is Executive Chef of Grand Central Oyster Bar in New York City.

Catfish Risotto (Or What to Do When Your Fryolator Breaks)

Serves 4 to 6

Two cups of Arborio rice will make enough risotto for four large or six medium servings. Adjust the number of catfish fillets used accordingly. The risotto is served with a smoked-tomato sauce—don't get scared, this is easy!

COOK'S STRATEGY: Begin by marinating the catfish one or two days before cooking. You may also prepare the Risotto ahead of time to the point the rice is nearly done. The tomatoes for the sauce may be smoked in advance as well. Cook the fish and finish the Risotto last.

4 to 6 catfish fillets, 5 to 7 ounces each
1 cup heavy cream
1 tablespoon chopped fresh rosemary
6 whole cloves garlic
3 tablespoons olive oil
1 quart chicken broth (vegetable or
    mushroom broth can be substituted)
Salt and freshly ground black pepper

2 cups grated mozzarella or fontina cheese
2-1/2 cups grated Parmesan cheese
12 ounces fresh spinach, stemmed and
    washed, leaves roughly chopped
Fresh Italian flat-leaf parsley, chopped
❧ Risotto
❧ Smoked-Tomato Sauce

Put the cream and rosemary in a dish large enough to hold the fish fillets. Brown the garlic in the olive oil, cool, and add to the dish. Stir and add the catfish fillets. Cover and refrigerate for 1 or 2 days.

To finish the risotto and serve, pull the catfish from the marinade and cut into half-inch strips. Reserve 1 cup of the marinade. In a large pot, or even a wok, bring the broth to a boil and add the catfish and reserved marinade. On medium-high heat, add the nearly cooked rice and stir carefully (it is okay for the catfish to break into pieces). When the catfish is cooked, turn off the heat and gently fold in the mozzarella or fontina cheese and 2 cups of the Parmesan cheese. Fold in the spinach. Serve with the Smoked-Tomato Sauce and sprinkle with the remaining Parmesan. Garnish with parsley. If you happen to have some truffle oil lying around, put 1 or 2 drops over each serving. Your guests will put you on a pedestal. *É molto buono!*

❧ Risotto

2 cups chicken broth

2 cups clam stock (chicken, vegetable, or half chicken/half vegetable can be substituted; if using clam stock, either homemade or bottled is fine)

1/4 cup vegetable oil

1 large onion, cut into small dice

2 medium carrots, cut into small dice

1 tablespoon chopped garlic

2 cups Arborio rice

2 small yellow squash, cut into small dice

1 medium zucchini, cut into small dice

8 ounces shiitake mushrooms, sliced (substitute any fresh mushroom)

1 tablespoon fresh thyme leaves

1 teaspoon dried basil

1 teaspoon dried hot red pepper flakes

1 tablespoon salt

2 teaspoons freshly ground black pepper

In a saucepan over low heat, heat the chicken broth and clam stock. Heat the oil over medium-high heat in a separate 2-quart saucepan and sauté the onion until clear. Add the carrots and garlic. Add the rice and stir to coat. Add one-third of the liquid. Pull a spoon through the rice a few times to keep it from sticking, but don't over stir. When the liquid has been absorbed, add the next third of the broth. Stir from the bottom up. When the liquid has been absorbed, add the squash, zucchini, and mushrooms, along with the thyme, basil, red pepper flakes, salt and pepper, and the remaining broth. Stir carefully to incorporate the vegetables. When the liquid has been absorbed, pour the al dente rice into a shallow pan to cool. The rice is not cooked all the way because it will be reheated when the catfish is cooked. The rice can be prepared to this point a day ahead to save time the day of the feast. Once cool, scoop it into a container and refrigerate until ready to use.

❧ Smoked-Tomato Sauce

10 to 12 vine-ripened medium tomatoes (Romas are good)

1 cup small hickory or alderwood chips

2 tablespoons vegetable oil

1 small onion, chopped

1 teaspoon chopped garlic

1 teaspoon salt

1 teaspoon freshly ground black pepper

1/2 cup olive oil

Cut a small slit in each tomato. Possibilities for smoking include: (1) a steamer pot with a high basket (use outdoors or have a great exhaust fan), (2) an outdoor grill with a lid, (3) a smoker, or (4) a household oven smoker. Soak wood chips in water for 15 minutes,

(Continued)

then strain. Using smoking method 1 or 4, place foil on the bottom of a pan and place chips in pan. Cover and turn heat to high. When heavy smoke appears, reduce heat to medium high, add the tomatoes to the basket, cover, and smoke for 10 minutes. You should be able to put your finger into a tomato and taste smoke. If not, smoke 5 minutes longer. Tomatoes should be soft. Cool the chips, fold foil around them, and toss into the trash. For method 2 or 3, place chips on coals, smoke tomatoes for 10 minutes, then check.

Heat the vegetable oil in a large skillet over medium heat. Sauté the onion until soft. Add the garlic and cook for 1 to 2 minutes. Add the smoked tomatoes, salt and pepper, and 1 cup water. Bring to a boil, breaking up the tomatoes with a spoon, and simmer for 30 minutes. Cool. Add olive oil and transfer to a blender. Purée until smooth. Strain and adjust seasonings to taste.

Debra Paquette is Chef/Owner of ZOLA in Nashville, Tennessee.

Blackened Tilapia

Serves 4 to 8

Although the original blackened-fish recipe called for redfish, any rather small fish with mild flavor can be used, provided that the fillets are a little more than 1/2-inch thick—3/4 at the most. I prefer a fish with lean, white flesh. Farm-raised tilapia, sometimes marketed in my neck of the woods as Nile perch, is perfect. Fresh tilapia fillets can be purchased in many markets, but frozen fillets that have been vacuum sealed in individual bags also work well, allowing me to get out as many fillets as I need from the package without having to thaw the whole works. If you purchase whole market tilapia, you'll have to fillet them. This isn't hard, but note that tilapia have a row of short, odd bones on either side of the backbone, somewhat like saw teeth. The ends of these stubby bones can be cut off during the filleting process, in which case they should be removed by cutting out a thin triangular strip of meat from the fillet.

I often serve a dollop of sour cream or yogurt with the fish. Many people want a glass of iced water at hand as a chaser when eating spicy dishes, but it really won't help much. The heat of chile peppers comes from capsaicin, which isn't diluted by water. It's sort of like pouring water onto a grease fire, making it spread. Dairy products help tame the capsaicin.

Tilapia fillets (count on about 1/4 pound of fish per person—the Blackening Dust will be enough for about 2 pounds of fish)	Butter ➤ Blackening Dust (page 157)

Special Equipment: Cast-iron skillet or griddle (not Teflon or ceramic)

Many recipes for blackened fish make an issue of the amount of smoke the process generates, suggesting that maybe you ought to notify the local fire department before you start cooking. There is some smoke, but proper

Tilapia

SCIENTIFIC NAMES: Various species of *Oreochromis*, usually the Nile tilapia, *O. niloticus*

OTHER NAMES: Tilapia are sometimes marketed as Saint Peter's fish, redbreasted bream, or Nile tilapia.

U.S. DISTRIBUTION: Originally from Africa, tilapia is now farmed all over the globe. Most U.S. tilapia farms are in the southern states, but some are as far north as Maine and others as far west as California.

WHAT TO LOOK FOR: Tilapia are sold as whole 1-1/2-to-2-pound fish or as fillets. The fillets should look extremely fresh and white to pinkish white. Frozen fillets are also available.

COLOR, TASTE, AND TEXTURE: Tilapia is very similar to catfish except the fillets are thinner and not quite as firm, and the flesh has a smaller flake. The skin is edible.

COOKING METHODS: Panfrying, broiling, or braising are good bets for tilapia.

(Continued)

cooking technique will hold it to a minimum, while making a perfect blackened fillet: crisp and black on the outside, moist and white on the inside. Soggy blackened fish isn't the real stuff and was probably not cooked at high heat. How high? About as hot as you can get a cast-iron skillet or griddle on an electric stove and hotter than some briquette-burning grills will obtain. My favorite rig for blackening is a high-BTU outdoor gas burner used to heat large pots for boiling crawfish or frying a whole turkey. Of course, you can use an iron skillet or griddle instead of a big pot.

Rig a hot fire or gas burner on the patio, or pull out some red-hot wood coals from a campfire. Heat the skillet until it is very hot. Melt the butter in a suitable container. Pour some of the blackening dust into an oblong container, a little larger than the fillets. Dip a fillet into the melted butter to coat 1 side; turn to coat the other side. Shake off the excess butter, place the fillet down on the blackening dust, then turn and coat the other side. Shake off the excess dust and carefully place the fillet on a platter or plate. Coat the rest of the fillets. Then look at the fillets again, starting with the first, and sprinkle on enough of the dust to cover any wet spots. Now, take a deep breath and hold it. Using tongs, place a fillet onto the hot skillet. Let it sizzle for about 1-1/2 minutes. Turn and sizzle the other side for the same length of time. (The cooking time varies according to the thickness of each fillet: 1-1/4 minutes for 1/2-inch thickness, 2 minutes for 3/4-inch thickness.) You should now have a fillet that is dry and charred on the outside, but moist and white inside. Blacken the rest of the fillets, then serve them hot along with whatever accompaniments you want.

Note that a number of blackened-fish recipes call for coating the bottom of the skillet or griddle with butter or oil before proceeding. Don't do it; that's where most of the smoke comes from. Don't worry, the fish won't stick if it is properly coated with the blackening dust and the skillet is hot enough.

❧ Blackening Dust

1/4 cup ancho or New Mexico chile powder (not commercial chili powder)	1 tablespoon finely ground black pepper
2 tablespoons mild paprika	1 tablespoon finely ground white pepper
1 tablespoon cayenne (or to taste)	1 tablespoon finely ground sea salt
	1 tablespoon onion powder

Mix all the seasonings and set aside until you are ready to cook. Note that this mix contains more mild red pepper than most recipes or commercial blackening seasonings. I use it rather like a filler, permitting me to make a rather thick coating on the fillet as compared to a mere sprinkle. The same effect can be achieved by adding quite a bit of mild paprika or ground chile powder to a commercial blackening mix. I might add that most other recipes also call for thyme, oregano, and other spices. Suit yourself. Experiment.

This recipe was adapted from A. D. Livingston's *Cast-Iron Cooking* (Lyons Press, 1991).

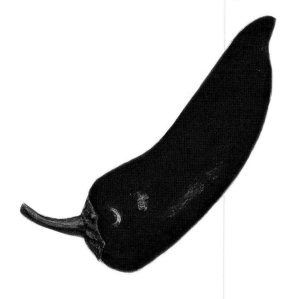

Wasabi Tilapia with Macadamia Rice, Napa Slaw, and Asian Vinaigrette

Serves 4

COOK'S STRATEGY: The fish can be marinated and the slaw made as the rice starts to cook.

4 tilapia fillets, 4 to 6 ounces each
2/3 cup oyster sauce
1/2 cup rice vinegar
1 teaspoon wasabi powder

2/3 cup panko (Japanese bread crumbs)
1/3 cup grated fresh horseradish
❋ Macadamia Rice
❋ Napa Slaw and Asian Vinaigrette

In a shallow dish, combine the oyster sauce, vinegar, and wasabi. Add the tilapia, turning to coat, and let marinate for 10 minutes. Preheat the oven to 350°F. Line a baking sheet with sides with parchment paper. Combine the panko and horseradish. Place the fish on the baking sheet and sprinkle the horseradish bread crumbs on top. Roast for 10 to 12 minutes.

Spoon warm Macadamia Rice onto the center of each plate. Mound the Napa Slaw on top of the rice. Place the Wasabi Tilapia on top of the slaw. Drizzle with extra vinaigrette and serve.

❋ Macadamia Rice
1 cup basmati rice
1 teaspoon olive oil
Salt and freshly ground black pepper to taste

1-1/2 cups chicken broth
1/2 cup macadamia nuts

Preheat the oven to 350°F. Toss the rice with the olive oil and salt and pepper in an ovenproof container. Bring the chicken broth to a boil and add to the rice. Cover and bake for 20 to 25 minutes until all liquid is absorbed. The rice can also be prepared on the stovetop. Meanwhile, spread the macadamias in a pie plate and toast in the oven for 10 minutes. Roughly chop.

When the rice is done, add the toasted macadamias and toss together. Keep warm until the fish is done.

❧ Napa Slaw and Asian Vinaigrette

1/2 cup rice vinegar

1-1/2 tablespoons oyster sauce

1 tablespoon Dijon mustard

3/4 cup vegetable oil

3/4 cup sesame oil

Salt, freshly ground black pepper,
    and sugar to taste

1/2 head napa cabbage, very thinly sliced

1/4 head red cabbage, very thinly sliced

1/2 bunch scallions, sliced

1/2 large carrot, grated

In a small bowl, whisk together the vinegar, oyster sauce, and mustard. Slowly whisk in the vegetable and sesame oils. Season with salt, pepper, and a pinch of sugar. In a salad bowl, toss the 2 cabbages, scallions, and carrot together. Toss this mixture with enough of the vinaigrette to lightly coat. Reserve some vinaigrette for the final drizzle.

Mark Swomley is Executive Chef and Jessica Gibson is Sous Chef of The Carlton Restaurant in Pittsburgh.

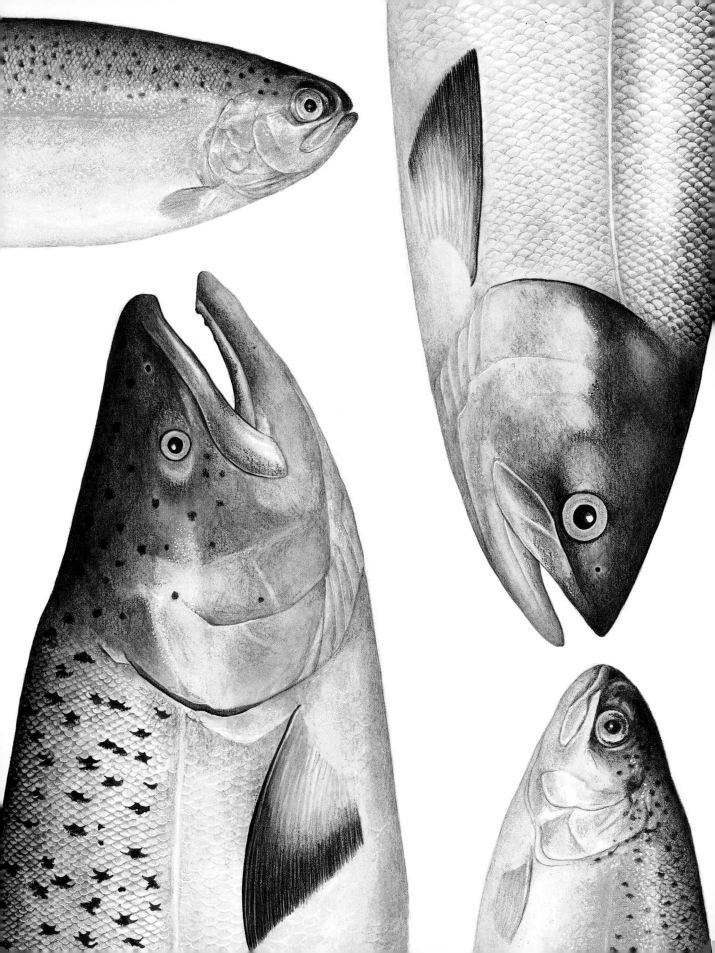

Salmon, Trout, and Arctic Char

*f*OR MANY, A SIZZLING SALMON STEAK HOT OFF THE grill, a delicately poached whole salmon, or a sliver of cold-smoked salmon brings the wild essence of the Pacific Northwest to the table. In reality, however, most salmon consumed in the United States has nothing to do with the wilderness: It is

Rainbow trout *(top left and bottom right)*, Sockeye salmon *(top right)*, Chinook salmon *(bottom left)*

In the Wild

Some salmonids are landlocked and live their entire lives in freshwater, but most are anadromous, returning from ocean waters to native streams to spawn. Anadromous salmon may have played a role in the growth of the giant forests of the northwestern United States. The nitrogen, phosphorus, and minerals from the salmon, consumed, digested, and left behind by bears, are in turn taken up by nearby plants. A recent study by scientists at Washington State University found that as much as 20 percent of the nitrogen in trees growing adjacent to salmon-spawning streams can be traced through the bears and salmon to its original source in the Pacific Ocean.

farmed, with huge numbers of salmon crowded in coastal pens. In an attempt to satisfy a salmon-loving nation after natural populations of Atlantic salmon were overfished, salmon farming has developed into a giant industry in cold-water inlets around the world. A good idea gone awry, it seems, because the environmental problems associated with coastal salmon farms are many (see "Issues Regarding U.S. Seafood").

On the other hand, five species of wild Alaska salmon have been certified by the Marine Stewardship Council as well managed and sustainable: pink, sockeye, chum, Coho, and king. Most commercially caught wild Pacific salmon is pink salmon, but it is a small fish and most is canned. The most valuable species for the fresh market is sockeye, which has bright red-orange flesh and more omega-3 fatty acids than any other known fish. King salmon are the most prized because they can grow so large (greater than 100 pounds), yet they account for only about 3 percent of the total Pacific salmon catch. Coho and chum, smaller than king, are more important commercially.

Fresh only in season, wild Alaska salmon can be considerably more expensive than the ubiquitous farmed Atlantic salmon, but conscientious consumers should choose wild Alaska salmon over imported farmed salmon. The beautiful orange or pink flesh of wild salmon comes from their diet of krill and other carotenoid-pigmented crustaceans (white, or ivory king, salmon don't accumulate these pigments). Farmed salmon are fed manufactured food pellets, and must be given a synthetic carotenoid to achieve that distinctive orange color.

Other members of the salmon family are the rainbow trout and arctic char. Like salmon, rainbow trout is farmed, but trout farms are inland and considered environmentally sound. The United States has raised rainbow trout for more than 150 years and ranks second in world production. Arctic char is predominantly fished and farmed in waters north of the United States; salmon or trout can be substituted for it.

Gravlax with Juniper and Mustard-Dill Sauce

Serves 8 to 12 as a first course,
4 to 6 as a main dish

COOK'S STRATEGY: Prepare the salmon at least two days in advance of serving.

2 pounds sushi-grade king
  salmon fillet, skin on,
  pin bones removed
1/4 cup packed brown sugar
2 tablespoons salt
1 teaspoon crushed juniper
  berries
4 bay leaves, crushed
1/4 teaspoon ground allspice
1/4 teaspoon freshly
  ground black pepper
1/4 to 1/2 cup gin
Rye or pumpernickel
  bread
Tiny dill sprigs,
  for garnish
✦ Mustard-Dill Sauce

With a new razor blade, cut 5 or 6 slits through the salmon skin, each running lengthwise about 2 inches. Be careful not to cut too deeply into the flesh. Set the salmon, skin-side up, in a long shallow dish just large enough to hold the salmon. Blend the sugar, salt, juniper berries, bay leaves, allspice, and pepper and distribute evenly over salmon, first on the skin side, then flip over and pat lightly into flesh side. Dribble the gin over the fish to moisten the spice mixture. Cover the dish with plastic wrap. Place another dish (slightly smaller than the first dish) over it and place about 2 pounds of weight in it—cans of beans work well. Refrigerate for at least 2 days; spoon the juices over the fish occasionally during this time. After the first day, remove the weights. The salmon will keep up to 1 week in the brine, but it gradually becomes too salty.

(Continued)

Pacific Salmon

Pink, Sockeye, Chum, Coho, King

SCIENTIFIC NAMES: *Oncorhynchus gorbuscha* (pink), *O. nerka* (sockeye), *O. keta* (chum), *O. kisutch* (Coho), and *O. tshawytscha* (king)

OTHER NAMES: Pink (humpy), chum (keta or dog), sockeye (red), Coho (silver), and king (chinook, or white or ivory king if it has pale—not bright orange—flesh). King, sockeye, and Coho may be marketed as Copper River Salmon, indicating the point of capture.

U.S. DISTRIBUTION: Alaska to California. Most Pacific salmon is wild, but king salmon is now farmed in Canada.

SEASON: Fresh Pacific salmon is available from mid-April to early October. Improved freezing techniques mean high-quality salmon is available throughout the year.

WHAT TO LOOK FOR: Whole fish weigh 3 to 5 pounds or much more; their silvery sides should glisten and their eyes should be clear. The flesh of fillets and steaks should look moist and not gape. The fish should smell sweet, not at all strong. Sockeye salmon has the deepest red color, whereas pink and chum are the lightest.

COLOR, TASTE, AND TEXTURE: Wild Pacific salmon has a fuller, more pronounced flavor than farmed salmon. The flesh of king and sockeye is moderately firm. Coho contain a little less fat (7 grams per 3-ounce serving versus 11.5 grams for king and 9.5 grams for sockeye) and tend to be flakier when cooked. Chum and pink salmon contain even less fat, 4 grams each per 3-ounce serving.

COOKING METHODS: Salmon may be served raw, cured, marinated, smoked, poached, grilled, broiled, sautéed, or slow-roasted.

TIP: Whole fillets have a row of pin bones. Run your finger along the length of the fillet to locate them and use tweezers or needlenose pliers to pull them out.

With a long, thin, very sharp knife, slice the salmon thinly across the grain on a diagonal down to the skin, and cut the flesh away from the skin.

A dab of Mustard-Dill Sauce on a small piece of rye bread or pumpernickel, topped with a thin slice of Gravlax, makes for a fine hors d'oeuvre. Garnish with a tiny sprig of dill.

✦ Mustard-Dill Sauce

1/4 cup Dijon mustard	1/3 cup olive oil
1 teaspoon dry mustard	1/4 cup chopped fresh dill or
3 tablespoons sugar	2 tablespoons dried
2 tablespoons white-wine vinegar	

Mix the mustards, sugar, and vinegar. Drizzle in the oil slowly, whisking constantly to make a light, mayonnaise-like consistency. Stir in the dill.

Narsai David is Food and Wine Editor at San Francisco's KCBS radio station, cohost of *Cookoff America* on PBS, and host of a weekly cooking class at Macy's in San Francisco and San José, California.

Grilled Baby Coho Salmon with Lemon-Ginger Marinade

4 coho salmon (about 8 to
  10 inches each), cleaned,
  with heads on
1/2 cup freshly squeezed
  lemon juice
2 cloves garlic, minced
1 tablespoon minced fresh ginger
1/4 cup olive oil
1/4 cup vegetable oil, plus more
  for brushing grill

Salt and freshly ground
  black pepper
8 sprigs fresh thyme
4 scallions, trimmed and cut
  lengthwise
Chopped fresh parsley
Lemon wedges

To make the marinade, combine the lemon juice, garlic, ginger, olive oil, and vegetable oil. Rinse the salmon and pat them dry. Generously salt and pepper the cavity of each fish and place 2 thyme sprigs and 1 split scallion into each cavity. Place the salmon in the dish with the marinade, turn to coat, and refrigerate for about 1 hour.

Light a charcoal fire or heat a gas grill to medium high. Generously brush the grill with lots of vegetable oil. Remove the salmon from the marinade and place on the grill. Cook for 4 to 5 minutes per side, gently turning the fish and brushing liberally with the marinade, until the fish flesh is opaque and flakes lightly.

Serve each fish garnished with chopped fresh parsley and lemon wedges.

Lucia Watson is Chef/Owner of Lucia's in Minneapolis, Minnesota. She is co-author of *Savoring the Seasons of the Northern Heartland* (Alfred A. Knopf, 1995) and writes a column for *In Fisherman* magazine.

Cured Salmon with Basil Oil and Soy-Glazed Almonds

Serves 4

1 pound sushi-grade sockeye salmon
  fillet, pin bones removed
1/2 cup sea or kosher salt
1/4 cup packed brown sugar
1/4 cup roughly chopped fresh mint
1/4 cup roughly chopped fresh basil
2 tablespoons grated lemon zest
2 tablespoons grated lime zest
2 cups white wine, preferably
  Sauvignon Blanc

2 tablespoons shaved Pecorino-Romano
  cheese
Mixed fresh Asian greens, optional,
  dressed lightly with olive oil
  and citrus juice if desired
➤ Basil Oil
➤ Balsamic-Soy Reduction
➤ Soy-Glazed Almonds, cut in half

Lay plastic wrap in a 9-by-12-inch baking dish and cover with a layer of salt. Lay salmon, skin-side down, on the layer of salt. Cover the salmon with the rest of the salt. On top of salt, evenly spread a layer of brown sugar, mint, basil, and citrus zests. Wrap plastic wrap tightly around the entire salmon 3 or 4 times, being careful not to leave any openings. Refrigerate for 48 hours. Remove, unwrap, and wash under ice-cold water. Dry with paper towels. Place the fish back in the cleaned baking dish, add the wine, and let soak for 30 minutes. Remove and refrigerate until ready for use.

With a long, thin, very sharp knife, slice the salmon into 1/4-inch slices and fan out slices on 4 plates. Drizzle each serving with 1 tablespoon Basil Oil and 1 tablespoon Balsamic-Soy Reduction. Sprinkle with Soy-Glazed Almonds and Pecorino-Romano cheese. Add the Asian greens if desired.

➤ Basil Oil
1 bunch (1/4 pound) basil leaves,
  stemmed

1/4 cup olive oil

Bring a pot of water to a boil and add a pinch of salt. Plunge the basil leaves into the boiling water, then strain and place leaves in an ice bath. Squeeze out extra water from the basil. Blend in a blender with the olive oil. Strain the mixture through a cheesecloth-lined strainer, reserving the oil and discarding the solids. Store in the refrigerator for up to 2 weeks.

❖ Balsamic-Soy Reduction

1 cup balsamic vinegar   2 tablespoons soy sauce

In a small pan, bring the vinegar and soy sauce to a boil. Reduce the heat immediately and simmer the mixture until reduced to a syrupy consistency.

❖ Soy-Glazed Almonds

1/2 cup whole almonds   1 teaspoon mirin (Japanese
1 teaspoon soy sauce   seasoning wine)
1 teaspoon sake

Preheat the oven to 300°F. Spread the almonds in a pie pan and toast in the oven for about 20 minutes, shaking the pan occasionally. In a frying pan over medium heat, cook the toasted almonds with the soy sauce, sake, and mirin until the nuts absorb the liquid. Remove quickly so that the almonds do not burn; set aside to dry.

Nobuo Fukuda is Chef/Owner of Sea Saw in Scottsdale, Arizona.

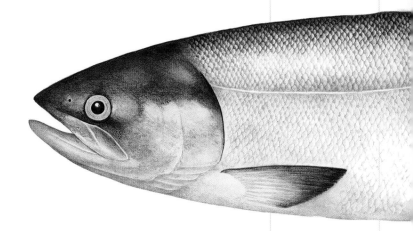

Salmon Steaks Braised in Grape Juice with Whipped Red Potatoes and Horseradish

Serves 4

This recipe features an unusual combination: salmon and white grape juice. During the autumn months at Wildwood, we acquire fresh grape juice from Pinot Noir, Pinot Gris, or any available variety of grapes that a winemaker can supply. Salmon pairs well with this fresh grape juice, as the natural sugars from the juice complement the rich texture of the fish. Fresh wine-grape juice is rarely available, so I recommend substituting a white grape juice that is not overly sweet. Salmon steaks on the bone with the skin intact are ideal for this preparation, for the bone adds that extra little bit of flavor to the sauce and the fish. A touch of horseradish added to the Whipped Red Potatoes contrasts with the sweetness of the grapes.

An organic Chardonnay makes an excellent accompaniment for this salmon dish.

4 Pacific salmon steaks
    (8 to 10 ounces each)
    or fillets (6 to 8 ounces each)
1 to 2 tablespoons olive oil
1-1/2 teaspoons salt
1 teaspoon freshly ground black pepper
2-1/2 cups white grape juice
1/4 cup Chardonnay
1 small red onion, cut vertically
    into thin crescents

1 cup Thompson or other seedless
    green grapes
1 teaspoon fennel seeds, crushed with
    the flat side of a large knife
1/4 cup minced fresh Italian
    flat-leaf parsley
2 tablespoons unsalted butter
2 tablespoons freshly squeezed
    lemon juice
✦ Whipped Red Potatoes

Preheat the oven to 350°F. In an ovenproof skillet large enough to hold the salmon, heat the oil over medium heat on the stovetop. Season the salmon with the salt and pepper and brown for 3 minutes on each side. Remove the fish from the skillet and set aside.

Wipe out the skillet and add the grape juice, wine, onion, grapes, and fennel seeds. Bring to a simmer. Return the salmon to the skillet and transfer to the oven. Braise for about 20 minutes for steaks and 10 minutes for fillets, or until the salmon flakes easily and is opaque throughout. Remove the salmon from the skillet and keep warm. Return the pan to the stovetop and bring the sauce to a simmer over medium heat. Stir in the parsley, butter, and lemon juice. Cook for 1 minute.

Spoon the Whipped Red Potatoes onto each plate. Place a salmon steak or fillet on the potatoes and spoon on the sauce.

✦ Whipped Red Potatoes

1 pound Red Bliss or Yukon Gold potatoes, scrubbed but unpeeled, halved	3/4 teaspoon freshly ground black pepper
2-1/2 teaspoons salt	1 tablespoon prepared horseradish
1 cup milk	1 tablespoon snipped fresh chives
1 tablespoon unsalted butter	2 tablespoons olive oil

In a medium saucepan, cover the potatoes with water. Add 1 teaspoon of the salt and bring the water to a boil. Reduce the heat and simmer uncovered for 20 to 25 minutes, or until fork tender. Drain and let stand for 5 minutes. In a small pan, heat the milk and butter until just steaming. In a bowl, using an electric mixer, mash the potatoes on medium speed. Season with the remaining 1-1/2 teaspoons salt and the pepper. Gradually add the hot milk mixture, whipping the potatoes until light and fluffy. Fold in the horseradish and chives. Set aside and keep warm.

Cory Schreiber is Chef/Owner of Wildwood in Portland, Oregon. This recipe is adapted from his cookbook *Wildwood: Cooking from the Source in the Pacific Northwest* (Ten Speed Press, 2000).

Slow-Cooked King Salmon

Of the various ways king salmon can be cooked, this one is shockingly simple and strikingly good. The salmon is baked in a very slow, humidified oven, which yields a moist, tender, velvet-textured fish. When it is served at room temperature with fennel and fava beans, or tomatoes and green beans, or beets and garden lettuces, we find it has versatility and appeal the entire season. And since it holds well for a few hours, it's also perfect for a picnic or buffet.

1 king salmon fillet, about 3 pounds
Extra-virgin olive oil
Salt and freshly ground black pepper

✤ Aïoli (pages 52 to 53) or
✤ Meyer-Lemon Relish or
✤ Sauce Gribiche

Preheat the oven to 200°F. Place a pan of warm water on the lowest rack in the oven. This creates a humid environment that helps keep the salmon moist.

Lightly brush a baking pan with olive oil. Brush the salmon with olive oil and season generously with salt and pepper. Place the salmon in the baking pan and put it in the oven. Allow about 1 hour for the salmon to cook through. If it seems to be cooking too fast, turn the oven down a bit. The salmon is cooked when it is just barely firm to the touch and juices are beginning to collect on top of the fillet. Let it rest at least 10 minutes, or up to 3 hours, at room temperature.

To serve, break the salmon into rough pieces, surround with summer vegetable salads, and accompany with Aïoli, Meyer-Lemon Relish, or Sauce Gribiche.

Variation: Season the salmon with roughly chopped fresh herbs (such as basil or tarragon), grated citrus peel, and finely sliced shallots before baking.

✤ Meyer-Lemon Relish

Meyer lemons are sweet, thin-skinned, and famous for their ethereal perfume. Although common in California backyards, they are just beginning to be commercialized. Ask your friends or relatives in California to send you some. This simple relish is good with most fish and shellfish. Unfortunately, it cannot be made with ordinary lemons. It is best made fresh and served within a few hours.

1 large shallot, finely diced
1 tablespoon white-wine vinegar
    or lemon juice
Salt
1 large Meyer lemon

1/2 cup extra-virgin olive oil
2 tablespoons chopped fresh parsley
1 tablespoon chopped fresh
    chervil or chives
Freshly ground black pepper

Combine the shallot, vinegar, and a pinch of salt in a small bowl. Set aside for 10 to 15 minutes. Cut the lemon into 8 wedges. Remove the seeds and central core from each piece, then cut each wedge in half lengthwise. Slice the wedges crosswise into thin slivers. You will have about 1/2 cup. Combine the slivered lemon and shallot and add a little more salt. Stir in the olive oil, parsley, chervil, and some pepper. Taste and adjust the seasoning. Makes about 1 cup.

✦ Sauce Gribiche
Fresh herbs are essential for this zesty herb sauce. If you don't have all the different kinds, it's fine— the sauce is delicious even when made only with good fresh parsley.

1 egg	Zest of 1/2 lemon, finely chopped
1 medium shallot, finely diced	1 tablespoon capers, rinsed and chopped
2 tablespoons chopped fresh parsley	3 gherkins, diced fine
2 tablespoons chopped fresh chervil	3/4 cup extra-virgin olive oil
2 tablespoons thinly sliced fresh chives	Salt
1 teaspoon chopped fresh tarragon	

Over high heat, bring to a full boil enough water to cover the egg. Lower the egg gently into the water with a slotted spoon, turn down the heat slightly, and cook for exactly 9 minutes. Prepare a bowl of water and ice. When time is up, remove the egg and immediately plunge into the ice bath to cool. After a minute or so, when the egg is cool enough to handle, crack on the tabletop and return to the ice water for another 5 minutes. This will make peeling easier. Remove from the ice bath and peel away the shell under cold water. In a bowl, combine the shallot, parsley, chervil, chives, tarragon, lemon zest, capers, gherkins, and olive oil and season with salt to taste. Chop the egg yolk, dice the white, and stir into the herb-oil mixture.

Alice Waters is Owner of Chez Panisse Restaurant in Berkeley, California. This recipe was adapted from her *Chez Panisse Café Cookbook,* copyright © 1999 by Alice Waters and reprinted by permission of HarperCollins Publishers Inc.

Pan-Roasted Wild Ivory Salmon, Braised Fennel and Grapefruit Ragoût, and Truffle-Potato Purée

Serves 4

I was first introduced to wild ivory salmon as a child, fishing with my brothers in Alaska. We caught an ivory king salmon and at first were not sure what we had caught. We grilled it right over an open pit and thought we were in heaven. That experience I will never be able to duplicate. I hope that when my four-year-old son is ready we will have a similar experience. Until then, this is a dish that is full of flavor that is good anytime.

COOK'S STRATEGY: Start the Braised Fennel and Grapefruit Ragoût about an hour before serving. The Truffle-Potato Purée takes about fifteen minutes.

4 Copper River wild ivory salmon fillets,
    6 ounces each
2 tablespoons olive oil
Sea salt and freshly cracked black pepper

3 tablespoons unsalted butter
Leaves from 3 sprigs fresh thyme
➤ Braised Fennel and Grapefruit Ragoût
➤ Truffle-Potato Purée

Heat the oil in a sauté pan over high heat. Season the salmon fillets with salt and pepper and sear for 3 minutes on 1 side. Turn the fillets over, turn heat down to medium, and add the butter and thyme. Baste the fish with the herb butter and cook until the salmon is medium rare.

To serve, spoon the Braised Fennel and Grapefruit Ragoût and Truffle-Potato Purée into each of 4 warm soup plates. Top with the salmon.

➤ Braised Fennel and Grapefruit Ragoût
2 tablespoons extra-virgin olive oil
2 medium fennel bulbs, trimmed and
    sliced into julienne strips (2 cups)
1 medium onion, sliced into julienne
    strips (1 cup)
2 cloves garlic, sliced
Grated zest of 1 grapefruit
1/2 cup fresh grapefruit juice

1/4 cup imported green olives,
    crushed, pitted, and chopped
2 tablespoons chopped fresh thyme leaves
2 sprigs fennel fronds
2 tablespoons chopped fresh chervil
    or tarragon
1/4 cup grapefruit sections
Sea salt and freshly cracked black pepper

Heat the oil in a saucepan over medium heat. Add the fennel strips, onion, and garlic and sauté for 5 minutes. Add grapefruit zest, grapefruit juice, and olives; cook for an additional 2 minutes. Add thyme, fennel fronds, and chervil or tarragon, turn heat to low, and cook for 45 minutes. When ready to serve, add the grapefruit sections and season with salt and pepper.

✦ Truffle-Potato Purée

3 Yukon Gold potatoes, peeled and chopped

2 tablespoons unsalted butter

Sea salt and freshly ground white pepper

White-truffle oil

Cook the potatoes in salted water until tender. Remove and drain the water from the pan. Mash the potatoes and run them through a sieve or colander. Return the potatoes to the pan and cook them over low heat to remove as much water as possible. Work the potatoes with a wooden spoon, then add the butter a little at a time until all the butter is incorporated into the potatoes. Remove and sieve the potatoes again, then add salt and pepper to taste. Add a little truffle oil to taste and serve.

Tom Condron is Executive Chef of Upstream in Charlotte, North Carolina.

Slow-Roasted Sockeye Salmon on a Fennel and Herb Salad

Serves 6

1-1/2 pounds sockeye salmon fillet, skinned
1 tablespoon coriander seeds
1 tablespoon fennel seeds
1/2 cup plus 2 tablespoons extra-virgin olive oil
3 cups thinly sliced fennel bulb
1/2 cup very thinly sliced red onion

6 tablespoons seasoned rice-wine vinegar
Kosher salt
1/2 cup parsley leaves, gently packed
1/2 cup cilantro leaves, gently packed
1/4 cup tarragon leaves, gently packed
1/4 cup spearmint leaves, gently packed, torn if large
Coarse sea salt

Trim the salmon of any gray fat and pull out the pin bones with fish tweezers or needle nose pliers. Holding a knife at a 30° angle to the cutting board, cut the salmon into 6 wide slices, about 1/2-inch thick. Arrange them in a shallow baking dish. Lightly crush the coriander and fennel seeds in a mortar and pestle or by putting them in a skillet and using the bottom of a heavy pot to crush them. Sprinkle them over the fish, then pour on 1/2 cup olive oil. Marinate the fish in the refrigerator for at least 1 hour. Toss the fennel and onion with the vinegar and let the salad sit at room temperature while the fish is marinating.

Preheat the oven to 225°F. Remove the fish from the oil and use your fingers to wipe off most of the marinade, but allow some of the oil and seeds to remain on. Arrange the fillets on a baking sheet and sprinkle lightly with kosher salt. Bake for 15 to 20 minutes, or until the fat between the layers of fish just begins to turn opaque and the fish flakes slightly when nudged with your finger. It will appear to be underdone because the color will be vivid, but it will be fully cooked.

Meanwhile, finish the salad: Tip the bowl with the fennel and onion to drain any excess liquid. Toss in the herb leaves, drizzle with the remaining 2 tablespoons of olive oil, and toss again.

Spread out the salad on 6 dinner plates and carefully place a fish fillet in the center of each. Sprinkle the fish with a pinch of sea salt. Serve right away.

Jerry Traunfeld is Executive Chef of The Herbfarm in Woodinville, Washington. He is the author of *The Herbfarm Cookbook* (Scribner, 2000).

Fish Galettes with Black Butter Sauce

Serves 6 to 8

A fish mousse is a purée of high-quality fish into which you beat as much heavy cream as it will take and still hold its shape, either to be sautéed in butter (galettes), poached in liquid (quenelles), or baked in a mold (e.g., crown mousse). In the old days, a fish mousse took several hours of hand labor and was strictly in the realm of the professional kitchen and "haute cuisine." Because of that wonderful machine, the food processor, there is so little fuss to making a mousse that it is now part of plain everyday cooking. Flimsy fish like California halibut are hopeless mousse candidates, while fish with a certain gelatinous quality, like freshwater trout, salmon, and Alaska halibut, are just what you want. Shrimp can be combined with a flimsy fish to bolster a mixture that otherwise lacks texture.

ALL-PURPOSE FISH MOUSSE (MAKES ABOUT 4 CUPS)

1 pound (2 cups) best-quality chilled skinless and boneless fish from list above (or if your fish is light in texture like California halibut, include 1/2 cup raw shrimp)

1 large egg, chilled

1/2 to 1 cup (or more) heavy cream, chilled

1 teaspoon salt

Freshly ground white pepper

Pinch of grated nutmeg

Up to 1 cup lightly pressed down crumbs from fresh homemade-type crustless white bread with body (if needed)

1 teaspoon brandy, optional

Cut the fish into 1-inch pieces. (If you are using shrimp chop them roughly.) Drop the fish into the bowl of the food processor along with the egg, 1/2 cup of the cream, and the seasonings to taste. Process, using half a dozen 1-second spurts; process several seconds continuously, then start checking. The mousse should be perfectly smooth; scrape down the bowl and process a few seconds more if necessary. For galettes and quenelles, the mousse should hold a definite shape in a spoon, its peaks and valleys quite well defined. If it seems loose and lacking in body, process in bread crumbs by 1/4 cupfuls (or you could add 1/4 cup or more raw shrimp). On the other hand, if too stiff, process in more cream by small dollops. Process in a teaspoon or so of brandy if you wish. Taste very carefully, and correct seasoning. The mousse may be done several hours in advance; pack into a covered container and refrigerate in a bowl of ice. Alternatively, you may freeze the mousse.

(Continued)

FISH GALETTES WITH BLACK BUTTER SAUCE

4 cups All-Purpose Fish Mousse, chilled
   (make it firm enough to hold its shape)
3 to 4 tablespoons unsalted butter
1 cup flour on a sheet of wax paper

3 tablespoons minced fresh parsley
1-1/2 sticks (12 tablespoons) unsalted
   butter, cut into slices
3 tablespoons capers

Special Equipment: A bowl of cold water (for dipping your hands)

Divide the mousse into 6 to 8 portions. Just before sautéing, film 1 or 2 nonstick frying pans with a 1/16-inch layer of butter and set over low heat. Dip your hands in the cold water, form a portion of the mousse into a cake, turn lightly in the flour, and set it in the warm frying pan. Continue rapidly with the rest. *Note:* If too soft to form into cakes, you may drop portions into the hot butter from a spoon. Sauté slowly for 2 to 3 minutes (while you wash your hands!), turn, and sauté on the other side. The galettes are done when just springy rather than squashy to the touch, and they should barely color. Transfer the galettes to hot plates or a platter and sprinkle with parsley.

Return the pan to the heat to make the sauce. Toss the butter into the hot pan and increase heat to high. Swirling the pan by its handle, swish the butter around as the bubbles subside, and in a few seconds the butter will begin to turn a walnut brown (not black!). Pour the hot butter over the galettes; the parsley will sizzle. Drop the capers into the pan, heat them briefly until they bubble, and spread them over the galettes. Serve at once.

Note: If you prefer to make quenelles (delicate fish dumplings) with the mousse instead of galettes, pour 2 inches of water into a saucepan and add 1-1/2 teaspoons of salt per quart of water. Bring to the simmer. Dip a wet soup spoon into the chilled mousse and bring up a rounded gob; shape the top neatly by inverting the bowl of a second wet spoon over it. Nudge it into the water with a rubber spatula. Rapidly continue with the rest of the mousse. Maintain the water at just below the simmer for 6 to 8 minutes; if the water simmers or boils, the quenelles may disintegrate. The quenelles are done when they roll over easily. Remove them with a slotted spoon to a rack.

Julia Child has devoted much of her life to bringing the art of French cooking into the American kitchen. She is co-author, with Louisette Bertholle and Simone Beck, of *Mastering the Art of French Cooking* (Alfred A. Knopf, 1961); *Volume Two* followed in 1970. Since that time, she has written more than a dozen cookbooks including *The Way to Cook* (Knopf, 1989), from which this recipe was adapted. Her most recent work, *Julia's Kitchen Wisdom: Essential Techniques and Recipes from a Lifetime of Cooking* (Knopf) was published in 2000.

Trout Hemingway

Serves 4

4 whole rainbow trout, 8 to 10
    ounces each
1/2 cup cornmeal
1/2 cup unbleached all-
    purpose flour
Salt and freshly ground
    black pepper
Dash cayenne pepper

1/2 cup freshly squeezed
    lemon juice
1/2 cup sesame seeds
2 tablespoons butter
2 tablespoons grapeseed or
    vegetable oil
Chopped fresh parsley and
    lemon wedges for garnish

Rinse the trout and pat dry. Slit each trout open along the belly, starting just under the gills and ending just short of the tail. Rinse out the guts. Run a knife along the top of the rib cage to separate the bones from the flesh on both sides. Then work the knife under the spine. Break the spine at the tail and head. Using the knife, work out the spine and ribs, leaving the flesh exposed like an open book.

Combine the cornmeal and flour on a plate and season with salt, pepper, and cayenne. Pour the lemon juice into a shallow bowl. Season the fish liberally with salt and pepper. Dip the flesh side of the trout in the lemon juice, dust lightly with the seasoned cornmeal-flour mixture, dip again in the lemon juice, then coat the fish with the sesame seeds.

Heat the butter and oil in a heavy skillet over medium heat, add the trout, skin-side up, and panfry for about 3 minutes. Gently flip the fish and fry for another 3 minutes, until the sesame seeds are golden brown.

Serve immediately with chopped fresh parsley and lemon wedges.

Lucia Watson is Owner/Chef of Lucia's in Minneapolis, Minnesota. She is co-author of *Savoring the Seasons of the Northern Heartland* (Alfred A. Knopf, 1995) and writes a column for *In Fisherman* Magazine.

Rainbow Trout

SCIENTIFIC NAME: *Oncorhynchus mykiss*

OTHER NAMES: Wild rainbow trout may be called steelhead, silver trout, or brook trout.

U.S. DISTRIBUTION: Lakes and streams throughout the country. The rainbow trout sold in markets is farm raised, most in Idaho and some in West Virginia and North Carolina.

WHAT TO LOOK FOR: Trout skin should be a glistening gray, covered with a slippery transparent layer. If whole, the eyes should not be sunken or clouded; flesh should be firm. Most farmed rainbow trout weigh 10 to 16 ounces and are sold whole, dressed, or filleted. Fillets are sold with the bones removed; however, the fish will have more flavor if cooked with the bones.

COLOR, TASTE, AND TEXTURE: Color ranges from cream to pink to a rich salmon. The flesh is soft to moderately firm, with a delicate, almost grassy flavor.

COOKING METHODS: Smoke, panfry, grill (using a wire fish basket), or poach. The delicate flavor may be overpowered by strong herbs and spices. Very fresh trout is probably best cooked à la meunière—dusted in flour and sautéed in butter.

TIP: Trout scales are so tiny, there's no need to scale the fish.

Blue Cornmeal–Crusted Trout with Tomatillo-Chipotle Sauce and Chile-Corn Custard

Serves 4

This is a great recipe because the cornmeal mixture can be made ahead in larger quantities to use at a later date. It is also very good on other types of fish. At the restaurant, we like to serve this dish with long-simmered pinto beans.

COOK'S STRATEGY: The Tomatillo Sauce, Chipotle Crema, and Cornmeal Crust Mixture can be prepared a day or two in advance. The custard is easily assembled and baked. When it's done, remove the pan from the oven and increase the oven heat to 400°F. Sauté the trout fillets on top of the stove, then finish in the hot oven.

4 rainbow-trout fillets, 6 to 8 ounces each, skin on	✦ Cornmeal Crust Mixture
1/2 cup buttermilk	✦ Tomatillo Sauce
2 tablespoons canola oil	✦ Chipotle Crema
Cilantro sprigs, for garnish	✦ Chile-Corn Custard

Pour the buttermilk into a shallow dish. Spread 1/2 cup of the Cornmeal Crust Mixture in another shallow dish. One at a time, dip the fillets into the buttermilk and then dredge through the crust mixture. Place fillets on a plate and refrigerate, uncovered, for about 30 minutes. Preheat the oven to 400°F.

Heat the oil in a large ovenproof sauté pan over medium-high heat. Sauté the fillets flesh-side down until golden brown. Turn the fish over and transfer the pan to the oven to finish cooking for about 5 minutes.

To serve, place the trout fillets skin-side down on 4 dinner plates. Spread 1 tablespoon Tomatillo Sauce over the fish. Drizzle a teaspoon of the Chipotle Crema over the Tomatillo Sauce. If you like, garnish with a sprig of cilantro. Serve with the Chile-Corn Custard.

✦ Cornmeal Crust Mixture

1/2 tablespoon mustard seeds	1/2 tablespoon sugar
1 cup blue cornmeal (regular cornmeal will also work fine, the blue just gives it an interesting color)	1 teaspoon granulated garlic
	1 teaspoon salt
	1 teaspoon freshly ground black pepper
1 tablespoon dry mustard	1/2 teaspoon chili powder
2 teaspoons ground coriander	(homemade or commercial blend)

Lightly toast the mustard seeds in a small skillet over medium heat. When cool, grind the seeds in a spice grinder or mortar and pestle. Combine the mustard and remaining ingredients in a bowl. This will make enough to crust about a dozen fillets. The extra cornmeal crust stores quite well in an airtight container for future use.

✦ Tomatillo Sauce

5 tomatillos, papery husks removed

1/2 poblano chile, seeds discarded, coarsely chopped

2 cloves garlic

Salt and freshly ground black pepper

1/2 avocado

1/4 bunch cilantro, stemmed

Combine the tomatillos, chile, garlic, and 2 cups water in a small saucepan, bring to a boil, and simmer for about 5 minutes. Remove from the heat and let cool. Strain out the solids (reserving the water) and place them into a blender along with the avocado and cilantro leaves. Turn blender on and slowly add the reserved water until the sauce is blended to a smooth, ketchuplike consistency. The Tomatillo Sauce may be prepared 2 or 3 days in advance and stored in the refrigerator.

✦ Chipotle Crema

1/2 cup sour cream

1 chipotle pepper canned in adobo sauce

2 to 3 tablespoons heavy cream

Salt and freshly ground black pepper

Place the sour cream and chipotle pepper in a small food processor, process until mixed, then slowly add a small amount of the cream until mixture reaches a smooth, ketchuplike consistency. Add salt and pepper to taste. The Chipotle Crema may be prepared 2 or 3 days in advance and stored in the refrigerator.

(Continued)

❧ Chile-Corn Custard

1 tablespoon butter
1/2 cup whole milk
1/2 cup heavy cream
2 eggs, beaten
1 egg yolk, beaten

Dash of grated nutmeg
2 tablespoons finely diced poblano chile
2 tablespoons fresh or frozen corn kernels
4 tablespoons grated Monterey Jack cheese

Preheat the oven to 325°F. Melt the butter and coat 4 ovenproof ramekins. In a large glass measuring cup, combine the milk, cream, eggs, egg yolk, and nutmeg. Sprinkle diced poblanos into each ramekin; add 1/2 tablespoon corn and 1 tablespoon cheese. Set the ramekins in a small baking dish and fill them with the egg mixture. Add hot (not boiling) water to the dish so that it goes 3/4 of the way up the side of the ramekins. Cover with foil and perforate several places with the point of a knife to let steam escape. Bake for 25 to 30 minutes. The custards are done when a knife inserted in a custard comes out clean. Remove from the oven and let sit 5 to 10 minutes. To unmold each custard, run a knife around the edge of the ramekin, invert it, and the custard should slip out.

Barbara Hill is Executive Chef/Owner of the Snake Creek Grill in Heber, Utah.

Rainbow Trout with Balsamic Syrup and Honey-Citrus Vinaigrette

Serves 2

2 cleaned rainbow trout, 10 ounces each
Salt and freshly ground black pepper
2 tablespoons olive oil, plus more
    for drizzling
2 thick slices crusty French or Italian bread

1 bunch watercress, stemmed, washed,
    and spun dry
1 large vine-ripened tomato, diced
1/2 cup almonds, toasted
✦ Honey-Citrus Vinaigrette
✦ Balsamic Syrup

Preheat the oven to 350°F. Heat an ovenproof sauté pan over medium-high heat. Season the trout with salt and pepper. Add the 2 tablespoons oil to the pan; carefully add the trout and sauté for 3 minutes. Turn the fish over and transfer the pan to the oven. Bake for 5 to 7 minutes. Drizzle both sides of the bread with olive oil and season with salt and pepper. Toast on a stovetop grill or under the broiler.

Toss the watercress, half of the diced tomato, and half the toasted almonds with a little of the Honey-Citrus Vinaigrette. Place the toasted bread in the middle of each plate. Mound the watercress on the toasts and set the trout on top. Drizzle more Honey-Citrus Vinaigrette over the trout. Sprinkle the remaining almonds and tomato over the trout and plates. Finish by drizzling Balsamic Syrup over the trout.

✦ Honey-Citrus Vinaigrette
2 tablespoons cider vinegar
1-1/2 teaspoons Dijon mustard
1 tablespoon frozen orange-juice
    concentrate
1-1/2 teaspoons honey

1/2 cup vegetable oil
2 tablespoons snipped chives
2 tablespoons chopped fresh parsley
Salt and freshly ground black pepper

Whisk together the vinegar, mustard, orange-juice concentrate, and honey. Slowly whisk in the oil until the vinaigrette thickens. Whisk in chives and parsley. Add salt and pepper to taste.

✦ Balsamic Syrup
1 cup balsamic vinegar

Simmer the balsamic vinegar in a sauté pan over medium-low heat until a syrupy consistency is achieved, about 20 to 30 minutes.

Mark Swomley is Executive Chef and Jessica Gibson is Sous Chef of The Carlton Restaurant in Pittsburgh, Pennsylvania.

Sautéed Rainbow Trout with Brussels Sprouts, Bacon, and Braised Red-Cabbage Sauce

Serves 4

COOK'S STRATEGY: The cabbage for the sauce must be marinated overnight. The next day, you may prepare the sauce well ahead of the dinner and rewarm it just before serving to give you time to focus on preparing these nutty, delicious trout "sandwiches."

4 rainbow-trout fillets, 6 ounces each,
    pin bones removed, skin on
1-1/2 teaspoons olive oil
3 shallots, thinly sliced
1/4 teaspoon minced garlic
1 tablespoon hazelnuts, toasted
    and chopped
2 teaspoons chopped parsley
2 teaspoons snipped chives
12 long, whole chives, blanched for
    a few seconds

Salt and freshly ground black pepper
Wondra flour, for dusting
2 teaspoons canola oil
1 tablespoon butter
2 teaspoons chopped shallots
1 teaspoon chopped fresh thyme
➤ Red-Cabbage Sauce
➤ Brussels Sprouts

In a sauté pan, heat the olive oil over medium heat. Add the sliced shallots and sauté until soft and translucent, being careful to not let them burn, about 5 minutes. Once soft, add garlic and sauté for 1 to 2 minutes longer. Add the hazelnuts, parsley, and snipped chives and season with salt and pepper. Remove from the heat and divide into 4 equal portions.

Cut each trout fillet in half. Place half of these pieces skin-side down on the work surface and spread the pieces with the shallot-nut mixture. Top with the other fillet halves, skin-side out. (You should have a trout sandwich with filling in the center and skin sides of fillet facing out.) Tie each trout sandwich together with 3 chives, making 3 horizontal bands across fish. Season each sandwich with salt and pepper and dust lightly with Wondra. Heat the canola oil in a sauté pan, and cook fish on 1 side until crisp, about 3 minutes. Turn, add the butter, chopped shallots, and thyme, and baste fish with foaming butter for about 1 to 2 minutes.

To serve, spoon a circle of Red-Cabbage Sauce onto 4 warmed plates. Spoon Brussels Sprouts in center of sauce. Top the vegetables on each plate with a trout sandwich.

❧ Red-Cabbage Sauce

1/4 medium red cabbage, cored
    and shredded
1 cup red wine
1/2 cup ruby port

1/2 Granny Smith apple, peeled and grated
Grated zest of 1 orange
Juice of 1 orange
Salt and freshly ground black pepper

Combine all of the ingredients in a mixing bowl. Cover and marinate in the refrigerator overnight. Pour the cabbage and marinade into a saucepan (the liquid should cover the cabbage; if necessary add a little water or chicken broth to submerge). Simmer cabbage over medium heat until tender. Remove from the heat, transfer to a blender and purée until smooth. Strain the purée through a fine-mesh sieve. Set aside and keep warm. (The sauce can be made in advance and reheated.)

❧ Brussels Sprouts

1 cup Brussels sprouts
1 tablespoon diced bacon
Salt and freshly ground black pepper

1 tablespoon chopped shallot
1 tablespoon chopped fresh parsley

Pull apart the leaves from the Brussels sprouts—as when preparing a salad—and set aside. Heat a sauté pan over medium heat. Add the bacon and cook until crisp, about 5 minutes. Add the Brussels sprouts leaves and sauté until wilted. Season with salt and pepper (add salt carefully as bacon is already quite salty). Add shallot and sauté about 1 minute. Stir in the parsley. Set aside and keep warm.

Brian Bistrong is Executive Chef of Citarella The Restaurant
in New York City.

Rainbow-Trout Tacos

Serves 4 to 6

These crispy tacos are garnished with Monterey Jack cheese, Avocado Sauce, and Corn Relish. It is crucial to assemble and serve the tacos as soon as possible after the fish is cooked because the fish is light in texture and will not hold heat for long. If you're really adventurous, panfry the fish in bacon drippings —but you didn't hear this from me!

COOK'S STRATEGY: The Corn Relish may be prepared several hours in advance. Before you begin panfrying the trout, make sure the toppings and Avocado Sauce are lined up and ready for assembly. Finish crisping the taco shells in the oven while you fry the fish.

8 rainbow-trout fillets, 3 to 4 ounces each, skinned
12 taco shells
1 cup cornmeal
1/2 cup flour
1/4 cup salt
2 teaspoons each of ground cumin, chile powder, garlic powder, freshly ground black pepper, paprika, and dried thyme

1 teaspoon cayenne
Canola oil for panfrying
3 cups shredded pepper Jack cheese (Monterey Jack with jalapeños)
3 cups finely shredded lettuce
1 lime, cut into wedges
❧ Corn Relish
❧ Avocado Sauce

Preheat the oven to 300°F. Place the taco shells on a baking sheet and toast in the oven until crisp, about 10 minutes.

In a metal bowl, use a wire whisk to combine the cornmeal, flour, salt, and remaining spices and herbs. Heat a small pool of canola oil in large skillet over medium heat (high heat will scorch the fillets). Roll the fillets in the cornmeal mixture and cook them for 3 to 4 minutes per side. Remove the fish from the skillet and place on a clean cutting board. Each fillet has a wide end and a narrow end. Trim off the narrow end (about 1 inch or so) so that each fillet becomes 1 rectanglar and 1 triangular piece.

Working quickly, line each warm taco shell with approximately 1/4 cup cheese, then add 1 rectangular trout piece or 2 triangular pieces. Top each with a heaping spoonful of Corn Relish, a drizzle of Avocado Sauce, and approximately 1/4 cup shredded lettuce. Garnish with a lime wedge, and serve with rice and beans, if desired.

❋ Corn Relish

6 cups fresh or frozen corn kernels
1 red bell pepper, finely diced
1 green bell pepper, finely diced
2 tablespoons coarse salt
1-1/2 teaspoons celery seed

1/4 teaspoon cayenne
2 tablespoons dry mustard
3/4 cup brown sugar
1-1/4 cups cider vinegar
1 white onion, finely diced

Combine all ingredients except the onion in a saucepan and bring to a boil. Reduce the heat and simmer until the liquid begins to disappear, about 20 minutes. Add the onion and simmer another 10 minutes. Leftover relish stores well in the refrigerator.

❋ Avocado Sauce

1 ripe avocado, peeled and seeded
1-1/2 cups sour cream

1 teaspoon freshly squeezed lemon juice
Salt

Purée the avocado and sour cream in blender or food processor. Stir in the lemon juice and season with salt to taste.

Dan Shapiro is Chef/Owner of Pine Creek Café in Livingston, Montana.

Dill-Crusted Arctic Char, Potato-Artichoke Ragoût, Pinot Noir Sauce

Artic Char

SCIENTIFIC NAME: *Salvelinus alpinus*

OTHER NAMES: Char, common char, Alpine trout, Alpine char, charr

U.S. DISTRIBUTION: Icy lakes and rivers north of the 60th parallel. Most of the arctic char sold in the United States is farmed in Canada and Iceland.

SEASON: High-quality fresh and frozen fish is available all year.

WHAT TO LOOK FOR: Arctic char's pale-pink to dark-red flesh should be clear and unmarred, with a fresh, clean scent. Farm-raised char range in size from 2 to 6 pounds. May be sold whole or as fillets.

COLOR, TASTE, AND TEXTURE: The char's high fat content helps it survive in the cold north and makes the flesh flavorful, buttery, and moist. The flaky-to-firm flesh is pink when cooked. If you like salmon, you will love arctic char.

COOKING METHODS: Use in recipes that call for salmon or trout.

TIP: Arctic char's skin becomes leathery when cooked; remove it before serving.

Serves 4

COOK'S STRATEGY: A few hours in advance, cook the whole artichokes for the ragoût and reduce the stock and wine for the Pinot Noir Sauce. About an hour before dinner, prepare the ragoût and begin the fish. Once the fish is seared, you can quickly finish the sauce.

20 ounces arctic-char fillet (skin on), cut into 4 portions
2 fingerling potatoes, peeled
1 stick (8 tablespoons) unsalted butter
1/4 cup chopped dill
Salt and freshly ground black pepper
1 cup panko (Japanese bread crumbs) or other coarse bread crumbs
❧ Potato-Artichoke Ragoût
❧ Pinot Noir Sauce

Put the potatoes in cold water in a saucepan, bring to a boil, and cook until soft, 15 to 20 minutes. Drain and cool to room temperature. Mash with a fork, add the butter and dill, and season with salt and pepper. Divide potato mixture evenly onto the 4 fish portions and spread a thin layer on each fillet. Place fillets potato-side down in the panko. Heat a heavy sauté pan over medium-high heat. Sear the fillets on potato-panko side until golden brown, about 2 or 3 minutes. Turn over and cook on the skin side for 2 minutes over high heat. Remove from the pan and let cool.

To serve, spoon the Potato-Artichoke Ragoût onto the center of each of 4 dinner plates. Cut each fillet in half and arrange 1 piece skin-side up and the other crust-side up. Drizzle the Pinot Noir Sauce on each serving.

❧ Potato-Artichoke Ragoût

3 artichokes
1 cup white wine
2 sprigs fresh thyme
2 tablespoons salt, plus more to season
1 Idaho potato, peeled
1/2 cup cauliflower florets
1 tablespoon heavy cream
2 tablespoons butter
Freshly ground black pepper

Break off the outer leaves of the artichokes. Bring 1 quart water, the wine, thyme, and 2 tablespoons salt to a boil in a pot. Add artichokes and simmer for 15 to 20 minutes or until soft. Cool in the cooking liquid by placing the pot in an ice bath. Trim the artichokes and remove the choke. Cut the potato into 1/2-inch cubes. Cook in lightly salted water until soft, drain, and let cool. Cook the cauliflower in lightly salted water until soft. Strain and purée in a mixer; add the cream. Cut the artichoke hearts into 1/2-inch cubes and sauté with the potato in 1 tablespoon butter until golden brown. Add the cauliflower purée and remaining butter and season with salt and pepper.

✤ Pinot Noir Sauce

1 tablespoon butter

1 shallot, finely chopped

2 cloves garlic, finely chopped

1 cup veal stock

1 sprig fresh rosemary

1/2 cup Pinot Noir

Salt and freshly ground black pepper

Melt the butter in a saucepan over medium heat. Sauté the shallot and garlic, add the veal stock, rosemary, and 1/4 cup of the wine. Cook until about 1/2 cup liquid remains. Strain and pour into a small saucepan. Add the remaining 1/4 cup wine and season with salt and pepper.

Roger Johnsson was Chef de Cuisine of Aquavit in Minneapolis, Minnesota. He now resides in Sweden.

Opah, Pollock, and Grenadier

MANY AMERICAN CONSUMERS ARE UNFAMILIAR WITH opah, pollock, and grenadier, but for different reasons: Opah are rare, grenadier live so deep that few have ever seen them alive, and pollock are so common that they frequently go unnamed except as "fish fillets." Creative recipes provided here will inspire you to try them all, impressing your family and friends with your ability to serve up a broad array of delicious seafoods with flair.

Opah, also called moonfish, do not swim in schools, so they are caught one by one. They are extraordinary fish—found in deep tropical, subtropical, and temperate areas of the Atlantic, Indian, and Pacific oceans (especially around the underwater mountains of Hawaii), opah weigh from 60 to more than 200 pounds. They are beautifully colored both outside and inside. The body has an iridescent blue sheen, white spots, bright red fins, and yellow or gold eyes, and the flesh may vary from pink to orange to ruby red. Unlike most fish, opah swim by moving their pectoral fins up and down, much as a bird flaps its wings. Hawaiians believe the beautiful and unique opah brings good luck and may give the fish as a gift. Although it is rarely seen in grocery-store chains, opah is available from many seafood retailers throughout the country.

In contrast to the rare opah, pollock supports an enormous commercial fishery in the United States, with more than 30 billion pounds landed between 1991 and 2001, mostly from Alaskan waters. Most of this catch is from a single

Alaska pollock *(top)*, opah *(bottom)*, and surimi pieces *(top left, center right)*

In the Wild

Imagine climbing into a miniature four-person submarine and descending into the dark depths of the ocean, passing on the way down glowing jellyfish, squid, and fish, and finally landing at 3,000 feet on a bottom that resembles a moonscape—except that there is lots of life. There, in a submersible called the *Johnson Sea Link II* in the Pacific waters surrounding the Galápagos Islands, I saw my first living grenadiers. In fact, with the sub's illumination of the natural darkness of the deep, I saw more grenadiers than any other type of fish. They have large heads and long bodies that taper to a point at the tail end, and they swim using a rhythmic undulation of the body. Having previously seen grenadiers and many other deep-sea fishes only from rigid, preserved museum specimens, I could barely contain my glee at seeing them at home.

—CAROLE BALDWIN

species, the Alaska pollock, a member of the cod family. At processing plants, Alaska pollock is converted into three main products: fillets for fast-food restaurants; fish eggs or roe; and surimi, which is designed to imitate high-value shellfish such as crab or lobster. The "crab" centerpiece of the maki sushi known as the California Roll, surimi is produced by pressing boneless fillets of fish, most often pollock, through an extruder to produce a paste. Water, sugar, salt, and other ingredients may be added, and the surimi paste can be shaped to resemble pieces of real shellfish.

We include a recipe for another group of cod relatives, grenadier (also called rattail), which are part of a family of fishes that inhabit the deep, cold waters of both hemispheres. On the west coast of the United States, grenadier have been harvested commercially from California to Alaska.

Opah, when available, is a good seafood choice because its solitary habits help prevent it from being overfished. And despite heavy fishing pressure on Alaska pollock, there are no immediate conservation concerns regarding stocks off Alaska. In fact, Alaska pollock is being considered by the Marine Stewardship Council for one of its coveted eco-labels for sustainability and sound management. This is not the case for pollock populations in other parts of the world, and other members of the cod family such as Atlantic cod, where catches have declined dramatically in the past few decades. Grenadier are abundant in deep waters and, like opah, a good seafood choice when available. They are, however, long-lived species that will require conservative management strategies if the commercial fishery for them increases greatly.

Opah Baked in Parchment with Blackberry Butter Sauce

Serves 4

The baked opah is topped with a butter sauce accented with fresh blackberries.

4 opah fillets,
    4 to 6 ounces each
1/4 cup extra-virgin olive oil
1 clove garlic, minced
1 teaspoon chopped
    fresh thyme
Juice of 1 lemon

Salt and freshly ground
    black pepper
1 large carrot, peeled
1 leek, white part only
2 medium zucchini
✦ Blackberry Butter Sauce

Special Equipment: 4 pieces baking parchment, each 12 by 17 inches

Combine the olive oil, garlic, thyme, lemon juice, and a pinch each of salt and pepper in a ceramic baking dish. Add the opah fillets and coat well.

Preheat the oven to 400°F. Cut each vegetable into 3-inch sections and, using a mandoline or large chef's knife, slice the carrot and leek chunks into julienne strips. Julienne only the outside green portion of the zucchini (discard the soft interior).

Fold a parchment rectangle in half along the short side. Place a fillet inside the parchment along the fold line. Top with one-fourth of the juli-enned vegetables. Starting at 1 corner, fold each of the 4 corners of the parchment around the fillet. At the last fold, twist the parchment to seal. Place on a baking sheet. Repeat with the remaining parchment, fillets, and vegetables. Bake for 15 to 20 minutes, until the parchment is completely browned.

Carefully cut open the parchment (escaping steam will be very hot) and place the fish on a serving platter. Top with the vegetables and gar-nish with Blackberry Butter Sauce. Serve with a basmati rice pilaf.

Opah

SCIENTIFIC NAME: *Lampris guttatus*

OTHER NAMES: Moonfish

U.S. DISTRIBUTION: Deep waters off east and west coasts, and seamounts around Hawaii

SEASON: Available sporadically through the year, with a peak from April to August

WHAT TO LOOK FOR: Most opah goes to restaurants, but con-sumers will find opah fillets in quality fish markets.

COLOR, TASTE, AND TEX-TURE: Opah has four types of flesh, each a different color. Behind the head and along the backbone is orange flesh. Toward the belly, the flesh is pink and somewhat stringy. The fish's cheeks are dark red. These types of flesh all turn white when cooked and have a juicy, rich, supple qual-ity to them. Inside the fish's breastplate is another, smaller sec-tion of flesh that's ruby-red and cooks to a brown color, with a somewhat stringy texture.

COOKING METHODS: The large-grain flesh is rich and fatty. Opah is used for sashimi (raw), broiling, steaming, and, occasion-ally, for smoking. It can be pre-pared just like tuna.

TIP: If you are buying opah fillets, avoid cuts from the stomach sec-tion because they can be stringy.

(Continued)

⤳ Blackberry Butter Sauce

1 cup chicken broth	1/2 cup fresh blackberries
1/2 cup dry white wine	Salt and freshly ground black pepper
1 cup heavy cream	
1-1/2 sticks (12 tablespoons) cold unsalted butter, cut into pieces	

Bring the broth and wine to a boil in a medium saucepan over medium-high heat. Cook to reduce by half; you should have about 3/4 cup liquid. Add the cream and simmer until thick and bubbly. Whisk in the butter, 1 piece at a time. Add the blackberries. Remove from the heat and blend with a hand mixer or process in food processor until smooth. Season with salt and pepper.

Eric Sarnow is Executive Chef of The Hummingbird Room in Spring Mills, Pennsylvania.

Steamed Opah Wrapped in Herbs with Spanish Hollandaise and Spinach Orzo

Serves 4

Piquillo peppers are grown in the Navarra and La Rioja regions of Spain. The red, triangular peppers are no more than 4 inches long. They narrow to a beak, hence the name "piquillo," which means "little beak." Sold canned or in jars, piquillos are full of wood-roasted flavor and are so convenient because the roasting and peeling has already been done. For traditional Hollandaise sauce, replace the olive oil with clarified butter (2/3 cup total) in this recipe and eliminate the sherry vinegar, almonds, and pepper purée.

4 opah fillets, 7 ounces each
6 cloves garlic
2 cups loosely packed fresh herb leaves
    (Italian flat-leaf parsley, basil, chives,
    oregano), coarsely chopped

1/4 cup extra-virgin olive oil
Coarse salt and freshly ground black pepper
❧ Spinach Orzo
❧ Spanish Hollandaise

Special Equipment: Steamer basket

Boil the garlic in salted water for 2 to 3 minutes; cool on a cutting board and slice thinly. Mix the garlic with the herbs and olive oil in a small bowl. Season each opah fillet evenly with salt and pepper. Roll out a 10-by-10-inch piece of plastic wrap on the work surface and coat with one-eighth of the herb mixture. Place an opah fillet in the center and cover with another layer of the herb mixture. Wrap the plastic wrap tightly and set aside. Repeat with the other 3 fillets.

When the accompaniments are ready, steam the opah packets above simmering water for 12 minutes, flipping halfway through. Remove from the steamer and cut off the plastic wrap with kitchen shears.

To serve, place the opah fillets with the Spinach Orzo on 4 warm dinner plates. Top with Spanish Hollandaise.

❧ Spinach Orzo

6 cloves garlic, peeled
1 large bunch spinach, stemmed,
    washed, and dried
10 to 12 ounces orzo pasta

3 tablespoons extra-virgin olive oil
1/4 cup grated Parmesan
Coarse salt and freshly ground black pepper

(Continued)

In a pot that will hold a steamer basket and can be covered tightly, bring about 2 inches of salted water to a boil. Add the garlic cloves to the water and boil for 2 to 3 minutes; set them aside. Place the steamer basket above the simmering, salted water and steam the spinach leaves about 4 minutes, tossing occasionally. Remove the spinach from the steamer to a plate. When the spinach is cool enough to handle, squeeze to extract as much liquid as possible. In a small food processor, finely chop the spinach and garlic.

Cook the orzo in a generous amount of boiling salted water until just al dente, about 5 to 7 minutes; drain well. Meanwhile, heat the olive oil in a sauté pan over low heat, add the spinach mixture and heat through. Add the warm, cooked orzo and stir to coat well. Stir in the grated cheese; taste and adjust seasonings. Keep warm until serving time.

✦ Spanish Hollandaise

2 egg yolks

Juice of 1/2 lemon

Coarse salt and freshly ground black pepper

1/3 cup clarified butter (see Glossary)

1/3 cup extra-virgin olive oil

1-1/2 tablespoons aged sherry vinegar

1/4 cup crushed toasted almonds

1/4 cup puréed roasted piquillo peppers

 (or red bell peppers or pimientos)

Place a metal mixing bowl on top of a pot half-full of simmering water. In the bowl, vigorously whisk together the egg yolks, 1 tablespoon water, the lemon juice, and salt and pepper and cook until mixture is light and fluffy, 3 to 5 minutes. The yolks should leave a trail when you lift the whisk. Remove from the heat. Gradually whisk in the clarified butter a few drops at a time, beating vigorously. Add the oil in a steady stream while continuing to whisk. Add the sherry vinegar, almonds, and pepper purée. Taste and adjust seasonings. Keep covered in a warm place for up to 3 hours.

Mary Sue Milliken and Susan Feniger are the Chef/Owners of the Border Grill restaurants in Santa Monica, Pasadena, and Las Vegas, as well as Ciudad in downtown Los Angeles. They are authors of five cookbooks (four dedicated to the Latin kitchen), hosts of *Too Hot Tamales* and *Tamales World Tour* programs on the Food Network, and radio hosts of *Hot Dish* features heard daily in southern California.

California Rolls with Sunomono

Serves 4 (8 California rolls, 12 pieces per person)

Sunomono is a salad made with cucumber and surimi (imitation crabmeat) and seasoned with a Japanese vinaigrette. To make sushi rice for the California rolls, you can use a vinegar-mix powder available from Japanese grocery stores if you prefer.

8 ounces surimi (imitation crabmeat), leg style

1/2 cup Japanese rice-wine vinegar

6 tablespoons sugar

1 tablespoon salt

1-1/2 cups Japanese short-grain rice

4 sheets nori (Japanese seaweed), each cut crosswise into 2 pieces approximately 4 by 9 inches

1 ripe avocado

Toasted sesame seeds, optional

2 tablespoons wasabi powder

Soy sauce

✦ Sunomono

Special Equipment: A bamboo sushi rolling mat

Combine the vinegar, sugar, and salt in a small saucepan and bring to a boil over high heat. Remove from heat and let cool. Wash the rice in cold water until the water runs clear. Combine rice with 1-3/4 cups water and cook in a rice cooker for 45 minutes (or follow directions on package for stove-top cooking). Remove the cooked rice from the cooker and place in a large bowl. Pour 3/4 cup of the cooled vinegar mixture over the rice and stir. Wait until the rice cools to body temperature before making California Rolls, approximately 30 minutes.

Completely cover the bamboo rolling mat with plastic wrap and set aside. Peel the avocado and cut it into approximately 16 slices. Cut the cylinders of surimi lengthwise in half. Lay one 4-by-9-inch sheet of nori on the counter and, with hands moistened with water, pat rice onto the surface.

(Continued)

Alaska Pollock

SCIENTIFIC NAME: *Theragra chalcogramma*

OTHER NAMES: Pollack, whiting, Pacific tomcod, snow cod, bigeye pollock, walleye pollock, Pacific pollock

U.S. DISTRIBUTION: California to Alaska

SEASON: Year-round

WHAT TO LOOK FOR: You are more likely to encounter pollock in a fast-food fish sandwich or as frozen fillets or imitation crabmeat (surimi) in a supermarket than as fresh fillets at the fish counter. Most Alaska pollock is frozen on board ship and sold to large processors on shore. When you do see fillets at the market, the flesh should be snow white and smell fresh.

COLOR, TASTE, AND TEXTURE: Pollock is lean and firm with a pleasant flake. In the past ten years, it has all but replaced cod as the white fish of choice on restaurant menus.

COOKING METHODS: Use in all your favorite cod recipes.

Sprinkle toasted sesame seeds over rice if desired. Turn the nori over onto the plastic-covered bamboo rolling mat, rice-side down, with 1 of the long sides along the edge where you will begin rolling. With this long side facing you, place 2 pieces of sliced avocado and 2 pieces of surimi across the length of the seaweed side, about 1 inch up from the bottom. Lift the edge of the rolling mat and roll the long edge of the nori firmly over the avocado and surimi. Continue to roll firmly, remove roll from bamboo mat, and cut with a very sharp knife into 6 equal pieces. Repeat with the remaining nori. Rolls can be wrapped in plastic and left at room temperature for 1/2 hour. Do not refrigerate.

Mix wasabi with 2 tablespoons water. Arrange the pieces of California Roll on a single large platter or 4 small ones and garnish with a large pinch of wasabi paste. Serve with soy sauce and Sunomono in separate bowls.

✦ Sunomono

1/2 cup rice-wine vinegar

2 tablespoons water

1/4 cup sugar

1/2 teaspoon salt, plus more for sprinkling

Juice of 1/2 lemon

One 4-inch-square piece dashi kobu (dried seaweed), available in Japanese food markets

1 English cucumber

4 to 8 ounces surimi (imitation crabmeat) cut into thin strips

Combine vinegar, water, sugar, and 1/2 teaspoon salt in a small saucepan. Bring to a boil, stirring until the salt and sugar are dissolved. Remove from heat, add the lemon juice and dashi kobu, and let the mixture cool.

Slice the cucumber into thin strips and sprinkle with salt. Squeeze the cucumber strips hard to remove excess liquid. Rinse with water and squeeze again. Combine the cucumber and surimi in a bowl. Remove the dashi kobu from the vinegar mixture, then pour over the cucumber and surimi.

Steve Fujii is Chef at Ebisu in San Francisco, California.

Cucumber-Steamed Grenadier

Serves 4

4 grenadier fillets,
    5 to 6 ounces each
1 medium leek, trimmed,
    washed, and thinly sliced
1/2 cup clam juice, fish stock,
    or chicken broth
1/3 cup dry white wine

Salt and freshly ground
    black pepper
1 cucumber, peeled and sliced
    paper-thin
2 tablespoons chopped
    fresh dill

Place the leek in a frying pan that has a cover. Add the broth and wine.
Place the fish fillets in the pan and season lightly with salt and pepper.
Arrange the cucumber slices on the fish in very neat overlapping patterns
resembling fish scales. Cover the pan and cook over medium heat until the
fish flakes easily. Thin fillets will take 3 to 4 minutes; thick fillets may take
6 to 7 minutes.

Transfer the fillets to plates and surround with leeks and broth. Sprinkle
with the dill and serve.

Narsai David is Food and Wine Editor at San Francisco's KCBS radio station, cohost
of *Cook-Off America* on PBS, and host of a weekly cooking class at Macy's in San
Francisco and San José, California.

Grenadier

SCIENTIFIC NAMES:
*Coryphaenoides or Macrourus
species*

OTHER NAMES: Rattail,
onion-eye

LOCAL TO: Cold deep waters
from California to Alaska

SEASON: May to December

WHAT TO LOOK FOR: It's
unlikely you'll find whole
grenadier at the fish market.
The fish may be 2 feet in
length, and they have huge
heads and tapering bodies
with sharp scales. The fish
may be sold whole minus the
head, innards, and scales, or as
long fillets that are very thin at
the tail end.

COLOR, TASTE, AND
TEXTURE: When cooked,
the flesh is firm and very
white. The diet of grenadier
includes shrimp, squid, and
small fish, which are believed
to give the flesh its sweet and
succulent taste.

COOKING METHODS:
Grenadier can be roasted,
sautéed, steamed, or fried.

Sablefish and Butterfish

SABLEFISH AND AMERICAN BUTTERFISH ARE NOT closely related, but because both are often referred to as simply "butterfish," they are paired here to eliminate any confusion. As noted by Jay Harlow in the introduction to his recipe for steamed butterfish, the two fish couldn't be more different. So why the same name? Both have buttery, succulent flesh. Longtime favorites in Japan, where most of the U.S. catch is exported, sablefish and American butterfish are now slowly making their way into U.S. markets, and sablefish is appearing on menus of some of the finest U.S. seafood restaurants.

Sablefish (*Anoplopoma fimbria*), also known as Alaskan butterfish, butterfish, and black cod, are large fish, often caught at about 2 feet long, that live in the cold, deep waters of the northeastern Pacific. Most of the commercial catch is from Alaska. American butterfish (*Peprilus triacanthus*), by contrast, are small (usually 6 to 9 inches long), round, thin fish that inhabit the shallow waters off the east and Gulf coasts of the United States. Sablefish are related to the popular (but unfortunately overfished) Pacific rockfishes, whereas American butterfish are classified by biologists in the huge group of perchlike fishes. Additional confusion at the seafood market may arise because of the

American butterfish *(top left)*, harvestfish *(top right)*, and sablefish *(bottom)*

199

In the Wild

Young butterfish have an unusual way of protecting themselves from predators: They often take shelter among the tentacles of jellyfish—like sea nettles, apparently immune to the jellyfish toxins. As adults, butterfish travel in large schools, feeding on small pelagic fish, shrimp, squid, and sometimes even jellyfish.

occasional presence of another Pacific fish species, the Pacific pompano or Pacific butterfish (*Peprilus simillimus*), which is actually a butterfish closely related to the American butterfish. Neither the Pacific pompano nor an Atlantic relative of American butterfish, the harvestfish (*Peprilus alepidotus*), are of significant commercial importance.

Like salmon, tuna, and mackerel, sablefish is an excellent source of the beneficial omega-3 fatty acids. It tastes remarkably like the popular Patagonian toothfish (marketed as Chilean sea bass), but the commercial fishery is much better managed, especially in Alaskan waters. In fact, sablefish is the highest valued finfish per pound in Alaska's commercial fisheries. Although sablefish populations in the Gulf of Alaska have been declining recently, reduced fishing quotas have been established and many scientific studies are under way, including tagging to learn more about sablefish movements. Catches of American butterfish peaked in the 1980s when displaced cod fishermen turned to this and other species, but catches have been relatively stable during the past decade. The species is considered underexploited as a food resource, and it is managed under a plan that limits annual harvest to prevent overexploitation.

Hong Kong–Marinated Black Cod

Serves 4

I frequently serve this in a smaller portion (3 to 4 ounces) as an appetizer. Set on a bed of raw baby spinach or tatsoi leaves, it makes an attractive presentation. For a main course, I serve it with rice pilaf and a green vegetable in season, such as asparagus, broccoli, or green beans.

4 sablefish (black cod) fillets,
    5 to 6 ounces each
    (cut as thick as possible)
1/2 cup soy sauce
6 tablespoons sugar
1/4 cup rice wine or white wine

1 orange, zest shaved thin
    or grated
2 bunches scallions—1 bunch
    chopped (with all the
    green tops), 1 bunch
    trimmed and left whole

In a shallow dish, combine the soy sauce, sugar, wine, orange zest, and chopped scallions. Add the fish and marinate for 3 hours in the refrigerator.

Preheat the oven to 400°F. Lay the whole scallions in a baking dish. Wipe off the marinade from the fillets and place on the bed of scallions. Bake for 10 to 15 minutes, or just until the fish starts to flake.

Narsai David is Food and Wine Editor at San Francisco's KCBS radio station, cohost of *Cook-Off America* on PBS, and host of a weekly cooking class at Macy's in San Francisco and San José, California.

Sablefish

SCIENTIFIC NAME:
Anoplopoma fimbria

OTHER NAMES: Butterfish, Alaskan butterfish, black cod, coalfish, skilfish

U.S. DISTRIBUTION: Alaska to California

SEASON: January to September. Much of the catch is frozen onboard the boat, so high-quality fish is sold all year.

WHAT TO LOOK FOR: Fish typically weigh between 3 and 10 pounds. Fresh sablefish should glisten. The fish freezes well and is often shipped frozen. Smoked sablefish is superb.

COLOR, TASTE, AND TEXTURE: The fish takes its name from its black or dark green skin. The pearly white flesh has a high oil content and buttery, sweet, rich flavor. When cooked, the large flakes are somewhat firm.

COOKING METHODS: Bake, sauté, marinate and grill, hot smoke, or panfry. Asian seasonings with a hint of sweetness pair well with sablefish. Try mirin, ginger, and soy in a marinade or sauce.

Sablefish with Polenta Crust

Serves 4

The fish is served over a bed of tomato salsa with kalamata olives, lemon, and capers.

4 sablefish fillets, 5 to 6 ounces each

3 egg whites

Sea salt and freshly ground black pepper

1 cup polenta (coarse yellow cornmeal)

2 to 3 tablespoons olive oil

❧ Olive-Lemon Salsa

Combine the egg whites and 1 tablespoon water in a bowl and beat until frothy. Season the fillets with salt and pepper. Dip the fillets in the egg whites and then in the polenta to coat thoroughly. Heat the oil in a sauté pan over medium-high heat until hot but not smoking. Place the fillets in the pan and cook until golden and just cooked through, 3 to 4 minutes per side.

Spoon the Olive-Lemon Salsa onto 4 warmed dinner plates. Top with the fish fillets. Serve immediately.

❧ Olive-Lemon Salsa

2 cups quartered grape tomatoes
    (or small cherry tomatoes)

1/4 cup finely chopped kalamata olives

2 tablespoons grated lemon zest or 1/4 cup
    chopped Preserved Lemon (page 219)

1/4 cup minced red onion

1 tablespoon drained capers

1 teaspoon minced garlic

1 teaspoon fresh lemon thyme or
    thyme leaves

1 teaspoon Pernod or other anise-flavored
    liqueur

2 tablespoons olive oil

Sea salt and freshly ground black pepper

Stir together the tomatoes, olives, lemon zest or Preserved Lemon, onion, capers, garlic, thyme, Pernod, and olive oil. Season to taste with salt and pepper. Marinate at room temperature for 30 minutes.

Jacques Haeringer is Chef de Cuisine at L'Auberge Chez François in Great Falls, Virginia. He is the author of *The Chez François Cookbook* (Simon and Schuster, 1986) and *Two for Tonight* (Bartleby Press, 2001) and is the host of the PBS cooking show *Two for Tonight*.

Sablefish in Sake Kasu

COOK'S STRATEGY: This recipe requires two days' preparation time for marinating the fish. The rice can be cooked and refrigerated up to a day in advance.

1 sablefish fillet, 2 to 2-1/2 pounds, skin on,
    bones removed, cut into
    4 serving pieces
1/3 cup kosher salt, more if needed
3/4 cup kasu paste (available at
    Asian markets)

1/3 cup sugar
4 heads choy sum (Chinese flowering
    cabbage), steamed
Gari (pickled ginger), sliced
✦ Sesame Rice Cakes

Place fish pieces skin-side down in a shallow glass baking dish. Sprinkle a generous layer of salt over the fish, cover with plastic wrap, and refrigerate for 24 hours. Rinse the salt from the fish and pat dry. Place the fish skin-side down in a clean dish. Using an electric mixer, beat the kasu paste and sugar until smooth. Slowly add 3/4 cup water and mix until incorporated. Pour the kasu mixture evenly over the fish, cover, and refrigerate for another 24 hours.

Heat a charcoal or gas grill. When the grill is very hot, remove the fish from the marinade, allowing the excess to drip off. Grill the fish until nicely browned and just cooked through, about 5 minutes per side.

Transfer the fish to individual plates. Serve with the Sesame Rice Cakes, steamed choy sum, and gari.

✦ Sesame Rice Cakes
1 cup Japanese short-grain rice
2 teaspoons seasoned rice-wine vinegar
1 tablespoon white sesame seeds

1 tablespoon dark sesame seeds
3 tablespoons canola oil

Place rice and 1-1/4 cups water in a 2-quart saucepan and bring to a boil. Continue boiling for 1 minute, then cover pan and reduce heat to low. Simmer on low for 20 minutes. Remove from the heat and stir in the vinegar. Line the bottom of a 6-by-6-inch baking pan with parchment or waxed paper. Using a rubber spatula, transfer the rice to the pan. Spread the rice out evenly and pack it down tightly to about 3/4 to 1 inch deep. Cool the rice in the refrigerator.

(Continued)

While the rice is cooling, lightly toast the white and dark sesame seeds in a nonstick pan over medium-high heat. Constantly stir or toss seeds until the white seeds start to become golden, about 3 to 4 minutes. Remove from the heat and cool.

Preheat the oven to 350°F. When the rice has cooled, carefully invert the baking pan onto a clean, flat surface. Peel paper from the rice. Using a 3-inch biscuit cutter, cut the rice into 4 cakes. You can also make squares or other shapes, as desired. Sprinkle cakes evenly with sesame seeds and pat lightly. In an ovenproof nonstick pan, heat the oil over medium-high heat. Place the cakes seed-side down in the pan and sear until lightly browned, about 2 minutes. Turn the cakes over, place pan in oven, and bake for 3 to 4 minutes or until heated through.

Charles Ramseyer is Executive Chef of Ray's Boathouse in Seattle, Washington and author of *Ray's Boathouse: Seafood Secrets of the Pacific Northwest* (Documentary Media, 2003).

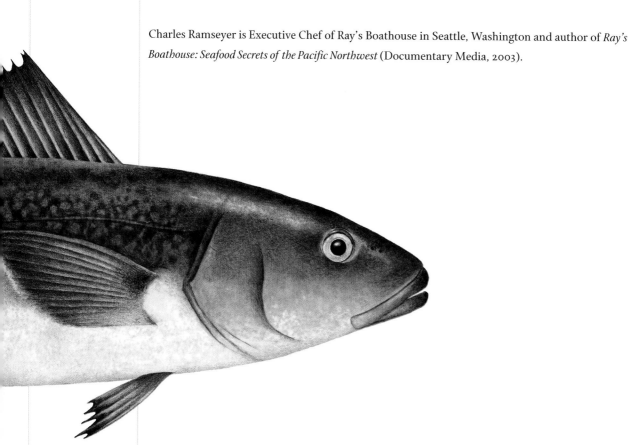

Sake and Miso–Marinated Alaskan Butterfish, Wasabi Oil, Soy Syrup, and Vegetarian Soba Sushi

Serves 4

I consider this my signature dish; in fact, it has been on Blue Ginger's menu since day one. People still can't seem to get enough of it! You could say that it is the synthesis of two great dishes I ate and admired: the miso-brushed yakitoris I enjoyed in Osaka and miso black cod (sablefish), a great dish created by Nobu Matsuhisa. This dish pairs well with a toasted oak–vanilla Chardonnay.

COOK'S STRATEGY: Begin marinating the fish the night before or in the morning. You may prepare the Soy Syrup at that time as well. About an hour before serving, make the Wasabi Oil and start the Vegetarian Soba Sushi. Grill the fish last.

4 pieces sablefish (Alaskan butterfish),
  each about 5 by 3 inches
  and 7 ounces, cut from a fillet
1 cup light miso (shiro miso)
1/2 cup mirin (Japanese seasoning wine)
1/2 cup sake
1/2 cup grapeseed or canola oil
1/4 cup sugar
1 tablespoon finely chopped fresh ginger

Freshly ground black pepper
10 ounces wakame (Japanese seaweed)
  salad, optional
1/4 cup toasted sesame seeds
2 tablespoons gari (pickled ginger)
❀ Vegetarian Soba Sushi
❀ Wasabi Oil
❀ Soy Syrup

In a medium bowl, combine the miso, mirin, sake, oil, sugar, and fresh ginger; stir to blend. Add the fish, turn to coat, and marinate, covered and refrigerated, overnight or at least 8 to 12 hours. Prepare an outdoor grill or preheat the broiler. Wipe the marinade from the fish and season it with pepper to taste. Grill or broil the fish, turning it once, until just cooked through, 10 to 12 minutes.

To serve, cut each Vegetarian Soba Sushi roll into 5 pieces, 3 straight across and 2 diagonally. Divide the sushi pieces among 4 plates. Add a small mound of the seaweed salad, if using, to each and top each with a piece of the Sake and Miso–Marinated Alaskan Butterfish. Drizzle with the Wasabi Oil and Soy Syrup, and garnish with the sesame seeds and gari.

(Continued)

❖ Vegetarian Soba Sushi

1/2 pound dried soba noodles

1/4 cup chopped fresh cilantro

1/4 cup chopped scallions
(green parts only)

2 tablespoons soy sauce (naturally brewed)

2 tablespoons rice-wine vinegar

2 tablespoons Wasabi Oil (recipe below)

2 tablespoons chopped gari
(pickled ginger)

1 tablespoon finely chopped fresh ginger

Salt and freshly ground black pepper

4 sheets toasted nori (Japanese seaweed)

1 cucumber, peeled, seeded, and julienned

1 red bell pepper, cored, seeded,
and julienned

1 yellow bell pepper, cored, seeded,
and julienned

Special Equipment: Bamboo sushi-rolling mat

Bring a large quantity of salted water to a boil. Fill a medium bowl with cold water and add ice. Add the noodles to the boiling water and cook until slightly softer than al dente, about 8 minutes. Drain and transfer the noodles to the ice water. When the noodles are cold, drain well.

In a large bowl, combine the cooked noodles, cilantro, scallions, soy sauce, vinegar, Wasabi Oil, gari, and the fresh ginger; toss to blend. Season with salt and pepper to taste. Have a small bowl of water handy. Place a sheet of nori shiny-side down on the rolling mat with a long edge toward you. Evenly spread a 1/4-inch layer of the noodle mixture on the bottom half of the nori. Top the upper third of the mixture with 3 to 4 strips of cucumber and 2 pieces of each of the peppers. To roll, lift the mat, compressing it against the filling as you roll the bottom edge in on itself. Continue rolling toward the top edge until only 1/4 inch of the nori remains unrolled. Moisten a finger and wet the edge of the nori. Press the mat to seal the roll. Allow the roll to rest, seam-side down, for 2 minutes. Repeat with the remaining nori and filling ingredients. Cover the rolls lightly with plastic wrap and set aside while you prepare the fish.

✦ Wasabi Oil

1/2 cup wasabi powder

2 tablespoons mirin
(Japanese seasoning wine)

2 teaspoons sugar

1/2 cup grapeseed oil

In a small stainless-steel bowl, combine the wasabi powder, mirin, and sugar; whisk to blend. Gradually add a little less than 1/2 cup water, whisking, until a purée the consistency of pancake batter is formed. Whisk in the oil. Let stand for 10 minutes before using. (Makes about 1 cup; leftover oil may be stored in the refrigerator, covered, for 1 week.)

✦ Soy Syrup

2 cups soy sauce

1/2 cup brown sugar

Juice of 1 lime

In a medium saucepan, combine the soy sauce, brown sugar, and lime juice. Bring to a boil slowly over medium heat, turn down the heat, and simmer the mixture until syrupy, about 30 minutes—you should have about 1/2 cup. Strain, cool, and use.

Ming Tsai is Executive Chef and Owner of Blue Ginger in Wellesley, Massachusetts. He is the host of *East-Meets-West* and *Ming's Quest* on the Food Network and author of *Blue Ginger* (Clarkson N. Potter, 1999). Ming's second cookbook, *Simply Ming,* will be published by Clarkson N. Potter in fall 2003.

Steamed Butterfish in Bean Threads

American Butterfish

SCIENTIFIC NAME: *Peprilus triacanthus*

OTHER NAMES: Butterfish, dollarfish, harvestfish, skipjack

U.S. DISTRIBUTION: East and Gulf coasts

SEASON: Available fresh in east-coast markets during the spring, when the fish move inshore and northward as the water warms.

WHAT TO LOOK FOR: Small, thin, round, silvery fish approximately 6 to 9 inches long and weighing only a few ounces. You will need at least two fish per person.

COLOR, TASTE, AND TEXTURE: The raw flesh is dark but turns white once cooked. The flake is fine and the taste pleasant and slightly buttery from the moderate fat content.

COOKING METHODS: Butterfish are usually cooked whole because only tiny fillets can be obtained from the thin fish. Remove or have the fishmonger remove the innards and fins. Butterfish are excellent panfried, grilled, steamed, or baked.

Serves 2

Chinese fish markets in California frequently display piles of small, silvery, almost disc-shaped fish invariably labeled "pompano." Although these little fish are not related to the true Florida pompano, the similarity in appearance is obvious—the compressed shape ("tall" from dorsal fin to belly and quite thin from side to side), the blunt snout, deeply forked tail, and raked fins—and given the fine reputation of real pompano, it's no surprise that they are sold under that name rather than their proper name, butterfish.

Another reason for the pompano tag is that the name "butterfish" causes some confusion around here. Ask for butterfish in most California markets and you will get fillets of the much larger sablefish. The two couldn't be more dissimilar: Sablefish is a large, rather codlike fish, producing thick, narrow fillets a foot or more in length. Butterfish is a small fish, needing several to make up a single pound, and the compressed shape yields thin fillets almost as wide as they are long. About the only thing the two share is a soft texture and high fat content, thus the name "butterfish."

Butterfish are caught commercially on the West Coast, but the supply is sporadic, and the fish in the market are more likely to be a very similar species of butterfish from Florida, brought in frozen and thawed for sale in the "fresh" market. Although it's not the equal of true pompano, butterfish does have rich, fine-textured meat that starts out dark but cooks up white and sweet. At 2 to 3 ounces each, butterfish are usually treated as a pan fish, simply dusted with flour or cornstarch and fried in deep or shallow oil. But they are also good broiled, grilled, steamed in the Chinese style, or baked in a sauce. In any case, the thin skin is likely to come apart in cooking. The scales are so tiny they can be eaten along with the skin.

The small butterfish are best cooked whole (head and insides removed) in this recipe, but be careful of the bones when eating.

1 pound whole butterfish (about 6),
    cleaned
8 to 10 dried or fresh shiitake mushrooms
1-1/2-to-2-ounce bundle dried bean
    threads (available at Asian markets)
1-1/2 tablespoons soy sauce

1/3 cup chicken broth
2 scallions, julienned
1-1/2 tablespoons julienned
    fresh ginger
1 teaspoon Asian sesame oil

Special Equipment: Bamboo steaming basket or wok

In separate bowls, soak the dried mushrooms (if using) in warm water and the bean threads in hot water until soft, 20 to 30 minutes. Drain the dried mushrooms. Discard the mushroom stems and toss the caps with 1 teaspoon of the soy sauce. Drain the bean threads and place in a deep heat-proof plate or glass pie pan that will fit inside a wok or other steaming pot.

Arrange the fish on top of the bean threads, tucking the mushroom caps in around them. Pour in the chicken broth, scatter the scallions and ginger on top of the fish, and sprinkle with the remaining soy sauce.

Bring the water in the steamer to a rolling boil and place the plate on a rack 1 inch above the water. Cover and steam for 20 minutes. Sprinkle with the sesame oil and serve from the steaming dish.

Jay Harlow is a Northern California food writer, culinary instructor, and author or co-author of twelve books. This recipe was excerpted from *West Coast Seafood,* copyright © 1999 by Jay Harlow, and reprinted with permission of Sasquatch Books.

a STRIPED BASS, BAKED WHOLE AND BEAUTIFULLY garnished with lemon twists or roasted vegetables, is among the most spectacular and delicious seafood presentations. Black sea bass has perhaps the whitest, most delicate flesh of any ocean fish when cooked. And the colorful yellow perch is a similarly mild fish selection for those seeking simplicity rather than bold flavors.

If you find yourself with a striped bass at the end of your fishing line, you may know it long before you land it. Striped bass, also called rockfish and stripers, can grow up to 5 feet long and are powerful. They live from Canada to the Gulf of Mexico, where they swim in fresh, brackish, and marine waters. Black sea bass, of the same family as groupers, live from Maine to the Gulf of

Hybrid striped bass *(top)*, yellow perch *(middle)*, black sea bass *(bottom)*

In the Wild

Black sea bass moms never have to wonder whether dads have it easier (or the other way around); as "protogynous hermaphrodites," these fish are born with all the necessary parts for each lifestyle and change from females to males partway through their lives. Although the size and age at which they make this transformation vary, the process generally begins when the fish is between 7 and 10 inches long and two to five years old.

Mexico, but they are strictly marine, usually congregating around hard-bottom areas or reefs—even artificial reefs made from sunken automobiles or car tires. Yellow perch are primarily freshwater fish; in the United States they thrive from the Great Lakes west to Nebraska, throughout the Mississippi River Basin, and in Atlantic drainages south to the Santee River in South Carolina.

Striped bass has been enjoyed as a food since colonial days, and commercial catches increased gradually in the Chesapeake Bay (the main spawning area for the species) until peaking at almost 15 million pounds annually in 1973. By 1983, however, for reasons that are still not clear today (though overfishing and pollution are suspected), less than 2 million pounds was landed, resulting in a stringent management plan that included a complete moratorium on striped-bass fishing for parts of the bay from 1985 to 1989. In 1990 the fishery was reopened under tight regulations, and commercial landings have been a stable 6 to 7 million pounds a year since about 1997.

Much of the striped bass currently available to consumers is a farm-raised cross between striped bass and white bass. Farms exist throughout the south, in some northeastern states, and in California. Striped bass farms are inland operations and are considered environmentally sound. There are also few problems with conservation of yellow perch in the United States, and black sea bass, although heavily fished, are now under the protection of size and catch restrictions. (According to a recent study, the potential for farming black sea bass is excellent.) Note that the black sea bass species highlighted here (*Centropristis striata*) is not the one known by that name in California. That huge fish, *Stereolepis gigas*, was hunted nearly to extinction and has only recently shown minimal signs of recovery. Nor is it related to Patagonian and Antarctic toothfishes (*Dissostichus* species), which, although sold as Chilean sea bass, are not members of the sea-bass family.

Steamed Striped Bass in Tomato-Verbena Water with Crisp Marinated Vegetables with Capers, Apples, and Tarragon

Basses

Striped Bass, Black Sea Bass

Serves 4

I love this dish in the late summer when all the tomatoes are perfectly ripe. Although it takes some advance preparation, all the techniques are very simple.

COOK'S STRATEGY: The Nage and Tomato-Verbena Water can be made a day in advance and rewarmed before using. The Crisp Marinated Vegetables can be tossed together up to one hour before serving.

4 fillets striped bass,
    7 ounces each
Fine sea salt and freshly ground
    white pepper
2 tablespoons julienned fresh
    ginger (2 inches long)

12 leaves fresh lemon verbena
✦ Tomato-Verbena Water
✦ Nage
✦ Crisp Marinated Vegetables
    with Capers, Apples, and
    Tarragon

Preheat the oven to 500°F. Season each fillet with salt and white pepper on both sides. Place the fillets in a heavy-bottomed baking dish big enough to accommodate all the fillets without overlapping or touching. Pour 1 cup of warm Nage over the fish and cover with aluminum foil. Place in the oven and bake for 7 minutes.

Meanwhile, put the ginger in a small saucepan. Cover with cold water, bring to a boil, and cook until tender, about 5 minutes. Drain.

To serve, place some ginger julienne and 3 lemon verbena leaves around the outside of each of 4 plates. Place the Steamed Striped Bass in the center of each plate and spoon about 1/4 cup of the Tomato-Verbena Water over each plate. Top each serving with a portion of the Crisp Marinated Vegetables.

✦ Tomato-Verbena Water

8 vine-ripened tomatoes, lightly puréed
1 cup Nage (recipe below)
6 leaves fresh lemon verbena

Fine sea salt and freshly ground
    white pepper

Place the lightly puréed tomatoes in a colander lined with cheesecloth. Place the colander in a bowl to catch the "tomato water" and put in the refrigerator

SCIENTIFIC NAMES: *Morone saxatilis* (striped bass), *Centropristis striata* (black sea bass)

OTHER NAMES: Striped bass are also called rockfish, stripers, or greenheads. Black sea bass are also known as blackfish, rock bass, bluefish, or simply sea bass.

U.S. DISTRIBUTION: Maine to the Gulf of Mexico. A striped bass/white bass hybrid is now farmed.

SEASON: Year-round

WHAT TO LOOK FOR: Whole fish should be gorgeous, with bright red gills. Striped bass usually weigh 2 to 4 pounds; black sea bass, 1 to 2 pounds. Fillets should be moist and firm with a grassy, mild aroma.

COLOR, TASTE, AND TEXTURE: Either bass is a favorite with chefs and fish fans. The lean, pinkish-to-white flesh has a sweet, crustacean-like flavor and tender flakes.

COOKING METHODS: Black sea bass and striped bass are excellent grilled, steamed, panfried, baked, or braised.

(Continued)

overnight. The next day, you should have about 2 cups of tomato water in the bottom of the bowl. Discard the tomatoes, place the tomato water in a small saucepan, and bring to a boil over high heat. Strain the tomato water through cheesecloth. Return it to the pan and add 1 cup of Nage and the lemon verbena; simmer to infuse for 2 minutes. Season to taste with salt and white pepper.

✦ Nage

2 cups dry white wine	1 medium carrot, halved
1/2 cup Champagne vinegar	4 cloves garlic
2 ribs celery, halved	1 tablespoon fine sea salt
1 large onion, halved lengthwise	1 tablespoon white peppercorns
1 medium fennel bulb, trimmed, halved lengthwise	1 bay leaf

Place all ingredients and 2 quarts water in a large pot. Bring to a boil over high heat, immediately lower the heat, and simmer for 2 hours. Remove from the heat and let stand until cool. Strain through a fine-mesh sieve or cheesecloth and discard the solids. Store the liquid tightly covered in the refrigerator for up to 3 days, or in the freezer for up to 2 months.

✦ Crisp Marinated Vegetables with Capers, Apples, and Tarragon

1/2 cup red cherry tomatoes, cut in half	1 scallion, thinly sliced, white and tender green parts only
1/2 cup yellow pear tomatoes, cut in half	1/2 tablespoon capers, chopped
1/2 apple, diced (1/4 cup)	1/2 teaspoon chopped fresh tarragon
1/2 small cucumber, peeled, seeded, and diced (1/4 cup)	1/4 cup extra-virgin olive oil
1/4 cup diced fennel bulb	Fine sea salt and freshly ground white pepper

Combine all ingredients and marinate in the refrigerator for up to 1 hour before serving.

Eric Ripert is Executive Chef/Co-owner of Le Bernardin in New York City and author (with Maguy Le Coze) of *Le Bernardin Cookbook: Four-Star Simplicity* (Broadway Books, 1998).

Steamed Striped Bass and Mussels with Lemongrass Broth, Red-Satin Radishes, Braised Swiss Chard, Soba, Cucumber, and Onion Sprouts

4 pieces striped bass, 3 ounces each

16 fresh mussels

4 cups fish stock

2 stalks lemongrass, 12 inches each, coarsely chopped

Salt and freshly ground black pepper

1 cup blanched, coarsely chopped Swiss chard

4 ounces soba (buckwheat noodles), cooked according to package directions

1/2 cup julienned red-satin radish (regular red may be substituted)

1/2 cup julienned cucumber

1 jalapeño, seeded and finely julienned

16 thin slices of water chestnuts

1/4 cup julienned nori (dried seaweed)

1/4 cup julienned shiso (perilla or Japanese basil)

1/2 cup onion sprouts

4 teaspoons sesame oil

Serves 4

Scrub the mussels clean under cold running water. Remove the beards. Bring 1 inch of water to a simmer with herbs and aromatic vegetables of your choice. Add the mussels to the pot and cover. Steam the mussels for 2 to 3 minutes or until the shells pop open. Discard any mussels that do not open completely.

Place the fish stock in a medium saucepan with the lemongrass. Simmer over medium heat for 20 minutes to infuse the lemongrass. Strain and season to taste with salt and pepper. Season the striped bass with salt and pepper and score the skin. Place in a steamer for 3 to 5 minutes, or until just done. Warm the Swiss chard in the fish stock over low heat for 2 minutes.

To serve, place some of the soba noodles, radish, cucumber, and jalapeño in the center of each of 4 soup bowls. Place a piece of the steamed striped bass on top of the noodles. Place a slice of water chestnut at the 4 corners of the fish, and set a mussel on top of each water chestnut. Ladle 1 cup of the fish stock and Swiss chard into each bowl. Sprinkle the nori, shiso, and onion sprouts around the bowl. Drizzle the sesame oil around the bowl and top with freshly ground black pepper. Serve immediately.

Charlie Trotter is Executive Chef at Charlie Trotter's in Chicago, Illinois. He is the author of nine cookbooks, including *Charlie Trotter's Seafood* (Ten Speed Press, 1997) and *The Kitchen Sessions with Charlie Trotter* (Ten Speed Press, 1999), the companion book to his PBS cooking show of the same name.

Steamed Black Sea Bass "Hong Kong" Style

Serves 2

A good dry Riesling would accompany the fish nicely.

COOK'S STRATEGY: Mix the Soy Deglaze and have all the garnish ingredients measured and sliced before you begin steaming the fish.

1 whole black sea bass, 1 to 1-1/2 pounds,
    head on and gutted
2 bok choy
3 tablespoons peanut oil
2 tablespoons thinly sliced jalapeños
2 tablespoons sliced garlic

2 tablespoons julienned fresh ginger
2 tablespoons sliced shallots
1/4 cup scallions, thinly sliced on a bias
1/4 cup cilantro leaves
➤Soy Deglaze

Special Equipment: Bamboo steamer basket

Prepare a pot of boiling water and a bamboo steamer. Place the fish in the steamer. Steam covered for 10 to 12 minutes, until cooked through. When the fish is about halfway cooked, place the bok choy in the steamer with the fish.

While the fish is steaming, prepare the garnish. Starting with a cold sauté pan, fry the jalapeños in the peanut oil until aromatic. Add the garlic and ginger and continue to cook until they just begin to brown. Toss in the shallots and remove from heat.

Just before serving, place the bok choy and black sea bass on a serving dish. Pour the garnish over the fish. Put the pan back over the heat, add the Soy Deglaze, and stir. Pour the pan sauce over the fish and sprinkle with the scallions and cilantro. Serve immediately.

➤ Soy Deglaze
2-1/2 tablespoons rice-wine vinegar
1 tablespoon mushroom soy sauce
1/4 cup light Japanese soy sauce

1/2 tablespoon sugar
1 teaspoon fermented Chinese black beans

Combine all ingredients in a small bowl or glass measuring cup.

Wolfgang Puck is Chef/Owner of Spago Beverly Hills and numerous other fine dining and casual restaurants and cafés throughout the United States. He has written several cookbooks, including *Live, Love, Eat!: The Best of Wolfgang Puck* (Random House, 2002) and *Adventures in the Kitchen* (Random House, 1991).

Black Sea Bass Veracruz

Serves 4

Veracruz is where the Spanish first landed in the sixteenth century. The Spanish brought their Mediterranean ingredients to the coastal area and influenced the cuisine common to Veracruz today. A Sauvignon Blanc or Pinot Gris would be lovely with Sea Bass Veracruz, or any dry white wine with a hint of fruit.

2 pounds black sea bass fillets
    (or any perchlike fish), skin on
2 tablespoons canola oil
1 jalapeño pepper, sliced
4 cloves garlic, chopped
1 small leek, trimmed, washed, and sliced

1/2 cup pimiento-stuffed olives
1/4 cup capers
2 fresh bay leaves
1/2 teaspoon freshly ground black pepper
1/4 cup dry white wine
1 large plum tomato, julienned

Preheat the oven to 350°F. Heat the oil in a large skillet over medium-high heat until it shimmers. Brown the fish skin-side up until golden, about 5 minutes. Remove and place fish skin-side down on a baking sheet. Top the fish with the jalapeños. Place in oven and cook for 10 minutes or until the fish barely flakes. While the fish is in the oven, use the oil remaining in the skillet to sauté the garlic until golden. Add the leek, olives, capers, bay leaves, pepper, and wine. Stir in the tomato.

To serve, place the fish on warmed dinner plates or a platter. Top with the leek-olive mixture.

Joanne Bondy is Executive Chef/Partner of Ciudad's Restaurant in Dallas, Texas.

Black Sea Bass in Saffron Nage with Chickpea Dumplings and Preserved Lemon

Serves 2

COOK'S STRATEGY: The Preserved Lemon should be prepared three weeks in advance. Start the Saffron Nage and, while it is simmering, assemble the Chickpea Dumplings. The dumplings can be boiled and the fish sautéed at the last minute.

2 black sea bass fillets, 8 ounces each
Salt and freshly ground black pepper
1 tablespoon unsalted butter

✦ Saffron Nage
✦ Chickpea Dumplings
✦ Preserved Lemon

Season the fillets with salt and pepper. Heat the butter over medium heat in a nonstick sauté pan. Cook the fish for 3 to 4 minutes on each side.

To serve, ladle the Saffron Nage into soup plates with the fish fillet in the center. Place the Chickpea Dumplings around the plates and garnish with a few thin strips of Preserved Lemon.

✦ Saffron Nage
1 tablespoon olive oil
1 leek, white part only, julienned
1 small carrot, julienned
1 stalk celery, julienned
1 teaspoon saffron

1 clove garlic, minced
1 bay leaf
1 sprig fresh thyme
2 cups chicken broth or fish stock
Salt and freshly ground black pepper

Heat the oil in a saucepan over medium heat. Sauté the leek, carrot, and celery with the saffron and garlic for 3 minutes. Add the bay leaf, thyme, and stock and simmer for 20 minutes. Season with salt and pepper. Remove the bay leaf and thyme sprig before serving.

✦ Chickpea Dumplings
2-1/2 cups cooked chickpeas
1 tablespoon chopped fresh cilantro
1 teaspoon sesame oil
1 tablespoon sambal oelek
   (Indonesian chile sauce)

Juice of 1 lemon
Salt and freshly ground black pepper
8 wonton skins

In a food processor, combine the chickpeas, cilantro, sesame oil, sambal oelek, and lemon juice; purée until smooth and season with salt and pepper. Spoon some of the mixture onto the center of a wonton skin and fold into a dumpling. Repeat with all the wonton skins. Bring a pot of water to a boil and simmer the dumplings for 3 minutes. Remove dumplings from the water with a slotted spoon and drain excess water.

❧ Preserved Lemon

2 lemons, quartered
1 cup freshly squeezed lemon juice

1/2 cup salt

Combine ingredients in a sterilized glass jar, cover tightly, and let sit at room temperature for 3 weeks.

Paul Kendeffy is Executive Chef/Proprietor of Zola New World Bistro in State College, Pennsylvania.

Yellow Perch

SCIENTIFIC NAME: *Perca flavescens*

OTHER NAMES: Perch, ring perch, striped perch, Jack perch, redfin. (Note that this is not ocean perch, which may be west-coast rockfish or fillets from the eel-like eel pout.)

U.S. DISTRIBUTION: Primarily freshwater—Great Lakes, Mississippi River basin, and Atlantic drainages

SEASON: Frequently caught during spawning runs between February and July

WHAT TO LOOK FOR: Whole fish will be about 1 pound or less and easily recognizable by the yellowish body color with dusky vertical bars.

COLOR, TASTE, AND TEXTURE: Yellow perch has a mild, sweet flavor, relatively fine flake, low fat content, and white flesh when cooked.

COOKING METHODS: Whole fish may be difficult to scale. If purchasing whole fish, fillet and skin the fish before cooking. Perch is excellent panfried, deep fried, broiled, or baked.

Panfried Yellow Perch with Blue-Crab Rémoulade, Roasted-Corn Risotto, and Sautéed Mixed Greens

Serves 4

If you want to prepare the risotto in advance, undercook the rice, spread the risotto on a baking sheet, and place in the refrigerator. When ready to serve, reheat the remaining broth, fold the risotto into the warm liquid, stir, and add Parmesan and a little butter.

COOK'S STRATEGY: Prepare Blue-Crab Rémoulade up to one day in advance. About forty-five minutes before serving, have all ingredients for the fish, Roasted-Corn Risotto, and Sautéed Mixed Greens washed, cut, and lined up. When the risotto is nearly done, quickly sauté the greens and panfry the fish.

8 yellow perch fillets, 4 ounces each,
    skin on
1-1/2 cups panko (Japanese bread crumbs)
1/2 cup yellow cornmeal
Salt and freshly ground black pepper

1/4 cup oil
Chopped mixed herbs, for sprinkling
❧ Blue-Crab Rémoulade
❧ Roasted-Corn Risotto
❧ Sautéed Mixed Greens

Finely grind the panko in a food processor and combine with cornmeal. Season with salt and pepper. Dredge both sides of fillets in panko and cornmeal mixture. Heat the oil in a heavy-bottomed sauté pan or skillet over medium heat. Place the fish skin-side up in the pan. Turn fish over when edges begin to brown. Remove from heat when second side is done, about 2 minutes per side.

Place a nice mound of Roasted-Corn Risotto in the center of each plate, being careful to keep it in a circle, then gently pile the Sautéed Mixed Greens on top, careful to keep them centered and fresh looking; do not pack down. Then place the 2 fillets leaning up against the rice and greens toward the front of the plate to form an inverted V. Take a spoonful of Blue-Crab Rémoulade and place a dollop on top of the fish at the point where the fillets meet. Sprinkle a bit of leftover herbs around the plate to garnish.

❧ Blue-Crab Rémoulade

1 tablespoon olive oil
1/4 cup each diced onion, red bell pepper,
    green bell pepper, yellow bell pepper
    (1/4-inch dice)
1/2 teaspoon Old Bay seasoning
1/4 pound lump blue crabmeat
2 tablespoons sweet pickle relish
1/2 tablespoon capers, rinsed and chopped

1 teaspoon shallot, minced
1 tablespoon minced Italian flat-leaf parsley
1/4 cup mayonnaise
1/2 teaspoon Dijon mustard
4 dashes Tabasco
Kosher salt and freshly ground
    black pepper

Heat the oil in a sauté pan over medium heat. Cook the onion until translucent. Add the diced bell peppers and the Old Bay; cook until aromatic. Lightly toss in the crabmeat but do not cook further; remove from the heat and set aside. In a small bowl, combine all the remaining ingredients and mix until incorporated. Fold in the crab mixture and chill.

✦ Roasted-Corn Risotto

2 ears fresh corn	1/4 cup diced red bell pepper
2 tablespoons olive oil	(1/4-inch dice)
1 tablespoon minced scallions (whites only)	A big pinch each minced thyme, rosemary,
1/2 teaspoon minced garlic	and Italian flat-leaf parsley
1 cup Arborio rice	(1 tablespoon total)
1/4 cup white wine	1/4 cup grated Parmesan
2 cups chicken broth	Salt and freshly ground black pepper to taste

Preheat the broiler. Cut the corn kernels off the cobs with a serrated knife. Spread the kernels on a baking sheet with sides and roast under the broiler until lightly browned. Set aside.

Heat the oil in a heavy saucepan over medium heat and cook the scallions and garlic. Add the rice and cook, stirring until the grains are translucent. Add the wine and cook until almost no liquid remains. Add the broth 1/2 cup at a time, cooking until liquid has been absorbed before the next addition. After the last addition, stir in the corn, diced pepper, herbs, and Parmesan. Taste and adjust the seasoning. The rice should be al dente when finished.

✦ Sautéed Mixed Greens

2 tablespoons olive oil	1 teaspoon garlic, minced
2 cups baby spinach leaves, washed	1/4 cup chicken broth
2 cups chopped Swiss chard, washed	Salt and freshly ground black pepper
2 cups mustard greens, stemmed, washed, and chopped	

Heat the oil in a sauté pan over high heat, quickly add the greens and garlic while mixing at the same time. Add the broth and salt and pepper to taste. Remove from the heat once the greens have wilted. Prepare at the last moment before serving.

Dandi Bockius is Executive Chef of Mitchell's Fish Market in Homestead, Pennsylvania.

Amberjack and Pompano

AMBERJACK AND POMPANO ARE TWO OF THE OCEAN'S culinary treasures. Florida pompano, considered the "filet mignon of the sea," is renowned for its succulent, fine-textured, creamy flesh. And the rich, buttery yellowtail amberjack is one of the highest-priced items on sushi menus around the world.

Pompano are thin fish that may reach 2 feet in length and weigh at most about 8 pounds. In the United States, Florida pompano live in coastal areas and bays from Massachusetts to the Gulf of Mexico. They may enter surf zones along beaches throughout their range, making them popular with recreational fishers casting baited hooks directly at pompano schools visible in the waves. By contrast, the large greater amberjack, which is commercially and recreationally the most important U.S. amberjack species, can reach approximately 6 feet and 180 pounds while cruising in shallow to very deep waters from Canada to the Gulf of Mexico. Called "AJ" by sport fishermen, its feistiness on the line inspires some of the best fish stories; hooking a greater amberjack has been likened to snaring a train. Red muscle, which helps power the amberjack's antics, lends an assertive flavor that some like best when smoked. But the firm flesh is also delicious fried or grilled.

Smaller amberjacks with much less commercial significance in the United

Florida pompano *(top),* greater amberjack *(bottom and right)*

In the Wild

Amberjacks are often loners. But sport fishers have discovered that amberjacks like to follow the pack when it comes to feeding; they will chase a hooked fellow amberjack or swarm with other amberjacks interested in bait. Greater amberjack have two stripes, one amber and a dark one through the eye; the dark one curiously lights up while in feeding mode.

States include the almaco jack, which lives only in the Atlantic, and lesser amberjack, which is distributed around the globe, including off the east and west coasts of the United States. The largest of the U.S. amberjacks is the yellowtail amberjack, from the Pacific coast, which may exceed 8 feet and 200 pounds. The yellowtail amberjack is usually sold as "yellowtail" or as "hamachi," the Japanese name for a western Pacific amberjack. In the United States, the pricey yellowtail or hamachi sold in sushi bars may be U.S.-caught yellowtail amberjack or Japanese cultivated amberjack known as buri. Greater amberjack, sushi-grade yellowtail amberjack, and Florida pompano are available through various U.S. seafood retail markets. Greater amberjack is also available frozen as individual, vacuum-packaged fillets.

In addition to their appeal to sport fishers, amberjacks and pompano support an important commercial fishing industry, and U.S. landings have been relatively stable. The management plan for greater amberjack includes seasonal restrictions to protect spawning fish, and Florida has banned the use of gill nets, which are extremely effective in catching pompano. No U.S. fish-farming operations exist for pompano or amberjack, but there is potential for both.

Smoked Pompano Bourgeois

Serves 4

This presentation also works well with smoked Alaska salmon.

COOK'S STRATEGY: Keep in mind that brining the fish takes eighteen to twenty-four hours and the smoking takes about twelve hours, so you will want to begin two to three days in advance.

✣ Smoked Pompano
    (16 thin slices)
1/2 cup sour cream
8 thin slices bread, crusts
    removed, toasted,
    cut on the diagonal into
    16 toast points
2 hard-cooked eggs, whites
    and yolks separated
    and finely chopped

1 red onion, finely chopped
1/4 cup capers
Finely chopped parsley
    for garnish
Fresh sprigs of dill for
    garnish

Roll 4 slices of Smoked Pompano and arrange in an X shape in the center of each of 4 chilled dinner plates. Place a dollop of sour cream where the 4 rolls meet. Place chopped egg whites and yolks, onion, and capers in the spaces between the fish and position 2 toast points at the outer edge of each space. Garnish with parsley and dill.

Amberjack and Pompano

Greater Amberjack, Yellowtail Amberjack, Florida Pompano

SCIENTIFIC NAMES: *Seriola dumerili* (greater amberjack), *S. lalandi* (yellowtail amberjack), *Trachinotus carolinus* (pompano)

OTHER NAMES: Greater amberjack is also called AJ or yellowtail, and yellowtail amberjack is called yellowtail, great amberjack, or hamachi. Pompano is also known as butterfish or sunfish.

U.S. DISTRIBUTION: Greater amberjack and pompano—east and Gulf coasts; yellowtail amberjack—west coast

SEASON: Greater amberjack are taken in the summer off the Carolinas, during the winter in the Gulf. Yellowtail are caught year-round but more commonly in the summer. Pompano is available year-round but is less expensive in spring and summer.

WHAT TO LOOK FOR: Pompano have a metallic, silvery sheen. The fish should be fresh smelling and look almost lively. Whole fish usually weigh between 1 and 2 pounds. Pompano are sold as whole fish and fillets. The tiny scales are best removed by the fish seller. Amberjacks (average size about 12 pounds) are sold as skin-on or skinless fillets. Yellowtail is also available as sashimi- or sushi-grade fillets.

COLOR, TASTE, AND TEXTURE: Pompano has a sweet, mild flavor that's buttery and distinctive. Amberjack has pinkish, firm flesh with a somewhat stronger flavor. The texture of both is dense with a fine flake.

COOKING METHODS: Pompano and amberjack are ideal on the grill. Keep the skin on when grilling. The fish are also excellent smoked, sautéed, seared, or roasted. Yellowtail (hamachi) is magnificent as sushi or sashimi or in ceviche.

TIP: Amberjack contains red and white muscle, and the red can have a strong flavor. Some chefs recommend removing the red muscle from fillets before cooking.

(Continued)

✦ Smoked Pompano

3 whole pompano

1-1/2 pounds kosher salt

2 tablespoons cracked
    black pepper

2 tablespoons sodium nitrate
    (available at Asian markets)

1 teaspoon ground cloves

1 pound (2 cups) light
    brown sugar

1 bay leaf

1 teaspoon granulated garlic

Special Equipment: Smoker

Fillet the fish, leaving the skin on. Clean off any entrails or blood. Thoroughly mix the remaining ingredients (reserving 1 tablespoon of brown sugar) to make a dry brine. In a dish large enough to hold the fillets without overlapping, spread enough of the dry mixture to cover the bottom. Lay the fish over the dry mix. Pour more dry mix over to cover all surfaces of the fillets. Cover the dish well with plastic wrap. Place weights on top of the fish—a board or platter and canned goods work well. The weight must press directly on the fish, not rest on the edge of the dish. Refrigerate for 18 to 24 hours, checking after 12 hours. Pat the fillets dry with paper towels. Add more dry mix if necessary.

Smoking the fish takes 10 to 12 hours. It will be necessary to add charcoal and hickory at least midway through the cooking if not sooner. Amounts and timing will depend on the capacity of the individual smoker. Consult the manufacturer's booklet.

Place hickory chips in a container with water to cover. Set aside for 1 hour. Start the smoker. Place the water pan in position in the bottom of the smoker. Fill with water. Position the fire pan over the water pan, fill with charcoal, and ignite. Burn until the charcoal is uniformly covered with gray ash. Remove enough hickory chips from the water to fill a clean metal coffee can. Set on the charcoal. When the chips start to smoke, approximately 8 to 10 minutes, cover the can with foil. Poke holes in the foil about 1/2 inch apart around the rim and in the center. Spoon 1 tablespoon of light brown sugar onto the foil. Place the grill rack in its highest position over the fire pan and place the fish, skin-side down, on the grill. Close the lid. Check regularly. Add water, charcoal, and hickory chips as necessary.

Tommy DiGiovanni is Executive Chef of Arnaud's Restaurant in New Orleans, Louisiana.

Hamachi Sashimi with Avocado, Cucumber, and Crabmeat in a Wasabi-Soy Vinaigrette

Serves 4

6 to 8 ounces yellowtail amberjack
(hamachi) fillet, sashimi quality
8 ounces blue-crab meat, picked free of shells
2 tablespoons wasabi powder
Soy sauce
2 avocados

1/2 cucumber, peeled, seeded,
and julienned
1 scallion, thinly sliced
1 tablespoon toasted sesame seeds
Gari (pickled ginger), optional

Special Equipment: Bamboo mat for rolling sushi

Make a paste of the wasabi and a little water and set aside for 10 minutes until the flavor is strengthened. Add some soy sauce to smooth out the paste, and add enough water to dull the salt in the soy sauce, tasting as you go. Slice the fish into very thin slices on the bias. Set aside and keep cold. Line the sushi roller with plastic wrap. Slice the avocados very thin and fan out on the roller. Lay the crabmeat and cucumber evenly over the avocado. Roll the mat and squeeze. Unroll and remove the avocado roll from the mat. Lay the hamachi slices over the entire roll. Slice the roll into 4 to 8 pieces.

Place pieces of Hamachi Sashimi on a plate. Garnish with the scallion and sesame seeds. Serve gari (if desired) and wasabi sauce on the plate.

Jeremy Marshall is Executive Chef of Aquagrill in New York City.

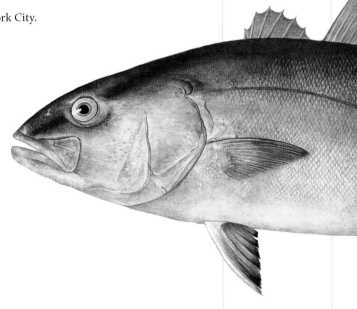

Wood-Grilled Louisiana Pompano with Mango Slaw

Serves 4

Pompano is a great Louisiana fish, full flavored with a firm meaty texture. It particularly lends itself to wood grilling and needs only a little salt and pepper to bring out the flavor. The mango slaw is a fresh counterpoint to the richness of the fish.

2 whole fresh pompano, 2 to 2-1/2 pounds each, filleted but not skinned

2 tablespoons olive oil

Sea salt and freshly ground black pepper

1 lime, cut into wedges

❧ Mango Slaw

Prepare a hot charcoal fire or a gas grill with wood chips. Have all other items for the meal prepared so that the fish can be served directly from the grill. Lightly brush the fillets with olive oil and season liberally with salt and pepper. Place the fish on a hot, clean, lightly oiled grill rack fairly close to the coals. Cook for about 3 to 4 minutes on each side, until medium-well done.

Serve the Grilled Pompano with the Mango Slaw and lime wedges.

❧ Mango Slaw

2 ripe mangoes

1/2 ripe cantaloupe

1/2 ripe honeydew melon

1 cup seasoned rice vinegar

1/4 cup honey

2 tablespoons chopped fresh cilantro

2 tablespoons chopped fresh mint

1/2 teaspoon chile paste with garlic

Peel the mangoes and melons and slice into thin julienne strips. Combine the rice vinegar and honey; stir in fresh herbs and chile paste. Toss all the ingredients in a large bowl until mixed; refrigerate.

Tenney Flynn is Chef/Partner of GW Fins in New Orleans, Louisiana.

Fillet of Florida Pompano with Wild Mushroom Risotto

4 skinless pompano fillets, 6 ounces each
1 tablespoon olive oil

8 cooked asparagus spears, optional
❧ Wild Mushroom Risotto

Preheat the oven to 400°F. Heat the oil in an ovenproof sauté pan over medium-high heat. Sear the pompano fillets on both sides until golden brown. Transfer the pan to the oven and roast the fish for about 8 minutes longer.

Place a couple of spoonfuls of Wild Mushroom Risotto in the center of each plate. Lay the pompano on top. Garnish with asparagus spears if you like.

❧ Wild Mushroom Risotto

1/4 cup olive oil
1/4 cup minced onion
1 shallot, minced
1-1/2 cups mixed fresh wild
    mushrooms, sliced
1 cup Arborio rice

1 cup red wine
2 bay leaves
Salt and freshly ground black pepper
3-3/4 cups chicken broth
1/2 cup grated Manchego cheese
1/2 stick (4 tablespoons) unsalted butter

Heat the olive oil in a heavy-bottomed saucepan over medium heat. Add the onion and shallot and cook until translucent. Add the mushrooms and sauté until they wilt. Stir in the rice and sauté until the edges become translucent. Add the wine and bay leaves; cook until the rice absorbs the wine. Season with salt and pepper at this stage. Add the chicken broth in 6 stages (1/2 to 2/3 cup at a time), stirring often and letting the rice absorb the liquid after each addition. After all the liquid has been added, stir in the cheese followed by the butter. Taste and adjust seasoning. Serve immediately.

Anthony Sindaco is Chef/Owner of Sunfish Grill in Pompano Beach, Florida.

Bluefish and Mullet

COOKS LOOKING TO DIVERSIFY THEIR SEAFOOD selections definitely should consider the tasty bluefish and mullet. Although not closely related and with somewhat different culinary characteristics, bluefish and mullet are presented together here because their slightly oily or fatty flesh is frequently available smoked. Indeed, A. D. Livingston's avocado with smoked mullet is elegant enough to tempt any home chef to try the lowly mullet; and several other chefs jumped at the chance to help us promote the under-utilized bluefish, which when served fresh is full of bold flavor and omega-3 fatty acids. But you don't have to tell the kids it's so good for them; they'll like Todd English's take on bluefish just for the crunchy cornflake crust and side of creamy corn.

Bluefish live in subtropical areas of all oceans except the eastern Pacific. Off the United States, they can occur from Maine to Texas, but they are not always present in any given location because they migrate south seasonally to spawn. Schools of migrating bluefish can span tens of square miles and engage in spectacular feeding frenzies. Bluefish have rows of razor sharp teeth and during a frenzy may snap at any creature—even a person—that gets in the way.

Bluefish *(top and bottom)* and mullet *(center)*

In the Wild

Mullet are known for their habit of leaping out of the water. Why do they jump? Apparently to avoid predators and also to fill a special internal pocket with air. Fish normally obtain oxygen from the surrounding water, but where oxygen is scarce, such as among the bottom sediments where mullet feed, obtaining enough can be difficult. The air the mullet takes in while jumping is believed to give the fish enough oxygen for about five minutes of bottom feeding.

Striped mullet live in tropical and subtropical areas of all oceans, including off the United States from Cape Cod to the Gulf of Mexico and the coast of California. Adults migrate offshore in schools to spawn, and the young move inshore, sometimes far up into tidal creeks. Although the flesh of mullet is also delicious, the species is fished heavily for the roe. In the United States, mullet roe is traditionally fried or broiled. In Japan and Italy, dried mullet roe is considered a delicacy, usually served shaved thin as an appetizer or grated over pasta.

Known for their fighting ability, bluefish have long been popular with sport fishers and more recently have become a choice pursuit in saltwater fly fishing. In fact, in the Chesapeake Bay, five or six times as many fish are landed by recreational fishers as are commercially caught. Because of heavy fishing pressure on the species throughout its U.S. range, both the recreational and commercial fishing of bluefish are regulated. Although catches of bluefish have dropped considerably in the Chesapeake Bay in recent years, the bay accounts for only 20 percent of the commercial catch; total U.S. landings of bluefish have remained around 8 to 10 million pounds a year over the past decade, down only slightly from peak catches in the 1980s. In April 2003, NOAA Fisheries reported to Congress that bluefish are not being overfished. Likewise, landings of striped mullet remain high—about 20 million pounds each year. The 1995 ban on gill nets in Florida waters is credited with annually protecting a large portion of the spawning mullet stock. The potential for farming striped mullet for the flesh and roe is being evaluated in Mississippi and South Carolina.

Pan-Seared Bluefish with Porcini-Mushroom and Lobster-Cream Sauce

Serves 2

A local favorite on the east coast, bluefish can range from mild to heavy oil content. To ensure that the fish is not too oily, buy only the freshest fish available.

2 bluefish fillets, 6 ounces each, skin on and scaled

2 ounces (1/2 cup) cooked lobster meat, diced

3 tablespoons olive oil

1/3 cup chopped shallots

4 ounces fresh porcini mushrooms, sliced (or 2 ounces dried, rehydrated)

1 teaspoon chopped fresh oregano, plus whole sprigs for garnish

1/4 cup Chardonnay

1 cup heavy cream

Salt and freshly ground black pepper

2 tablespoons all-purpose flour

In a medium sauté pan heat 1-1/2 tablespoons of the oil. Add the shallots and cook until translucent. Add the porcini and lobster meat. Cook for about 4 minutes, and then add the chopped oregano and Chardonnay. Simmer until the pan is almost dry, then add the cream and let simmer until reduced by half. Season with salt and pepper. Set aside and keep warm.

In another sauté pan, heat the remaining 1-1/2 tablespoons oil over medium-high heat. Season the fish fillets with salt and pepper and lightly coat with the flour. Place the fillets flesh-side down in the hot pan and cook for about 3 to 4 minutes. Turn the fish over and finish cooking for another 4 minutes or until done.

Place the fish on 2 dinner plates and cover with sauce. Garnish with fresh oregano sprigs. Serve immediately.

Rob Klink is Executive Chef of Oceanaire Seafood Room in Washington, D.C.

Bluefish

SCIENTIFIC NAME: *Pomatomus saltatrix*

OTHER NAMES: Choppers, snappers, tailors

U.S. DISTRIBUTION: East and Gulf coasts

WHAT TO LOOK FOR: If you haven't caught the fish yourself, buy it locally and when it's plentiful. Bluefish is available as whole fish under 5 pounds and as steaks or skin-on fillets. Whole fish should glisten, and fillets should have no off odors. Highly perishable, bluefish must be iced when you buy it and kept on ice until it's cooked.

COLOR, TASTE, AND TEXTURE: The soft, tender, bluish flesh is assertive and rich but not overpowering. Small bluefish—1 to 3 pounds—taste sweeter than larger fish.

COOKING METHODS: Best when grilled, roasted, broiled, or seared; also excellent in chowders or smoked. Bluefish's high oil content calls for an acidic counterpoint such as lemon or lime juice or garden-fresh tomatoes. Its full-bodied flavor works well with bold seasonings. Bluefish skin is edible.

TIP: Most cooks remove the line of dark flesh that runs down the center of large fillets. Use a sharp knife to make a v-shaped cut on either side of the line and remove the flesh along with any pin bones.

Savory Summer Fish Chowder

Serves 10 to 12 as a first course, 6 as a main course

As a cook, I love bluefish and striped bass for their rich deep flavor, luscious texture, and versatility. They can be grilled, broiled, roasted, or panfried and are excellent in stews and chowders. I created this recipe especially for bluefish and striped bass. The chowder bursts with the flavors of summer: fresh, wild fish paired with sweet corn, ripe tomato, fresh basil, and a little bite of hot chile. My recipe ignores the tomato-versus-cream debate and incorporates both, a practice that comes from Connecticut and parts of southern Massachusetts and Rhode Island. I use only fresh tomatoes for this chowder, because my goal is not to make a "red" chowder but to produce a creamy fish-and-corn chowder with tomatoes as an accent.

2 pounds bluefish or striped bass fillets, skinless, boneless, trimmed of all dark meat and cut into chunks (The dark meat [bloodline] of bluefish and rockfish must be removed and discarded, so be sure to buy extra to allow for trim. To yield 2 pounds of usable fish, buy about 2-1/2 pounds fillets or a 5-to-6-pound whole fish.)

3 ears sweet corn

4 ounces slab (unsliced) smoked bacon, rind removed, diced small (3/8 inch)

1/2 stick (4 tablespoons) unsalted butter

3 cloves garlic, finely chopped (1 tablespoon)

1 large jalapeño chile, seeded and minced

1 large onion, chopped

2 medium celery stalks, finely chopped

1-1/2 pounds Yukon Gold, Maine, P.E.I., or other all-purpose potatoes, peeled and sliced 3/8-inch thick

4 cups fish stock, chicken broth, or water (You can use the head and frame from a bluefish or striped bass to make strong fish stock especially for this recipe. If you do, add the corn cobs as well. This creates a perfect stock for this chowder—but not for anything else.)

1 pound vine-ripened red tomatoes, peeled, seeded, and diced

Kosher or sea salt and freshly ground black pepper

1-1/2 cups heavy cream (optional) or additional fish stock

4 sprigs fresh basil, leaves chopped (1/4 cup)

Husk the corn. Carefully remove most of the silk by hand and then rub the ears with a towel to finish the job. Cut the kernels from the cobs with a serrated knife. There should be about 2 cups. Reserve.

Heat a 4- or 6-quart heavy-bottomed soup or sauce pot over low heat and add the bacon. Once it has rendered a few tablespoons of fat, increase the heat to medium and cook the bacon until crisp and golden brown. Pour off all but 1 tablespoon of the bacon fat. Leave the bacon in the pan.

Add the butter and garlic to the pan. Cook for 30 seconds then add the jalapeño, onion, and celery. Sauté for about 5 minutes over medium heat, stirring occasionally with a wooden spoon, until the onion and celery are softened but not browned. Add the corn kernels, potatoes, and stock. If the stock doesn't cover the potatoes, add water to cover. Turn up the heat and bring to a boil, cover, and cook the potatoes vigorously for about 10 minutes, until they are firm in the center and soft on the outside. If the stock hasn't thickened lightly, smash a few of the potato slices against the side of the pot and cook for a minute or two longer to release their starch. Add the tomatoes, and reduce the heat to low. Season the mixture assertively with salt and pepper, as very little stirring will occur from this point on.

Add the fish. Leave on the heat for 5 minutes, then remove the pot from the heat and let sit another 10 minutes: The cooking of the fish will be completed during this time. Gently stir in the cream and basil. Taste for salt and pepper. If you are not serving the chowder within the hour, let it cool a bit, then refrigerate. Cover the chowder after it has chilled completely. Otherwise, let it sit for up to 1 hour to allow the flavors to meld.

When ready to serve, reheat the chowder over low heat but don't let it boil. Use a slotted spoon to mound the chunks of fish, onion, and potato, as well as the colorful bits of corn and tomato, in the center of large soup plates or shallow bowls and ladle the creamy broth around.

Jasper White is Chef/Owner of Summer Shack in Boston and Cambridge, Massachusetts, and Mohegan Sun, Connecticut. This recipe is adapted from his cookbook *50 Chowders* (Simon and Schuster, 2000).

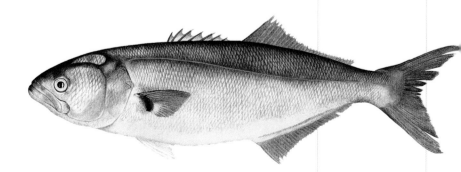

Grilled Whole Bluefish with Lime-Coriander Vinaigrette

Serves 8

During the warm-weather months, I spend most of my free time in a small coastal town on Buzzard's Bay in southeastern Massachusetts. In my 18-foot outboard, I cruise the waters in this area in search of striped bass, bluefish, scup, and the occasional small tuna or bonito. In the rivers, we hunt for blue crabs and dig hard-shell clams. All of this adds up to lots of good eating. Perhaps the best species for sport fishing and eating is the feisty bluefish. They are delicious when caught and eaten in the same day, cooked simply over a hardwood fire. The flesh of the bluefish is rich and full of flavor, reminiscent of mackerel. The flavor and texture stand up well to strong seasonings such as spices, fresh herbs, and citrus. The following recipe accentuates the best qualities of this wonderful fish. I recommend grilling the bluefish whole, but grilled fillets work well too. As with beef steaks, grilling or roasting fish with the bones intact gives more flavor and moisture to the flesh.

1 medium bluefish, about 3 to 4 pounds
    (scaled and gutted but with head
    intact, or filleted if desired)
1 tablespoon olive oil for the fish, plus
    a little extra for the grill

Kosher salt and freshly ground
    black pepper
➹ Lime-Coriander Vinaigrette

In a kettle grill using traditional all-natural lump charcoal, build a medium fire on 1 side. Place the grill over the fire when it is hot, and brush it vigorously with a wire brush to clean it. Quickly wipe off the grill with a wadded-up paper towel.

Rub the fish on both sides with the olive oil. Sprinkle lightly with salt and a little pepper.

Just before putting the fish on the grill, brush the grill with a little olive oil. Place the bluefish on the grill parallel to the edge of the fire, but not over it, the dorsal fin toward the fire. Allow the fish to roast for about 7 to 8 minutes on the first side, being careful to move it if flare-ups occur. When the skin is crispy and slightly blistered from the heat, roll the fish over and turn it so that the dorsal fin is still facing towards the fire, but be sure that the fish is not directly over the fire. Important: If the skin sticks to the grill when you try to pry it loose with your tongs and spatula, just wait another minute and try again—it will release itself when ready.

When you have turned the fish, put on the lid and set the vents to the open position so that air continues to feed the fire. With the lid on and the fish next to, but not over, the fire, the fish will roast through as it grills, resulting in a moist flesh that is flavored with the wood smoke. The second side will take about another 7 to 8 minutes to fully cook the fish. When the flesh is ready to come free from the backbone with the tip of a knife, carefully remove the fish from the grill and transfer it to a serving platter.

At the table, peel away the crispy skin and remove the dark line of meat that runs down the side of each fillet. Serve each guest a portion of the fish and drizzle the chunky Lime-Coriander Vinaigrette over the top.

❧ Lime-Coriander Vinaigrette

1/4 cup freshly squeezed lime juice
2 shallots, sliced
1 tablespoon minced fresh ginger
2 teaspoons crushed fresh coriander berries
   (or 1 tablespoon toasted and
   ground dried coriander seeds)

1/2 teaspoon dried hot red pepper flakes
1 tablespoon fish sauce
1 tablespoon chopped fresh cilantro
1 tablespoon chopped fresh mint
3/4 cup canola oil
Kosher salt

In a mixing bowl, stir together all of the vinaigrette ingredients. Double check the seasoning. Set aside until ready to use.

Steve Johnson is Chef/Owner of The Blue Room in Cambridge, Massachusetts.

Corn Flake–Crusted Bluefish with Creamy Corn

Serves 2

This is my twist on the classic bluefish recipe that New England locals have been using for a long time. Bluefish is a fish that has been frowned upon and rarely seen on menus, but if cooked correctly, using the freshest possible fish, it can be an interesting and tasty fish to eat. Bluefish are fun to catch, and with their sharp teeth and vicious behavior, it is no wonder that they are known as the "piranhas of the North Atlantic."

2 bluefish fillets, 8 ounces each
Salt and freshly ground black pepper
2 tablespoons olive oil
2 tablespoons Miracle Whip

2 tablespoons Dijon mustard
1 cup corn flakes
Salt and freshly ground black pepper
❧ Creamy Corn

Preheat the oven to 375°F. Season the fish with salt and pepper. Heat an ovenproof sauté pan over medium heat, add the oil, and sauté the fish flesh-side down for 2 minutes. Turn the fish over and transfer the pan to the oven. Bake the fish for 5 to 8 minutes, depending on thickness, until cooked through. Mix the Miracle Whip and mustard together and smother the fish with it. Evenly distribute the corn flakes over the fish and bake for 1 more minute, being careful the flakes do not burn.

To serve, spoon the hot Creamy Corn onto 2 dinner plates. Set the bluefish on top.

❧ Creamy Corn

1 tablespoon olive oil
1/2 onion, diced
1 cup corn kernels, fresh or frozen
1 teaspoon fresh thyme, chopped

2 cups heavy cream
1 tablespoon butter
Salt and freshly ground black pepper

Heat the oil in a sauté pan over medium-high heat and cook the onion for about 2 minutes. Add the corn and thyme and cook for 2 more minutes. Add the cream and simmer until the cream is thick and the liquid has reduced to about 1 cup. Finish with the butter and salt and pepper. Serve hot.

Todd English is the Chef/Restaurateur behind the Olives restaurants in Boston, New York City, Washington, Aspen, and Las Vegas, as well as Figs, Bonfire, Tuscany, and Kingfish Hall restaurants in Boston, New York, and Mohegan Sun, Connecticut. He is the author of *The Olives Table* (Simon and Schuster, 1997), *The Figs Table* (Simon and Schuster, 1998), and *The Olives Dessert Table* (Simon and Schuster, 2000).

Baker's-Style Bluefish and Potatoes

Serves 6

Poor old cheap bluefish—it's definitely not at the top of the gourmet fish hierarchy. I try to put it on my special menu a few times a year, without much response. It is such a misunderstood yet abundant and delicious fish. The recipe below is about 28 years old. I used to make it for friends when I was living and working in Provincetown, Massachusetts. The fish was so fresh and cheap that we could feed friends for pennies. It also is a one-dish meal that doesn't create lots of fish odor in your kitchen.

The original recipe can be modified by adding corn kernels, fennel, or celery root. If tomatoes are in season, sliced or chopped ripe tomatoes go well with this dish. In the spring, boned shad fillets make a delicious substitute for bluefish.

6 bluefish fillets, 6 to 7 ounces each,
    skin on and scaled
9 medium Yukon Gold potatoes, peeled
3 tablespoons butter
2 cloves garlic, sliced
4 fresh thyme sprigs, leaves picked
Sea salt and freshly ground black pepper

3 medium white onions
1 lemon
1 quart hot fish stock, chicken broth,
    or water
1 cup bread crumbs, optional
1/2 cup coarsely chopped Italian
    flat-leaf parsley

Preheat the oven to 400°F. Cut the potatoes into 1/4-inch slices. Melt 2 tablespoons of the butter and combine with the potatoes, garlic, thyme, and a sprinkle of salt and pepper. Set aside.

Cut the onions in half, then into thin slices. Heat the remaining 1 tablespoon butter in a small sauté pan over high heat. Add the onions and cook quickly to wilt. Season with salt and pepper. Slice the lemon into 1/4-inch slices and remove the seeds with the tip of your knife. In a 10-inch baking dish, place half of the potatoes in an even layer and top with half of the onions and lemon slices. Arrange the bluefish fillets skin-side down on the potatoes. Sprinkle with salt and pepper. Repeat the layers, covering first with the remaining onions and lemon slices, then with the remaining potatoes. Add the heated stock or water. Cover with foil.

Place the fish in the oven and bake for 25 minutes. Remove the foil. Sprinkle with the bread crumbs, if desired, and return to the oven. Bake another 15 minutes to brown the top.

Serve 1 bluefish fillet per person with the luscious potatoes and onions, including the lemon slices. Top with a good amount of parsley.

Carole Peck is Executive Chef of Good News Café in Woodbury, Connecticut.

CHEF A. D. LIVINGSTON

Avocado Stuffed with Smoked Mullet

Serves 4 as a light lunch or salad

The best avocados I have ever eaten came from a large tree near Tampa Bay in Florida. This area is also noted for its smoked mullet, but I confess that I didn't connect the two until I ran across a bell-ringing recipe from Ghana. In Florida smoked mullet can be purchased in many coastal fish markets and raw bars, or you can purchase market mullet and smoke your own (as follows).

To prepare fresh mullet for smoking, it should first be butterflied. To do this, remove the head and run a sharp knife along the top from shoulder to tail, being careful not to cut through the belly skin. Clean out the innards and open the fish out flat, using the belly skin as a hinge. The butterflied fish is smoked unscaled and skin-side down. For this recipe, fresh mullet can be treated with brine and cold smoked, but in Florida it is usually much more practical to hot smoke them. Most outdoor charcoal-burning grills with a cover can be used. Simply put the fish, skin-side down, on one side of the grill and the fire on the other, along with a few wood chips for smoke (any good hardwood will do just fine). The mullet is a fatty fish and needs no marinade or baste, although recipes for both abound. (The hot-smoked mullet served at the Boggy Bayou Mullet Festival in Niceville, Florida, is basted with a mixture of butter, lemon juice, and Worcestershire sauce.) I like to sprinkle the flesh with a little salt and Tabasco. The fish is done when the meat flakes off the skin, but remember that a low heat and a longer cooking time will increase the exposure to smoke. Special electrically heated smokers can also be used, following the manufacturer's instructions.

If you purchase whole fresh mullet during the fall of the year, or if you catch your own with a cast net, you may have roe fish fat with yellow roe (female roe, also called hard roe) or white roe (milt from males, also called soft roe), neither of which should be cut into with a knife. Both types of roe are delicious. The yellow roe from Mediterranean gray mullet has long been dried and sold at outrageous prices in gourmet markets—$268 per kilo the last time I checked. I dry my own mullet roe for practically nothing, using only a little salt to help draw out the moisture. Dried roe may be an acquired taste, but I am addicted to the stuff. The yellow roe can also be used in recipes that call for shad roe. And white roe is Florida's best-kept culinary secret. Simply dust it with flour and fry it.

An even stranger lagniappe among the mullet innards is the gizzard. This organ is a stomach made of rather tough white muscle that enables the fish to digest plant material. It is usually dressed pretty much like a chicken gizzard and fried along with the rest of the fish.

1-1/2 cups flaked smoked mullet or
    4 whole fresh mullet for smoking
4 large hard-cooked eggs
1/4 cup milk
1/2 teaspoon salt

1/4 teaspoon sugar
2 limes
1/4 cup peanut oil
1/4 cup olive oil
2 large, very ripe avocados

To prepare the smoked mullet stuffing for the avocados, separate the egg yolks from the whites. In a bowl, mash the yolks with the milk until you have a paste. Add salt, sugar, and the juice of 1 lime. Stir in the peanut oil a little at a time, then stir in the olive oil. Chop the egg whites and add them to the mixture. Carefully stir in the flaked fish, being careful not to break up the chunks. Refrigerate until you are almost ready to serve.

To serve, cut the avocados in half, peel, and remove the pits. Fill the cavities with the stuffing. Squeeze on a little lime juice and enjoy. In Ghana, this dish is served with strips of red bell pepper or pimiento as a garnish. Fire-roasted bell peppers, both red and green, are great. I also like to sprinkle the stuffing lightly with mild paprika and serve the avocado halves in a leaf of lettuce, along with a lemon or lime wedge for each person. If you have any stuffing left over, use it as a spread for crackers.

A. D. Livingston is the author of *Cold-Smoking and Salt-Curing Meat, Fish, and Game* (The Lyons Press, 1995), from which this recipe was adapted. A. D. lives in Wewahitchka, Florida.

Striped Mullet

SCIENTIFIC NAME: *Mugil cephalus*

OTHER NAMES: Mullet, flathead mullet, grey mullet, black mullet, fatback

U.S. DISTRIBUTION: Cape Cod to the Gulf of Mexico and shallow bays along the California coast

SEASON: Available year-round. The Gulf season culminates in October at the Boggy Bayou Mullet Festival in Niceville, Florida, when several tons of mullet are consumed.

WHAT TO LOOK FOR: Sold as whole fish (about 1 to 4 pounds) or skin-on fillets; the roe may be sold separately. Like bluefish, fresh mullet doesn't travel well, so buy only very fresh fish. Mullet is also available smoked.

COLOR, TASTE, AND TEXTURE: The light-colored flesh is firm, rich, and delicious. Mullet is also a good source of Omega 3 fatty acids.

COOKING METHODS: Fillets are best fried, broiled, roasted, or smoked. Much of the harvested roe is flown to Japan, where it is salted and dried. Gulf Coast Floridians like to fry fresh roe and eat it with scrambled eggs for breakfast.

TIP: Trim the dark strip that runs down the center of the fillet; it can have an earthy flavor.

*i*IF YOU ONLY KNOW TUNA AS THE CENTERPIECE of a tuna-salad sandwich, read on. Whether you like it raw or thoroughly cooked, our contributing chefs suggest dramatic ways to take advantage of the distinctive taste and texture of fresh tuna, as well as mackerel and what may be the most exuberantly named fish in the sea, the wahoo.

The U.S.-caught tuna species included in our seafood species list are

Atlantic mackerel

In the Wild

Why is fresh tuna so red? Because tunas and their relatives have a larger proportion of red muscle than most fish, which is useful in prolonged physical activity. Tunas and their kin are built for swimming, and nearly every aspect of the body is designed to maximize hydrodynamic efficiency. Tuna can travel thousands of miles in several months, and wahoo have been clocked at nearly 50 mph. Most of these fishes can swim far and wide; albacore, yellowfin, skipjack, and bigeye tuna, as well as wahoo, live in tropical and subtropical areas of three oceans—the Atlantic, Pacific, and Indian. Blackfin tuna and Atlantic and Spanish mackerel stay in the Atlantic, but their ranges are broad.

albacore, yellowfin, skipjack, and blackfin, in order of highest to lowest commercial importance. Mackerels include the highly commercial Atlantic (or Boston) mackerel and the Spanish mackerel. Wahoo (the name is actually the way European seafarers often spelled "Oahu," a Hawaiian island where wahoo are found in abundance) and Spanish mackerel are among the mildest-tasting of the tuna family; Atlantic mackerel is among the strongest.

Canned tuna may be albacore, yellowfin, or skipjack, the last two sold as "light" tuna. Yellowfin tuna *(ahi)* has taken the place of bluefin tuna *(maguro)* in many Japanese restaurants in the United States, although yellowfin is often sold as *maguro* at sushi bars. The succulent *toro*, sold at a much higher price in sushi bars, is the richer flesh from the belly of a tuna, traditionally bluefin. When fishing technology for tuna improved in the 1950s and 1960s and Japan began taking an interest in Atlantic bluefin for sashimi in the 1970s, heavy fishing pressure led to dramatic declines in the northwestern Atlantic, and prices of bluefin skyrocketed.

Unlike bluefin tuna, fortunately, albacore, yellowfin, skipjack, and blackfin tunas, Spanish and Atlantic mackerels, and wahoo are abundant. Wahoo are a particularly good seafood choice because they grow and reproduce so quickly that they can rebound from even heavy fishing.

Some fishing methods for tuna are not environmentally sound, however. Longlines and purse seines may be associated with a large bycatch, which for purse seines can include dolphins; when tuna fishermen first realized that tuna sometimes congregate beneath dolphins, they began to follow schools of dolphins, set the purse seine, and haul in the tuna below. Eventually, hundreds of thousands of dolphins were killed each year. The label "dolphin-safe" does not necessarily guarantee that nets weren't set on dolphins; it means that an onboard observer certified that no dolphins were killed or seriously injured during the catch. An ecologically sound alternative is Ecofish's albacore tuna, caught by a troll fishery on the west coast.

Tuna-Sashimi Salad with Matsuhisa Dressing

Serves 4

A favorite with customers since Matsuhisa first opened, Matsuhisa dressing is an appetizing soy sauce–based mixture enhanced by sweet onions and aromatic sesame oil.

7 ounces sushi-grade
   fresh yellowfin tuna fillet
Sea salt and freshly ground
   black pepper
2 ounces assorted salad
   vegetables (e.g., micro greens
   and young bean sprouts)

➤ Matsuhisa Dressing
➤ Udo Curls
Red shiso leaves for garnish,
   optional

Preheat a grill or broiler. Sprinkle a little sea salt and black pepper on the tuna. Briefly sear the tuna until its surface turns white but the center remains red. Plunge the fillet into iced water to stop it from cooking any further, then shake off the excess water.

Pour 5 tablespoons plus 1 teaspoon Matsuhisa Dressing into a serving dish. Arrange the salad vegetables, 15 Udo Curls, and red shiso leaves, if using, in the center of the dish. Cut the tuna into slices (about 1/4-inch thick). Roll each slice into a cylinder and place them in a petal-like pattern with the vegetables in the center.

(Continued)

Tuna

Albacore, Skipjack, and Yellowfin

SCIENTIFIC NAME: *Thunnus alalunga* (albacore), *T. albacares* (yellowfin), *Katsuwonus pelamis* (skipjack)

OTHER NAMES: Albacore is known as *tombo ahi,* skipjack is also called ocean bonito or *aku,* and yellowfin is *ahi.*

U.S. DISTRIBUTION: Atlantic and Pacific Oceans

SEASON: Year-round

WHAT TO LOOK FOR: Fresh tuna fillets should have slightly translucent and iridescent flesh, its color ranging from pale pink to deep red, depending on the species. Skipjack is smaller than the others and is the only one that may be sold whole.

Premium quality tuna is sold as sashimi- or sushi-grade tuna. Albacore tuna should smell clean and fresh; the other tunas have a more assertive aroma.

COLOR, TASTE, AND TEXTURE: The color varies, with albacore having the lightest and skipjack the darkest flesh. Dark-colored tuna blanches to reddish beige when cooked. Tuna's dense, close-grained flesh is appealing and savory without being fishy. The flavor of skipjack tuna is more pronounced than that of yellowfin.

COOKING METHODS: When serving tuna raw as in tuna tartare or ceviche, buy sushi- or sashimi-grade tuna. Meaty tuna is succulent when marinated and grilled or broiled. Like a good piece of beef, it dries out when overcooked. Braising—slow cooking in an aromatic broth—will also prevent tuna from drying out.

✦ Matsuhisa Dressing

3/4 cup finely chopped onion
    (Maui, Vidalia, or other sweet onion)
2 tablespoons plus 2 teaspoons soy sauce
2 tablespoons plus 1 teaspoon rice vinegar
2 teaspoons water
1/2 teaspoon sugar

A pinch of sea salt
1/4 teaspoon powdered mustard
Pinch of freshly ground black pepper
4 teaspoons grapeseed oil
4 teaspoons sesame oil

Combine all ingredients except the oils. When the salt has fully dissolved, add the oils. Makes 1-3/4 cups.

✦ Udo Curls

1 udo (a Japanese vegetable in the
    ginseng family); Japanese radish
    (daikon) may be substituted

Peel the udo in a thin, unbroken strip 1-1/2 inches wide. On a 45° angle, cut the udo into 1/2-inch-wide strips. Wind the strips around a 1/2-inch-diameter rod and place in cold water until curls are formed.

Chef Nobu Matsuhisa is Chef/Owner of Matsuhisa in Beverly Hills, California; Nobu in New York City; and numerous other fine dining establishments throughout the United States, Europe, and Asia. Matsuhisa is also author of *Nobu: The Cookbook* (Kodansha International, 2001), from which he submitted this recipe.

Grilled Tuna Steak with Tomato-Caper Chutney

Serves 4

4 tuna steaks, about 10 ounces each
1/2 cup chopped onion
2 teaspoons chopped fresh ginger
2 teaspoons chopped garlic
2 teaspoons honey
2 teaspoons Dijon mustard

1/2 cup soy sauce
1 cup peanut oil
Very thinly sliced daikon radish
✦ Tomato-Caper Chutney

In a food processor or blender, purée the onion, ginger, and garlic. Add the honey and mustard. Pulse once or twice to blend. Add the soy sauce and oil and pulse to blend. Pour the marinade into a bowl. Add the tuna steaks and set aside to marinate for about 10 minutes.

Preheat a gas or charcoal grill. Shake off excess marinade and grill the tuna for about 4 minutes on each side, depending on the thickness of the steaks.

To serve, garnish the grilled tuna with the daikon slices and warm Tomato-Caper Chutney.

✦ Tomato-Caper Chutney

2 large vine-ripened tomatoes,
    seeded and chopped
1 small cucumber, peeled, seeded,
    and diced
2 tablespoons thinly sliced scallions

2 teaspoons capers, drained and rinsed
1/2 teaspoon minced fresh ginger
1 clove garlic, minced
Pinch freshly ground black pepper

Combine all ingredients in a sauté pan and cook over medium-low heat for about 15 minutes, stirring often.

Timothy McNulty is Chef of The Lobster Pot Restaurant in Provincetown, Massachusetts. He is the author of *The Lobster Pot Cookbook* (LP Products LTD, 1991), from which this recipe is adapted.

Skipjack-Tuna Ceviche and Pepitas on Grilled-Nopales Salad with Botarga Vinaigrette

Serves 4

COOK'S STRATEGY: Prepare the salad first because the nopales need to be chilled after grilling. Then make the vinaigrette and the ceviche, which only needs twenty minutes to marinate.

1/2 pound skipjack tuna, cleaned
    of skin and blood line
Salt and freshly ground black pepper

2 tablespoons pepitas (pumpkin seeds),
    toasted and crushed
➤ Botarga Vinaigrette
➤ Grilled-Nopales Salad

Make sure the tuna is very cold. Dice the tuna into 1/4-inch cubes using a very sharp knife; always make sure all the pieces are the same size. In a stainless-steel or glass bowl, mix the tuna with 1/2 of the Botarga Vinaigrette and salt and pepper. Refrigerate for 20 minutes.

Add another 1/2 cup Botarga Vinaigrette to the chilled ceviche. Adjust the seasonings again. Spoon the Grilled-Nopales Salad onto plates or into martini glasses, top with the ceviche, and garnish with more of the vinaigrette and some crushed pepitas. Serve chilled.

➤ Botarga Vinaigrette

2 tablespoons pepitas, toasted and crushed
1 ounce tuna botarga (dried caviar, or any
    other botarga will do), chopped
1/4 cup freshly squeezed lime juice

3/4 cup extra-virgin olive oil
1/4 cup pumpkinseed oil, preferably Austrian
Salt and freshly ground black pepper

With the blade running, add the pepitas, botarga, and lime juice to the food processor. Add the oils and process until incorporated. Season with salt and pepper.

➤ Grilled-Nopales Salad

2 large nopales (prickly pear cactus leaves),
    cleaned of thorns
1/2 cup plus 1 teaspoon extra-virgin olive oil

Salt and freshly ground black pepper
1/2 cup freshly squeezed lime juice
2 teaspoons coarsely chopped cilantro leaves

Preheat the grill until it is very hot. Submerge the nopales leaves in ice water for 20 minutes, then pat dry and toss with 1/2 cup olive oil and salt and pepper. Place nopales on the grill and cook quickly for about 2 minutes per side. Remove from the grill and chill in the refrigerator until cool. Slice the leaves horizontally into 1/4-inch strips, place in a stainless-steel or glass bowl, and mix in the lime juice and cilantro; set aside.

Guillermo Pernot is Chef/Partner of ¡Pasión! in Philadelphia, Pennsylvania.

Spicy Tuna Tartare with Japanese Flavors

The inspiration for this dish is a combination of my fondness for sushi and the flavors of Japan and Southeast Asia. It consists of raw tuna combined with avocado in a spicy Japanese citrus sauce.

Serves 4 to 6

1 pound sashimi-grade yellowfin tuna

1 to 2 slightly firm avocados

1/3 cup snipped chives

1 ounce orange tobiko (flying-fish caviar, available at Japanese markets), optional

1 ounce green tobiko, optional

1 tablespoon chile oil, optional

Fresh cilantro leaves

Sesame crackers

✦ Spicy Citrus Sauce

With a very sharp knife, dice the tuna into tiny (1/8-inch) cubes. Dice the avocados into tiny cubes as well. In a bowl, combine the tuna, avocados, chives, and 1/4 cup of the Spicy Citrus Sauce. Gently stir the ingredients together, being careful not to crush the avocados.

To serve, mound the tuna tartare mixture in the center of a large plate. Garnish the top with the orange and green tobikos, if you like. Drizzle the chile oil, if using, and some of the remaining Spicy Citrus Sauce around the plate. Place some cilantro leaves around the base of the tartare. Serve with sesame crackers.

✦ Spicy Citrus Sauce

1/3 cup soy sauce

2 tablespoons freshly squeezed lime juice

2 teaspoons freshly squeezed orange juice

2 teaspoons grated fresh ginger

2 teaspoons minced jalapeño, seeds removed

1 teaspoon sesame oil

1 teaspoon grated fresh horseradish

1 teaspoon sugar

1/4 to 1/2 teaspoon togarashi (Japanese red chile powder)

In a large bowl, whisk together all of the ingredients for the sauce. For best results allow the mixture to sit for an hour to combine and enhance the flavors.

Jeffery Powell is Chef de Cuisine at PlumpJack Squaw Valley Inn, Olympic Valley, California.

Thai-Inspired Spicy Tuna Tartare

Serves 4

The raw tuna is here mixed with flying-fish caviar and a wasabi-spiked marinade. The tartare is then topped with taro chips and Thai Dressing.

1 pound sashimi-grade yellowfin tuna,
    diced small
Salt
1 tablespoon sambal oelek
    (Indonesian chile sauce)
1/2 teaspoon wasabi powder or paste
6 tablespoons soy sauce

48 thin cucumber slices
16 thin taro chips
1/4 cup sliced gari (pickled ginger)
1/4 cup sliced scallions
➻ Thai Dressing
6 teaspoons tobiko (flying-fish caviar,
    available at Asian markets), optional

Place tuna in a mixing bowl and season lightly with salt. Combine the sambal oelek, wasabi, and soy sauce; pour over the tuna. Gently mix together.

To serve, fan 12 cucumber slices in a circle on each of 4 plates. Using a ring mold if desired, mound 4 ounces of the Tuna Tartare on each cucumber fan. Place the taro chips upright, dividing the tuna into 4 equal portions. Sprinkle with the gari and scallions. Top with the Thai Dressing. Spoon the tobiko, if using, between the taro chips.

➻ Thai Dressing

3 tablespoons sugar
3 tablespoons wine vinegar
2 teaspoons chopped garlic
1-1/2 tablespoons fish sauce
1-1/2 tablespoons freshly squeezed
    lemon juice

1/2 medium onion, sliced very thinly
1/2 cup diced red bell pepper
1 teaspoon minced jalapeño pepper
Pinch dried hot red pepper flakes
Pinch cayenne pepper
1/4 cup canola oil

Mix all ingredients together in the order given.

Jeremy Marshall is Executive Chef of Aquagrill in New York City.

Classic Ceviche

1 pound fresh albacore tuna loin, cut into
1/2-inch cubes or slightly smaller

1-1/2 cups freshly squeezed lime juice

1 medium white onion, chopped into
1/4-inch pieces

2 medium-large (1 pound total)
vine-ripened tomatoes,
chopped into 1/4-inch pieces

Fresh hot green chiles to taste
(roughly 2 to 3 serranos or 1 to 2
jalapeños), stemmed, seeded,
and finely chopped

1/3 cup chopped fresh cilantro, plus a
few leaves for garnish

1/3 cup chopped pitted green olives
(choose manzanillos for a typical
Mexican flavor)

1 to 2 tablespoons olive oil, preferably
extra-virgin, optional but
recommended to give a
glistening appearance

Salt

3 tablespoons freshly squeezed orange juice
or 1/2 teaspoon sugar

1 large or 2 small ripe avocados,
peeled, pitted, and diced

Tostadas, tortilla chips, or saltine
crackers for serving

Makes about
4-1/2 cups,
enough for 8
as an appetizer,
12 as a nibble

In a 1-1/2-quart glass or stainless-steel bowl, combine the fish, lime juice, and onion. You will need enough juice to cover the fish and allow it to float somewhat freely; too little juice means unevenly cooked fish. Cover and refrigerate for about 4 hours, until a cube of fish no longer looks raw when broken open. Pour into a colander and drain off the lime juice.

In a large bowl, mix together the tomatoes, green chiles, cilantro, olives, and optional olive oil. Stir in the fish, then taste and season with salt, usually about 3/4 teaspoon, and orange juice or sugar (the sweetness of the orange juice or sugar helps balance some of the typical tanginess of the ceviche). Cover and refrigerate if not serving immediately.

Just before serving, stir in the diced avocado, being careful not to break up the pieces. For serving, you have several options: Set out your ceviche in a large bowl and let people spoon it onto individual plates to eat with chips or saltines; serve small bowls of ceviche (I like to lay a bed of frisée lettuce in each bowl before spooning in the ceviche) and serve tostadas, chips, or saltines alongside; or pile the ceviche onto chips or tostadas and pass around for guests to consume on these edible little plates. Whichever direction you choose, garnish the ceviche with cilantro leaves before setting it center stage.

Rick Bayless is Chef/Owner of Frontera Grill and Topolobampo in Chicago, Illinois. He is the author of several books, including *Authentic Mexican* (William Morrow and Co., 1987), *Rick Bayless's Mexican Kitchen* (Charles Scribner's and Sons, 1996), and *Salsas That Cook* (Simon and Schuster, 1998).

Grilled Spanish Mackerel with Apricot-and-Caper Duxelles, Chanterelle Mushrooms, and Almond Cream

Mackerel

Atlantic Mackerel, Spanish Mackerel

SCIENTIFIC NAMES: *Scomber scombrus* (Atlantic), *Scomberomorus maculatus* (Spanish)

OTHER NAMES: Atlantic mackerel is also called Boston mackerel, and Spanish mackerel may be called spotted cybium or bay or spotted mackerel.

U.S. DISTRIBUTION: Atlantic mackerel—North Atlantic; Spanish mackerel—Gulf of Mexico to Cape Cod

SEASON: Year-round

WHAT TO LOOK FOR: Very fresh mackerel are vividly colored, and whole fish look almost alive. Marketed whole Atlantic mackerel are about 1-1/2 to 2-1/2 pounds, and Spanish mackerel are usually under 3 pounds. Because they're rich in fish oils, mackerel must be iced immediately after being caught and should be kept on ice. Mackerel are sold whole, dressed, or cut into fillets and steaks. Mackerel is also available smoked.

COLOR, TASTE, AND TEXTURE: The beige flesh of Spanish mackerel is firmer and more delicately flavored than the Atlantic mackerel. The scale-free skin is delicious.

COOKING METHODS: Lemon, lime, vinegar, and tomato offer appropriate acidic counterpoints to the high oil content in the fish. Mackerel is an ideal fish for grilling; for added flavor, place soaked rosemary stems or bay leaves on the coals while grilling.

Serves 4

Mackerel has been underappreciated for too long. I began eating mackerel at a young age and have grown to enjoy its wonderful, distinctive flavor and succulence. The mackerel's flavor is best enhanced by simple cooking techniques: in this case, through light grilling. Sweet apricots, tangy capers, almonds, and a twist on the traditional "duxelle" in the guise of a salad were added to complement the fish's unique characteristics. This combination is best enjoyed in the spring, when all of the ingredients are at their peak.

COOK'S STRATEGY: Make the Apricot-and-Caper Duxelles and Almond Cream an hour or two before dinner. Sauté the chanterelles shortly before grilling the mackerel, which should be done at the last minute.

1 pound Spanish mackerel, skin on, cut into 4 portions
Salt and freshly ground pepper
Snipped chives

➤ Apricot-and-Caper Duxelles
➤ Almond Cream
➤ Chanterelle Mushrooms

Season the mackerel with salt and pepper. On a clean, hot grill, place the mackerel skin-side down and cook for 2 minutes. Lift and reverse the angle of the fish to create crosshatch marks on the skin. Grill 2 minutes more. Turn the mackerel over carefully then cook for 1 to 2 minutes more.

Just before serving, warm the Apricot and Caper Duxelles (add a touch of water or stock if needed) and stir in the chives. Heat the mushrooms. On 4 dinner plates, make a quenelle (a small oval, using 2 teaspoons) of the duxelles and place to one side. Spoon a wide ribbon of Almond Cream down the other side. Place Chanterelle Mushrooms just slightly next to the sauce. Place the mackerel atop the mushrooms. Serve and enjoy!

❧ Apricot-and-Caper Duxelles

12 dried apricots, diced small

1 teaspoon sugar

1 teaspoon butter

1 teaspoon chopped capers

In a small saucepan, combine the apricots, sugar, and butter. Add just enough water to cover. Cook over low heat until the apricots are soft and glazed. Stir in the capers. Use immediately or chill and store for later use; if making ahead, add the capers just before serving.

❧ Almond Cream

3 ounces sliced almonds, toasted

3/4 cup heavy cream

In a small saucepan, combine almonds and cream. Steep over low heat until cream is infused with almond flavor. Season to taste, strain, and keep warm.

❧ Chanterelle Mushrooms

8 ounces chanterelle mushrooms, cleaned and sliced

1 tablespoon extra-virgin olive oil

1 shallot, minced

Salt and freshly ground black pepper

Heat the oil in a sauté pan over medium-high heat. Sauté the chanterelles until tender. Season with minced shallot and salt and pepper.

Thomas Keller is Executive Chef and Owner of the French Laundry in Yountville, California, and the founder and owner of EVO, a nationally distributed retail line of premium California olive oils and vinegars. He is the author of *The French Laundry Cookbook* (Workman Publishing Co., 2000).

Mackerel in Scapece with Lemon Thyme and Sweet Peppers

Serves 4 as an appetizer

An oily fish like mackerel is often a difficult sell, even in New York. This dish makes it easy to love because poaching the fish in a delicate yet acidic bath of onions and thyme cuts the oily quality.

1 pound Atlantic mackerel fillet, cut
    diagonally into 2-inch diamonds
Kosher salt and freshly ground
    black pepper
2 cups red-wine vinegar
3 tablespoons sugar
2 tablespoons freshly squeezed lemon juice
2 tablespoons lemon-thyme leaves

1 tablespoon dried hot red pepper flakes
10 to 15 saffron threads, crushed in a
    mortar with a pestle
1/4 cup extra-virgin olive oil
1 red bell pepper, cut into 1/4-inch dice
1 teaspoon mustard seeds
4 cloves garlic, thinly sliced

Season the fish with salt and pepper. In a wide, deep sauté pan, combine the vinegar, 2 tablespoons of the sugar, the lemon juice, lemon thyme, red pepper flakes, saffron, and salt and pepper to taste and bring to a simmer. Add the fish chunks, adding a bit of water if needed to cover the fish, and simmer until the fish is just cooked through, about 5 minutes. Remove from the heat and allow the fish to cool in the liquid.

In a 12-to-14-inch sauté pan, heat 3 tablespoons of the olive oil over medium-high heat. Add the bell peppers, reduce the heat to low, and cook slowly to wilt the peppers. Once the peppers have begun to soften, sprinkle with the remaining tablespoon of sugar, the mustard seeds, and garlic. Cook until the garlic is softened, 3 to 4 minutes. Season with salt and pepper and set aside.

To serve, remove the fish from the scapece and arrange in stacks on 4 chilled plates. Spoon 1 tablespoon of the saffron liquid over each serving and then sprinkle with the red pepper mixture.

Mario Batali is Chef/Owner of Babbo in New York City. He hosts *Molto Mario* and *Mario Eats Italy* on the Food Network and is the author of *The Babbo Cookbook* (Clarkson N. Potter, 2002), *Simple Italian Food* (Clarkson N. Potter, 1998), and *Mario Batali Holiday Food* (Clarkson N. Potter, 2000).

Spanish-Mackerel Ceviche with Pomelo and Peruvian Huacatay Mint

There are many varieties of mackerel, a dark-meat fish in the same family as tuna and bonito. I use Spanish mackerel, which has a brownish, rough-textured skin. I charbroil the skin, using the pyromaniac chef's favorite tool: a blowtorch, straight from the hardware store. Several cookware catalogs now sell smaller, less fearsome blowtorches that are ideal for that task. Some gourmet shops carry small jars of Huacatay-mint purée, a delicious rainforest product from Peru. Because this mint has such a special flavor, I don't recommend any substitutions.

Serves 4

3/4 pound fresh Spanish mackerel
    fillet with skin

1 pomelo or white grapefruit divided
    into sections
➤ Huacatay-Mint Sauce

Clean the mackerel by placing it skin-side down on a cutting board. Using a sharp knife, cut down along either side of the dark "blood line" that runs along the center. Remove and discard this dark flesh. Using a blowtorch, charbroil the skin of the mackerel until charred and bubbling. Cover and refrigerate the fish until it is firm, about 30 minutes.

Cut the mackerel crosswise into 1/2-inch-thick slices. Pour about 2 tablespoons Huacatay Mint Sauce into a dish and dip each slice of fish in the sauce. Cover and refrigerate the fish for about 30 minutes so that it absorbs the flavor of the sauce.

When ready to serve, dip the mackerel slices once again in mint sauce. On a large serving platter, place one pomelo section alongside one slice of the mackerel. Leave some space between each pair of pomelo and mackerel slices. Drizzle the platter with any remaining mint sauce and serve.

➤ Huacatay-Mint Sauce

2 tablespoons Huacatay-mint purée
1/4 cup freshly squeezed lime juice
1/4 cup mild olive oil
1/2 teaspoon finely chopped garlic

1 teaspoon kosher salt
2 tablespoons fresh mint leaves,
    cut into thin ribbons

Combine all the ingredients in a blender and purée. Transfer the sauce to a bowl. Refrigerate covered if not using immediately.

Guillermo Pernot is Chef/Partner of ¡Pasión! in Philadelphia. Used by permission of *¡Ceviche!* ©2001 by Guillermo Pernot and Aliza Green, photographs ©2001 by Steve Lagato, published by Running Press Book Publishers, Philadelphia and London.

Grilled Atlantic Mackerel, Heirloom Tomatoes, and Pancetta-Studded Mashed Potatoes

Serves 4

This recipe works well with other strong-tasting fish, such as bluefish, but also with tuna and halibut.

1 pound Atlantic mackerel fillet,
   cut into 4 portions
1/4 cup extra-virgin olive oil
2 cloves garlic, thinly sliced
Salt and freshly ground black pepper
1 cup raw pancetta, cut into small dice
2 yellow heirloom tomatoes
2 red heirloom tomatoes

2 sprigs fresh basil, leaves only,
   cut into thin ribbons,
    plus 4 sprigs for garnish
2 sprigs fresh thyme, leaves only
2 sprigs fresh oregano, leaves only
8 Yukon Gold potatoes, peeled
1/2 stick (4 tablespoons) butter
1 bunch scallions, minced
Cracked black pepper

Rub the mackerel with 2 tablespoons of olive oil and 1 sliced clove of garlic. Season with salt and pepper; set aside.

Cook the pancetta in a medium skillet until lightly browned and crisp; drain and set aside. Slice each of the tomatoes into 4 thick slices. Combine sliced basil leaves with the thyme and oregano leaves. Sprinkle each tomato slice with the thinly sliced second garlic clove and the fresh herb mix. Season with salt and pepper; set aside.

Boil the potatoes until soft. Drain and mash potatoes with a fork. Add the butter, pancetta, and scallions. Season with salt and pepper; keep warm and set aside.

Place a sheet of aluminum foil on the grill and moisten it with olive oil. Place the mackerel on the foil and grill on both sides until warmed through. Place the tomatoes on the foil and grill until they begin to soften. Work quickly to remove tomatoes so they don't fall apart.

To serve, arrange 1 yellow tomato slice and 1 red tomato slice in the center of each plate. Place a piece of mackerel on the tomatoes. Set a small scoop of pancetta potatoes next to the mackerel. Drizzle with the remaining olive oil. Sprinkle cracked black pepper over the plate and garnish with a sprig of basil. Serve without delay.

Debbie Gold and Michael Smith are Chef/Owners of Forty Sardines in Overland Park, Kansas.

Seared Wahoo, Truffle Grits, Asparagus, Tomatoes, and Sautéed Carolina Shrimp

COOK'S STRATEGY: Start the Truffle Grits about forty-five minutes before serving. While they are cooking, prepare the wahoo, shrimp, and vegetables for cooking and cook ten to fifteen minutes before serving.

Serves 2

12 ounces wahoo fillet, skin removed
6 large U.S.–farm raised or trawled
    white shrimp, peeled and deveined
Salt and freshly ground black pepper
1/4 cup olive oil
1/2 stick (4 tablespoons) butter
2 tablespoons thinly sliced garlic
3 tablespoons thinly sliced shallots
1 cup asparagus tips

3/4 cup white wine
3 tablespoons cold butter, cut into pieces
Juice of 1/2 lemon
1/2 cup grape tomatoes, sliced in half
3 tablespoons chopped fresh basil
1 teaspoon salt
Pinch freshly ground white pepper
❧ Truffle Grits

Cut the fish into 2 equal pieces and season with salt and pepper. Heat oil in a skillet over medium-high heat. Add the wahoo to the skillet. Sear on the first side for 2 to 3 minutes, turn over, and add the butter, shrimp, garlic, and shallots. Continue to cook for 2 to 3 minutes. Remove the wahoo from the pan. Add the asparagus to the pan and cook for 1 to 2 minutes. Remove the shrimp from the pan. Deglaze pan with the white wine and reduce liquid by half, about 2 minutes. Over low heat, stir in the cold butter until melted and creamy. Add the lemon juice, tomatoes, basil, salt, and white pepper.

To serve, spoon Truffle Grits onto each plate and top with the shrimp and wahoo. Next place the asparagus and tomato mixture on top of the fish. Finally spoon the pan sauce around the fish.

❧ Truffle Grits

1 cup stone-ground white grits
1/4 cup heavy cream
3 tablespoons butter
2 tablespoons truffle oil

1-1/2 tablespoons honey
1-1/2 tablespoons sea salt
1/2 teaspoon freshly ground white pepper

Bring 3 cups water to a boil in a saucepan. Add the grits; cook for 25 to 30 minutes over medium-low heat, stirring occasionally until water is absorbed and grits are slightly creamy. Add the remaining ingredients and cook another 5 to 10 minutes.

Craig Deihl is Executive Chef of Cypress Grille in Charleston, South Carolina.

Pan-Roasted Wahoo on Arugula Salad with Red Onions, Clementines, and Citrus Vinaigrette

Serves 4

COOK'S STRATEGY: Be sure to slice the red onion and marinate it in rice-wine vinegar in advance. This softens and sweetens the onions and leaves them a pretty pink color.

4 pieces wahoo fillet, 2 ounces each
Salt and freshly ground black pepper
2 tablespoons olive oil

2 tablespoons canola oil
➤ Arugula-Clementine Salad
➤ Citrus Vinaigrette

Season the wahoo with salt and pepper and brush with olive oil. Add the canola oil to a hot sauté pan; oil should be smoking a little bit. Place the wahoo pieces one at a time into the pan and cook until golden brown on each side, about 3 to 5 minutes per side.

To serve, divide the Arugula-Clementine Salad among 4 plates. Place a piece of pan-roasted wahoo on each.

➤ Arugula-Clementine Salad
1 small red onion, thinly sliced
1 cup rice-wine vinegar
8 cups arugula

1 clementine, peeled and segmented
➤ Citrus Vinaigrette

Marinate the sliced onion in the vinegar for at least 1 hour and up to several hours. Drain and add the onions to a bowl along with the arugula and clementine segments. Add 1/2 to 3/4 cup Citrus Vinaigrette and toss lightly.

✢ Citrus Vinaigrette

2 tablespoons freshly squeezed
    orange juice
1 tablespoon freshly squeezed
    lime juice
1 tablespoon freshly squeezed
    lemon juice
2 teaspoons rice-wine vinegar

1/4 teaspoon Dijon mustard
1/2 teaspoon sugar
2/3 cup blended oil
    (75% canola, 25% olive oil)
Salt and freshly ground black
    pepper

In a small bowl, combine the citrus juices, vinegar, mustard, and sugar. Whisk in oil slowly to emulsify. Season with salt and pepper.

Dale Reitzer is Chef/Owner of Acacia Restaurant in Richmond, Virginia.

Wahoo

SCIENTIFIC NAME:
Acanthocybium solandri

OTHER NAMES: Ono

U.S. DISTRIBUTION: Tropical and subtropical waters of Atlantic and Pacific, including Hawaii. Most commercial catches are from North Carolina to Louisiana.

SEASON: Year-round, but most available from May to October

WHAT TO LOOK FOR: Although a member of the mackerel family, wahoo flesh is pale pink—almost like a pale version of tuna—with a barely detectable aroma. They are large fish sold, like tuna, as fillets or steaks.

COLOR, TASTE, AND TEXTURE: Ono in Hawaiian means "sweet and delicate," an apt description of cooked wahoo. The flesh turns white and flaky when cooked and is dense and slightly chewy. Wahoo is often used in place of mahi mahi, but it's not as sweet.

COOKING METHODS: Because it is low in fat, wahoo is best prepared in a way that helps keep it moist, such as searing, poaching, or braising.

SPOT, CROAKER, SPOTTED SEA TROUT, WEAKFISH, black drum—if you live on the east or Gulf coasts of the United States, you probably know them well; otherwise, you've probably never heard of them. They are all part of the family of fishes known as drums, and if you've ever savored a meal of Cajun blackened redfish, you too have tried drum (*Sciaenops ocellatus*, or red drum). Around the world, the drum family, which includes more than 250 species, is an extremely important source of protein. In the United States, drums are usually available only seasonally and in local markets, but these fish are always worth a taste. The flesh of most is lightly colored, tender, and relatively mild. Large black drum (more than 5 pounds) have coarse flesh that some have likened to pork, but the small ones are choice fish for chefs.

Recreational and subsistence fishing bring in most of the drums caught each year in the United States, but there are commercial fisheries for many species. The most commercially important U.S. species is the croaker. Spot, spotted sea trout, and the Gulf of Mexico black drum are among other commercially caught U.S. drums.

Croaker, which may grow to be about 2 pounds, live from Maine to Argentina, migrating to the coastal mid-Atlantic for the spring, summer, and fall, and moving south and offshore during the winter. This species is one of

Spot *(top)* and weakfish *(center and bottom)*

In the Wild

Drums are so called because they produce a drumming sound using muscles to vibrate the swim bladder, an internal pocket of air otherwise used for buoyancy. Why do they do it? Perhaps for the same reason that many animals do surprising things: to court a mate. Whatever the inspiration, these fish are noisy; some have likened the sound of a group of knocking red drum to galloping horses or even a Harley-Davidson motorcycle.

Virginia and Maryland's most abundant finfish. Spot, which grow to only about a pound in size, are also widely distributed along the Atlantic coast and migrate much like the croaker.

The two sea-trout species included here, spotted sea trout and weakfish, grow much larger than spot and croaker, as large as 13 pounds. Unrelated to freshwater trout, which are in the salmon family, spotted sea trout and weakfish swim fast and are caught recreationally by trolling or bait casting. Spotted sea trout are taken commercially from the Gulf of Mexico to Maryland, and the slightly more northern weakfish are harvested from the east coast of Florida to Massachusetts.

Black drum are the heavyweights of the family, the largest on record at 146 pounds. They live along the east coast from New York south to the Gulf states and may be found in water so shallow that their backs are exposed—or deeper than 100 feet.

If you're looking for an economical and ecologically sound seafood for your table, croaker and its relatives are excellent choices. All are taken commercially with small nets that are not habitat destructive. Landings of all drums included here except spotted sea trout have been relatively stable. Spotted sea trout abundance has fluctuated over the past couple decades, and South Carolina has declared it a game fish only; we include spotted sea trout because both recreational and commercial fisheries for the species are being closely monitored under a 2002 management plan.

Because of their small size, spot and croaker are usually sold whole or dressed (head and innards removed), and black drum, spotted sea trout, and weakfish are sold whole or as fillets. A. D. Livingston suggests here that if you are looking for a good substitute for the Gulf of Mexico red drum, which was overfished in the 1980s, try blackened tilapia.

Fennel-Crusted Sea Trout with Vidalia Onions, Fennel, Orange, and Tarragon

Drums

Spot, Croaker, Weakfish, Spotted Sea Trout, and Black Drum

SCIENTIFIC NAMES: *Leiostomus xanthurus* (spot), *Micropogonias undulatus* (croaker), *Cynoscion nebulosus* (spotted sea trout), *C. regalis* (weakfish), *Pogonias cromis* (black drum)

OTHER NAMES: Spotted sea trout is also called speckled trout or sea trout, and weakfish is also called gray trout, gray weakfish, or summer trout; black drum may be called oyster drum or sea drum, and small ones are also called puppy drum.

U.S. DISTRIBUTION: Atlantic and Gulf coasts

SEASON: Many varieties can be caught throughout the year, but drums are most abundant during summer and fall.

WHAT TO LOOK FOR: Red gills, bright skin, and a fresh smell are all signs of fresh fish. Spot (about 8 ounces) and somewhat larger croaker (about 1 pound) are sold whole or dressed. Spot are easy to recognize by the spot right beside the gill opening. Weakfish, spotted sea trout, and black drum are larger and are sold whole or as fillets.

COLOR, TASTE, AND TEXTURE: Drums are white to off-white when cooked, with a fine flake. Large black drum have much coarser flesh. The flavor is delicate sweet.

COOKING METHODS: The smaller members of the drum family such as spots and croakers are among the best pan fish. Panfry or deep fry. Avoid eating raw.

Serves 4

4 spotted sea trout fillets (skin on), 6 ounces each
2 navel oranges
1/4 cup olive oil, plus more for brushing
2 Vidalia onions, very thinly sliced
1 bulb fresh fennel, trimmed, cored, and julienned
1 cup fresh orange juice
Juice of 1 lemon
2 teaspoons sugar
1/2 teaspoon finely chopped fresh ginger
2 teaspoons finely chopped fresh tarragon
Kosher salt and freshly ground white pepper
2 tablespoons fennel seeds, chopped

With a sharp vegetable peeler or paring knife, pare thin strips of zest (without the bitter white pith) from the oranges. With a large knife, slice the zest into julienne strips. Measure and reserve 2 tablespoons zest. With a serrated knife, cut the remaining peel and pith from the oranges. Separate the orange segments and cut the segments into wedges. Reserve.

Heat the oil in a medium saucepan. Add the onions and fresh fennel; stir over medium heat until tender, about 4 to 5 minutes. Add the orange juice, lemon juice, reserved orange zest, sugar, and ginger. Bring to a simmer over medium-high heat and cook to reduce to 3/4 cup liquid. Stir in the reserved orange segments and tarragon. Cook for 1 minute longer and remove from the heat.

Preheat the broiler or an outdoor charcoal grill to medium-high heat. Brush the trout fillets lightly with oil and season with salt, pepper, and fennel seeds. Grill under the broiler or over hot coals for about 3 to 4 minutes per side.

To serve, spoon the Vidalia onion–fennel mixture onto 4 dinner plates. Place the trout fillets in the center of each plate.

Jeffrey Buben is Chef/Owner of Vidalia and Bistro Bis in Washington, D.C.

Cornmeal-Crusted Croaker on Grilled Asparagus with Yellow-Tomato Sauce

Serves 4

Garlic mashed potatoes are great with this dish.

COOK'S STRATEGY: If you prepare the Yellow-Tomato Sauce in advance and the asparagus up to the point of grilling, when dinnertime comes you'll be able to get this dish to the table in no time.

8 croaker fillets
Canola oil, for frying
3 eggs
1 cup flour
2 cups cornmeal

Chopped Italian flat-leaf parsley, for
   garnish, optional
✦ Grilled Asparagus
✦ Yellow-Tomato Sauce

Heat a cast-iron pan over medium to high heat; fill the pan 1/2-inch deep with oil. Beat the eggs lightly in a shallow dish to make an egg wash. Dust the croaker fillets in the flour and shake off the excess. Dip them in the egg wash, then coat in cornmeal so they are nicely breaded. Cook for 1 to 2 minutes or until they are golden brown on each side. Do this in batches if you don't have a large enough pan to do them all at once. Keep the fish warm in the oven on a plate lined with paper towels.

To serve, lay the Grilled Asparagus spears flat in the center of 4 warmed dinner plates. Place a cornmeal-crusted croaker fillet on top. Spoon the Yellow-Tomato Sauce around the asparagus. Garnish with chopped Italian parsley if desired.

✦ Grilled Asparagus

1/2 cup kosher salt
2 pounds green asparagus (pencil size),
   bottoms trimmed

1 to 2 tablespoons good olive oil
Salt and freshly ground pepper

Bring 4 quarts water to a boil in a large pot; add the kosher salt. Add the asparagus and cook for 4 minutes. Remove the asparagus from the water and immediately transfer to a large bowl of water and ice: this sweetens the asparagus. Drain well, toss with some olive oil, and add a pinch of salt and pepper. (The asparagus may be prepared to this point several hours ahead.)

Heat a stovetop grill pan or an outdoor grill. Grill the asparagus until hot and nicely grill marked, about 2 to 4 minutes. Do not burn.

✦ Yellow-Tomato Sauce

1 teaspoon unsalted butter
1 shallot, minced
1/2 cup white wine
1 large or 2 medium vine-ripened yellow
    tomatoes, seeded and chopped

1 cup vegetable broth
3 basil leaves
Salt and freshly ground black pepper
2 tablespoons good olive oil

Heat the butter in a saucepan over medium heat. Add the shallots and cook until soft. Add the white wine and boil until only 2 tablespoons remain. Add the tomatoes and broth, bring to a boil, lower the heat to a simmer, and cook for about 10 minutes. Pour the sauce into a blender, add the basil, and purée; strain the sauce through a fine-mesh sieve. Season with salt and pepper. Finish the sauce by whisking in the olive oil.

Dale Reitzer is Chef/Owner of Acacia in Richmond, Virginia.

Speckled Trout Meunière

Serves 6

6 spotted sea trout (speckled trout) fillets, 6 to 7 ounces each
Cottonseed oil or a blend of cottonseed and corn oils, for frying
1/2 cup milk
1/4 cup buttermilk

1 cup all-purpose flour seasoned with salt and freshly ground black pepper
2 lemons, cut into wedges
Fresh parsley sprigs
✦ Meunière Sauce

Preheat the oil to 350°F in a deep fryer or large heavy pan. The oil should be deep enough for the fish to float freely. Combine milk and buttermilk in a bowl. Dredge the trout fillets in the seasoned flour and then in the buttermilk bath to coat both sides. Dredge again in flour and shake off excess. Place the fish in the fryer basket 2 at a time to avoid crowding, and fry for 4 to 5 minutes. When they are golden brown, remove and place on a paper towel–lined baking sheet and pat off excess oil. Keep warm while other fillets are being fried. Transfer to a hot platter or serving plate.

Ladle the Meunière Sauce into a sauceboat and serve with the fish. Garnish with lemon wedges and parsley.

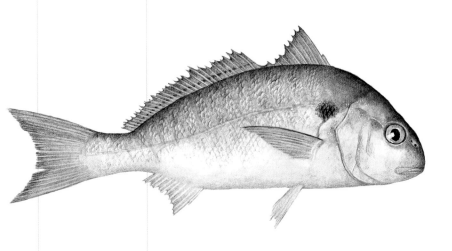

✦ Meunière Sauce

2 tablespoons butter
1/4 cup chopped fresh parsley
1/2 white onion, cut in half again
1/4 cup chopped green bell pepper
1/2 lemon, cut in half again
1 bouquet garni (several parsley stems,
   3 bay leaves, 1 branch fresh thyme,
   and 1 stalk celery tied together—leave
   a long tail tied to the handle
   for easy removal)

1 whole clove
1-1/2 cups veal stock (or chicken broth)
1 tablespoon freshly squeezed
   lemon juice
Salt and freshly ground black pepper
✦ Roux

Melt the butter in a saucepan over high heat. Add the parsley, onion pieces, green pepper, lemon pieces, bouquet garni, and clove; sauté until brown. Stir in the veal stock and lemon juice and bring to a boil for 2 minutes. Lower the heat and simmer for 10 minutes. Whisk in 3 tablespoons of Roux, 1 tablespoon at a time, until the sauce coats a spoon. Season to taste with salt and pepper. Strain the sauce into a clean saucepan and reheat if necessary before taking to the table.

✦ Roux

Roux is made with fat (butter, oil, bacon grease) and flour. We make the roux at Arnaud's with 1/2 stick butter and 1/2 cup flour.

Melt the butter over high heat. Add the flour gradually, stirring constantly with a wire whisk or wooden spoon. Cook until it becomes a paste. Remove from heat. Cool, then cover and store at room temperature until needed. Roux will keep for up to 1 week.

Tommy DiGiovanni is Executive Chef of Arnaud's Restaurant in New Orleans, Louisiana.

Pan-Roasted Black Drum over Goat-Cheese Gnocchi in a Saffron Fumet

Serves 4

At the restaurant, we place a mound of wilted Louisiana kale down as a base and place the fish on top of it. We add oven-dried grape tomatoes, Niçoise olives, haricots verts, poached garlic, and chervil to the Saffron Fumet and then garnish the entire dish with a drizzle of French Pistou.

COOK'S STRATEGY: The French Pistou can be made up to a week in advance and refrigerated, and the Saffron Fumet can be prepared a day or two in advance and refrigerated (or frozen in small batches). The Goat-Cheese Gnocchi dough needs to be refrigerated for thirty to forty minutes before forming into pieces and cooking.

4 skin-on black-drum fillets, 7 ounces each
Salt and freshly ground white pepper
1 tablespoon peanut oil
❧ Saffron Fumet
4 teaspoons unsalted butter
❧ Oven-Dried Grape Tomatoes
16 to 20 pitted Niçoise olives

1/2 cup haricots verts, snipped into
   1-1/2-inch lengths on the bias and
   blanched in salted water
1 teaspoon chopped fresh chervil
❧ Poached Garlic Cloves
❧ Goat-Cheese Gnocchi
❧ French Pistou

Wrap the fish fillets in paper towels to dry them well prior to cooking. Season the fish on both sides with salt and white pepper. Heat the oil in a 12-inch sauté pan and place the fish skin-side down in the pan. Cook over medium-high heat until the fish has formed a crust and is golden. Using a spatula, flip the fillets and continue to cook until the fish is just done, about 2 to 3 minutes.

In a 2-quart sauce pot, bring 1-1/2 cups of the slightly thickened fumet to a boil. Add the butter, the Oven-Dried Grape Tomatoes, olives, the haricots verts, chervil, the Poached Garlic Cloves, and the Goat-Cheese Gnocchi (fresh from the hot water).

Taste the sauce and place it into 4 shallow entrée bowls. Place a piece of the seared fish on top of each.

Garnish the entire dish with a drizzle of French Pistou.

❧ Saffron Fumet

1 tablespoon unsalted butter, softened (not melted)

1 tablespoon all-purpose flour

1 pound fish trimmings and bones, free of blood line and guts, soaked in cold water for at least 30 minutes, rinsed well

2/3 cup yellow-onion trimmings or leek greens, chopped large

2/3 cup fennel trimmings, chopped large

1 cup chopped vine-ripened tomatoes

4 cloves garlic, smashed

1 teaspoon chopped saffron threads (chop then measure)

1-1/3 cups white wine, such as Chardonnay

1 sprig fresh thyme

1 sprig fresh Italian flat-leaf parsley

4 sprigs fresh tarragon

1 bay leaf

10 white peppercorns

Combine the butter and flour thoroughly and refrigerate. This will be used to thicken the sauce. Place the fish trimmings and bones, onion, fennel, tomatoes, garlic, saffron, and white wine in a 4-quart stockpot, and cover with 1-1/2 quarts of cold water. Bring to a boil, reduce to a simmer, and cook for 30 minutes. Add the thyme, parsley, tarragon, bay leaf, and peppercorns. Cook for 5 more minutes, remove from the heat, and allow to sit for 30 minutes. Strain through a fine-mesh sieve or chinoise into a container and cool in an ice bath. Cover and refrigerate or freeze in small batches until needed.

Bring the fumet to a boil. Force the chilled piece of butter/flour onto the end of a whisk and whisk it into the sauce until it is dissolved and incorporated. Simmer the sauce for 5 minutes (don't boil it). Remove and cool until needed. You can also use the sauce as soon as it has simmered down for 5 minutes.

❧ Poached Garlic Cloves

32 cloves garlic, peeled

Cut all the cloves into uniform wedges. Poach until tender in water or Chardonnay, and allow to cool.

(Continued)

✦ Goat-Cheese Gnocchi

1-1/4 pounds Idaho baking potatoes, all similar in size, not peeled	Kosher salt and freshly ground white pepper
1/2 cup flour	3 tablespoons fresh goat cheese
1/3 cup potato flour	1 egg yolk, beaten

Preheat the oven to 400°F. Bake the potatoes until very tender (start checking after 45 minutes). While the potatoes are hot, peel (protect your hands with gloves) and put them through a ricer. It is very important that this is done while they are hot. Mix the flours in a large bowl and season with salt and white pepper. Mix together the goat cheese and the egg yolk until smooth. Add the potatoes and cheese-egg mixture to the flours and mix together very methodically. Do not overmix. Form into one piece and refrigerate until firm, about 30 to 40 minutes. Cut into smaller pieces and roll into long, thin cylinders (3/4 inch wide and 8 to 10 inches long) Cut into 1-1/2-inch pieces and roll each piece onto the tines of a floured fork to give it grooves.

Blanch the gnocchi in boiling salted water. As they rise to the top, remove with a slotted spoon and transfer to a bowl of iced water. When they are all done, drain and toss with a little olive oil. If preparing them in advance, reheat in a simmering pot of water and drain before adding them to the Saffron Fumet.

✦ French Pistou

1 large clove garlic	1/2 cup fresh basil leaves
1/2 cup pure olive oil	1/2 cup fresh chervil leaves
Kosher salt and freshly ground black pepper	1/2 cup fresh parsley leaves

Place the garlic and oil in the blender and season it lightly with salt and pepper. Purée for 30 seconds. Add the herbs and process the mixture for 30 seconds. Transfer to a small squirt bottle for easy use. The pistou will keep for 1 week in the refrigerator.

✤ Oven-Dried Grape Tomatoes

16 to 20 grape tomatoes

Olive oil, for drizzling

Salt and freshly ground black pepper

Preheat the oven to 200°F. Line a baking sheet (with sides) with baking parchment, Slice grape tomatoes in half through the middle and lay them out on the prepared sheet. Drizzle with oil and season with salt and pepper. Bake the tomatoes until they are shrunken and somewhat dry, about 2 hours.

Anne Kearney is Chef/Proprietor of Peristyle in New Orleans, Louisiana.

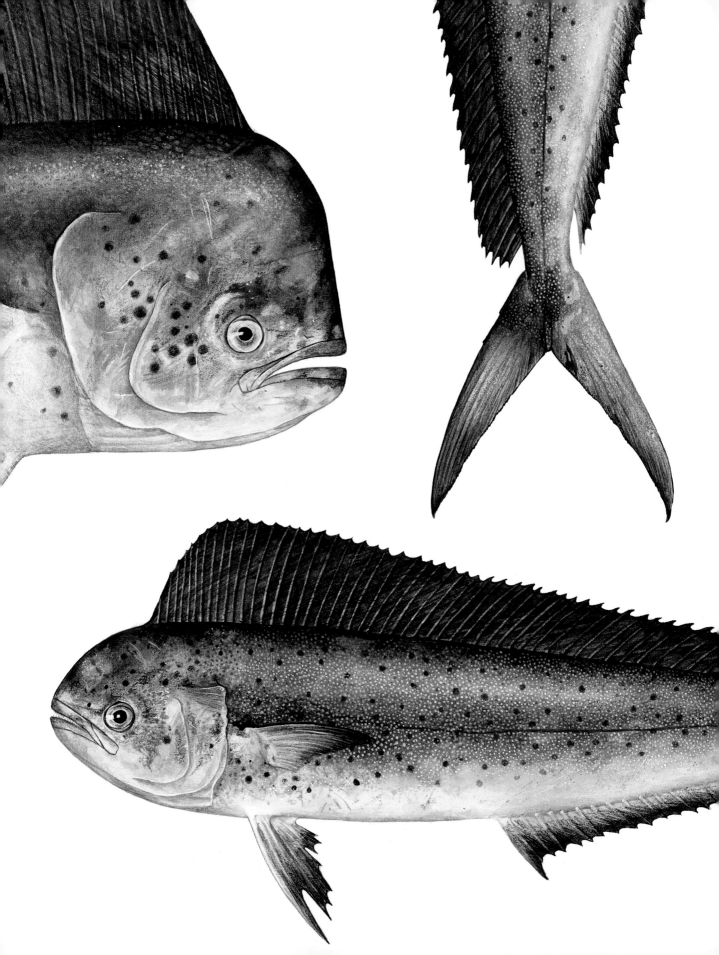

MAHI MAHI AND COBIA ARE GLAMOROUS BOTH
in the wild and on the plate. Mahi mahi follow ships, dazzling all with their brilliant hues of gold and metallic blues and greens. And the hulking cobia, which can get as large as 150 pounds, thrills fishers with its sharklike single dorsal fin and spirited antics. With their firm, moist flesh and mild flavor, these fish are also delightfully versatile in recipes.

As adults, mahi mahi and cobia look nothing alike, in part because the mahi mahi is so brightly colored and the cobia dark brown. Only during their young, nearly identical larval stages do they show their common heritage as pelagic fishes related to jacks and pompano. Both species migrate among the tropical and subtropical waters of the Atlantic, Indian, and Pacific oceans. Mahi mahi form schools, whereas cobia are solitary, but both are attracted to drifting objects, which has led commercial fishers to float bamboo mats or other objects behind their boats as lures. In the United States, mahi mahi and cobia are caught commercially and recreationally from the northeast to the Gulf of Mexico (as well as Hawaii), but most commercial landings are from the east and west coasts of Florida and from Louisiana and North Carolina. Mahi mahi is far more important commercially than cobia, with landings between

Mahi Mahi

In the Wild

There is a common misconception about the identity of mahi mahi. Because in English it is popularly known as common dolphinfish (mahi mahi is the Hawaiian name), many mistakenly believe it's the mammal called dolphin (think Flipper) being harvested. But dolphins are gray and much larger than mahi mahi, and as air-breathing mammals they must surface regularly to breathe. Mahi mahi is a fish, which "breathes" by obtaining oxygen from the water through its gills. Furthermore, mahi mahi undergoes a dramatic color change when caught— almost immediately after it is landed, its brilliant yellow darkens into a greenish hue and the dramatic blue-green dulls to a deep blue or purple.

1991 and 2001 usually exceeding 1 million pounds annually for mahi mahi but less than 400,000 pounds each year for the solitary cobia.

National seafood-watch programs have paid little attention to the conservation status of cobia, probably because it is of relatively minor commercial importance, but the Gulf of Mexico and South Atlantic Fishery Management Councils do manage the species through size and catch restrictions for both recreational and commercial harvesters. Mahi mahi is considered an ecologically sound seafood choice mostly because it grows and reproduces so quickly; the species grows to about 20 pounds in one year, reproduces at a young age, and lives only four or five years. The largest mahi mahi recorded was 90 pounds, although they average only 10 to 30 pounds. Both cobia and mahi mahi are caught commercially using single fishing lines, but they may also be taken as incidental catches on longlines for other commercially important species. Because of the enormous numbers of target animals caught and high bycatch associated with longlining, try to avoid cobia and mahi mahi taken using this method.

Mahi mahi and cobia are usually sold as fresh or frozen fillets. Mahi mahi in U.S. markets may be from U.S. waters or from Ecuador, Taiwan, or Costa Rica. The availability and price of mahi mahi captured by Central and South American fisheries may be strongly affected by the warming of coastal waters during El Niño, which drives the fish offshore. Cobia is not common in national seafood markets, though it can be found in some; it is available seasonally in local markets. It may be more abundant in the future, however: Cobia is a focus of a multi-institutional project to bring recently developed offshore-aquaculture technology to the commercial level in the United States.

Mahi Mahi on Rye with Meyer Lemon and Brussels Sprouts

Serves 8

The fish is served with tender cippolini (an Italian version of pearl onion) and blanched Brussels-sprouts leaves. The Meyer-Lemon Purée and Meyer-Lemon Sauce garnish the dish.

COOK'S STRATEGY: The Meyer-Lemon Purée, Brussels Sprouts, and Cippolini can be made several hours in advance. The Mahi Mahi on Rye and Meyer-Lemon Sauce should be prepared just before serving.

8 mahi mahi fillets, about
    8 ounces each
1 teaspoon kosher salt
✦ Meyer-Lemon Purée
8 thin slices rye bread
1 cup canola oil
✦ Brussels Sprouts

Butter
Salt
✦ Cippolini
1/4 cup caraway seeds,
    toasted and ground
✦ Meyer-Lemon Sauce

Season the fillets with salt and spread with a thin amount of Meyer-Lemon Purée. Place a slice of rye on top of each piece of fish and press to adhere. Heat the oil in a large sauté pan over medium heat. Add the fish bread-side down and cook until bread turns golden. Flip fish and cook for 3 additional minutes. Reheat Brussels Sprouts in a small amount of butter and season with salt to taste.

To serve, place the Mahi Mahi on Rye on 4 large dinner plates. Spoon mounds of Brussels Sprouts and Cippolini to 1 side of the mahi mahi. Streak Meyer-Lemon Purée down 1 side of the plate parallel to the fish. Sprinkle the plate with toasted caraway powder. Spoon Meyer-Lemon Sauce close to the fish.

✦ Meyer-Lemon Purée
2 Meyer lemons
3 tablespoons sugar

1 teaspoon salt

Mahi Mahi

SCIENTIFIC NAME: *Coryphaena hippurus*

OTHER NAMES: Dolphin, common dolphinfish, or dorado

U.S. DISTRIBUTION: All coastal tropical and subtropical waters. Mahi mahi is most often associated with Hawaii, and it's the state's best-known fish.

SEASON: Year-round

WHAT TO LOOK FOR: Local Hawaiian fishermen market mahi mahi as fresh, whole fish. At retail, these large (usually 8 to 25 pounds) fish are cut into fillets or steaks. The pinkish flesh should have a clean, delicate aroma and consistent color with no brown streaks (although a dark band of flesh along the fillet is normal). Fillets may be sold with the thin skin on.

COLOR, TASTE, AND TEXTURE: The flesh turns off-white when cooked and is meaty and dense, similar to swordfish but moister. The flavor is mild and pleasantly sweet.

COOKING METHODS: Mahi mahi can be grilled, broiled, panfried, sautéed, steamed, or braised. Mahi mahi should be cooked just until it flakes. If fillets were not skinned before cooking, the tough, flavorless skin should be removed before eating. The dark band of flesh in fillets is a bit stronger than the rest of the fish and can be removed before cooking if desired.

(Continued)

Cut the lemons into quarters and remove the seeds but leave the skin on. Pour 4 cups water into a saucepan; add the sugar, salt, and lemons. Simmer until the lemons are tender and most of the liquid is gone. Transfer the lemons and liquid to a blender and purée until smooth. Strain the purée through a fine-mesh sieve and transfer to a squeeze bottle or small pitcher.

✤ Brussels Sprouts

1 pound Brussels sprouts

Peel all the leaves from the core of each sprout and blanch in salted boiling water for 3 minutes. Drain and plunge the leaves into a bowl of ice water, then drain again.

✤ Cippolini

16 cippolini (or pearl onions), peeled	1 teaspoon sugar
2 tablespoons butter	1 teaspoon salt

Add the cippolini to a small pot with butter, sugar, salt, and 2 cups water. Bring to a boil and simmer until tender, about 10 minutes.

✤ Meyer-Lemon Sauce

1 Meyer lemon	1 tablespoon sugar
2 sticks (16 tablespoons)	1 teaspoon salt
unsalted butter, cut into small cubes	

Peel the rind from the Meyer lemon and mince it finely. Juice the lemon into a small pot, bring to a simmer, and begin to reduce the juice. When the juice has reduced to a light syrup, whisk in the butter a couple of pieces at a time until it is all incorporated. Add the rind to the sauce and season with the sugar and salt.

Grant Achatz is Executive Chef of Trio Restaurant in Evanston, Illinois.

Mahi Mahi with Italian Sausage, Mussels, and Gremolata

COOK'S STRATEGY: The Roasted Tomatoes, Clam-Juice Reduction, and Gremolata can be prepared an hour in advance of cooking the mahi mahi, sausage, and mussels.

1 pound mahi mahi fillet, cut in half
10 live mussels, scrubbed and debearded
Salt and freshly ground black pepper
4 tablespoons canola oil
4 ounces spicy Italian sausage,
 removed from casing

1 tablespoon chopped garlic
2 tablespoons butter
➤ Roasted Tomatoes
➤ Clam-Juice Reduction
➤ Gremolata

Season the mahi mahi with salt and pepper. Heat 2 tablespoons of the canola oil in a sauté pan and sauté the fish for 4 minutes per side.

In another pan, heat the remaining 2 tablespoons oil. Add the sausage, breaking it up with a wooden spoon, and cook until browned, about 3 minutes. Add the garlic and one-third of the chopped Roasted Tomatoes; cook for 1 minute. Add the Clam-Juice Reduction and mussels. Cook until all mussels are open; discard any unopened mussels. Add the butter and Gremolata. Whisk until the butter is emulsified. Season with salt and pepper to taste.

To serve, place 5 mussels and half of the broth in each of 2 bowls. Top with a piece of sautéed mahi mahi and sprinkle with the remaining Roasted Tomatoes.

➤ Roasted Tomatoes

3 ripe Roma tomatoes
2 tablespoons olive oil
1/2 teaspoon salt

1/2 teaspoon freshly ground
 black pepper

Preheat the oven to 250°F. Line a baking sheet with parchment paper. Slice tomatoes into 1/2-inch slices and remove seeds. Toss with the olive oil, salt, and pepper. Evenly space the tomato slices on the prepared baking sheet. Bake for 45 minutes, reducing the oven temperature if tomato edges blacken or burn. Remove from oven and roughly chop.

(Continued)

❧ Clam-Juice Reduction

1/2 cup clam juice or fish stock
1/2 cup white wine
2 shallots, chopped

2 tablespoons freshly
   squeezed lemon juice

Put clam juice, wine, shallots, and lemon juice in a saucepan, bring to a simmer, and cook to reduce the liquid by half.

❧ Gremolata

1/2 bunch Italian flat-leaf parsley,
   leaves picked
2 tablespoons chopped garlic

Grated zest of 1 lemon
1 tablespoon extra-virgin olive oil

Chop the parsley, garlic, and lemon zest together and toss with the olive oil.

Craig von Foerster is Executive Chef of Sierra Mar at Post Ranch Inn in Big Sur, California.

Sautéed Mahi Mahi with Asian Noodles and Thai Curry Sauce

COOK'S STRATEGY: Once the Thai Curry Sauce has been made, it takes just a few minutes to cook the bok choy, noodles, and fish.

Serves 6 to 8

2 pounds mahi mahi or wahoo fillets, cut into 6 to 8 pieces

2 pounds baby bok choy

2 pounds fresh Asian noodles, such as Azumaya-brand medium flat noodles

2 tablespoons canola oil

Cilantro sprigs for garnish

➜ Thai Curry Sauce

Bring 2 saucepans of salted water to a boil. Add the bok choy to 1 pan, cook for about 2 minutes, and strain. Cook the noodles in the other pan of water for about 90 seconds. Drain, place in a bowl, and add enough Thai Curry Sauce to coat the noodles well.

Heat a large sauté pan over high heat. Add the oil and cook the fish for 2 minutes on each side or until desired doneness.

To serve, put a "nest" of curry noodles in the center of each plate. Place the bok choy on top of the noodles. Remove the skin from the fish, place a fillet on the top of each stack, and put a little more sauce around the plate for color. Add a sprig of cilantro for garnish. Extra sauce can be frozen.

➜ Thai Curry Sauce

1/3 cup canola oil

1 tablespoon chile oil

2 yellow onions, chopped

1/3 cup Thai yellow curry paste (Mae Ploy or Thai Kitchen)

3 kaffir lime leaves

9 cloves garlic, smashed

2 tablespoons ground turmeric

1 cup freshly squeezed lime juice

2 tablespoons fish sauce

Four 12-ounce cans coconut milk

3 tablespoons finely grated galangal

1/4 cup honey (or to taste)

Salt

Place the canola oil, chile oil, onions, curry paste, kaffir lime leaves, garlic, and turmeric in a large nonreactive pot over medium heat. Cook the mixture until the onions are translucent and soft. Do not brown the mixture or it will become bitter. Add the lime juice and fish sauce, stir to dislodge browned bits, and simmer for 10 minutes. Add the coconut milk and galangal; bring to a simmer. Gently cook the curry until it has reduced by one-third. Season to taste with honey and salt.

Jeffery Powell is Chef de Cuisine at PlumpJack Squaw Valley Inn, Olympic Valley, California.

Grilled Mahi Mahi with Thai-Style Coconut Paella

Serves 4

Paella is one of my all-time favorites. This is my version of an Asian-style paella recipe, showcasing our style of cooking—Hawaiian fusion. We utilize local ingredients, bold Asian spices, and European sauces with an emphasis on seafood.

COOK'S STRATEGY: The aromatic Paella Broth takes about forty-five minutes from start to finish; make it before you begin cooking the paella itself.

4 mahi mahi fillets, 4 ounces each
3 tablespoons butter
20 saffron threads
2 shallots, minced
1 tablespoon minced garlic
1 teaspoon minced fresh ginger
2 cups rice
3 cups chicken broth
2 chicken thighs, each cut into
    4 pieces (8 pieces total)

12 large shrimp (U.S. farmed
    or trawled)
About 1 pound Polish sausage (Kielbasa),
    sliced into 3/4-inch lengths
8 pearl onions, cooked for 1 minute
    in boiling water
Salt and freshly ground black pepper
↠ Paella Broth

Melt the butter in a large sauté pan over medium heat and sauté the saffron, shallots, garlic, and ginger until the shallots are translucent, about 2 minutes. Add the rice and stir for another minute. Add the chicken broth, cover, and cook for about 5 minutes. Remove the lid and line the surface of the rice with the chicken, shrimp, sausage slices, and pearl onions. Cover and continue to cook until all ingredients are fully cooked, about 10 to 15 minutes.

While the rice is cooking, preheat the grill. Salt and pepper the mahi mahi. Grill the fish to desired doneness, about 3 or 4 minutes per side.

To serve, spoon some of the rice into each of 4 large pasta bowls. Top each with equal amounts of chicken, sausage, shrimp, and pearl onions. Place the grilled mahi mahi on top and ladle Paella Broth over each serving.

❖ Paella Broth

1 tablespoon cooking oil

2 tablespoons minced Maui onion or other sweet onion, such as Vidalia

2 tablespoons chopped scallions

1 teaspoon minced garlic

1 teaspoon minced fresh ginger

1 cup coconut milk

1 teaspoon freshly squeezed lemon juice

1 teaspoon fish sauce

1 teaspoon palm sugar

5 basil leaves

1 kaffir lime leaf

2 cups full-flavored chicken broth, preferably double strength

15 saffron threads

Salt and freshly ground black pepper

Heat the oil in a saucepan over medium heat. Sauté the onion, scallions, garlic, and ginger. Add the coconut milk, lemon juice, fish sauce, palm sugar, basil, kaffir lime leaf, and chicken broth. Simmer the liquid to reduce by one-third. Strain into another saucepan. Add the saffron and reduce again by half. Season with salt and pepper.

Roy Yamaguchi is Chef/Founder of thirty-one Roy's Restaurants located in Hawaii, Japan, Guam, and the U.S. mainland.

Cobia

SCIENTIFIC NAME: *Rachycentron canadum*

OTHER NAMES: Ling, lemonfish, crabeater, runner, sergeant fish

U.S. DISTRIBUTION: East and Gulf coasts

SEASON: In the Chesapeake Bay, cobia are most common from May to October, migrating from north to south from spring to fall. Off the southeastern United States and in the southern Gulf of Mexico, cobia are found from November to March, and in the northern Gulf from March to October.

WHAT TO LOOK FOR: Fillets should be slightly pink in color and with a sheen from the moderate oil content.

COLOR, TASTE, AND TEXTURE: The cooked flesh is firm, off-white, and dense, somewhat like swordfish. Cobia is flavorful but not overly strong.

COOKING METHODS: Grilling is a popular way of cooking cobia, but the fish also can be broiled, baked, or sautéed.

Grilled Cobia with Fried Green Tomatoes, Stewed Yellow Wax Beans, Green-Tomato Broth, and Limoncello Aïoli

Serves 4

Homemade limoncello needs one month to mellow before serving. A citrus-flavored vodka with the addition of a simple syrup may be substituted.

COOK'S STRATEGY: While the yellow wax beans are slowly stewing, marinate the cobia, prepare the Limoncello Aïoli, and start the Green-Tomato Broth. Finish the Green-Tomato Broth, grill the cobia, and fry the green tomatoes just before serving.

4 cobia steaks, 4 ounces each
2 tablespoons cider vinegar
1 tablespoon soy sauce
1 tablespoon walnut oil
Salt and freshly ground black pepper

✦ Stewed Yellow Wax Beans
✦ Fried Green Tomatoes
✦ Green Tomato Broth
✦ Limoncello Aïoli

Whisk together the vinegar, soy sauce, and oil. Pour over the fish and marinate for up to 3 hours. Remove the cobia from the marinade and season with salt and pepper. Light a charcoal or gas grill. Grill the cobia over high heat for about 2 minutes per side. Cobia should be grilled just to medium doneness; it will dry out if cooked too long.

Spoon the stewed yellow wax beans into 4 large soup plates. Arrange Fried Green Tomatoes on top. Set the grilled cobia on the tomatoes. Ladle the Green-Tomato Broth around the perimeter of the bowl and top with a dollop of Limoncello Aïoli.

✦ Stewed Yellow Wax Beans

3 tablespoons butter
1/2 pound yellow wax beans,
   halved lengthwise
4 Roma tomatoes, peeled, seeded,
   and diced

1/2 jalapeño pepper, seeds and ribs
   removed, minced
2 cloves garlic, minced
1 cup white wine
2 sprigs fresh thyme

Melt the butter in a sauté pan over low heat. Add the beans, tomatoes, jalapeño, and garlic; cook until the beans soften, about 10 minutes. Add 1 cup water, the wine, and the thyme and slowly simmer until the liquid evaporates, about 2 hours.

✦ Green-Tomato Broth

8 to 10 hard green tomatoes
1/2 stick (4 tablespoons) cold butter, cubed

Juice of 1/2 lemon
Salt and freshly ground black pepper

Juice the tomatoes in a vegetable juicer and strain through a fine-mesh sieve. You should have about 2 to 2-1/2 cups liquid. Pour into a saucepan and cook over medium heat until reduced to 1/2 cup liquid. Whisk in the cold butter. Season with lemon juice and salt and pepper to taste.

✦ Limoncello Aïoli

1 egg yolk
1/2 teaspoon Dijon mustard
Juice of 1/2 lemon
Grated zest of 1/2 lemon

✦ Limoncello (1 tablespoon; recipe below)
1/2 cup olive oil
Salt and freshly ground black pepper

Whisk the egg yolk, mustard, lemon juice, lemon zest, and 1 tablespoon of Limoncello together. Slowly drizzle in the olive oil while briskly whisking. Season with salt and pepper.

✦ Limoncello

5 lemons, scrubbed
One 750-ml bottle of vodka

1-1/2 cups sugar

With a sharp vegetable peeler or paring knife, cut the zest in strips from the lemons. Add the strips to a bottle of vodka. Close the bottle and let stand for 2 weeks. Bring 2 cups water and the sugar to a boil. Add the vodka, strain into a larger bottle, cover and let stand at room temperature for 2 more weeks. (Note: Alternatively, make a simple syrup, using the 1-1/2 cups sugar and water, and mix with a bottle of citrus-flavored vodka.) After 1 month, store Limoncello in the freezer. Limoncello makes an excellent digestif; serve chilled.

✦ Fried Green Tomatoes

Vegetable oil for frying
3 large, hard green tomatoes,
    each cut into 4 slices
1/4 cup flour, seasoned with salt and pepper

2 eggs, beaten
1/4 cup cornmeal, seasoned with salt
    and pepper

Pour oil to a 1/4-inch depth in a sauté pan and heat to 350°F. Dredge the tomatoes in the flour, then the beaten eggs, then the cornmeal. Immediately panfry in the hot oil until golden. This should be done last, as the tomatoes should be served hot.

Shane Ingram is Chef/Owner of Four Square Restaurant in Durham, North Carolina.

*f*LATFISH IN GENERAL ARE AMONG THE MILDEST
flavored fish—the perfect choice for those who relish a "nonfishy" flavor.
Named "flatfish" because they are thin and usually lie or swim along the bottom on one side, the species featured here range from the small Pacific sand
dabs, which are usually cooked whole after being cleaned, to the huge Pacific
halibut, fillets from which are very thick and hold up well in a variety of
recipes—like the excellent cider-based matelote by Greg Higgins.

From greatest to least commercial value, the flatfishes included in our
species list are Pacific halibut, Greenland halibut, Pacific sand dab, and
California halibut. Annual commercial landings of those species from 1991 to
2001 averaged approximately 70 million, 11 million, 2 million, and 1 million
pounds, respectively.

Pacific halibut *(center)* and speckled
sand dabs *(bottom left and right)*

In the Wild

Have you ever wondered how well a flatfish can see while lying on the ocean bottom on one side of its body? It actually sees very well, because it has both eyes on the same side of its head. But it doesn't start out this way: All flatfishes, including halibut and sand dabs, begin life with their eyes in the usual place—one on each side of the head, and they swim upright like other fish. As the flatfish grows into a juvenile, one eye makes its way to the other side to join the other. The adult then lies on the bottom, "blind"-side down, and both eyes point up into the water, where the flatfish can locate its prey. Masters at camouflage, the settled flatfish can change colors to blend in with the surrounding habitat, making it almost impossible to spot from above.

The Pacific halibut is one of the largest known food fishes. The largest ever recorded was 800 pounds and nearly 9 feet long (such large fish are rare, though; 20-to-100-pound fish are more commonly caught). Although it may live for more than forty years and so seems a likely candidate for overfishing, Pacific halibut is abundant off Alaska, and the species is considered an ecologically sound seafood choice. The fishery is managed through an unusual, and very successful, quota system that issues commercial fishermen in Alaska a percentage of the annual legal halibut harvest.

The Greenland halibut is tiny compared to the Pacific halibut, less than 100 pounds and 4 feet long. It lives in both the northern Atlantic (south to New Jersey) and northern Pacific (south to Baja California), but nearly all U.S. commercial catches are from Alaska. Note that this is not the Atlantic halibut (*Hippoglossus hippoglossus),* landings of which dropped approximately 87 percent between 1981 and 2001.

California halibut is similar in size to Greenland halibut but has a more limited distribution (Washington to Baja California), and nearly all U.S. commercial catches come from California. Pacific sand dabs, the smallest of the included species, reach about 1.3 feet. Landings of this species have remained relatively constant over the past two decades.

There are more than thirty commercially important U.S. flatfishes, including species of flounder, halibut, plaice, sole, sand dab, and turbot. Many are either of minor commercial importance or commercial landings have plummeted. In fact, all commercially fished flounder in the Atlantic are considered overfished or depleted, although the U.S. National Marine Fisheries Service reports progress in restoring stocks of summer flounder (*Paralichthys dentatus*). All of the flatfish species included here are sound choices, although consumers should avoid trawl-caught sand dabs when possible and opt for line-caught fish.

Macadamia Nut–Crusted Halibut with Mango Purée and Scallion Oil

Serves 10 as an appetizer, 4 as an entrée

I first fixed this dish while still Executive Chef at The Grill Room of the Windsor Court Hotel in New Orleans. I created it one night for my father, who was in town visiting and dined at the Chef's Table. My father liked the dish so much that I put it on the menu. It soon became second only to lobster in popularity, thereby securing its place on the menu at DC Coast, where it has been a top seller since the restaurant opened in 1998.—Jeff Tunks

COOK'S STRATEGY: The Scallion Oil and the Mango Purée may be prepared several hours in advance.

2 pounds Pacific halibut fillets, thickly cut
1/2 cup macadamia nuts
1/4 loaf brioche
Salt
2 eggs
3/4 cup light olive oil
1 teaspoon black sesame seeds
✦ Mango Purée
✦ Scallion Oil

Preheat the oven to 350°F. Spread the macadamia nuts in a pie pan and toast until golden, about 5 to 7 minutes. Cool and reserve. Pulse the brioche in a food processor until crumbs form. Pulse in the toasted nuts until a crumbly mixture forms. Reserve. Leave the oven on.

Cut the halibut into 3-ounce pieces for appetizer portions or 8-ounce pieces for entrées and season with salt. In a shallow bowl, beat the eggs and 2-1/2 tablespoons water to make an egg wash. Dredge the fish in egg wash, then coat completely in the nut-crumb mixture to make a nice crust. Heat the oil in a nonstick pan over medium-high heat. Sauté the fish until golden brown on both sides, about 1 minute per side. Remove from the heat and place fish on a baking sheet; set aside.

Spread the black sesame seeds in a pie plate and toast in the oven for approximately 5 minutes. Reserve.

(Continued)

Halibut

Pacific Halibut, Greenland Halibut, California Halibut

SCIENTIFIC NAMES: *Hippoglossus stenolepis* (Pacific), *Reinhardtius hippoglossoides* (Greenland), *Paralichthys californicus* (California)

OTHER NAMES: Pacific halibut is also called Alaska halibut, California halibut, and giant flounder. Greenland halibut is marketed as Greenland turbot in the United States. California halibut is also known as California flounder.

U.S. DISTRIBUTION: Pacific halibut—Alaska to California. California halibut—California to Alaska but most commonly caught in southern California. Greenland halibut is caught commercially off Alaska.

SEASON: The quota system now in place for Pacific halibut allows fresh fish to make its way to the market regularly. High-quality frozen halibut is available all year.

WHAT TO LOOK FOR: Halibut flesh should be white, translucent, and somewhat shiny. The fish are generally frozen to maintain the flesh at peak quality. Avoid flesh that has a milky white color or brownish blotches.

COLOR, TASTE, AND TEXTURE: For a lean fish, halibut has a mild but distinctive, pleasant flavor. When cooked, the large ivory-to-white flakes are firm and hold together well.

COOKING METHODS: Large chunks are good for soups, chowders, and stews. Fillets and steaks are excellent sautéed, roasted, or grilled. It can be dry if overcooked, so other options for cooking include braising, poaching, or steaming.

To serve, place the baking sheet with halibut in the hot oven and bake for about 4 minutes. Ladle a generous amount of warm Mango Purée onto each plate, and place a piece of halibut on the purée. Garnish with a ribbon of Scallion Oil and sprinkle the sesame seeds around the plate. Serve immediately.

✦ Mango Purée

1 mango	1/4 cup cream
1/2 cup white wine	Juice of 1 lime
1 tablespoon sugar	Salt

Peel the mango and remove all flesh. Place the mango chunks in a small saucepan over medium heat. Add the wine and sugar. Cook to reduce the volume by three-fourths, then add the cream. Bring to a boil and simmer for 5 minutes. Let cool slightly, then purée in a food processor. Strain the mixture into a bowl. Add the lime juice and salt to taste. Cover and set aside. Gently warm the sauce before serving.

✦ Scallion Oil

1 bunch scallions, green parts only	Pinch of sugar
1/2 cup olive oil	Pinch of salt

Bring a pot of salted water to a boil. Quickly blanch the scallion greens, then immediately plunge them into cold water. Remove and dry scallions. Place them in a blender with the olive oil, sugar, and salt; purée until smooth. Place the scallion oil in a squeeze bottle and reserve. The oil may be prepared several hours ahead of serving time.

Jeff Tunks is Executive Chef of TenPenh and DC Coast in Washington, D.C. Cliff Wharton is Chef de Cuisine of TenPenh.

Halibut, Crabmeat, and Mussels in Hot-and-Sour Broth

2 fillets Pacific (Alaska) halibut,
8 ounces each, skinned
8 fresh mussels, steamed and shucked
1 ounce fresh lump blue-crab meat
3 tablespoons olive oil
Salt and freshly ground black pepper
2 dried shiitake mushroom caps,
soaked in hot water and
thinly sliced
1 teaspoon sliced cilantro stems

2 cups chicken broth
8 hard-cooked quail eggs, peeled
2 tablespoons soy sauce
2 teaspoons sugar
1 teaspoon sriracha (Thai chile sauce)
1 teaspoon (heaping)
cornstarch mixed with
2 tablespoons cold water
8 sprigs cilantro, for garnish

Serves 2 to 4

Heat the olive oil over high heat in a nonstick frying pan. Sprinkle both sides of the halibut fillets with salt and pepper and place in the pan. Lower the heat to medium high. Lightly sear the halibut for about 2 minutes per side, until just cooked and lightly golden. Remove the fillets from the pan and set aside on a warm serving plate. Leave any remaining oil in the pan, keeping heat on medium high.

Add the mussels, mushrooms, and cilantro stems and sauté for 30 seconds. Add the chicken broth and, once the broth begins to boil, add the crabmeat, quail eggs, soy sauce, sugar, and sriracha, followed last by the cornstarch mixture. Lower the heat and simmer for 1 minute.

To serve, place the halibut fillets in deep serving plates. Ladle the hot-and-sour broth over the fish and garnish with cilantro sprigs.

Pookie Duangrat is Chef/Owner of Duangrat's Thai Restaurant in Falls Church, Virginia.

Halibut à la Grecque

Serves 2

2 Pacific halibut fillets, 6 to 8 ounces
  each, skin removed
Salt and freshly ground black pepper
1/2 cup crumbled feta cheese
1 large vine-ripened tomato,
  seeded and chopped
10 imported black olives
1 clove garlic, chopped

1 tablespoon chopped fresh oregano
1 tablespoon sliced basil leaves
1 bunch scallions, trimmed and sliced
12 cilantro leaves, chopped
8 tablespoons olive oil
Freshly squeezed lemon juice
Lemon wedges for garnish

Season the halibut fillets with salt and pepper. In a bowl, combine the cheese, tomato, olives, garlic, oregano, basil, scallions, and cilantro. Add 6 tablespoons of the olive oil. Season to taste with lemon juice, salt, and pepper; set aside (this mixture will serve as a topping for the fish).

Preheat a grill or heat the 2 remaining tablespoons of olive oil in a pan. Grill or sauté the fish for about 2 minutes on each side. Preheat the broiler. Place the cheese-herb mixture on top of the fish and broil for a few minutes until light golden brown.

Andre Bienvenu is Executive Chef of Joe's Stone Crab in Miami Beach, Florida.

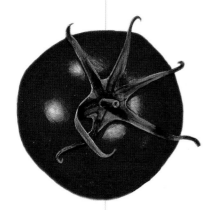

Shanghai Evano Halibut

Serves 4

While researching a paper about cooking on submarines, I came across a cook by the name of Nelson. During World War II, his sub made repeated trips to Shanghai, and he became known as "Shanghai Nelson." This halibut-and-linguine dish is a fusion of Chinese and Italian cookery. It is also my son Evan's favorite, so I've named it after him—"Evano" is Italian for Evan. My recipe is the accumulation of all of these thoughts.

The broiled halibut is served with sautéed vegetables and an Asian-inspired broth over linguine and topped with crispy strips of egg-roll wrappers and Parmesan cheese. A hot tangy salad, such as a cabbage slaw with hot pepper and seaweed salad, works well on the side.

COOK'S STRATEGY: Make the Asian-Inspired Broth first, then prepare the vegetables for the sauté. Next cook the linguine, fry the garnish, and broil the fish. Sauté the vegetables as a last step.

1 pound Pacific halibut fillet, cut into
    1-inch cubes
1 tablespoon red miso (red fermented
    soybean paste), preferably organic,
    such as Southriver adzuki-bean miso
1 teaspoon sesame oil
Pinch of freshly ground black pepper

1/2 pound linguine
1 teaspoon olive oil
1 teaspoon hot chile oil
✦ Sautéed Vegetables
✦ Asian-Inspired Broth
✦ Chinese-Italian Garnish

Toss the halibut cubes with the miso, sesame oil, and black pepper. Place on a foil-lined baking sheet and set aside. Cook the linguine in a pot of boiling salted water until al dente. Drain, rinse with cold water, drain again, and toss with the olive and chile oils. Set aside.

Preheat the broiler. Broil the fish (on 1 side only) on the baking sheet until lightly brown, about 8 minutes.

To serve, divide the linguine among 4 large soup bowls and top each with Sautéed Vegetables, a ladleful of Asian-Inspired Broth, and the broiled halibut. Finish with the Chinese-Italian Garnish.

(Continued)

❧ Sautéed Vegetables

2 tablespoons extra-virgin olive oil

1 teaspoon hot-pepper sesame oil

2 cups thinly sliced napa cabbage

1/4 cup sliced red bell pepper

2 cups bean sprouts

1/2 cup pea shoots, available at Asian markets

2 stalks celery, sliced

6 fresh shiitake mushrooms

6 button mushrooms

1 teaspoon chopped fresh ginger

Heat the olive and sesame oils in a large sauté pan over medium-high heat. Sauté the vegetables and ginger in the oil until just wilted, about 3 to 4 minutes.

❧ Asian-Inspired Broth

1 quart chicken broth

4 cloves, crushed

2 stalks celery

One 2-inch piece kombu (dried kelp), available at Asian food markets

1/4 cup shiro miso (white fermented soybean paste)

1 bay leaf

1 teaspoon rice-wine vinegar

1/4 teaspoon dried thyme leaves

1/4 teaspoon freshly ground black pepper

1/4 teaspoon dried hot red pepper flakes

Combine all ingredients in a stockpot, bring the mixture to a boil, and simmer for 20 minutes. Strain and keep the broth warm on the stove.

❧ Chinese-Italian Garnish

Olive oil for frying

2 egg-roll wrappers, cut into thin strips

1 cup freshly grated Parmesan

Heat 1 inch oil in a saucepan to 350°F. Add the strips of egg-roll wrapper and fry until crisp. Drain on paper towels and set aside. Use, along with the Parmesan, to garnish the halibut.

Chef/Author Greg Upshur is the personal chef of William Clay Ford Jr.; formerly, he brought his Motor City style of cuisine to the Food Network's *Ready, Set, Cook.*

Potato-Wrapped Halibut

1-1/2 pounds California halibut
2 large russet potatoes, peeled
Salt and freshly ground black pepper
1/4 cup olive oil
1/2 stick (4 tablespoons) unsalted butter
2 tablespoons freshly squeezed lemon juice

2 tablespoons diced tomato
1 tablespoon sliced Fresno chile
  (seeds removed)
1 tablespoon capers, lightly chopped
1 tablespoon chopped fresh parsley

Serves 4

Preheat the oven to 400°F. Bring a pot of water to a boil. Slice the potatoes lengthwise as thinly as possible—use a mandoline slicer if you have one. Boil the potato slices for 2 minutes and remove immediately. Place on paper towels to dry. Skin the halibut, cut into 4 equal portions, and season with salt and pepper. Wrap the potato slices tightly around the fish, making sure they overlap. In a nonstick ovenproof skillet, heat the oil and sear the potato-halibut parcels on both sides. Transfer the pan to the oven to finish cooking, about 8 to 10 minutes depending on the thickness of the fish.

Remove the pan from the oven and transfer the parcels to a warm plate. Pour off the extra fat in the skillet and wipe clean with a paper towel. In the same pan over medium heat, melt the butter and add the lemon juice, tomato, chile, capers, and parsley. When the butter is golden, remove from the heat.

To serve, place the potato-halibut parcels on 4 dinner plates and pour the butter sauce over them.

Luke Sung is Chef/Co-Owner of Isa in San Francisco, California.

Chermoula Halibut with Preserved-Lemon Bulgur and Asparagus Spears

Serves 4

Chermoula is a Moroccan green sauce flavored with garlic, lemon, cilantro, parsley, and spices.

COOK'S STRATEGY: Make preserved lemon well in advance to use in the bulgur. The bulgur may be prepared earlier in the day and stored in the refrigerator, but remember to let it come back to room temperature before serving. The fish itself is very easy—simply mix the herbs and spices for the chermoula and smear on the halibut before baking. The Lemon Beurre Blanc is an optional, yet delicious, indulgence.

4 Pacific halibut fillets, 6 to 8 ounces each
2/3 cup finely chopped fresh cilantro
1/3 cup finely chopped fresh parsley
4 cloves garlic, minced
1-1/2 teaspoons paprika
1/2 teaspoon ground cumin
1/8 teaspoon cayenne

1/4 cup extra-virgin olive oil
Juice of 2 lemons
Salt
✦ Preserved-Lemon Bulgur
✦ Asparagus Spears
✦ Lemon Beurre Blanc (optional)

To make chermoula, combine the cilantro, parsley, garlic, paprika, cumin, and cayenne in a bowl. Whisk in the oil and lemon juice. Add salt to taste.

Preheat the oven to 350°F. Place the halibut fillets in a baking dish and spread some chermoula over them. Bake for 5 to 7 minutes.

Mound the Preserved-Lemon Bulgur with the asparagus onto 4 dinner plates. Lay the halibut over the bulgur and top with a little more chermoula. If desired, garnish with the Lemon Beurre Blanc, pouring it in a ring around the edge of the plate.

✦ Preserved-Lemon Bulgur
2 tablespoons olive oil
1 small red onion, finely chopped
1-1/2 cups bulgur

1/2 teaspoon salt
✦ Preserved-Lemon Dressing

Heat the oil in a saucepan over medium heat. Sauté the onions for 1 minute. Add the bulgur and cook, stirring, until lightly toasted, about 4 to 5 minutes. Add 2 cups water and the salt; bring to a boil. Cover, reduce the heat to low, and simmer until the bulgur is tender, about 12 minutes. Let cool. Toss with Preserved-Lemon Dressing. Taste and adjust seasoning if necessary. The recipe may be prepared a day or 2 in advance and refrigerated.

❧ Preserved-Lemon Dressing

1/2 cup Preserved Lemon (page 219),
   chopped
1/4 teaspoon ground cumin

1/2 teaspoon salt
1/4 teaspoon freshly ground black pepper
1/2 cup olive oil

In a bowl, stir together the chopped Preserved Lemon, cumin, salt, and pepper. Whisk in the olive oil.

❧ Asparagus Spears

8 asparagus spears
Olive oil

Salt and freshly ground black pepper

Peel the asparagus if they are large; cut spears on the diagonal. Cook the asparagus in boiling salted water for 2 minutes; remove spears and place in ice water. Drain and dry well. Toss the asparagus with olive oil and salt and pepper to taste. Briefly grill or sauté shortly before serving.

❧ Lemon Beurre Blanc

1/4 cup freshly squeezed lemon juice
1/4 cup white wine
1/2 shallot, sliced
1/4 teaspoon black peppercorns

1-1/2 sprigs fresh thyme
1/2 pound (2 sticks) cold unsalted butter,
   cut into pieces

In a saucepan, combine the lemon juice, wine, shallot, peppercorns, and thyme. Cook over medium to high heat until about 1 tablespoon of liquid remains. Strain into another saucepan and place over medium heat. Whisk in the cold butter piece by piece. Keep warm (not too hot, not too cold).

Monica Pope is Owner/Chef of Boulevard Bistrot in Houston, Texas. She has been called "Alice Waters of the Third Coast."

Grilled Halibut with Orange-Tarragon Beurre Blanc

Serves 4

COOK'S STRATEGY: Prepare the sauce to the point of whisking in the butter and set aside while you grill the fish. Finish the sauce at the last minute.

4 Pacific halibut fillets, 6 to 8 ounces each
Salt and freshly ground white pepper

1 tablespoon olive oil
❧ Orange-Tarragon Beurre Blanc

Light a charcoal or gas grill. Gently season the halibut on both sides with salt and white pepper. Lightly oil the grill with olive oil. Grill the fillets over high heat for about 3 minutes per side.

Place the grilled fish on dinner plates and pour the Orange-Tarragon Beurre Blanc over and around it.

❧ Orange-Tarragon Beurre Blanc
1 tablespoon finely minced shallots
2 tablespoons white-wine vinegar
1-1/2 tablespoons Grand Marnier
   or other orange liqueur
1-1/2 tablespoons fresh orange juice
1 tablespoon chopped fresh tarragon

1/2 cup heavy cream
2 sticks (16 tablespoons) unsalted butter,
   at room temperature, cut into pieces
1 teaspoon grated orange zest
Salt and freshly ground white pepper

Combine the shallots, vinegar, Grand Marnier, orange juice, and tarragon in a saucepan. Cook rapidly over high heat until the liquid has almost evaporated, 1 to 2 minutes. Add the cream and cook over medium heat until the mixture has reduced and thickened slightly, 1 to 2 minutes. Remove the pan from the heat and set it aside while you grill the halibut.

Just before serving, pour the sauce into the top of a double boiler over hot, not boiling, water. Add the butter piece by piece, along with the orange zest, salt, and white pepper; whisk until all the butter has been incorporated. Serve immediately.

John Toulze is Executive Chef of the girl & the gaucho in Glen Ellen, California, and the girl & the fig in Sonoma and Petaluma, California.

Matelote of Pacific Northwest Seafood

"Matelote" is French for a seafood stew made with a cider broth. It's a traditional dish in Normandy and Brittany.

Serves 12

1-1/2 pounds Pacific halibut, cut into
    1-inch pieces
1-1/2 pounds wild salmon, cut into
    1-inch pieces
1-1/2 pounds fresh mussels, cleaned
    and debearded
24 shucked Pacific yearling or
    Kumomoto oysters
12 live crawfish
Salt and freshly ground black pepper
1 cup all-purpose flour
1/4 cup canola oil

1 pound chanterelle mushrooms, sliced
1/4 cup minced shallots
2 tablespoons minced garlic
Pinch cayenne pepper
One 750-ml bottle hard cider
1-1/2 pounds fingerling potatoes,
    split lengthwise and poached
    until just tender
1 cup heavy cream
3 sprigs fresh thyme
Cider vinegar, optional
1/2 cup chopped fresh parsley

Season the pieces of halibut and salmon with salt and pepper and dredge them in the flour, shaking off the excess. Heat the oil in a large, heavy-bottomed nonreactive saucepan over medium-high heat. When the oil just begins to smoke, carefully sear the fish on both sides until nicely browned, 3 to 5 minutes; do this in several batches so as not to crowd the fish. Remove the browned pieces of fish to a warm platter. Add the mushrooms, shallots, garlic, and cayenne to the pan and sauté until the chanterelles are tender, 3 to 5 minutes. Deglaze with the cider and then add the potatoes, mussels, oysters, crawfish, cream, and thyme sprigs. Cover tightly and bring to a low boil. Adjust the seasoning to taste with salt, pepper, cayenne, and perhaps a dash of cider vinegar. Add the salmon and halibut and continue cooking until the mussels open, taking care to not break up the fish and shellfish.

To serve, ladle the matelote into 12 large bowls and sprinkle with chopped parsley. Serve with crusty bread and more cider.

Greg Higgins is Chef/Owner of Higgins Restaurant and Bar in Portland, Oregon.

Sautéed Sand Dabs with Coriander Potatoes, Sautéed Spinach, Capers, Sage, and Lemon

Serves 4

Sand dabs are the favored fish here in the Bay area. You will find them on the menus of all the venerable San Francisco restaurants, and for good reason. When cooked whole, the flesh is easily separated from the bone and the small effort is greatly rewarded with a meat that is moist, sweet, and succulent.

Because of a naturally occurring enzyme that causes the fish to break down quickly after being caught, it does not transport or freeze well, ensuring its place as a local treat and helping sustain the species.

8 sand dabs
2 pounds Yukon Gold potatoes,
    washed but not peeled
Salt and freshly ground black pepper
1 cup all-purpose flour
1 cup pure olive oil
1 tablespoon finely chopped shallots
2 bunches fresh spinach leaves,
    stemmed and washed

4 tablespoons (1/2 stick) unsalted butter
1 tablespoon whole coriander,
    lightly toasted then ground
16 leaves fresh sage
4 tablespoons capers
Juice from 1 lemon

Simmer the unpeeled potatoes in salted water until cooked through. Remove the potatoes from the water, pour the water out of the pot, and put the potatoes back in the pot; cover and keep warm.

Preheat the oven to 350°F. Place a large nonstick pan over medium heat. While the pan is heating, season the sand dabs with salt and pepper and dredge through the flour, shaking off any excess flour. Add approximately 1/4 cup olive oil to the pan and, when the pan is hot, add the fish gently so as not to splash any hot oil. Turn up the heat to high and sauté to a golden brown on each side. Remove the fish from the pan and place them on a baking sheet; finish cooking the fish in the preheated oven for approximately 4 to 5 minutes.

While the fish is in the oven, cook the spinach: Preheat a large sauté pan, and add 2 tablespoons of olive oil. Add the chopped shallots and cook until soft. Add the spinach and just a touch of salt and sauté until it gives up all of its liquid. Gently squeeze to remove excess liquid and season to taste. Keep warm.

Remove the skin from the still-warm potatoes. With a fork, lightly crush the potatoes with the butter. Add the coriander and season with salt and pepper. Reserve.

Heat the remaining olive oil (approximately 2/3 cup) in a sauté pan. When hot, add the sage leaves. Cook just until they stop sizzling. Add the capers and lemon juice, and season the sauce with salt and pepper. Remove the pan from the heat.

When ready to serve, mound the crushed buttered potatoes in the center of each plate and place the spinach around the sides. Prop the sand dabs up against the potatoes, and pour the sauce over them. Serve and enjoy.

Bob Hurley is Chef/Owner of Hurley's Restaurant and Bar in Yountville, California.

Sand Dabs

SCIENTIFIC NAME: *Citharichthys sordidus* (Pacific sand dab)

OTHER NAMES: Mottled sand dab, soft flounder

U.S. DISTRIBUTION: Alaska to California but occurs in great abundance off California

SEASON: Year-round

WHAT TO LOOK FOR: Sand dabs are small, up to 1 pound, and may be sold as small as 4 ounces. They are sold whole.

COLOR, TASTE, AND TEXTURE: Sand dabs have mild, white, and moist flesh. The taste and texture is much like flounder or sole.

COOKING METHODS: Cook them whole, either by sautéing or frying them.

Issues Regarding U.S. Seafood

The oceans are in trouble. Our coasts are in trouble . . . all, perhaps, in serious trouble.

—U.S. Commission on Ocean Policy, September 2002

OVERFISHING AND FISHERIES MANAGEMENT

Marine animals are the only wildlife still hunted commercially on a large scale, but in recent decades many marine species have been overfished or depleted to the point of commercial extinction. Consumer demand and advances in commercial fishing technology have driven this trend, spurring record catches of marine fish and shellfish, with peak catches for many species occurring in the 1980s and 1990s. In 2001, for example, 3 million pounds of bluefin tuna were landed in the United States, down 75 percent from 12 million pounds in 1996; 33 million pounds of Atlantic cod were caught, down 72 percent from 118 million pounds in 1980; and 25 million pounds of snow crab were brought to shore, down 92 percent from 325 million pounds in 1991.

Management plans that include limits on size and overall catch, as well as gear, locality, and seasonal restrictions, have been implemented for many commercially and recreationally fished U.S. seafood species. Ideally, following passage of the 1996 Sustainable Fisheries Act, every species available to consumers should be considered well managed, but this is not the case. Regional fishery councils that make management decisions are supposed to represent a balance of commercial and recreational fishermen, marine scientists, and state and federal fishery managers, but sometimes they are composed predominantly of individuals whose livelihoods depend on the seafood industry. The National Marine Fisheries Service (NMFS), the federal agency charged with managing most U.S. seafood stocks, has only limited influence because state governments recommend individuals to serve on fishery management councils.

Sometimes, too, the discrepancy between what biologists report about the status of a species and what fishermen report they see is so great that the integrity of the data on which management plans are based is questionable. In 2002, for example, NMFS admitted that a trawl used to sample groundfish off New England was unintentionally set so that one side fished slightly higher off the bottom than the other, possibly resulting in low estimates of actual fish biomass and more-stringent-than-necessary regulations. Yet despite this possibility, several environmental groups recently filed a lawsuit against NMFS for failing to protect these same fish stocks. The issues are complex and involve more than turf battles between the fishing industry and conservationists. Properly managing commercially important species requires knowledge of their natural history—including life expectancy, growth rate, age at maturation, geographical range, abundance, genetics, spawning areas, and nursery areas—a tall order when studying species that live underwater and are thus difficult to observe.

Further, these data may not be available at the inception of a given fishery, and in such cases managers frequently find that they're one step behind in the game, implementing emergency management plans for stocks already in serious decline. For example, overfishing and environmental stresses, or both, resulted in a severe decline in landings of striped bass in the Chesapeake Bay in the early 1980s. In response, a complete moratorium on striped-bass fishing for parts of the bay was implemented from 1985 to 1989. Although such measures are frequently imposed late and have economically harsh consequences for the affected fishermen, they are often successful: By 1990, the Chesapeake Bay striped-bass fishery was reopened, and the stock is considered fully recovered. Likewise, stringent fishing regulations were established for Georges Bank groundfish after the collapse of cod and other fisheries.

Management problems are compounded when a widespread or highly migratory species is involved; in these cases, international management plans must be developed. The United Nations has responsibility for such species, which it handles through the Food and Agriculture Organization and regional commissions. The broadbill swordfish, widely distributed in tropical to temperate areas of the North Atlantic, South Atlantic, and Pacific, is a case in point. Relatively well managed in U.S. fishing operations off the west coast, swordfish stocks in the Atlantic declined dramatically when a few nations apparently ignored size and catch restrictions set by the International Commission for Conservation of Atlantic Tunas (ICCAT). New regulations to enhance compliance with ICCAT were established in 1997, and swordfish in the North Atlantic are reported to have recovered to 94 percent of the predecline level (although most of the gain is from greater numbers of younger fish, which cannot yet reproduce).

The Patagonian and Antarctic toothfishes, more commonly known collectively as Chilean sea bass, are other commercially important, widespread species, occurring throughout the cold, deep waters of the southern hemisphere. The fish was essentially unknown in North American cuisine fifteen years ago, but today it is enormously popular. Although quotas exist for the species in Antarctic and neighboring waters through the international Commission for the Conservation of Antarctic Marine Living Resources (CCAMLR), poaching is common. The species could become overfished before sufficient natural history data are available to construct and enforce a global management plan. Even the geographical distributions of the species aren't known: The Patagonian toothfish was recently discovered for the first time in the northern hemisphere, off Greenland. The CCAMLR, of which the United States is a member, has implemented a program to document landings and international trade of Chilean sea bass. The United States supports the documentation requirement, has seized illegally caught Chilean sea bass entering the country, and encourages consumers to verify with a seller that the fish being purchased was caught in accordance with CCAMLR regulations.

DESTRUCTIVE FISHERY PRACTICES

Overfishing and poor management are not the only ecological concerns surrounding the commercial fishing industry: In addition, methods used to catch seafood can harm the environment. Trawl nets or dredges that are dragged along the bottom, for example, can alter habitat. When trawling is done over sand, large-scale damage may be minimal; trawling for groundfish off the east and west coasts of the United States, however, has destroyed forests of deep-sea corals that may have been hundreds or thousands of years old. These forests, like those on land, provide essential habitat for animal life. The destroyed corals may take decades or even much longer to recover. Trawling through grass beds, such as turtle grass in the Gulf of Mexico, can both damage nursery grounds for commercially important species and result in high catches of those juvenile fish as "bycatch"—nontargeted animals that are caught and usually killed when fishing for the target species. Bycatch is a serious concern in many parts of the world that have trawl fisheries, such as for shrimp and groundfish, as well as longline fisheries as for tuna and swordfish. With trawls, it is estimated that 3 to 100 hundred pounds of sealife may be killed for every pound of the target species harvested. In the United States, 2.3 billion pounds of sealife were discarded as bycatch in 2000 alone. The United States is addressing the issue in its shrimp-trawl fisheries in the Gulf of Mexico by requiring that trawl nets be fitted with bycatch-reduction devices, which reportedly reduce the unintended capture by more than half without affecting the shrimp catch. In 2003, all shrimp trawlers in the western Atlantic and Gulf of Mexico also will be required to fit their nets with new turtle-excluder devices, which are more effective than previous models in enabling all species of sea turtles to escape. Longliners, which lay thousands of baited hooks on or within miles of ocean, frequently catch sea birds, sharks, and sea turtles, including the endangered leatherback turtle. Seafood in markets labeled as "line caught" may be from longlining; more ecologically sound line-caught methods include trolling (single lines towed behind a boat) or other solitary hook-and-line methods such as hand lines and rod and reel. Some environmental and scientific groups are calling for bans of certain types of fishing gear to protect ocean resources. Another strategy involves establishing areas that are off limits to fishermen. In an attempt to protect sea scallops, for example, areas off New England have been closed to dredging; because the animals are not strong long-distance swimmers, doing so allows them to grow undisturbed. Scallop abundance increased exponentially in closed areas after only a few years of closure.

FISH FARMING

As an alternative to harvesting seafood from the ocean, some fish and shellfish species are now farmed using various aquaculture methods. Although ostensibly providing the ultimate solution to expanding seafood production, not all fish-farming practices are ecologically sound, and some may have deleterious effects on human health. Farming operations for clams, oysters, mussels, and scallops have few environmental problems as long as the animals are grown in clean water—an important consideration because these shellfish are filter feeders and can accumulate pollutants. Inland finfish operations, such as those for rainbow trout, catfish, striped bass, white sturgeon, and tilapia, also elicit few environmental concerns. Most of the negative issues involve coastal farming operations, such as those for Atlantic salmon and shrimp. Issues include the destruction of wetlands or mangroves (which serve as nursery areas for many finfishes) for construction of farms; discharge of waste into surrounding water; the spread of disease from farmed fish into wild populations; the interbreeding of wild populations with exotic or genetically altered farmed fish that escape from ponds; and, in some shrimp and crawfish operations in underdeveloped countries, the use of the potent antibiotic chloramphenicol, for which the U.S. Food and Drug Administration states there is no known safe level of human exposure. The United States is not a major producer of farmed Atlantic salmon or shrimp, and most of the complaints are directed toward foreign producers whose products the United States imports in vast quantities. U.S. shrimp farms—such as those in Texas—are well regulated and pose fewer environmental concerns relative to some foreign operations. Chemicals such as chloramphenicol are strictly forbidden in U.S. farming. As part of a settlement agreement, one salmon farm in Maine has agreed to strict environmental control measures.

An additional concern about salmon farming that does extend to U.S. operations is the large amount of fish that must be killed to feed farmed salmon: It takes 2 to 3 pounds of wild-caught fish to produce 1 pound of farmed salmon. At least one potential solution involves using by-products from fish processing plants as salmon food, as one manufacturer of fish food for salmon hatcheries and other aquaculture ventures is doing in the Pacific Northwest, Canada, and Alaska. This operation maximizes the yield and minimizes waste from fish caught for seafood. Grain-based pellets manufactured as food for other U.S.-farmed finfish such as catfish and tilapia do not include protein from wild-caught fish.

Concerns about farmed fish escaping into the wild—or even being intentionally released from hatcheries for stock enhancement—arise from the potential for the natural genetic diversity of a species to become so compromised that it cannot respond and adapt to normal challenges of survival. Additionally, characteristics that make certain fish good candidates for farms or hatcheries may be very different from those that are advantageous in the wild. If farmed and wild fish reproduce, these "bad genes" could be incorporated into the gene pool to the detriment of the wild fish.

The United States ranks approximately eleventh in global aquaculture but hopes to increase seafood farming significantly in the future. The ecological effects of various farming methods are being monitored and addressed, and new technology for open-ocean farming of finfish (such as mahi mahi, red snapper, cobia, tuna, halibut, flounder, and amberjack) and coastal farming of shellfish (like sea scallops) is under study or development. By increasing the national production of farmed seafood, the United States hopes to shrink its annual $9-billion trade deficit stemming from foreign seafood imports.

U.S. MARINE RESOURCE ASSESSMENT

Two U.S. panels are assessing how this country affects and protects its coastal zones and oceans. One is the U.S. Commission on Ocean Policy, members of which were recommended by Congress and appointed by the president. This commission was created by a bill that Senator Ernest "Fritz" Hollings (D-South Carolina) sponsored in 2000 and is headed by retired admiral James Watkins. The other is the Pew Oceans Commission, created by the Pew Charitable Trusts (also in 2000) and headed by former White House chief of staff Leon Panetta. The issues being addressed by the U.S. Commission are broader in scope than those of the independent panel, but both are providing recommendations on protection of U.S. marine resources. Although there were initial concerns by some environmental groups that the U.S. Commission might favor resource exploitation over protection, the first lines of an interim report released in September 2002 and quoted as an epigraph here suggest that the group is fully aware of the gravity of the situation. Recommendations from the Pew Commission were released in June 2003, and those of the U.S. Commission are expected in late 2003.

SUSTAINABLE SEAFOOD

The concept of sustainability is at the core of marine resource protection. As noted in the Introduction, sustainable seafood is fish or shellfish caught or farmed in a manner that doesn't risk the future of the species. A variety of factors affects the sustainability of a given fishery, including fishing pressure and features of the species, such as lifespan and age of sexual maturity. The orange roughy fishery off New Zealand, for example, collapsed because of heavy fishing pressure on a fish that can live 150 years and doesn't reach sexual maturity until 25 to 30 years of age. The resilience of such a long-lived species to heavy fishing pressure is low because the fish may be caught before they can reproduce, thus preventing maintenance of normal population sizes. Fast-growing species such as herring, mahi mahi, and wahoo have much greater resilience to fishing pressure. FishBase (www.fishbase.org), an extensive compilation of information for more than 27,000 fish species, rates the resilience of commercially harvested finfish as very low, low, medium, and high, based on the minimum time required for a population of the species to double in size (greater than 14 years, 4.5 to 14 years, 1.4 to 4.4 years, and less than 15 months, respectively). Even long-lived species can be fished sustainably if well managed; an example of such a success story is Alaska halibut.

CONSERVATION INITIATIVES

Many conservation-oriented organizations are working to protect marine resources, in part by informing consumers about ecological issues surrounding their seafood choices. Efforts by U.S. organizations have included the National Audubon Society's Seafood Lover's Almanac, Monterey Bay Aquarium's Seafood Watch Program, American Oceans Campaign's Ocean-Friendly Seafood initiative, the South Carolina Aquarium's Sustainable Seafood Education Project, the Seafood Choices Alliance's SeaSense Database, and the Environmental Defense's Seafood Selector. Most of these organizations provide lists of seafood species to be avoided because of overfishing, poor management, or ecologically unsound fishing or farming methods; seafood species that are good choices; and seafood species that fall somewhere in between. The Marine Stewardship Council (MSC) actually awards certifications to fisheries throughout the world for good management and sustainability. Conservation organizations do not restrict their lists of good seafood choices to stocks with MSC certifications in part because, to date, only six fishing industries have received the certification (handline-caught Atlantic mackerel off the southwest coast of England, cockles from the Burry Inlet in South Wales, hoki from the west coast of New Zealand's South Island, rock lobster from western Australia, driftnet-caught herring from the Greater Thames Estuary in the United Kingdom, and five species of Pacific salmon from Alaska). Farmed species have not been addressed by MSC.

Other groups, such as the California Seafood Council and some news reporters, are critical of steps taken by certain environmental organizations regarding seafood choices. For example, the 1998 "Give Swordfish a Break" campaign, designed to encourage chefs and consumers to boycott North Atlantic swordfish, was criticized for penalizing U.S. fishermen who have complied with federal fishing regulations, for not acknowledging that Pacific swordfish populations are in excellent shape, and for not giving the management plan implemented for Atlantic swordfish a chance to succeed. The more recent "Take a Pass on Sea Bass" drive to discourage consumption of Chilean sea bass also has met with resistance, with one writer labeling it an unnecessary scare tactic aimed at a species the U.S. Departments of State and Commerce recently indicated is not endangered.

SPECIES LIST

Our species list is far more encompassing than those offered by most conservation groups because we include species that are only regionally available or of minor commercial importance as well as those found commonly throughout the nation. Reasons for including or excluding a particular U.S. seafood species are detailed in the Smithsonian Web site at www.mnh.si.edu/seafood, but these decisions incorporated information from NMFS commercial landings, NMFS fishery status reports to Congress, FishBase, and conservation organizations. The species list was modified considerably during the project, in part because fish populations and fishery regulations continue to change, and in part because as we researched the more than 150 seafood species fished or farmed commercially in the United States, issues surfaced of which we were previously unaware. For example, our list initially did not include shrimp trawled and farmed in the southern United States because our research indicated general problems with trawl bycatch and coastal fish farms. But after learning about the bycatch-reduction devices now required in the Gulf of Mexico shrimp-trawl fishery and talking with a marine biologist at a Texas shrimp farm about how well regulated that operation is, we added brown, pink, white, and U.S.-farmed shrimp to the list. Species with which U.S. consumers are familiar that are not on the list may have been excluded because of problems with the way they are fished, farmed, or managed (for example, snow crab, king crab, sharks, grouper, snapper, bluefin tuna, most flounder, and Pacific rockfish); because they are considered to be recovering stocks (like Atlantic swordfish, Gulf of Mexico red drum, and wild Atlantic salmon); because they are not fished or farmed in U.S. waters (for example, most bay scallops and New Zealand hoki); or because of some combination of these reasons (such as Chilean sea bass and imported farmed Atlantic salmon and shrimp). We included a few species that appear to be vulnerable only in certain areas of their range (like blue crab and American shad in the Chesapeake Bay)—but only a few, because consumers often aren't provided with information on origins of seafood. We are certain that with time and additional research, the seafood list will continue to evolve, and we will provide updated information on the Smithsonian Web site as it becomes available to us.

OBTAINING SEAFOOD

Catching your own seafood is both fun and the surest way of obtaining a fresh meal in an ecologically sound manner. Recreational fishing is an enormous industry worldwide, and catch-and-release programs that help to conserve marine resources are abundant and beneficial. However, if a recreational fisher catches something legal and edible that is well managed but then releases it and purchases a species for dinner that is more problematic, that scenario isn't necessarily helpful. Despite the fact that more than half of the U.S. population lives in coastal areas, most of us rely on purchasing seafood rather than catching it. For all consumers buying seafood from grocery stores or seafood markets, then, we have attempted to describe the best choices from what is available. In addition, the advent of online shopping has greatly increased the diversity of seafood species available to the American public regardless of where they live. For species or stocks highlighted herein that are rare or available only regionally, we provide a listing of retail sources, many of which offer online ordering and overnight shipping.

SEAFOOD CAUTIONS

A few additional comments regarding seafood consumption: First, fish contain varying levels of methylmercury, chemically transformed mercury that accumulates in streams, rivers, lakes, and oceans. Because mercury accumulates in tissues over time, large old fish harbor more than small young fish. The U.S. Food and Drug Administration cautions pregnant or nursing women and children to limit consumption of shark, swordfish, king mackerel, and tilefish (none of which is part of our species list). Those wishing to learn more about methylmercury in seafood might consult the following Web site: www.cfsan.fda.gov/~dms/hgpdftoc. Second, consuming raw seafood that has not been properly handled or was harvested in polluted waters can be harmful because of the presence of certain microorganisms. Always purchase fish or shellfish for raw consumption (for example, oysters or clams on the halfshell, sashimi, sushi, ceviche, or tartare) from a reputable market. Finally, seafood can be part of a kosher diet, but not all fish species are considered kosher. A good guide to kosher fish can be found in the appendix of Yacov Lipschutz's book *Kashruth*, published in 1998 by Mesorah Publications.

SEAFOOD LABELING

Knowing what is being sold, where it is from, and how it was harvested or if it was farmed are keys to making environmentally sound seafood choices, but U.S. retailers often provide little information on their labels. For example, "Atlantic salmon" is often Atlantic salmon raised in Pacific coastal farms, and "line-caught cod" or "line-caught Chilean sea bass" may refer to fish that have been taken by longline and not the more ecologically sound trolled lines. In 2001, the European Union implemented a mandatory seafood-labeling program designed to strengthen the ability to trace fisheries from the sea to market. Several U.S. organizations, including the Monterey Bay Aquarium, the Pacific Coast Federation of Fishermen's Associations, and the Institute for Fisheries Resources, have asked the federal government to implement mandatory informational seafood labeling. Seafood that has been taken in MSC-certified fisheries is labeled as such, and by 2004 U.S. wholesalers and retailers will be required to provide country-of-origin labels for imported seafood and to indicate whether seafood was fished or farmed.

Seafood Species

OYSTERS, MUSSELS, AND CLAMS
Kumomoto oyster, *Crassostrea sikamea*
Pacific oyster, *Crassostrea gigas*
Eastern oyster, *Crassostrea virginica*
European flat oyster, *Ostrea edulis*
Blue mussel, *Mytilus edulis*
Blue (Penn Cove) mussel, *Mytilus trossulus*
Mediterranean mussel, *Mytilus provincialis*
Hard clam (littleneck, topneck, cherry-stone, chowder clam, and quahog), *Mercenaria mercenaria*
Pacific littleneck clam, *Protothaca staminea*
Butter clam, *Saxidomus giganteous*
Manila clam, *Tapes philippanirum*

SCALLOPS
Atlantic sea scallop (farmed or diver only), *Placopecten magellanicus*
American bay scallop (farmed, e.g., Taylor bay), *Argopecten irradians*

OCTOPUS AND SQUID
Octopus, *Octopus* species
California market squid, *Loligo opalescens*

CRABS
Blue crab, *Callinectes sapidus*
Stone crab, *Menippe mercenaria*
Dungeness crab, *Cancer magister*

CRAWFISH AND LOBSTER
Crawfish (crayfish), *Procambarus clarkii*
American lobster, *Homarus americanus*

PRAWNS AND SHRIMP
California spot prawn, *Pandalus platyceros*
Northern pink shrimp (Maine shrimp), *Pandalus borealis*
U.S.-caught: white shrimp, *Litopenaeus setiferus;* brown shrimp, *Farfantepenaeus aztecus;* pink shrimp, *Farfantepenaeus duorarum*
U.S.-farmed shrimp, *Litopenaeus vannamei*

EEL AND FARMED WHITE STURGEON
American eel, *Anguilla rostrata*
Farm-raised white sturgeon, *Acipenser transmontanus*

HERRING AND SHAD
Atlantic herring, *Clupea harengus*
Pacific herring, *Clupea pallasii*
American shad, *Alosa sapidissima*

SARDINES, ANCHOVIES, AND SMELTS
Sardines: European pilchard, *Sardina pilchardus;* Pacific sardine, *Sardinops sagax;* Spanish sardine, *Sardinella aurita*
Northern anchovy, *Engraulis mordax*
Smelts: various species of *Osmerus*

CATFISH AND TILAPIA
Channel catfish, *Ictalurus punctatus*
Tilapia, *Oreochromis* species, usually, *O. niloticus*

SALMON, TROUT, AND ARTIC CHAR
Sockeye (red) salmon, *Oncorhynchus nerka*
King (Chinook) salmon, *Oncorhynchus tshawytscha*
Pink salmon, *Oncorhynchus gorbuscha*
Coho (silver) salmon, *Oncorhynchus kisutch*
Chum salmon, *Oncorhynchus keta*
Rainbow trout, *Oncorhynchus mykiss*
Arctic char, *Salvelinus alpinus*
Lake whitefish, *Coregonus clupeaformis*[2]

OPAH, POLLOCK, AND GRENADIER
Opah, *Lampris guttatus*
Alaska pollock, *Theragra chalcogramma*
Pollock (saithe), *Pollachius virens*[2]
Grenadier: various species of *Coryphaenoides* or *Macrourus*

SABLEFISH AND BUTTERFISH
Sablefish, *Anoplopoma fimbria*
Butterfish, *Peprilus triacanthus*
Harvestfish, *Peprilus paru*

BASSES AND PERCH
Striped bass, *Morone saxatilis*
Black sea bass, *Centropristis striata*[1]
Yellow perch, *Perca flavescens*
Tripletail, *Lobotes surinamensis*[2]

---

[1] This is the Atlantic black sea bass, not the Pacific black sea bass, *Stereolepis gigas,* which is critically endangered.

[2] Included on the species list sent to chefs, but they are not included in the text.

AMBERJACK AND POMPANO
Pompano, *Trachinotus carolinus*
Greater amberjack, *Seriola dumerili*
Yellowtail (hamachi), *Seriola lalandi*

BLUEFISH AND MULLET
Bluefish, *Pomatomus saltatrix*
Striped mullet, *Mugil cephalus*

TUNA, MACKEREL, AND WAHOO
Albacore tuna, *Thunnus alalunga*
Yellowfin tuna, *Thunnus albacares*
Blackfin tuna, *Thunnus atlanticus*
Skipjack tuna, *Katsuwonus pelamis*
Spanish mackerel, *Scomberomorus maculatus*
Atlantic mackerel, *Scomber scombrus*
Wahoo, *Acanthocybium solandri*

DRUMS
Atlantic croaker, *Micropogonius undulatus*
Spot, *Leiostomus xanthurus*
Spotted sea trout (speckled trout), *Cynoscion nebulosus*
Weakfish, *Cynoscion regalis*
Whiting, *Menticirrhus americanus*[2]
Black drum, *Pogonias cromis*

SHEEPSHEAD AND PORGY[2]
Sheepshead, *Archosargus probatocephalus*
Knobbed porgy, *Calamus nedosus*
Northern porgy (scup), *Stenotomus chrysops*

MAHI MAHI AND COBIA
Mahi mahi (common dolphinfish), *Coryphaena hippurus*
Cobia, *Rachycentron canadum*

HALIBUT AND SAND DABS
Greenland halibut (turbot), *Reinhardtius hippoglossoides*
California halibut, *Paralichthys californicus*
Alaska halibut, *Hippoglossus stenolepis*
Speckled sand dab, *Citharichthys stigmaeus*
Pacific sand dab, *Citharichthys sordidus*

PUFFERS[2]
Puffer, *Sphoeroides maculatus*

Sources for Selected Seafood

Most of the retail markets included here accept orders by telephone or e-mail and will ship their products anywhere in the United States. Sources for seafood species that are common in local, regional or national chain retail outlets are not included here. Contact information for each retailer is provided at the end of this list.

OYSTERS, MUSSELS, AND CLAMS

Kumomoto, Ameripure, Pacific and Eastern oysters: iSeafood.com, Lighthouse Seafood Market

Blue mussels: The Great Eastern Mussel Farms

Farmed Penn Cove mussels, manila clams, and oysters: Farm-2-Market, Northwest Seafood

Farmed oysters and manila clams: Hog Island Oyster Co.

SCALLOPS

Diver sea scallops: Browne Trading Co., Farm-2-Market, iSeafood.com, Lighthouse Seafood Market.

U.S.-farmed bay scallops: (Taylor bay scallops shipped live in the shell): Captain Marden's Seafood, Farm-2-Market

OCTOPUS AND SQUID

Squid (calamari): Alaska Seafood Connection, Braun Seafood Co., Charleston Seafood Express, Eco-Fish

Octopus: Citarella, Octopus Garden (fresh and frozen); Braun Seafood Co., Charleston Seafood Express (cooked whole baby octopus)

CRABS

Dungeness crabs: Alaska Seafood Connection, All Shores Seafood, Braun Seafood Co., Cap'n Zach's Crab House, Dave's Gourmet Albacore, Lighthouse Deli and Fish Co., Lighthouse Seafood Market

Blue crabs: Braun Seafood Co., Monterey Fish Market, Shore to Door Seafood (soft shell); Lighthouse Seafood Market (hard shell, cooked)

Stone-crab claws: Braun Seafood Co., Farm-2-Market, iSeafood.com, Lighthouse Seafood Market, Shore to Door Seafood

CRAWFISH AND LOBSTER

U.S.-farmed crawfish: Kyle LeBlanc Crayfish Farms, Louisiana Crawfish Co. (live crawfish—tails sold are imported); Cajun Grocer (live crawfish—tails sold are imported); Lighthouse Seafood Market

Maine lobsters (live): Available in most grocery stores and seafood markets as well as numerous online retailers, including Cape Porpoise Lobster Co., Gilmore's Seafood, Lighthouse Seafood Market

PRAWNS AND SHRIMP

U.S.-farmed shrimp: Harlingen Shrimp Farms, Ltd

U.S. white shrimp (caught with cast nets): Farm-2-Market

U.S.-trawled Gulf of Mexico or Atlantic shrimp (pink, white, or brown): Lighthouse Seafood Market, Shore to Door Seafood

Northern pink shrimp (Maine shrimp): Ecofish, Gilmore's Seafood, Integra Foods International, Sea Shore Seafood

Smoked northern pink shrimp (Maine shrimp): Ducktrap River Fish Farm

Spot prawns: Alaska Seafood Connection, Catalina Offshore Products (sushi quality amaebi), Coastal Seafood, Monterey Fish Market

EEL AND FARMED WHITE STURGEON

American eel: Braun Seafood Co.

Farmed white-sturgeon caviar (California cultured osetra): Farm-2-Market, iSeafood.com, Seattle Caviar Co., Stolt Sea Farm Americas

Farmed white-sturgeon fillets: Farm-2-Market, iSeafood.com, Lighthouse Seafood Market, Stolt Sea Farm Americas, Whole Foods

HERRING AND SHAD

Herring: Braun Seafood Co. (fresh or frozen); Charleston Seafood Express (in cream or in wine); Lighthouse Deli and Fish Co. (pickled)

Shad: Lighthouse Seafood Market, Braun Seafood Co. (shad and shad roe); Lusty Lobster, Captain Marden's Seafood (shad roe)

SARDINES, ANCHOVIES, AND SMELTS

Pacific sardines: Monterey Fish Market, Whole Foods

Sardines and Smelts: Braun Seafood Co.; Citarella, iSeafood.com (whole sardines, imported)

Atlantic rainbow smelt: Lighthouse Seafood Market, Wegmans

Anchovies: Karadenizhamsi (frozen); Pennsylvania Macaroni Co., Whole Foods (marinated, fresh)

CATFISH AND TILAPIA

Available in most grocery stores and seafood markets, as well as through numerous online retail outlets

SALMON, TROUT, AND ARCTIC CHAR

U.S.-farmed Atlantic salmon: Heritage Salmon

Wild Pacific salmon (various species, including Copper River King, Sockeye, and Coho): Alaska Seafood Connection, Copper River Seafoods, Dave's Gourmet Albacore, Diamond Organics, Eco-Fish, iSeafood.com, Lighthouse Deli and Fish Co., Lighthouse Seafood Market, Plankfish, Prime Select Seafood, Salmon Nation, Whole Foods

U.S.-farmed rainbow trout: Available in most grocery stores and seafood markets, as well as through numerous online retail outlets, including Charleston Seafood Express, Farm-2-Market, iSeafood.com, Lighthouse Seafood Market

Arctic char: Browne Trading Co., Citarella, Farm-2-Market, Lighthouse Seafood Market

Lake whitefish: Lighthouse Seafood Market

OPAH, POLLOCK, AND GRENADIER

Opah: All Shores Seafood, Coastal Seafood, Lighthouse Seafood Market, Wegmans

Pollock (Surimi/imitation crabmeat): Available in most grocery stores and National Fish and Shellfish

Grenadier: Eureka Fisheries

SABLEFISH AND BUTTERFISH

Sablefish (Alaskan butterfish/black cod): Alaska Seafood Connection, Eureka Fisheries, Lighthouse Seafood Market, Northwest Seafood.com, Pacific Seafood, Whole Foods.

Atlantic butterfish: Lighthouse Seafood Market, numerous local seafood markets seasonally

BASSES AND PERCH

Farm-raised hybrid striped bass: Farm-2-Market, iSeafood.com, Lighthouse Seafood Market, Lusty Lobster, Northwest Seafood, Monterey Fish Market

Black sea bass: Browne Trading Co., Citarella, Lighthouse Seafood Market (whole fish); iSeafood.com (whole fish and fillets)

Yellow perch: Charleston Seafood Express

AMBERJACK AND POMPANO

Yellowtail amberjack (hamachi): Catalina Offshore Products (sushi grade); All Shores Seafoods, Lighthouse Seafood Market, Lusty Lobster

Greater amberjack: Charleston Seafood Express, Lighthouse Seafood Market; Seafood Warehouse (individual Trigon-packed frozen fillets)

Pompano: Charleston Seafood Express, Citarella, Lighthouse Seafood Market, Lusty Lobster

BLUEFISH AND MULLET

Bluefish: Always Fresh Fish, iSeafood.com (whole and fillets); Lighthouse Seafood Market

Striped mullet: Lighthouse Seafood Market

TUNA, MACKEREL, AND WAHOO

Yellowfin tuna (ahi): Dave's Gourmet Albacore, iSeafood.com, Catalina Offshore Products (sushi grade); All Shores Seafood, Charleston Seafood Express, Lighthouse Deli and Fish Co., Lusty Lobster, Wegmans, Whole Foods

Albacore tuna: Catalina Offshore Products, Eco-Fish (sushi grade); Dave's Gourmet Albacore, Diamond Organics,

Lighthouse Deli and Fish Co., Lighthouse Seafood Market, Pacific Seafood

Wahoo: All Shores Seafood, Charleston Seafood Express, Lighthouse Seafood Market, Lusty Lobster, Wegmans

Spanish mackerel: Lighthouse Seafood Market, Lusty Lobster

DRUMS

Spotted sea trout: Citarella, Lighthouse Seafood Market

Black drum: Seafood Warehouse

SHEEPSHEAD AND PORGY*

Sheepshead: Lighthouse Seafood Market

Porgies: Citarella (whole)

MAHI MAHI AND COBIA

Mahi mahi: All Shores Seafood, Charleston Seafood Express, Eco-Fish, iSeafood.com, Lighthouse Seafood Market, Pacific Seafood, Seafood Warehouse, Shore to Door Seafood, Wegmans, Whole Foods

Cobia: Charleston Seafood Express, Lighthouse Seafood Market, Snapperfarm

HALIBUT AND SAND DABS

Alaska halibut: Alaska Seafood Connection, Charleston Seafood Express, Dave's Gourmet Albacore, Eco-Fish, Lighthouse Deli and Fish Co., Northwest Seafood, Pacific Seafood, Seafood Warehouse, Whole Foods

California halibut: Catalina Offshore Products

Sand dabs: Dave's Gourmet Albacore

PUFFER*

Puffer: Braun Seafood Co.

OTHER

Tobiko (flying fish roe): Charleston Seafood Express (red, spicy); iSeafood.com (orange, wasabi flavored); Lighthouse Seafood Market (wasabi, black, orange, and red)

---

*Included on the species list sent to chefs but not included in the text.

Bottarga di Muggine (dried mullet roe): Boutargue.org, Far Away Foods, Italtrade

Botarga or Bottarga di Tonno (dried tuna roe): Far Away Foods

CONTACT INFORMATION
FOR RETAILERS

Alaska Seafood Connection, 73–175 Highway 11, Suite D, Palm Desert, CA 92260; 760-346-6615; www.alaskaseafoodconnection.com

All Shores Seafood, 135 El Camino Real, San Bruno, CA 94066; 650-589-0532; www.allshoresseafood.com

Always Fresh Fish, www.alwaysfreshfish.com

Boutargue.org, www.boutargue.org

Braun Seafood Company, Main Road (Route 25), P.O. Box 971, Cutchogue, NY 11935; 631-734-6700; www.braun-seafood.com

Browne Trading Co., Merrill's Wharf, 262 Commercial Street, Portland, ME 04101; 207-775-7560; www.browne-trading.com

Cajun Grocer, Corporate Office, 208 West Pinhook Road, Lafayette, LA 70503; 1-800-CRAWFISH; www.cajungrocer.com

Cape Porpoise Lobster Company, 15 Pier Road, Cape Porpoise, ME 04014; 207-967-4268 or 1-800-967-4268; www.cape-porpoiselobster.com

Captain Marden's Seafood, 279 Linden Street, Wellesley, MA 02482; 1-800-666-0860; www.captainmardens.com

Cap'n Zach's Crab House, 1594 Reasor Road, McKinleyville, CA 95519; 707-839-9059; www.crabfeed.com

Catalina Offshore Products, 5202 Lovelock Street, San Diego, CA 92110; 619-297-9797; www.catalinaop.com

Charleston Seafood Express, 7195 Bryhawke Circle, Charleston, SC 29418; 888-609-FISH; www.charleston-seafood.com

Citarella, New York City, 212-874-0383; www.citarella.com

Coastal Seafood, 2330 Minnehaha Avenue South, Minneapolis, MN 55404-3153; 612-724-7425; www.coastalseafoods.com

Copper River Seafoods, One Cannery

Row, P.O. Box 158, Cordova, AK 99574; 888-622-1197; www.copperriverseafood.com

Dave's Gourmet Albacore, P.O. Box 1904, Soquel, CA 95073; 831-475-5847, www.davesalbacore.com

Diamond Organics, P.O. Box 2159, Freedom, CA 95019; 1-888–674–2642; www.diamondorganics.com

Ducktrap River Fish Farm, LLC, Fjord Seafood USA, 57 Little River Drive, Belfast, ME 04915; 207-338-6280 or 1-800-828-3825; www.ducktrap.com

Ecofish, 78 Market Street, Portsmouth, NH 03801; 603-430-0101; www.ecofish.com

Eureka Fisheries, P.O. Box 217, Fields Landing, CA 95537; 707-443-1673; www.eurekafisheries.com

Far Away Foods, 1443 Rollins Road, Burlingame, CA 94010; 650-344-1013; www.farawayfoods.com

Farm-2-Market, P.O. Box 124, Trout Town Road, Roscoe, NY 12776; 1-800-663-4326; www.farm-2-market.com

Gilmore's Seafood, 129 Court Street, Bath, ME 04530; 207-443-5231 or 1-800-849-9667; www.gilmoreseafood.com

Great Eastern Mussel Farms, P.O. Box 141, Long Cove Road, Tenants Harbor, ME 04860; 1-888-229-1436; www.eatmussels.com

Harlingen Shrimp Farms, Ltd., Los Fresnos, TX, 956-748-3976; www.harlingenshrimp.com

Heritage Salmon (products marketed through various outlets), Boston-area sales manager: 295 Turnpike Street Suite L1, Canton, MA 02021; 781-821-8900; www.heritagesalmon.com

Hog Island Oyster Company, P.O. Box 829, Marshall, CA 94940; 415-663-9218; www.hogislandoyster.com

Integra Foods International Corp. (Seattle office), 311 NW 177th Street, Shoreline, WA 98177; 206-546-5485; www.integrafoods.com

iSeafood.com, Grand Central Market, New York, NY 10017; 616-764-5732; www.iseafood.geomerx.com

Italtrade, 15500 SW Eighty-second Avenue, Miami, FL 33157-2217; 305-378-6235; www.italgroup.net

Karadenizhamsi, 950 Ridge Road, Unit B-16, Claymont, DE 19703; 302-798-9631; www.karadenizhamsi.com

Kyle LeBlanc Crayfish Farms, 302 Saint Peter Street, Raceland, LA 70394; 985-226-6444 or 985-537-6444; www.crawdads.net

Lighthouse Deli and Fish Co., 3640 SW Coast Highway, South Beach, OR 97366;1-800-834-1322 or 541-867-6800; www.lighthousedeli.com

Lighthouse Seafood Market, 640 Merrimon Avenue, No.105, Asheville, NC 28804; 828-281-3474; www.lighthouseseafoodmarket.com

Louisiana Crawfish Company, 1-888-522-7292; www.lacrawfish.com

Lusty Lobster, 88 Bay Avenue, P.O. Box 422, Highlands, NJ 07732; 732-291-4100; www.bestlobster.com

Monterey Fish Market, 1649 Hopkins, Berkeley, CA 94707; 510-525-5600; www.montereyfish.com

National Fish and Shellfish, 11–15 Parker Street, Gloucester, MA 01930-3017; 978-282-7880; www.seafoodlink.com

Northwest Seafood, 2012 East Illinois Street, Bellingham, WA 98226; 360-647-1181; www.northwest-seafood.com

Octopus Garden, 1780 Stillwell Ave., Brooklyn, NY; 718-946-9221

Pacific Seafood, Portland, OR; 503-226-2200; www.pacseafood.com

Pennsylvania Macaroni Co., 2010–2012 Penn Avenue, Pittsburgh, PA 15222; 412-471-8330; www.pennmac.com

Plankfish, 830 West Seventh, Eugene, OR 97402; 877-798-5988; www.plankfish.com

Prime Select Seafood, P.O. Box 846, Cordova, AK 99574; 907-424-7750 or 1-888-870-7292; www.pssifish.com

Salmon Nation, info@salmonnation.com

Seafood Warehouse, 1501 Whitney Avenue, Gretna, LA 70056; 877-973-2366; www.seafoodwarehouse.com

Sea Shore Seafood, 1128 Sawyer Road, Cape Elizabeth, ME 04107; 866-373-7473; www.seashoreseafood.com

Seattle Caviar Company, 2833 Eastlake Avenue, East Seattle, WA 98102; 1-888-323-3005 or 206-323-3005; www.caviar.com

Shore to Door Seafood, 67 Southwest Tenth Terrace, Boca Raton, FL 33486; 1-800-218-8147; www.shoretodoor.com

Snapperfarm, P.O. Box 685, Culebra, Puerto Rico 00775; 787-548-6134; www.snapperfarm.com

Stolt Sea Farm Americas, Sacramento Operations, Sacramento, CA; 1-800-525-0333; www.stoltseafarm.com

Wegmans (retail locations in New York, New Jersey, Pennsylvania, and Virginia) www.wegmans.com

Whole Foods (143 retail locations nationwide), www.wholefoods.com

Culinary Glossary

Aïoli. French garlic mayonnaise.

Aleppo chile. Moderately hot red chile from Turkey and Northern Syria, usually sold sun dried, seeded, and crushed.

Ancho chile powder. A seasoning made from the sweetest of the dried chiles, the ancho pepper; fresh, it is known as a poblano.

Arbol chile. Very hot dried, bright red chiles about 2-1/2 inches in length—related to cayenne.

Arborio rice. A medium-grain Italian rice, used for risotto because the plump, high-starch kernels give the cooked rice a creamy texture.

Arugula (also called roquette or rocket). A peppery salad green.

Beurre blanc. "White butter" in French, a sauce composed of wine, vinegar, shallots, and butter.

Blanch. To plunge herbs, vegetables, or fruits into boiling water briefly, then into cold water to stop the cooking process; used to firm the flesh, loosen skins, or to heighten and set color and flavor.

Bouquet garni. Herbs and spices wrapped in cheesecloth or tied with twine and placed in soups, stocks, or other cooking liquids for flavoring. Usually parsley, thyme, and bay leaf, but numerous herbs and spices can be used.

Brioche. A light, French bread made with butter and eggs.

Cachucha. A local name for a chile found in Brazil.

Canola oil. A bland-tasting oil lower in saturated fat (about 6 percent) than any other oil.

Caper. Flower bud of a bush native to the Mediterranean and parts of Asia, usually sun dried and pickled in a vinegar brine; capers lend piquancy to food because of their pungent flavor.

Carasau (Pane Carasau). A thin, crispy traditional Sardinian bread used dry or with wine, water, or sauces.

Ceviche. A Latin and South American dish made with raw seafood "cooked" in citrus (usually lime) juice, which turns the flesh opaque. Ceviche can be made with a variety of very fresh finfish and shellfish.

Champagne vinegar. A delicate, pale gold refined vinegar.

Chanterelle. A trumpet-shaped wild mushroom that ranges in color from bright yellow or orange to black; cooked chanterelles are slightly chewy with a nutty, sometimes fruity flavor.

Chipotle. A dried, smoked jalepeño; may be sold dried whole or ground, powdered, or pickled or canned in an adobo sauce of ground chiles, herbs, and vinegar.

Chinese black beans (or fermented black beans). Small black soybeans preserved in salt; to reduce saltiness, soak in warm water before using.

Choy sum (or pak choy). A Chinese plant with light or dark green, oval, or egg-shaped leaves.

Cilantro (Chinese parsley). The bright green leaves and stems of the coriander plant.

Clarified butter. Butter in which the milk solids have been removed. To make clarified butter, melt unsalted butter, skim any foam off the top, and then pour off the golden liquid at the surface that has separated from the solids that sink to the bottom.

Coconut milk. A liquid produced from soaking freshly grated coconut in hot water or milk.

Court bouillon. A simmering stock usually made with water and vinegar or wine, a bit of oil, onions, carrots, celery, leeks, garlic, and a bouquet garni.

Crème fraîche. A thick cream with a slightly sour flavor. Crème fraîche can be boiled and won't separate like sour cream. To make it at home, scald 1 cup heavy cream, stir in 1 cup buttermilk, sour cream, or plain yogurt. Let sit at room temperature until thick, about 3 or 4 hours. Crème fraîche will keep for several days in the refrigerator.

Daikon. A large, mild-tasting Asian radish.

Dashi kobu. *See* kombu.

Debeard. To remove the byssal threads or "beard" (fibers projecting outside shell) of mussels.

Deglaze. To dissolve hardened drippings with a liquid after sautéing or panfrying to further flavor a sauce.

Devein. To remove the gray-black intestinal vein from the back of shrimp or crawfish.

Duxelles. Finely chopped mushrooms, shallots, and herbs combined and slowly cooked in butter until thick.

Enoki (enokitake). Crunchy, delicate, mild-tasting mushrooms that grow in clumps and have long stems and tiny white caps; enoki can be eaten raw in salads or as a garnish.

Fennel (sweet anise). A plant with a bulbous base, celery-like stems, and feathery green tips that is cultivated throughout the Mediterranean and in the United States. The base and stems can be eaten raw or cooked and the green tips used as a garnish.

Fiddlehead fern. The young, dark green, tightly coiled fern frond before it opens into a fern leaf. Picked from Virginia to Canada during the spring, fiddleheads are a seasonal delicacy that can be enjoyed simply by trimming the ends and briefly steaming, simmering, or sautéing.

Filé powder. A spice made from dried sassafras leaves and used to flavor gumbo and other Cajun dishes.

Fines herbes. Finely chopped herbs (various but usually fresh chervil, chives, parsley, and tarragon) added to a dish shortly before serving.

Fingerling potato. Long, slender, sometimes lumpy small potatoes.

Fish sauce (nuoc mam, nam pla). A thin, salty liquid made from salted fish.

Frisée. A member of the chicory family often used in salads; frisée is feathery with delicate, slender, curly, pale green leaves.

Gaeta (Gyeta) olive. Small, black Italian olives that are dry cured (black and wrinkled) or brine cured (dark purple and smooth skinned). Kalamata olives may be substituted for brine-cured Gaetas.

Galangal (Galanga root, galangale). A rhizome with a spicy ginger flavor commonly used in Thai cooking.

Gari (beni shoga, pickled ginger). Sliced ginger, pickled in sweet vinegar and often colored pink to bright red.

Grape tomato. A small, oval tomato about

one-half to one-third the size of a cherry tomato.

Green garlic. Young garlic with a long green top, harvested before it begins to form cloves. The flavor is much milder than that of mature garlic.

Haricot vert. A very small, slender green bean.

Heirloom tomatoes. The fruit of old varieties of native, nonhybrid tomato plants.

Huacatay mint. A variety of South American marigold also known as black Peruvian mint.

Jalapeño pepper. A smooth, dark green (when fresh) chile that ranges from hot to very hot.

Japanese short-grain rice. A sweet rice that is soft and sticky when cooked.

Jicama (Mexican potato). A large, bulbous root with thin brown skin and white crunchy flesh. Raw, it has a sweet, nutty flavor; cooked, it maintains a crisp texture. Store up to 2 weeks in the refrigerator and peel just before using.

Kaffir lime leaves. Leaves of the kaffir lime tree grown in Southeast Asia and Hawaii; used dried or fresh in cooking.

Kasu paste. A paste made from the dregs (lees) at the bottom of tanks used for fermenting rice wine (sake).

Kombu (dashi kobu). A seaweed (kelp) used to make the fundamental soup stock in Japanese cuisine called dashi.

Kosher salt. An additive-free, coarse-grained salt used by some Jewish cooks in the preparation of meat, as well as by other cooks who prefer its texture and flavor.

Lemongrass. A stiff, reedlike grass with a citrus flavor.

Mace. A spice made from the red membrane covering the nutmeg seed.

Manchego cheese (curado, viejo). A golden, semifirm, mild-flavored cheese originally made only from the milk of the Spanish Manchego sheep; it melts beautifully in heated dishes.

Matelote. A French fish stew made with wine or cider.

Meyer lemon. A mild, sweet lemon relative to most supermarket lemons, such that both the peel and pulp can be eaten raw or cooked. Brought to the United States from China, Meyer lemons are available November through March in some specialty stores.

Mirin. A sweetened Japanese rice wine used for seasoning.

Miso (bean paste). Fermented soybean paste given various names depending on flavor and color (e.g., shiro miso is white miso).

Mojo. A Spanish sauce typically made with olives, tomato sauce, and vinegar; common variations have none of those ingredients except an acid.

Molho campanha. A Brazillian vinaigrette with finely diced vegetables; Molho (sauce), campanha (country) in Portuguese.

Morel. An edible wild mushroom related to but very different from yeast. The cap is light tan to black depending on the species, pine-cone shaped, spongy, and characterized by honeycomb-like indentations. A harbinger of spring, the morel is sought after for its earthy flavor.

Nage. An aromatic broth in which shellfish are cooked and served; from the French *nager*, to swim.

Napa. A Chinese cabbage with mild-flavored, crisp, crinkly leaves that are cream to pale green.

Niçoise. Traditionally refers to a cooking style of Nice characterized by the use of tomatoes, garlic, onion, and olives. Niçoise olives are small, oval olives ranging in color from purple-brown to brown-black and marketed cured in brine and packed in olive oil.

Nopales (pads, paddles). Fleshy oval leaves of the prickly pear cactus. Available year-round in South American food markets but best in the spring. Use a vegetable peeler or sharp knife to remove the thorns before cooking.

Nori. Sheets of dried seaweed that range in color from dark green to black; used in making maki sushi (rolls) as well as in other Asian dishes.

Onion sprouts. The young shoots (vs. roots for most sprouts) from onion seeds; they have a distinctive onion flavor.

Opal basil. A type of basil with purple leaves.

Orzo. A rice-shaped pasta.

Oyster sauce. A thick, concentrated, dark sauce made from oysters, brine, and soy sauce, used in oriental sauces and marinades.

Palm sugar (jaggery). A dark, coarse, unrefined sugar made from the sap of various palm trees or from sugarcane juice.

Pancetta. An Italian bacon cured with salt and spices but not smoked.

Panko. Japanese bread crumbs; coarser than those normally used to coat foods for frying, they create a crunchy crust.

Papas chorreades. Potatoes with tomato and cheese sauce.

Parboil. To boil food briefly to partially cook it; often used to ensure that ingredients requiring various cooking times will be done at the same time.

Pepitas. Pumpkin seeds popular in South American cuisine; may be sold salted, roasted, and raw, and with or without hulls.

Piquillo (pequillo). A small, red Spanish chile usually sold roasted and canned. Traditionally stuffed with salt-cod purée or other seafood mixtures.

Piment d'Espelette. A slender, mildly hot chile from Espelette, a village in the Basque region of France.

Pimentón de la Vera. A chile powder made from chiles grown and smoked in La Vera, Spain; paprika may be substituted.

Pimenton dulce. Spanish sweet paprika.

Pin bones. Intermuscular bones found in the center of an otherwise boneless fish fillet. The ends of these bones can be felt by running a finger down the flesh side of a fillet, and the bones can be removed by gripping the end of each bone with tweezers and pulling it out.

Poach. To cook gently in liquid kept just below the boiling point, so that the surface of the liquid quivers but does not simmer.

Rice vinegar. Vinegar made from fermented rice and widely used in Japanese and Chinese cooking.

Rock salt. Chunky, grayish salt crystals that are less refined than other salts. Used primarily as a bed on which to serve baked oysters and clams or in ice-cream makers but not consumed.

Roma tomato (Italian plum tomato). An oval tomato that comes in red and yellow varieties.

Rouille. A spicy, rust-colored French sauce of hot chiles, garlic, fresh bread crumbs, and olive oil.

Saffron. The yellow-orange stigmas from a small purple crocus; an expensive spice used to flavor and color dishes such as risotto, paella, and bouillabaisse.

Sambal (sambal oelek). A chile sauce popular throughout Indonesia, Malaysia, and southern India; the most basic form of sambal is sambal oelek, a mixture of chiles, brown sugar, and salt.

Sake. Japanese rice wine that is consumed as a beverage or used in sauces and marinades.

Scallion (green onion). A distinct variety of onion or the young of other onions or leeks; the base is white, and the tops are green.

Sea salt. A type of salt resulting from the evaporation of seawater.

Seviche. *See* ceviche.

Shallot. A member of the onion family but anatomically more like garlic than onion, with a head composed of multiple cloves, each covered with a thin, papery skin.

Shiso (perilla, Japanese basil). An aromatic, green serrate leaf from the perilla (or beefsteak) plant, belonging to the mint and basil family.

Soba. A Japanese noodle made from buckwheat and wheat flour.

Sriracha. A condiment made from sun-ripened chiles that are ground into a smooth paste along with garlic and packaged in a convenient squeeze bottle.

Thai chile (Thai bird chile). A small, fiery chile, 1 to 1-1/2 inches long, popular in southeast Asian cuisine.

Thai fish sauce. *See* fish sauce

Togarashi (ichimi). A small, hot red Japanese chile available fresh or as flakes or powder.

Tomatillo (Mexican green tomato, jamberry). A member of the tomato family resembling a small green tomato covered by a papery husk (which should be removed before using). Cooked tomatillos are used in a variety of Mexican and Southwest sauces, and the raw vegetable can be added to salads or fresh salsas.

Tomato confit. Tomatoes roasted slowly with a little olive oil, salt, pepper, and herbs.

Udo. A Japanese vegetable belonging to the ginseng family that looks like asparagus but tastes similar to fennel. It is used raw in salads or added to soups and other cooked dishes.

Verbena (lemon verbena). An herb with a strong lemon flavor, native to South America.

Ver jus (verjuice). A tart liquid made from unripe fruit, usually grapes, and used in sauces to heighten flavor; occasionally available in gourmet shops but difficult to find in the United States.

Wakame. A dark green seaweed used in Asian soups, cooked dishes, and salads. May be found in Asian markets fresh or dried.

Wasabi (Japanese horseradish). Derived from the root of an Asian plant and used to make a green condiment with a hot, pungent flavor. May be sold as a powder or a paste.

Yuzu. A sour Japanese citrus fruit typically used for its thick aromatic rind and for its juice.

Grant Achatz, *page 275*
Trio Restaurant
1625 Hinman Avenue
Evanston, IL 60201
847-733-8746

Jean Alberti, *page 131*
Kokkari Estiatorio
200 Jackson Street
San Francisco, CA 94111
415-981-0983

Mario Batali, *pages 115, 254*
Babbo
110 Waverly Place
New York, NY 10011
212-777-0303

Rick Bayless, *page 251*
Frontera Grill
445 North Clark Street
Chicago, IL 60610
312-661-1434

Andre Bienvenu, *pages 74, 290*
Joe's Stone Crab
11 Washington Avenue
Miami Beach, FL 33139
305-673-0365

Brian Bistrong, *page 182*
Citarella The Restaurant
1240 Avenue of the Americas at
    49th Street
Rockefeller Center
New York, NY 10020
212-332-1515

Dandi Bockius, *page 220*
Mitchell's Fish Market
185 West Waterfront Drive
Homestead, PA 15120
412-476-8844

Joanne Bondy, *page 217*
Ciudad's Restaurant
3888 Oak Lawn, No. 135
Turtle Creek Village
Dallas, TX 75226
214-219-3141

Jeffrey Buben, *page 263*
Vidalia
1990 M Street NW
Washington, DC 20036
202-659-1990

Jonathan Cartwright, *page 89*
The White Barn Inn
P.O. Box 560C
37 Beach Avenue
Kennebunkport, ME 04046
207-967-2321

Julia Child, *page 175*
Santa Barbara, CA

Tom Condron, *page 172*
Upstream
6902 Phillips Place Court
Charlotte, NC 28210
704-556-7730

Narsai David, *pages 163, 197, 201*
350 Berkeley Park Boulevard
Kensington, CA 94707
510-527-7900

Craig Deihl, *pages 10, 257*
Cypress Grille
167 East Bay Street
Charleston, SC 29401
843-577-7771

Marcel Desaulniers, *page 36*
The Trellis
Duke of Gloucester Street
Williamsburg, VA 23185
757-229-8610

Tracy Des Jardins, *page 139*
Jardiniere
300 Grove Street
San Francisco, CA 94102
415-861-5555

Gaetano "Tommy"
    DiGiovanni, *pages 11, 225,*
    266
Arnaud's Restaurant
813 Rue Bienville
New Orleans, LA 70112
866-230-8891

Roberto Donna, *page 48*
Galileo
1110 Twenty-first Street NW
Washington, DC 20036
202-331-0880

Pookie Duangrat, *page 289*
Duangrat's Thai Restaurant
5878 Leesburg Pike
Falls Church, VA 22041-2309
703-820-5775

Todd English, *page 238*
Olives
10 City Square
Charlestown, MA 02129
617-242-1999

Tenney Flynn, *page 228*
GW Fins
808 Bienville Street
New Orleans, LA 70112
504-581-3467

Steve Fujii, *page 195*
Ebisu
1283 Ninth Avenue
San Francisco, CA 94122-2306
415-566-1770

Nobuo Fukuda, *pages 43, 166*
Sea Saw
7133 East Stetson Drive
Scottsdale, AZ 85251
480-481-9463

Suzanne Goin, *page 103*
Lucques Restaurant
8474 Melrose Avenue
Los Angeles, CA 90069
323-655-6277

Debbie Gold and Michael
    Smith, *pages 134, 256*
Forty Sardines
11942 Roe
Overland Park, KS 66209
913-451-1040

Mark Gordon, *page 55*
Rose's Café
2298 Union Street
San Francisco, CA 94123
415-775-2200

Todd Gray, *page 63*
Equinox
818 Connecticut Avenue NW
Washington, DC 20006
202-331-8188

Jacques Haeringer, *page 202*
L'Auberge Chez François
332 Springvale Road
Great Falls, VA 22066
703-759-3800

Ryan Hardy, *page 106*
The Coach House in the Harbor
    View Hotel
131 North Water Street
Edgartown, MA 02539
508-627-7000

Jay Harlow, *pages 109, 208*
www.jayharlow.com

Chris Hastings, *page 86*
Hot and Hot Fish Club
2180 Eleventh Court South
Birmingham, AL 35205
205-933-5474

Greg Higgins, *pages 72, 297*
Higgins Restaurant and Bar
1239 SW Broadway
Portland, OR 97205-2915
503-222-9070

Barbara Hill, *page 178*
Snake Creek Grill
650 West 100 South
Heber, UT 84032
435-654-2133

Bob Hurley, *pages 120, 298*
Hurley's Restaurant and Bar
6518 Washington Street
Yountville, CA 94599
707-944-2386

Sandy Ingber, *pages 12, 118, 147*
Grand Central Oyster Bar
Grand Central Station
Lower Level
New York, NY 10017
212-490-6650

Shane Ingram, *page 282*
Four Square Restaurant
2701 Chapel Hill Road
Durham, NC 27707-1902
919-401-9877

Steve Johnson, *page 236*
The Blue Room
One Kendall Square
Cambridge, MA 02139
617-494-9034

Roger Johnsson, *pages 125, 186*
Norrvagen 3
18364 Taby
Sweden

Anne Kearney, *page 268*
Peristyle
1041 Dumaine Street
New Orleans, LA 70116
504-593-9535

Christine Keff, *pages 38, 56*
Flying Fish
2234 First Avenue
Seattle, WA 98121-1615
206-728-8595

Thomas Keller, *page 252*
French Laundry
6640 Washington Street
Yountville, CA 94599
707-944-2380

Paul Kendeffy, *page 218*
Zola New World Bistro
324 West College Avenue
State College, PA 16801
814-237-8474

Johanne Killeen and George
   Germon, *page 23*
Al Forno
57 South Main Street
Providence, RI 02903
401-273-9760

Robert Kinkead, *page 20*
Kinkead's
2000 Pennsylvania Avenue NW
Washington, DC 20007
202-296-7700

Rob Klink, *pages 143, 233*
Oceanaire Seafood Room
1201 F Street NW
Washington, DC 20004
202-347-2277

Emeril Lagasse, *page 79*
Emeril's Restaurant—New
   Orleans
Warehouse District
800 Tchoupitoulas
New Orleans, LA 70130
504-528-9393

A. D. Livingston, *pages 150, 155,
   240*
Wewahitchka, FL

Barbara Lynch, *page 32*
No. 9 Park
9 Park Street
Boston, MA 02108
617-742-9991

Armando "Tiny" Maes, *pages
   117, 141*
Rose Pistola
532 Columbus Avenue
San Francisco, CA 94133-2802
415-399-0499

Jeremy Marshall, *pages 18, 227,
   250*
Aquagrill
210 Spring Street
New York, NY 10013
212-274-0505

Nobuyuki Matsuhisa, *page 245*
Nobu
105 Hudson Street
New York, NY 10013
212-219-0500

Susan McCreight Lindeborg,
   page 16
Majestic Café
911 King Street
Alexandria, VA 22314-3018
703-837-9117

Timothy McNulty, *page 247*
The Lobster Pot Restaurant
321 Commercial Street
Provincetown, MA 02657
508-487-0842

Tory McPhail, *page 85*
Commander's Palace
1403 Washington Avenue
New Orleans, LA 70130
504-896-7600

Mary Sue Milliken and Susan
   Feniger, *pages 54, 193*
Border Grill
1445 Fourth Street
Santa Monica, CA 90401
310-451-1658

Masaharu Morimoto, *page 91*
Morimoto Restaurant
723 Chestnut Street
Philadelphia, PA 19106
215-413-9070

Christopher Nason, *page 98*
Sapphire Grill
110 West Congress Street
Savannah, GA 31401-2508
912-443-9962

Louis Osteen, *pages 14, 68*
Louis's at Pawleys
10880 Ocean Highway, U.S. 17
Pawley's Island, SC 29585
843-237-8757

Charlie Palmer and Dante
   Boccuzzi, *page 44*
Aureole
34 East Sixty-first Street
Manhattan, NY 10021
212-319-1660

Debra Paquette, *page 152*
ZOLA
3001 West End Avenue
Nashville, TN 37203
615-320-7778

Carole Peck, *page 239*
Good News Café
694 Main Street South
Woodbury, CT 06798
203-266-4663

Caprial Pence, *page 99*
Caprial's Bistro
7015 SE Milwaukie Avenue
Portland, OR 97202
503-236-6457

Jacques Pépin, *page 66*
Madison, CT

Guillermo Pernot, *pages 30,
   248, 255*
¡Pasión!
211 South Fifteenth Street
Philadelphia, PA 19102
215-875-9895

Monica Pope, *page 294*
Boulevard Bistrot
4319 Montrose Boulevard
Houston, TX 77006
713-524-6922

Nora Pouillon, *page 29*
Restaurant Nora
2132 Florida Avenue NW
Washington, DC 20008
202-462-5143

Jeffery Powell, *pages 9, 249, 279*
PlumpJack
1920 Squaw Valley Road
Olympic Valley, CA 96146
530-583-1576

Wolfgang Puck, *page 216*
Spago Beverly Hills
176 North Canon Drive
Beverly Hills, CA 90210
310-385-0880

Charles Ramseyer, *pages 19, 203*
Ray's Boathouse
6049 Seaview Avenue NW
Seattle, WA 98107
206-789-3770

Dale Reitzer, *pages 127, 142, 258, 264*
Acacia
3325 West Cary Street
Richmond, VA 23221
804-354-6060

Michel Richard, *page 33*
Citronelle
3000 M Street NW
Washington, DC 20007-3701
202-625-2150

Eric Ripert, *page 213*
Le Bernardin
787 Seventh Avenue
New York, NY 10019
212-554-1515

Eric Sarnow, *page 191*
The Hummingbird Room
Route 45
Spring Mills, PA 16875
814-422-9025

Cory Schreiber, *pages 24, 64, 168*
Wildwood
1221 NW Twenty-first Avenue
Portland, OR 97209
503-248-9663

Dan Shapiro, *page 184*
Pine Creek Café
2496 East River Road
Livingston, MT 59047
406-222-3628

Anthony Sindaco, *page 229*
Sunfish Grill
2771 East Atlantic Boulevard
Pompano Beach, FL 33062
954-788-2436

Frank Stitt, *page 17*
Highlands Bar and Grill
2011 Eleventh Avenue South
Birmingham, AL 35205
205-939-1400

Craig Stoll, *pages 50, 136*
Delfina
3621 Eighteenth Street
San Francisco, CA 94110
415-552-4055

Luke Sung, *page 293*
Isa Restaurant
3324 Steiner Street
San Francisco, CA 94123
415-567-9588

Mark Swomley and Jessica Gibson, *pages 158, 181*
The Carlton Restaurant
500 Grant Street
Pittsburgh, PA 15219
412-391-4099

Bradford Thompson, *pages 46, 82*
Mary Elaine's at The Phoenician
6000 East Camelback Road
Scottsdale, AZ 85251
480-423-2444

John Toulze, *pages 105, 296*
the girl & the gaucho
13690 Arnold Drive
P.O. Box 1433
Glen Ellen, CA 95442
707-938-2130

Jerry Traunfeld, *page 174*
The Herbfarm
14590 NE 145th Street
Woodinville, WA 98072
425-485-5300

Charlie Trotter, *page 215*
Charlie Trotter's
816 West Armitage Avenue
Chicago, IL 60614
773-248-6228

Ming Tsai, *page 205*
Blue Ginger
583 Washington Street
Wellesley, MA 02482
718-283-5790

Jeff Tunks and Cliff Wharton, *pages 110, 287*
TenPenh
1001 Pennsylvania Avenue NW
Washington, DC 20004
202-393-4500

Patricia Unterman, *page 71*
Hayes Street Grill
320 Hayes Street
San Francisco, CA 94102
415-863-5545

Greg Upshur, *page 291*
3663 Milner Road
Stockbridge, MI 49285
517-851-8588

Norman Van Aken, *page 34*
Norman's
21 Almeria Avenue
Coral Gables, FL 33134-6118
305-446-6767

Craig von Foerster, *page 277*
Sierra Mar
Post Ranch Inn
Highway 1, P.O. Box 546
Big Sur, CA 93920
831-667-2800

Robert Waggoner, *pages 61, 94*
Charleston Grill
Charleston Place Hotel
224 King Street
Charleston, SC 29401
843-577-4522

David Waltuck, *pages 21, 119*
Chanterelle
2 Harrison Street
New York, NY 10013
212-966-6960

Alice Waters, *pages 52, 70, 170*
Chez Panisse Café and Restaurant
1517 Shattuck Avenue
Berkeley, CA 94709
510-548-5072

Lucia Watson, *pages 165, 177*
Lucia's
1432 West Thirty-first Street
Minneapolis, MN 55408-2605
612-825-1572

Jerry Weinberg, *page 149*
Five Spice Café
175 Church Street
Burlington, VT 05401
802-864-4045

Jasper White, *pages 92, 96, 234*
Summer Shack
149 Alewife Brook Parkway
Cambridge, MA 02140
617-520-9500

Alan Wong, *page 22*
Alan Wong's
1857 South King Street
Honolulu, HI, 96826-2100
808-949-2526

Jonathan Wright, *page 80*
The Grill Room
Windsor Court Hotel
300 Gravier Street
New Orleans, LA 70130
504-596-4792

Roy Yamaguchi, *page 280*
Roy's—Honolulu
6600 Kalanaianaole Highway
Honolulu, HI 96825
808-396-7697

References

Web sites listed here also can be found at www.mnh.si.edu/seafood.

CLEANING, PURCHASING, AND COOKING SEAFOOD

Alaska Seafood. www.alaskaseafood.org.

Bittman, M. *Fish: The Complete Guide to Buying and Cooking.* New York: Wiley Publishing, 1994.

Fish and Seafood Online. Agriculture and Agri-Food Canada. http://atnriae.agr.ca/seafood/factsheet-e.htm.

"Foodnotes." *Thedacare Holistic Health.* www.thedacare.org/healthinfo.

Gorton's. www.gortons.com/cookbook. Includes a fish glossary.

Harlow, Jay. "Seafood." *Sally's Place.* www.sallysplace.com/food/columns/harlow/harlow_menu.

Pacific Seafood. www.pacseafood.com/products.

Peterson, J. *Fish and Shellfish.* New York: William Morrow and Co., 1996.

Randolph, S., and M. Snyder. *The Seafood List: FDA's Guide to Acceptable Market Names for Seafood Sold in Interstate Commerce.* U.S. Food and Drug Administration, Office of Seafood, 1993.

"Seafood." *Wegmans.* www.wegmans.com/kitchen/ingredients/fish/index.asp.

"Seafood Guide." *Simply Seafood.* www.simplyseafood.com/guide.

DIETARY CONSIDERATIONS OF SEAFOOD

"FAQs about Methylmercury." *Whole Foods.* www.wholefoodsmarket.com/healthinfo/methylmercury.

"FDA Increases Sampling of Imported Shrimp and Crayfish." *FDA.* www.cfsan.fda.gov/~lrd/fpshrimp.

Niazi, S. *To Fish or Not to Fish.* www.niazi.com/Omega/tofish.

"Manage Your Cholesterol One Day at a Time." *Reaping Benefits for a Lifetime.* Wake Forest University School of Medicine, Department of Family and Community Medicine. www.wfubmc.edu/fam_med/Cholest.

COMMERCIAL LANDINGS OF U.S. SEAFOOD SPECIES AND STATUS OF U.S. FISHERIES

"America's Living Oceans: Charting a Course for Sea Change." *A Report to the Nation: Recommendations for a New Ocean Policy.* May 2003. Pew Oceans Commission. www.pewoceans.org./oceans/oceans_report.asp

National Marine Fisheries Service Commercial Fishery Landings. www.st.nmfs.gov/st1/commercial.

NOAA Fisheries 2002 Report to Congress. www.nmfs.noaa.gov/sfa/reports.html.

Status of Fisheries of the United States. National Marine Fisheries Service. January 2001. www.nmfs.noaa.gov/sfa/status%20of%20fisheries2000.htm.

Status of the Fishery Resources off the Northeastern United States. www.nefsc.noaa.gov/sos/spsyn.

FISH AND SHELLFISH BIOLOGY

Brusca, R. C., and G. J. Brusca. *Invertebrates.* Sunderland, Mass.: Sinauer Associates, 1990.

Burnie, D., and D. E. Wilson, eds. *Animal—The Definitive Visual Guide to the World's Wildlife.* New York: DK Publishing, 2001.

Froese, R., and D. Pauly, eds. *FishBase.* June 4, 2003. www.fishbase.org.

Paxton, J. R., and W. N. Eschmeyer, eds. *Encyclopedia of Fishes.* San Diego: Academic Press, 1995.

SUSTAINABLE SEAFOOD CHOICES

"Ocean Friendly Seafood." *American Oceans Campaign.* www.americanoceans.org/fish/sustain.

"Seafood Selector." *Environmental Defense.* www.environmentaldefense.org/seafood/bestpicks.cfm.

"Audubon's Living Ocean's Seafood Guide." *National Audubon Society.* www.audubon.org/campaign/lo/seafood/guide.

"Fisheries." *Marine Stewardship Council.* http://eng.msc.org.

"Seafood." *Monterey Fish Market.* www.montereyfish.com/seafood.

Seafood Information Center. Monterey Bay Aquarium. www.seafoodinfocenter.org.

"Seafood Watch Program." *Monterey Bay Aquarium.* www.montereybayaquarium.com/cr/cr_seafoodwatch/sfw_factsheet.asp.

"Seasense Database." *Seafood Choices Alliances.* http://seafoodchoices.com.

U.S. PER CAPITA SEAFOOD CONSUMPTION

Americans Ate More Seafood in 1998. NOAA National Marine Fisheries Service news release. www.msstate.edu/dept/crec/fwmr98.

Shrimp Overtakes Canned Tuna as Top U.S. Seafood. NOAA news release. 2002. www.publicaffairs.noaa.gov/releases2002/aug02/noaa02113.

"Top Ten Seafoods." *National Fisheries Institute.* www.nfi.org.

"U.S. Top Ten Consumption List." *FDA.* www.fda.gov/OHRMS/DOCKETS/AC/02/slides/3816s1_05_Young/sld010.

OYSTERS, MUSSELS, AND CLAMS

AmeriPure Oysters. www.ameripure.com.

"Bivalvia, Mother of Pearl Oyster, Black-lip Pearl Oyster." *CIESM Atlas of Exotic Species in the Mediterranean Sea.* www.ciesm.org/atlas/Pinctadamargaritifera.html.

California's Living Marine Resources: A Status Report. California Department of Fish. www.dfg.ca.gov/mrd/status.

"Celebrating 100 Years of Oyster Culture in Washington State." *Oysters Are Cool.* Washington Sea Grant Program. www.wsg.Washington.edu/oysterstew/cool/waoyster.

"Clam Farming." *Indian River Lagoon National Estuary Program.* http://epa.gov/owow/oceans/lagoon/clamfarm.

"Clams Fishery—Pacific Region, Clam Biology." *Fisheries and Oceans, Canada.* www.pac.dfo-mpo.gc.ca/ops/fm/shellfish/Clam/biology_clam.

"Crabs and Shellfish." *Chesapeake Bay Program.* www.chesapeakebay.net/info/crabshell.

"Eastern Oyster." *Pelotes Island Nature Preserve.* http://pelotes.jea.com/eastern.htm.

Moskin, Julia. "The ABCs of Oysters." *New York Times News Service,* 2002.

www4.fosters.com/dining/articles/
food_12111_02.asp.

"Pearls—Marine Pearls." *American Museum
of Natural History.* www.amnh.org/exhi-
bitions/pearls/marine/index.

Robert Wan Pearl Museum.
www.tahiti-perles.com/Museum/.

SCALLOPS

Gugino, Sam. "Sunken Treasures." *Wine
Spectator,* August 28, 2002.

"Scallop Culture in British Columbia."
*British Columbia Shellfish Growers
Information Resource System.*
www.bcsga.ca/bcsgirs/scallops/
scallop.htm.

"Taylor Bay Scallops." *Eagan's.* www.
pandls.com/eagans/menus/
scallops.html.

"Sea Scallop." *Virginia Seafood.* Virginia
Marine Products Board. http://
virginiaseafood.org/foodService/
speciesFacts/seascallop.htm.

Weiss, Liz. "The Versatile Scallop." *CNN
Interactive,* March 27, 1997. http://
images.cnn.com/HEALTH/indepth.
food/meat/seafood/scallops.

OCTOPUS AND SQUID

About Octopuses. Mote Marine Laboratory.
www.marinelab.sarasota.fl.us/OCTOPI
.HTM

Hendrickson, L. *Northern Shortfin Squid.*
Northeast Fisheries Science Center.
www.nefsc.noaa.gov/sos/spsyn/iv/
sfsquid.

CRABS

Blue Crabs. Sea Science, Marine Resources
Division, South Carolina Department
of Natural Resources. www.dnr.
state.sc.us/marine/pub/seascience/blue
crab.html.

Guillory, Vince. *The Blue Crab Home Page.*
www.blue-crab.net/.

"Let's Give the Blue Crab a Break from the
Dredge." *Washington Times,* April 16,
1999. www.blue-crab.org/crab-
news/1999041601.htm.

Tales of the Blue Crab. Smithsonian
Environmental Research Center.
www.serc.si.edu/education/bluecrab/
exhibit/lifecycle.htm.

Zinski, Steve. *Blue-Crab Archives.*
www.blue-crab.org.

CRAWFISH AND LOBSTER

The American Lobster. Pictou-Antigonish
Regional Library Web site. www.parl.
ns.ca/projects/lobster/overview.htm.

Cajun's Crawfish Pond. www.worldzone.
net/lifestyles/pokeemom.

"Catching Stupid Lobsters: Study Finds
Most Lobsters Intelligent Enough to
Escape Traps." National Public Radio,
*All Things Considere*d, January 13, 2003.
Interview of zoology professor Win
Watson of University of New
Hampshire by Robert Siegel.

Crawfish. Auburn University Montgomery.
http://sciences.aum.edu/bi/bi4523/stu-
dent/Derrick/behavior.htm.

"Crayfish Information." *The Crayfish Corner.*
www.mackers.com/crayfish.

de la Bretonne, Larry Jr., and Robert P.
Romaire. *Crawfish Production Systems.*
University of Arkansas. www.uaex.edu
/aquaculture2/SRAC%20pubs/SRAC241
.htm.

France Ecrevisses. www.france-
ecrevisses.com.

Kurlansky, M. *Cod: A Biography of the Fish
That Changed the World.* New York:
Penguin Putnam, 1997.

"Leon Panetta on the Fishing Industry in
the United States." National Public
Radio, *Morning Edition,* December 25,
2002. Interview of Leon Panetta, chair,
Pew Oceans Commission, by Bob
Edwards.

"A Lobster by Any Other Name." *Lobsters.*
Gulf of Maine Aquarium. http://
octopus.gma. org/lobsters/
allaboutlobsters/species.html.

Sackton, John. "FDA Moves to Adopt EU
Standards on Chloramphenicol."
Seafood.com. June 17, 2002.
www.seafood.com/news/cur-
rent/69607.html.

PRAWNS AND SHRIMP

Brown Shrimp Catch Data. National Marine
Fisheries Service, Southeast Fisheries
Science Center, Galveston Laboratory.
http://galveston.ssp.nmfs.gov/
shrimpfishery/brown.htm.

*California's Living Marine Resources: A Status
Report.* California Department of Fish
and Game. www.dfg.ca.gov/mrd/status.

Higgins, Margot. "Texas Overhauls Shrimp
Trawling Policies." *Environmental News
Network,* September 2, 2000.
www.enn.com/news/
enn-stories/2000/09/09022000
/tshrimp_31097.asp.

Idoine, Josef. *Northern Shrimp.* Northeast
Fisheries Science Center.
http://nefsc.noaa.gov/sos/spsyn/iv/
shrimp.

Izena, Setsuko. *Coastal Shrimp Farming in
Texas.* www.memory.uci.edu/~sustain/
suscoasts/sizena.html.

McCrae, Jean. *Spot Prawn Pandalus platyceros.* Oregon Department of Fish and
Wildlife. www.hmsc.orst.edu
/odfw/devfish/sp/prawn.html.

*Northern Pink Shrimp, Pandalus borealis,
Distribution and Abundance in the Eastern
Bering Sea.* Alaska Fisheries Science
Center, Kodiak Laboratory. www.afsc.
noaa.gov/Kodiak/shrimpebs.htm.

U.S. Marine Shrimp Farming Program.
Oceanic Institute. www.oceanicinsti-
tute.org/research/
shrimp_proj_USMSF.html.

White Shrimp. NOAA. www.csc.noaa.gov/
acebasin/specgal/whshrimp.htm.

EEL AND STURGEON

Camuso, Pat. "Controversial,
Catadromous, Coveted, Contaminated:
The Continuing Saga of the American
Eel." *Outdoor Magazine.* 1998.
www.riverreporter.com/outdoor1/
eel.htm.

"Eel." *Barron's Educational Services.* Based
on *The Food Lover's Companion,* 2nd edition, by Sharon Tyler Herbst, 1995.
www.allrecipes.com/encyc/terms/E/
6349.asp.

Schweid, Richard. "Consider the Eel."
Gastronomica. www.gastronomica.
org/gastro/pages/sample2.2.html.

Sturgeon Conservation.
www.worldstar.com/~dlarson/
conofst.htm.

White Sturgeon. Pacific States Marine
Fisheries Commission. www.psmfc. org/
habitat/edu_wsturg_fact.html.

HERRING AND SHAD

"American Shad." *American Rivers.* www. amrivers.org/damremovaltoolkit/ shad.htm.

"American Shad (Alosa sapidissima)." *Worldwaters.com.* www.worldwaters. com/retail/common/currents/species/ american_shad.asp.

American Shad, Alosa sapidissima (A.K.A. White Shad, Common Shad, Atlantic Shad). Maryland Department of Natural Resources. www.dnr.state.md.us/fisheries/educa- tion/am_shad/american_shad.html.

"Herring." *New York Seafood.* www. nysea food.com/about/herring.asp.

"Life in the Bay." *Chesapeake Bay Programs.* www.chesapeakebay.net/pubs/sob/sob 02/Chap%201%20-%20Life%20in%20 the%20Bay.pdf.

SARDINES, ANCHOVIES, AND SMELTS

Atherinops californiensis. California Department of Fish and Game. www.delta.dfg.ca.gov/baydelta/ monitoring/jack.html.

Bacher, Dan. "California's Anglers Score Big Victory on Defeating Permit for Anchovy Reduction Fishery." *The Fish Sniffer Online,* July 7, 2000. www. fishsniffer.com/dbachere/070700 anchovies.html.

"Eulachon Facts." *Eulachon Conservation Society.* www.oolichan.org/ecs/ eulachonfacts.html.

"Sardinops sagax caerulea. California Pilchard, Pacific Sardine, Sardina Monterrey." *Ocean Oasis Field Guide.* www.oceanoasis.org/fieldguide/ sard-cae.html.

"The Smelt." *Nature Bulletin* 105, March 1, 1947. Forest Preserve District of Cook County, Illinois. www.newton. dep.anl.gov/natbltn/100- 199/nb105.htm.

Walton, Marsha. "Scientists Find El Nino's Grandparents." *CNN,* January 12, 2003. www.cnn.com/2003/TECH/ science/01/12/coolsc.sardines.

Wang, Johnson C. S. *Fishes of the Sacramento-San Joaquin Estuary and Adjacent Waters, California: A Guide to the Early Life Histories.* Berkeley Digital Library Project, Technical Report 9 (FS/B10-4ATR 86-9), January 1986. http://elib.cs.berkeley.edu/kopec/tr9/ html/ home.html.

CATFISH AND TILAPIA

American Tilapia Association. http:// ag.arizona.edu/azaqua/ata.html.

Farm-raised Channel Catfish. University of Florida. http://edis.ifas.ufl.edu/ BODY_FA010.

Fingerlakes Aquaculture, LLC. www.indoor- fish.com.

Introduction to Tilapia Culture. International Center for Aquaculture and Aquatic Environments, Auburn University. www.ag.auburn.edu/dept/faa/ tilap.html.

Libey, George S. *Aquaculture Extension in Fisheries Biology.* Virginia Polytech and State University. www.mdsg.umd.edu/ extensionconf/AQ47.html.

Tilapia. North Dakota State University. www.ext.nodak.edu/extpubs/ alt-ag/tilapia.htm

"Tilapia—An Old Fish Tale with a New Twist." *Aquanet.* www.aquanet.com/ features/tilapia/tilapia.htm.

"Tilapia and the Environment." *Trade and Environment Database.* www.american.edu/ted/TILAPIA.htm.

Tilapia Farming. www.fishfarming.com/tilapia.html.

Young, Kim R. *Aquaculture: A Need for Import Tolerances.* FDA. www.fda.gov/ OHRMS/DOCKETS/AC/02/slides/ 3816s1_05_Young/sld001.htm.

SALMON, TROUT, AND ARCTIC CHAR

"Amendment 1 to the Atlantic Salmon Fishery Management Plan." *Federal Register,* July 27, 1999 (vol. 64, no. 143). www.aquanic.org/news/1999/ amedsal.htm.

BC Salmon Farming. British Columbia's Salmon Farming Association www.salmonfarmers.org.

The Color of Salmon. Sysco Metro N.Y., LLC. www.rittersysco.com/salmon_color.htm.

Fresh Atlantic Salmon from Chile Injures U.S. Industry, Says IT. U.S. International Trade Commission. www.usitc.gov/er/ nl1998/ER0714V1.htm.

Hilderbrand, G. V., et al. "Role of Brown Bears (Ursus arctos) in the Flow of Marine Nitrogen into a Terrestrial Ecosystem." *Oecologia* 121 (1999): 546–550.

Nash, Colin, ed. *The Net-Pen Salmon Farming Industry in the Pacific Northwest.* NOAA Technical Memorandum NMFS-NWFSC-49. www.nwfsc. noaa.gov/pubs/tm/tm49/TM49.htm.

OPAH, POLLOCK, AND GRENADIER

"Alaska Pollock Catch Surges Despite World Decline." *Kenai Peninsula Online.* www.peninsulaclarion.com/sto- ries/011702/ala_011702alapm0030001.s html.

Deep Water Fish: Commission Proposes for the First Time Catch Limitations. European Commission. http://europa.eu.int/ comm/fisheries/news_corner/press/ info1_ 71_en.htm.

"Hawaiian Food Glossary." *About, Inc.* http://gohawaii.about.com/library/ weekly/aa032901a.htm.

McDonald's USA Ingredients Listing for Popular Menu Items. www.mcdonalds. com/countries/usa/food/nutrition/cat- egories/ingredients/index.jsp#1.

Miller, Daniel J., and Lea, Robert N. "Guide to the Coastal Marine Fishes of California." California Department of Fish and Game. *Fish Bull* 157 (1972): 84–85.

"Opah (It's a Fish)." *Simmer Stock.* www.simmerstock.com/archives/ performing/000618.html.

Opah. State of Hawaii. www.hawaii.gov/ dbedt/seafood/opah.html.

Welch, Laine. "Evaluators Assess Alaska Pollock for Possible 'Eco-Label' Certification." *Alaska Journal of Commerce.* www.alaskajournal.com/ stories/042902/fis_eco_label.shtml.

SABLEFISH AND BUTTERFISH

"Butterfish." *Food Network Encyclopedia.* http://web.foodnetwork.com/food/web /encyclopedia.

Essential Fish Habitat (EFH) for Butterfish. Northeast Fisheries Science Center.

www.nefsc.noaa.gov/ro/doc/
butterfish.htm.

*New Sablefish Research at the Auke Bay
Laboratory.* Alaska Fisheries Science
Center. www.afsc.noaa.gov/
Quarterly/jas99/jas99qrt/html/
feature.htm.

Overholtz, William. *Butterfish.* Northeast
Fisheries Science Center. www.nefsc.
noaa.gov/sos/spsyn/op/butter.

Sablefish Research. Alaska Fisheries Science
Center. www.afsc.noaa.gov/abl/
MarFish/sablecruise.html.

*Save the Bay: Guide to Common Life on
Narragansett Bay.* Rhode Island
Saltwater Anglers Association. www.
risaa.org/savethebay/archives.html.

BASSES AND PERCH

"Atlantic Striped Bass Conservation Act."
*Digest of Federal Resource Laws of Interest
to the U.S. Fish and Wildlife Service.*
http://laws.fws.gov/lawsdigest/
atlstri.html.

Cotton, C., and R. L. Walker. *Aquaculture of
Black Sea Bass (Centropristis striata).*
Southern Division of the American
Fisheries Society. www.sdafs.org/meet-
ings/00sdafs/posters/cotton1.htm.

Cotton, Chip. *Black Sea Bass Aquaculture.*
University of Georgia. www.uga.edu/
aquarium/NAT_HISTORY/seabass.
html.

Greer, Jack. "Aquaculture in the Mid-
Atlantic: A 20-Year Perspective."
Maryland Marine Notes. www.mdsg.
umd.edu/MarineNotes/May-
June94/side1.html.

"Black Sea Bass, *Centropristis striata.*"
eNature. www.enature.com/fieldguide/
showRguide.asp?rguideID=710&species
ID=3426.

Hanauer, Eric. "Comeback of the Black Sea
Bass." *Environmental News Network,* May
17, 2002. www.enn.com/news/enn-sto-
ries/2002/05/05172002/s_47121.asp.

Harrell, R. M., et al. (eds.) *Culture and
Propagation of Striped Bass and Its
Hybrids.* 1990. www.fisheries.org/
publications/catbooks/x53014.shtml.

*Division Adopts New Regulations for Black Sea
Bass, Porgy, and Tautog.* New Jersey
Division of Fish, Game, and Wildlife.

www.state.nj.us/dep/fgw/news/
newregs.htm.

*Emergency Regulations Announced for Summer
Flounder, Scup, and Black Sea Bass.* New
York State Department of
Environmental Conservation.
www.dec.state.ny.us/website/
press/pressrel/emerregs.html.

Fish ID and Regulations. South Atlantic
Fishery Management Council.
www.safmc.net/fishid/
fmpro?-db=content&-format=
default.html&-view.

Hybrid Striped Bass. Mississippi State
University Extension Service.
www.msstate.edu/dept/srac/bass.htm.

Parker, Nick C. *Striped Bass Culture in
Continuously Aerated Ponds.* U.S. Fish and
Wildlife Service, Southeastern Fish
Cultural Laboratory. www.tcru.ttu.edu/
tcru/kc/pubs/parker/p21.html.

*Report to Congress on Striped Bass Calls for
Sound Conservation.* Coastal
Conservation Association. www.
joincca.org/html/releases/2001/
bassreport.htm.

"Striped Bass." *Chesapeake Bay Program.*
www.chesapeakebay.net/info/
striped_bass.cfm.

Virginia Seafood. Virginia Marine Products
Board. www.virginiaseafood.org/
foodService/fs-factsheet.htm.

AMBERJACK AND POMPANO

Farren, Rick. "Net Ban Enforcement—
Some Improvements, But Problems
Persist." *Seawatch,* August 2001. www.
ccaflorida.org/seawatch/2aug01. htm.

Florida's Highest Valued Fish. Mariculture
Technologies International. www.
pompanofarms.com.

Florida Pompano. http://fwie.fw.vt.edu/
WWW/macsis/lists/M010011.htm.

"The Greater Amberjack." *Southern Charm
Sportsfishing.* www.floridasaltwater.com/
gamefish/ambrjack.htm.

"Greater Amberjack Trip Limit Approved."
Southeast Fishery Bulletins 2000.
http://caldera.sero.nmfs.gov/fishery/
newsbull.200/news200.htm.

Hawai'i Fisheries Development (USDC-NOAA).
www.oceanicinstitute.org/research/
finfish_proj_HFD.html.

Meadows, Jean. *Florida Food Fare.* University of Florida. http://sarasota.
extension.ufl.edu/FCS/flafoodfare/
pompano.htm.

"Not That Kind of Hamachi." *Hamachi.*
http://pages.prodigy.net/hamachi/
alternates.html.

Paul, Walter. "Reducing the Risk of Open-
Ocean Aquaculture Facilities to
Protected Species." *NOAA National
Strategic Initiative Project Summaries.*
1999. www.lib.noaa.gov/
docaqua/nmai1999.htm.

*Preliminary Elements of the Draft Rule.
Background on the Commercial Pompano
Fishery.* Florida Fish and Wildlife
Conservation Commission.
www.floridaconservation.org/
whos-who/00/reports/nov00/
pompano.html.

Walker, Charlie (Captain). "Pompano
Fishing in the Tampa Area." *Southern
Charm Sportsfishing.* www.flfish.com/
how_to/pompano_fishing.htm.

BLUEFISH AND MULLET

"Bluefish." *Chesapeake Bay Programs.*
www.chesapeakebay.net/info/
bluefish.cfm.

Bluefish. Maryland Department of Natural
Resources. www.dnr.state.md.us/
fisheries/education/bluefish/bluefish.
html.

"Bluefish." *New Jersey Fishing.* www.
fishingnj.org/problue.htm.

"Bluefish." *Flyfisher USA.* www.
flyfisher usa.com/bluefish.htm.

Gordon, Bernard. *The Secret Lives of Fishes.*
New York: Grosset and Dunlap, 1977.

Walker, Charlie (Captain). "Striped
Mullet." *Bait Profiles.* www.
fishingboating.com/baitprofiles/
sbmullet.htm.

"Striped Mullet." *Fishing in Indian River
County, FL.* indian river.fl.us/fishing/
fish/mullstri.htm.

"Striped Mullet." *Texas Parks and Wildlife.*
www.tpwd.state.tx.us/expltx/eft/gulf/
cspecies/mullet.htm.

"Striped Mullet." *Southland Fisheries,
Hopkins, S.C.* www.southlandfisheries.
com/striped_mullet.htm.

Striped Mullet Pond Production. Mississippi

State University. www.msstate.edu/
dept/crec/aquamull.html.

TUNA, MACKEREL, AND WAHOO

Collette, B. B. "Atlantic Bluefin Tuna." In
*Bigelow and Schroeder's Fishes of the Gulf
of Maine*, 3rd edition, edited by B. B.
Collette and G. Klein-MacPhee, 531–536.
Washington and London: Smithsonian
Institution Press (2002).

Davidson, Alan. *Seafood, A Connoisseur's
Guide and Cookbook*. New York: Simon
and Schuster, 1989.

"Dolphin Safe Tuna." *Protected Resources*.
NOAA Fisheries. www.nmfs.noaa.gov/
pr/PR2/Tuna_Dolphin/
dolphin-safe.html.

Lazaroff, Cat. "U.S. Changes Meaning of
Dolphin Safe Tuna Label."
Environmental News Service, January 6,
2003. www.flmnh.ufl.edu/fish/
InNews/dolphinsafe2003.htm.

DRUMS

Atlantic Croaker. Maryland Department of
Natural Resources. www.dnr.state.
md.us/fisheries/education/croaker/
croaker.

"Atlantic Croaker." *Fishing in Indian River
County, FL*. http://indian-river.fl.us/
fishing/fish/drumatla.html.

"Coastal Wildlife Species." *Exploring Texas:
Texas Parks and Wildlife*.
www.tpwd.state.tx.us/expltx/eft/gulf/
cspecies/wildlife.htm

Red Drum (Sciaenops ocellatus). East Carolina
University. http://personal.ecu.edu/
spraguem/fish/scioce.html.

Schultz, Ken. "Fish of the Week: Red
Drum." *Field and Stream*. www.
fieldandstream.com/fieldstream/
fishing/article/0,13199,336283,00.html

Virginia Seafood. Virginia Marine Products
Board. www.virginiaseafood.org/
foodService/fs-factsheet.htm.

MAHI MAHI AND COBIA

"Cobia." *William and Mary Fisheries Science*.
www.fisheries.vims.edu/femap/fish%20
pages/Cobia.htm.

"Cobia Aquaculture." *Snapperfarm Offshore
Aquaculture*. www.snapperfarm.com

/company/top.htm.

Cobia Issues and Recommendations. Florida
Conservation. www.floridaconserva-
tion.org/marine/Cobia082k.htm.

Johnson, G. D. "Percoidei." In *Ontogeny and
Systematics of Fishes*, edited by H. G.
Moser et al., 464-498. Special Publication
No. 1, American Society of Ichthyologists
and Herpetologists (1984).

"Mahi Mahi." *Seafood Business*.
www.seafoodbusiness.com/buyers-
guide03/issue_mahi.htm.

FLATFISHES

"Louisiana Foods Fish Fact for Halibut."
Louisiana Foods. www.louisianafoods.
com/fishfaq/halibut.html.

Greenland Halibut. Icelandic Freezing Plants
Corporation. www.icelandic.ru/
ifpc_all/halibut.htm.

"Pacific Halibut." *Piscatorial Pursuits*. www.
piscatorialpursuits.com/wafish.htm.

CULINARY GLOSSARY

Alden, Lori. *The Cooks Thesaurus*.
www.foodsubs.com.

Alderton, Eric W. *The Chef's Corner*.
www.ddc.com/cheferic.

"Asian Ingredients and Cooking Terms—
Glossary and Culinary Dictionary."
About.com. http://chinesefood.about.
com/library/bld_f.htm.

"Chile Encyclopedia." *OneCook.com*. www.
onecook.com/reference/chile.htm.

Caselton, Graeme. *Chile Head*. http://
easyweb.easynet.co.uk/~gcaselton/
chile/chile.html.

"Cooking Books, Recipes, Food." *Harvest
Fields Ltd*. www.harvestfields.
netfirms.com/food/index.htm.

"Cooking Glossary." *Waitrose.com*.
www.waitrose.com/food_drink/
Recipes/glossary/cookingglossary.

"Cooking Terms." www. cdkitchen.com.

"Culinary Techniques." *Prepared Foods*.
www.preparedfoods.com/archives/
2001/2001_12/1201education.htm.

DeWitt, Dave. *Dave's Pepper Pages*.
www.fiery-foods.com/dave/index.asp.

"Encyclopedia." *All Recipes*.
allrecipes.com/encyc.

"Encyclopedia." *Food Network*. www.
foodnetwork.com/food/ck_encyclopedia.

*Food and Fibre Industries in Queensland,
Australia*. www.dpi.qld.gov.au/home.

"Food Dictionary." *Epicurious*. http://
eat.epicurious.com/dictionary/food.

"Food Glossary." *Organic Food, Schnitzer*.
www.liesworld.com/shops/schnitzer/
index.htm.

"Food Terms." *The Gutsy Gourmet*.
www.thegutsygourmet.net.

"Glossary." *MyCookbook.net*. www.
mycookbook.net/Glossary.asp.

Huy Fong Foods, Inc. www.huyfong.com/
no_frames/sriracha.htm.

Longo's Online Cooking Glossary. www.
longos.com/cooks_corner/
cooking_glossary_new.asp?

Mexican Cooking and Culinary Terms Glossary.
www.gourmetsleuth.com/chipotle.htm.

Saaristo, Thomas. *Ingredients Defined*.
http://tomsaaristo.com/
ingredients.html.

Sprout People. www.sproutpeople.com/
seed/alliums.html.

Stradley, Linda. *Linda's Culinary Dictionary*.
http://whatscookingamerica.net/
Glossary/GlossaryIndex2.htm.

Wikipedia. www.wikipedia.org.

ECOLOGICAL ISSUES SUR-
ROUNDING SEAFOOD CHOICES

*The following entries are in the order in which
they apply to the text.*

Epigraph

*Developing a National Ocean Policy: Mid-term
Report of the U.S. Commission on Ocean
Policy*. www.oceancommission.gov/
documents/midterm_report/
midterm_report.html.

Overfishing and Fisheries Management

Lee, M. (ed.) *Seafood Lover's Almanac*. Islip,
N.Y.: Living Oceans Program, National
Audubon Society, 2000.

Jackson, J. B. C., et al. "Historical Overfishing
and the Recent Collapse of Coastal
Ecosystems." *Science* 293 (2001): 629–638.

Myers, R. A., and B. Worm. "Rapid
Worldwide Depletion of Predatory Fish
Communities." *Nature* 423 (2003).
"Oceans in Poor Shape." Editorial.
International Herald Tribune, January 23,
2003.

Fishery Management Councils. National Marine Fisheries Service. www.nmfs.noaa.gov/councils.

"Oceans in Trouble." Editorial. *New York Times,* January 19, 2003.

Hogarth, William T., director of National Marine Fisheries Service, NOAA. June 2002, Q&A period at National Press Club, Washington, D.C.

Bauers, S. "The Dogfish Debate." *Philadelphia Inquirer,* February 10, 2003.

Federal Science, Advice on Northeast Groundfish Is Sound. NOAA. www.publicaffairs.noaa.gov/pr98/jan98/noaa98-r102.html.

Scientific Survey Gear Inspected, Error in Rigging Found and Corrected. NOAA Northeast Fisheries Science Center. www.nefsc.noaa.gov/press_release/advisory02.16.html.

"Conservation Groups Announce Steps to Restore New England Fish Populations." *Oceana.* www.oceana.org/index.cfm?sectionID=10&fuseaction=35.detail&pressreleaseID=13.

Fletcher, Janet. "Troubled Waters: Fishermen, Chefs and Consumers Face a World-Wide Seafood Crisis." *San Francisco Chronicle,* August 1, 2001. www.sfgate.com/cgi-bin/article.cgi?f=/c/a/2001/08/01/FD144241.DTL.

"Striped Bass." *Chesapeake Bay Program.* www.chesapeakebay.net/info/striped_bass.cfm.

Atlantic Striped Bass Conservation Act. U.S. Fish and Wildlife Service. laws.fws.gov/lawsdigest/atlstri.html.

Regional Fishery Bodies. Food and Agriculture Organization of the United Nations. www.fao.org/fi/body/rfb/chooserfb.htm.

The International Commission for the Conservation of Atlantic Tunas. www.iccat.es.

"The Truth about Swordfish." *The California Seafood Council.* www.ca-seafood.org/news/swftruth.htm.

"Catch Documentation Scheme." *Convention on the Conservation of Antarctic Marine Living Resources (CCAMLR).* www.ccamlr.org/pu/e/cds/intro.htm.

"Chilean Sea Bass/Patagonian Toothfish."

Pacific Seafood. www.pacseafood.com/products/seabass.html.

"Toothfish (*Dissostichus* spp.)." *CCAMLR.* www.ccamlr.org/pu/e/sc/fish-monit/hs-tfish.htm.

Roach, John. "Do Fish Use Cold Current to Cross Tropics?" *National Geographic News,* February 5, 2003. http://news.nationalgeographic.com/news/2003/02/0205_030205_toothfish.html.

Illegal Harvests of Chilean Sea Bass Get Close Review. NOAA. www.publicaffairs.noaa.gov/releases2002/mar02/noaa02031.html.

Destructive Fishery Practices

"Oceans in Peril." *Environmental Defense.* www.edf.org/seafood/oceansinperil.cfm.

"Fishing Methods." *Monterey Fish Market.* www.montereyfish.com/sustainability/fishing_methods.htm.

Valles, Colleen. "Scientists Ask U.N. to Ban Certain Types of Fishing in Pacific." *Associated Press,* February 17, 2003, San Francisco.

Lazaroff, Cat. "Ocean Crisis Caused by Destructive Fishing." *Environmental News Service,* February 19, 2003. http://ensnews.com/ens/feb2003/2003e-02-19-01.asp.

New Device to Cut Shrimping Bycatch; Reduction May Prevent Cuts in Red Snapper Quota. NOAA. www.publicaffairs.noaa.gov/pr98/apr98/seronr98-022.html.

NOAA Fisheries Publishes Rules to Modify Turtle Excluder Devices (TEDs). NOAA. www.publicaffairs.noaa.gov/releases2003/feb03/noaa03r113.html.

"Scallop Fishery." *New England's Ocean News.* www.clf.org/NEON/0109_scallop_fishery.htm.

Fish Farming

"Farming Dilemma." *Environmental Defense.* www.edf.org/seafood/farmingdilemma.cfm.

Lazaroff, Cat. "Drug Traces Prompt Closer Look at Farmed Seafood." *Environmental News Service,* June 21, 2002. http://ensnews.com/ens/jun2002/2002-06-17-06.asp.

Nixon, Will. "Rainforest Shrimp." *Mother Jones.* www.motherjones.com/mother_jones/MA96/nixon.html.

Clancy, Mary Ann. "Emergency DMR Rules Protect Cobscook Bay." *Bangor Daily News,* August 15, 2002. www.bangordailynews.com/editorialnews/article.cfm?ID=62551.

"Lawsuit Provides Hope for Better Salmon Farming." *Natural Life Magazine* 86 (July–August 2002). www.life.ca/nl/86/salmon.html.

Page, Kim, biologist. Personal communication. Harlingen Shrimp Farms, Ltd., Los Fresnos, Tex.

Edgecomb, Misty. "Fish Farm Agrees to Strict Rules." *Bangor Daily News.* www.bangordailynews.com/editorialnews/article.cfm?ID=58551.

FDA Increases Sampling of Imported Shrimp and Crayfish (Crawfish). FDA, June 14, 2002. www.cfsan.fda.gov/~lrd/fpshrimp.html.

"About Us." *Bio-Oregon, Inc.* www.bio-oregon.com/flash/about.htm.

Aquaculture: A Need for Import Tolerances. FDA. www.fda.gov/OHRMS/DOCKETS/AC/02/slides/3816s1_05_Yong/index.htm.

The Florida Aquaculture Plan 1996-1997. Florida Department of Agriculture and Consumer Services. www.fl-aquaculture.com/newpages/Aquaculture_Plan/aqua2.html.

The 2000 Annual Report on the United States Seafood Industry. H. M. Johnson and Associates, Seafood Marketing Information and Analysis for Decision-Makers. www.hmj.com/highlights.html.

Kurlansky, Mark. *Cod: A Biography of the Fish That Changed the World.* New York: Penguin Putnam, 1997.

The State of World Fisheries and Aquaculture. Fisheries Department, Food and Agriculture Organization of the United Nations, Rome. 2002. www.fao.org/docrep/005/y7300e/y7300e00.htm.

U.S. Marine Resource Assessment

U.S. Commission on Ocean Policy. www.ocean-commission.gov.

Pew Oceans Commission. www.pewoceans.org.

Sustainable Seafood Concept

"Aquatic Stewardship." *American Fisheries Society.* www.fisheries.org/Stewardship.shtml.

"Sustainability." *Monterey Fish Market.* www.montereyfish.com/sustainability/htm.

"Sustainable Seafood." *South Carolina Aquarium.* http://206.74.146.33/scaquarium/scaweb/airindex.cfm?FAM=86&CLAN=5.

Connor, Jacquelyn. *Orange Roughy.* University of Minnesota. www.fw.umn.edu/fw5601/classproj01/roughy/roughy.htm.

Conservation Initiatives

See *The Truth about Swordfish* (above).

Martosko, David. "Something Fishy about Sea Bass Scare." *Seattle Post Intelligencer,* October 16, 2002. http://seattlepi.nwsource.com/opinion/91307_seabass16.shtml.

Chilean Sea Bass: Frequently Asked Questions. Joint U.S. Department of Commerce/U.S. Department of State fact sheet, March 26, 2002. www.state.gov/g/oes/rls/fs/2002/8989.htm.

Seafood Labeling

Informational Labeling of Seafood and Security. Letter to Tom Ridge, Director of Homeland Security. www.pcffa.org/foodsecurity.htm.

Benjamin, Natasha, Nicole Brown, and Allison Vogt. "Informational Seafood Labeling." *Pacific Coast Federation of Fishermen's Associations.* www.pcffa.org/fn-dec01.htm.

"Farm Bill 2002." *U.S. Department of Agriculture.* www.usda.gov/farmbill.